Lord Stanley

THE MAN BEHIND THE CUP

Lord Stanley
THE MAN BEHIND THE CUP

Kevin Shea and John Jason Wilson

Introduction by
The Right Honourable Adrienne Clarkson

Fenn Publishing Company Ltd.

Fenn Publishing Company Ltd.

LORD STANLEY
A Fenn Publishing Book / First Published in 2006

All rights reserved

We acknowledge the financial support of the Government of Canada through the Book
Publishing Industry Development Program (BPIDP) for our publishing activities.

Fenn Publishing Company Ltd.
Bolton, Ontario, Canada

Distributed in Canada by H. B. Fenn and Company Ltd.
Bolton, Ontario, Canada, L7E 1W2
www.hbfenn.com

Library and Archives Canada Cataloguing in Publication

Shea, Kevin, 1956–
    Lord Stanley : the man behind the cup / Kevin Shea and J. Jason Wilson.

ISBN-13: 978-1-55168-281-5
ISBN-10: 1-55168-281-8

    1. Derby, Frederick Arthur Stanley, Earl of, 1841-1908. 2. Governors general—
Canada—Biography. 3. Stanley Cup (Hockey). I. Wilson, Jason, 1970– II. Title.

DA566.9.D47S44 2006   971.05'4092   C2006-903769-8

This book is dedicated to every hockey player
whose dreams were fuelled by the hope of one day
hoisting the Cup that was so graciously provided
by Lord Frederick Arthur Stanley.

Contents

Foreword by
Adrienne Clarkson

The governor general stands for excellence in Canadian culture — and always has. Each new thing that is done in the governor general's name has to do with excellence, and it started way, way back. In many ways the Stanley Cup, Lord Stanley's trophy for outstanding hockey, was one of the first. It went on from there. There are literary awards in the governor general's name, visual arts awards, performing arts awards and every one represents a connection with excellence, with the best — with the best that we can do as a nation.

The Right Honourable Adrienne Clarkson
Toronto, Ontario
April 2006

Foreword by
The 19th Earl of Derby

In England, the name Lord Stanley means little to most people, but cross the Atlantic and things are very different. My great-great-grandfather's name is inextricably linked to Canada both as governor general and as the donor of the Stanley Cup.

The Stanley Cup is, undoubtedly, his lasting legacy today. It is interesting to note that he took it so personally that it was paid for by him and uses our family coat of arms and not that of the governor general.

He loved Canada and the Canadian people and returned to England upon inheriting the earldom to run the family estates, but I think he will have often looked back to reflect on his Canadian times.

Derby

The 19th Earl of Derby
Knowsley, Prescot, Merseyside
July 2006

Introduction

Frederick Arthur Stanley, Lord Stanley of Preston, was Canada's sixth governor general (1888–1893). Historians have thus far been satisfied to draw a brief timeline of Stanley's life to serve as the man's biography: born into privileged circumstances, personifying the archetypal robust English gentleman, embracing all that the family's position offered him and assuming his role as guardian of the Empire — working his way through a stint in the Royal military, then rising within the civil service before arriving at his ultimate appointment in Ottawa — and, of course, putting his name on the famous Cup.

Yet this oversimplified account does a great disservice to the stories that developed around Stanley's time as governor general and, indeed, to the refined man himself.

Stanley had some rather large footsteps to follow in: his father served as Britain's prime minister on three occasions and played a vital role in shaping the political landscape of Victorian England. As if that weren't enough, Lord Stanley often found himself standing in the shadow of his over-achieving older brother, Edward. These family dynamics, as well as a broader character sketch of Stanley and his Canadian experience, are fully revealed to us with the help of Lady Stanley's (the Governor General's wife) meticulous journals, which followed the family's travels across the new nation on the Canadian Pacific Railway.

Where political events are concerned, historians have wrongly dismissed Stanley's term as governor general, a position commonly referred to as the vice regal, as uneventful; they have also incorrectly accused Stanley of being unimaginative. Where Stanley was certainly inward-thinking, family-oriented and less given to pomp and circumstance than other governors general, he possessed a strong vision, demonstrated terrific political savvy and expert diplomatic skills at a time when the very existence of Canada was in question. Stanley's statesmanship and diplomacy were abetted through an extraordinary relationship with Sir John A. Macdonald — a fact that comes to life when reviewing the boxes of correspondence between these two colossal figures of Canadian history.

When the aggressive policies of the United States (aimed at starving the Dominion into annexation), threatened war with Canada and when racially motivated domestic strife jeopardized the very fabric of the nation, Stanley remained loyal to Canada first and helped Macdonald captain the Dominion's safe passage through some treacherous political waters.

Stanley believed that the Canadian militia was wanting in numbers and was thoroughly unfit to defend the nation. He was not alone. Many other social agents declared that a "crisis in masculinity" had woefully affected the nation's young manhood. One popular remedy to this issue was sport. The importance of sport to masculinity had been a notion that pervaded the Empire. From Dr. Thomas Arnold's "muscular Christianity" at Rugby School in England to the rule-making and standardization of amateur team sports like football, sport in general was increasingly regarded as an imperative part of nation-building — and, in the case of the militia, the maintenance of a nation.

Ice hockey fit perfectly with the social agents' war cry to ready the nation and repair the deficiencies in masculinity that industrialization and urbanization had brought on. The game had a profound impact on Lord Stanley and his family, who witnessed their first hockey game at the Montreal Winter Carnival during February 1889 and were hooked. Stanley's sons played with great fervour and were members of the famed Rideau Rebels. Daughter Isobel was one of the first women to try their hand at the fledgling game.

In 1892, Lord Stanley of Preston announced that he would donate a trophy for the amateur hockey championship of Canada. The next year, the Montreal Amateur Athletic Association became the first recipients of the Dominion Hockey Challenge Cup, better known as the Stanley Cup. Shortly thereafter, Lord Stanley returned to England and assumed the hereditary mantle of Earl of Derby.

Just as the game had made an impression on the Stanleys, conversely, the Stanleys made a terrific impact on the game. Prior to the First World War, vice regal influence in Canada was profound; in many respects, as direct satellites of the Queen and the Empire's head office, governors general helped shape the tastes and definitions of the Dominion. And so, with Stanley's direct stamp of approval, the already popular sport of hockey became the game of choice for the young nation — as it remains today.

While Stanley's complete life is interesting enough, our focus, given resources and access to research tools and documents, is primarily on Stanley's time in Canada. We only hope that this work will inspire others to flush out the great episodes of Stanley's life that are waiting to be rediscovered.

Lord Stanley of Preston could not have predicted the immense impact his gift to hockey would have. Possession of the battered mug has been contested for well over a century. Young men grow up dreaming of one day hoisting the Stanley Cup over their heads in triumph and having their names inscribed on the outside surface of sport's most cherished trophy. Still, Stanley's less visible legacy, however subtle and heavily nuanced, is equally as important to the nation of Canada, and it deserves to be shared and celebrated.

CHAPTER ONE

A Calling in Canada

"Welcome to the Dominion,"[1] wrote the *Ottawa Citizen* on 10 June, 1888 —
a greeting that echoed the sentiments of the great majority of Canadians,
who recognized the governor general as the country's head of state and the
Dominion's main link to the mother country. Lord Frederick Arthur Stanley
had arrived on Canadian soil and was ready to assume one of the Empire's
highest-ranking positions:

> *I hope that I may approach my duties in the spirit of feeling*
> *how much I may have to learn; that when my term of*
> *office is ended, Lady Stanley and myself, looking back with*
> *regard to those who have done so much to make our stay in*
> *this country happy, may also feel that our Administration,*
> *with the guidance of wisdom from up above, has not been*
> *without benefit to this great country.*[2]

The son of a British prime minister and brother of the 15th Earl of Derby
would himself be called upon for wisdom and guidance by the people of
the Dominion as they struggled to negotiate some very troubled waters in
the last decade of the nineteenth century. The sage and aging Stanley, who
became Canada's sixth governor general, would not disappoint a nation
that saw itself as a reflection of Britain and an integral part of an Empire
upon which the sun never set.

* * *

The principal role of the governor general in Canada was to carry out the duties and wishes of the King or Queen of England; ergo, the governor general was Canada's head of state, appointed by the British monarch. Since 1890, the reigning British monarch had looked to the prime minister of Canada for advice on the person who should fulfill the role of governor general, but when Lord Stanley was appointed vice regal in 1888, Queen Victoria acted on the advice of British authorities alone.[3]

The governor general's responsibilities included representing the Crown in Canada, representing Canadians, promoting sovereignty and unification within the Dominion and celebrating excellence. Stanley was to take the latter tenet to heart, given the legacy of the famous Cup awarded for excellence in hockey.

Another of the governor general's principal duties was to ensure that Canada was always operating with a prime minister. Other vice regal tasks included presenting the Speech from the Throne, giving Royal assent to bills passed by the House of Commons and the Senate, signing state documents, opening and ending sessions of Parliament, and dissolving Parliament for an election. As governor general, Stanley would also preside over the swearing-in of the Prime Minister, the Chief Justice of Canada and the various Cabinet ministers of a given government.[4]

When appropriate, usually at the request of the prime minister, the governor general might travel to other countries on official business. In turn, when the vice regal was at home in Ottawa, he was expected to welcome world leaders and other officials representing their countries.

The governor general presented numerous honours to Canadians whose achievements in their various fields of endeavour were deserving of recognition. The governor general also participated in various events across the country and actively interacted with Canadians from all walks of life in a bid to instil personal pride and community strength.[5]

In his memoir, Lord Minto, Canada's governor general between 1898 and 1904, said that the vice regal "walks inevitably on a razor edge. His powers are like those of a constitutional monarch — brittle if too heavily pressed, a shadow if tactlessly advertised, substantial only when exercised discreetly in the background."[6] In 1909, Prime Minister Wilfrid Laurier added:

> *The Canadian Governor General long ago ceased to determine policy, but he is by no means, or need not be, the mere*

figurehead the public imagine … He has the privilege of advising his advisers, and, if he is a man of sense and experience, his advice is often taken. Much of his time may be consumed in laying cornerstones and listening to boring addresses, but cornerstones must be laid, and people like a touch of colour and ceremony in life.[7]

Canada's prime minister between 1896 and 1911 further described the importance of strong ties between England and her colonies:

The Governor General's principal task was interpreting to Britain the ideals and aims of the Dominion, and, conversely, of expounding to the Dominion the intricate problems of the mother-country. Advice to Ministers in their administrative work and a constant effort to make sure that Britain and the Dominion see with the same eyes and speak the same language — these are duties which make far greater demands upon character and brain than the easy work of a dictator. The main qualification is experience and native shrewdness; the second, an alert sympathy and an open mind.[8]

The length of the governor general's term in office was not defined, although five or six years was customary. Stanley would see nearly five years in the post — a span that has historically been viewed as uneventful. However, a re-reading of Stanley's time in Canada, one that takes both domestic affairs and the Dominion's relationship with the United States into account, suggests a rather different view. Indeed, if not for some sound decisions on the part of the Baron of Preston, the age in which Stanley presided over the Dominion might have been far more unsettled and "eventful."

* * *

On 1 July, 1867, the day that Canada became a country, Sir Charles Stanley Monck, the 4th Viscount Monck, became governor general of the newly created Dominion, although he had in fact been Governor General of British North America since 1861. In 1883, the Most Honourable Henry Charles

Keith Petty-FitzMaurice, the 5th Marquess of Lansdowne, was appointed Governor General of Canada after having served in the House of Lords since 1866. Lansdowne's term concluded in 1888, and he was subsequently appointed Viceroy of India. On 28 December, 1887, prior to his departure, the press reported that Lord Stanley of Preston had accepted the post.[9] To bridge the time between Lansdowne's departure and Stanley's arrival, Sir John Ross, a decorated fifty-nine-year-old British soldier who, earlier that year, had been appointed the General Officer Commanding the forces in Canada, was sworn in as Administrator of the Government of Canada.[10]

On 1 February, 1888, the British prime minister, Lord Salisbury, acting on behalf of Queen Victoria, formally offered Lord Frederick Stanley the position of Governor General of the Dominion of Canada. Stanley, recently minted the 1st Baron Stanley of Preston, was president of the Board of Trade under Salisbury at the time. As one Canadian newspaper reported, "His Excellency at first declined the office he now holds, but it was pressed on him by Lord Salisbury, and as he himself has told it, he was finally 'persuaded.'"[11] On 1 May, Stanley was sworn in as Lansdowne's successor.

⁎ ⁎ ⁎

Captain Josceline Bagot, the grandson of Sir Charles Bagot, the Governor General of British North America in 1842, had served as aide-de-camp to the Marquis of Lorne during his tenure as governor general, and was secured by Lord Stanley as his acting military secretary. In the meantime, Lieutenant Aubrey McMahon, an aide-de-camp to the new governor general, left England ahead of Stanley and his party. In a letter to Sir John A. Macdonald written 2 May, 1888, Stanley asked the Prime Minister to afford McMahon an audience:

> *Mr. McMahon, one of my ADC's, sails in advance of our party and I take advantage of the opportunity thus afforded him to ask you to be good enough to let him present himself to you that he may receive your instructions upon any points which may arise in connection with my official arrival, and which might affect the convenience of your colleagues or your own, my desire being to do that which is most agreeable to yourself and to all concerned.*[12]

Stanley, who as Secretary of State for the Colonies had previously known Macdonald, added:

> *I need not tell you what a sincere pleasure it is to me to find myself again placed in official relations with those whose ability and power do justly command the confidence of those with whom he is associated, and I have a very strong hope that the feelings inspired by our communications, such as they were whilst I was at the Colonial Office, may be strengthened by our future connection in the affairs of the Dominion.*[13]

With his calling in Canada awaiting him, Stanley embarked on what would be five of the most memorable years of his life. In Canada, the future Earl of Derby would soon develop a glorious bond with the people of the Dominion and forge an extraordinary relationship with its Scottish-born prime minister.

---

[1] *Ottawa Daily Citizen* (10 June, 1888), *edition cover page.*

[2] From address to Methodist Conference. See, *Toronto Globe* (11 September, 1888).

[3] Toronto-born Vincent Massey, appointed in 1952, was the first Canadian-born governor general. Each of his seventeen predecessors had been a person of title from the United Kingdom.

[4] From the official website of the Governor General of Canada (*www.gg.ca*).

[5] Ibid.

[6] John Buchan, *Lord Minto: A Memoir* (London: T. Nelson, 1924).

[7] Ibid.

[8] Ibid.

[9] Article from *Manchester Courier* as reprinted in *Qu'Appelle Vidette* (5 January, 1888), *edition cover page.*

[10] *Halifax Morning Herald*, (9 July, 1890), *edition cover page.*

[11] *Victoria Daily Colonist*, (1 November, 1889), *edition cover page.*

[12] F. A. Stanley, *Letter to John A. Macdonald* (2 May, 1888).

[13] Ibid.

CHAPTER ONE

The Derbys

Nineteenth-century British politics are not easily understood: the political landscape was ever-evolving and the parties of the day, although recognizable in name, can not be tidily categorized as they did not always behave as one might assume. To understand the political leanings of the Stanley family, it is necessary to review the political environment in which the youngest child, Frederick Arthur, was raised. Indeed, Stanley's father, the Prime Minister of Britain in 1852, 1858–1859 and again from 1866–1868, was an opinionated man and is considered one of the pioneers of the modern Conservative Party. Yet, once one feels one has a handle on how the prime minister might react to a given situation, the exact opposite response is often manifest. The fact that Prime Minister Stanley started his political career as a Whig also goes some way towards further confusing the already-convoluted political history of the Stanleys.

Traditionally, the Derby family enjoyed a "country seat" in Knowsley, Prescot, in the heart of Merseyside. The seat was of the "rotten" variety, one that reformers hoped to remedy, but which nevertheless remained a Stanley possession even after the great reform. Although descendants came over with Richard the Conqueror, the Stanley family name began to appear in the late fourteenth century. Sir John Stanley, perhaps the most famous of the early Stanleys, had served King Henry IV well and was duly rewarded by him with the Isle of Man. This possession, later lost, was added to the list of lands the family already owned, including Lathom (which was received by way of marriage and, like the Isle of Man, was also lost) and the famous Knowsley, which remained in the family.

Sir John Stanley's grandson Thomas joined the British Parliament in 1456. Between this time and the early seventeenth century, the Stanleys were one of the most important families in England, and certainly the most powerful of all Lancashire houses.

During the reign of Henry VII, the Stanley family was closely associated with the famous War of the Roses, to the extent that the name is celebrated in the ballad of *Lady Bessie*, which described the role of Thomas, the 2nd Lord Stanley, at the battle of Bosworth Field. Stanley deserted Richard III at Bosworth, a move that sealed the fate of the battle — and that of the monarch, too — as Henry Tudor promptly took over the crown. Lord Stanley was thus rewarded with the Earldom of Derby, and he married the King's mother, Lady Margaret Beaufort.

In 1513, Edward Stanley, a son of the 1st Earl of Derby, was put in charge of the English left wing at the Battle of Flodden. While the Scots made great inroads into the English right wing during the fight, Stanley countered on the left. As one historian explained, the Scots were:

> *a disorganized mass, they threw themselves on Constable's brigade, where for a while they wrought havoc with their claymores. But Stanley came up and took them on the flank. Then they broke like a wave, and melted away in scattered groups, some still fighting desperately, some fleeing for their lives.*[1]

The end result, due in no small part to Stanley's efforts, was a disaster for Scotland: the loss of approximately ten thousand Scottish lives, including thirteen earls, fifteen lords and their king, James IV. The young Edward Stanley was handsomely rewarded for his legendary demonstration and was later immortalized in Sir Walter Scott's *Marmion*:

> *Charge, Chester, charge!*
> *On, Stanley, on!*

The generation of Stanleys that followed lived in a style that was "second only to that of the King."[2] The Stanley name is, in many respects, unrivalled in English history; as Randolph S. Churchill has asserted, "no English family can show a longer record of public activity and public service than the Stanleys. None has exercised political power and influence for so many centuries."[3]

While the family was among the richest and most powerful during the Tudor reign, the same can not be said during the time of the Great Rebellion. The 7th Earl of Derby, Sir James Stanley, was sentenced to death for his role in the Battle of Worcester in 1651. Stanley was a cavalier and a loyal royalist, and as such was beheaded by the Parliamentary Army at Bolton. His loyalty was hardly repaid by Charles II, who chose not restore the entire estate (and all that that entailed) to the Stanleys following his coronation in 1661.

And so, following the Rebellion, there followed a period when the Stanley family were estranged from the machinations of the realm, an era that lasted until the arrival of William of Orange. The 9th Earl was dismissed from his lieutenancy during the campaign against the Church of England.[4] It was during this time that the family, traditionally Tory, became aligned with the Whig party and were among the earliest to make William of Orange welcome in England.[5]

During the reign of Charles II, the Stanley family, in terms of political and social importance, was at a nadir. Indeed, as one historian candidly confirmed, "there can hardly be said to have been a Stanley who was a really prominent politician between Earl James' death on the scaffold at Bolton and the reappearance of Edward Stanley in the Commons as a kind of Canningite Whig after his election for Preston in 1826."[6]

There were, however, other Stanleys that left some mark on English society following the death of Sir James Stanley. Lord Frederick Stanley's great-grandfather, the 12th Earl of Derby, is best remembered for giving the horse-racing world its most cherished event: the Derby, held annually at Epsom. He also founded the Oaks, another time-honoured and important date on the racing calendar. The 13th Earl, Lord Stanley's grandfather, married his cousin Charlotte Margaret Hornby, and collected at Knowsley, one of Europe's best private zoological collections.

The 12th Earl was also highly involved in politics and was one of the "leading spirits" of the liberal faction of the Whig party.[7] He was somewhat obsessed with making his grandson (Frederick Stanley's father) a brilliant and proud Whig. Unfortunately for the 12th Earl, he was only partially successful in this bid.

Frederick's father, Edward George Geoffrey Smith-Stanley, made his

political mark in the heart of the "age of improvement," when both enlightenment and prejudice dictated the course of British politics. It was an age
when a larger (albeit modestly so) portion of Englishmen were enfranchised
for the first time. More men could vote, various sectors of society were being
cautiously afforded more say, and social and parliamentary reform was the
order of the day.

The Whig party marched through various initiatives during their nineteenth-century ascendancy. The Reform Bill was seen as a measure to placate
public sentiment (which, for the first time, was becoming more and more
important) by making some substantive improvement in the parliamentary
system and, subsequently, British life in general. As historian Asa Briggs
offered, demand for some reform "had appeared for many years on Whig
party banners side by side with 'retrenchment', 'civil and religious liberty', and
'the abolition of colonial slavery.'"[8] Make no mistake: the Whigs were by no
means socialists; rather, they sought to address certain social issues as a
means to fastening the lock on the status quo. As Briggs further explained:

> *The Whigs, exclusive and aristocratic though they were in*
> *their attitude to government, were ready to accept political*
> *innovations. Indeed, they believed that unless the privileged*
> *sections of the community were prepared to adapt and to*
> *'improve', waves of dangerous and uncontrollable innova-*
> *tion would completely drown the existing social order.*[9]

The incredibly involved nature of British politics of the time makes it
nearly impossible to quickly describe the various parties. As Tory historian
and Stanley contemporary George Saintsbury explained, when Stanley's
father "entered politics, it cannot be said that the great parties in England
were divided from each other by any thoroughgoing and logical difference
of principle."[10] Regardless of how hard it is to discern where one party
stopped and the other began, it could be argued that Whigs were rather
more interested in pursuing measures of reform than Tories were, though
not all Whigs were reformers. It might also be argued that members in both
parties were committed to, as Edward Geoffrey himself said, "stemming the
tide of democracy."[11]

Of course there were factions within various parties: some radically
right, like the "Ultra Tories," who were far less likely to support measures of

reform where moderate Tories might. Likewise, there existed a small band of revolutionary liberals whose ideas did not always reflect the prevailing attitudes of the Whig party.

Frederick Stanley's father found his place within the various factions of the British Parliament in a career that would prove to be somewhat apolitical. Edward Geoffrey may have pleased his grandfather by beginning his career as a Whig — the party of the 11th, 12th and 13th Earls of Derby, all of whom had sat in the House of Commons as Whigs prior to their ascent to the peerage — but he would not remain one. As a card-carrying member of the "privileged sections" of the English community, Edward Geoffrey Stanley was behind many Whig initiatives, but he remained very much his own man. The 14th Earl of Derby's conspicuous political career would restore the lustre to the Stanley name, but the bulk of the Earl's political life would be spent as a Tory.

Prior to the Restoration, in what were, as Saintsbury suggested, in "happier times,"[12] the Stanleys had perennially sat in Parliament as Tories, representing a seat in Lancashire. They even had a traditional refrain that accompanied their election campaigns:

> *Ho! Ho! Stanley for ever!*
> *He shall marry a wife that's rich,*
> *And shall ride in a coach and six,*
> *Ho! Ho! Stanley for ever!*

Still, it was as a Whig that Edward Geoffrey Stanley began his parliamentary career. Educated at Eton and Christ Church, Oxford, the senior Stanley was elected to Parliament in 1820, where he joined forces with some extremely influential politicians of the day just as the whole basis of English politics underwent a profound shift. More specifically, Edward Geoffrey was part of the Lansdowne faction of the Whig Party, and in 1827, upon the recommendation of Lord Lansdowne himself, Edward Geoffrey joined the government benches under the newly elected Prime Minister, George Canning. Three years later, Stanley was given his first appointment, as Chief Secretary for Ireland under Lord Grey, and he entered the Cabinet in 1831.

Edward Geoffrey was, as Saintsbury described:

Not very tall, not regularly handsome, Lord Derby pos-
sessed an indefinable bearing and air which combined ease
and authority, distinction and freedom from pose. With the
physical advantages of an orator, including a tenor voice of
great beauty, he was excellently furnished, and though he is
said to have been very shortsighted, this did not exercise
ungraceful effect on his manner.[13]

The famous Reform Bill of 1832 was regarded as a triumph by most. Certainly, the reformed system of representation increased the total electorate by an incredible fifty percent. Simultaneously, the "rotten boroughs"[14] that had plagued the democratic system for years were largely cleaned up. Edward Geoffrey, who had voted against a similar reform only two years previously, recalled those days before the Bill. "It was known that when a man attempted to estimate the probable result of a county election in England it was ascertained by calculating the number of the great landed proprietors in the county and weighing the number of occupiers under them."[15]

The 14th Earl wanted reform on a piecemeal basis, reviewing each corrupt borough as it presented itself. Ironically, Edward Geoffrey's own career was given a push via the rotten-borough system when his grandfather, the 12th Earl, purchased a seat for him in the corrupt constituency of Stockbridge in 1820. As his father was holding the family's borough seat, Edward Geoffrey came to take the borough of Stockbridge, which belonged to a West Indian Tory who was willing to sell the borough for money. Still, not long after the underhanded, if typical, way by which Edward Geoffrey came to power, the future prime minister complained about the very existence of rotten boroughs and lamented how people would hardly look upon those "elected" as their true representatives. Ironically, as elections were indeed rendered less predictable following reform, it would have been more difficult for Edward Geoffrey to embark on a parliamentary career.

Edward Geoffrey left his seat at Stockbridge in 1826 for one at Preston, which had been occupied by his father, the 13th Earl. The first Preston election is noteworthy in that Stanley was put up against one of the inspirational champions of reform. William Cobbett had written his famous *Rural Rides*, a political assay of English agrarian life. Cobbett surveyed the feelings of members of many different classes in his work, giving much more than his ear to the people of the country and tabling sweeping reforms that most people dearly desired. *Rural Rides* influenced and informed a great number of parliamentary reformers, many of whom used the work as a social toolkit.

Edward Geoffrey had only a "lukewarm affection" for parliamentary reform and loathed many of the subsequent pieces of legislation that followed it.[16] Yet, mindful as he was of aristocratic stability, Edward Geoffrey was certainly not disinclined to reform in itself and supported, throughout his career, many initiatives that bettered the common man's lot. Still, his approach to reform was cautious and measured. With this in mind, it is remarkable that Edward Geoffrey Stanley so comprehensively defeated William Cobbett, the principal advocate of reform, at a time when reform and Cobbett's work were foremost in the minds of most every influential person in England. This victory speaks directly to the popularity of the family in the Preston seat.[17]

By 1833, Stanley had become Secretary for War and the Colonies. As such, he was no longer Chief Secretary for Ireland when the ramifications of his directives in that post were fully realized. Still, it was an Irish matter that served as the prime motive behind Stanley's decision to cross over to the Tory side of the Commons.

The main question, at least historically speaking, was the fact that the Church of Ireland (the Irish branch of the Anglican Church) had been funded through tithes and taxes that all Irishmen, whether of Anglican faith or otherwise, were legally obligated to pay. In other words, Catholics were forced to contribute to a Protestant church. This came at a time when various Catholics and leading Protestant reformers were lobbying Parliament for the emancipation of Catholics and to bridge the social and economic gaps between members of the two faiths. Riding on the wave of such initiatives, reformers were able to bring forth the Catholic Emancipation Act and table a proposition for the disestablishment of the Church of Ireland. The latter issue was one that Edward Geoffrey Stanley was resolutely against, to the extent that it became the cornerstone of the future prime minister's political philosophy.[18]

This philosophy was based on the premise that, as Saintsbury explained, "no circumstances could justify an interference with the property of the Church which would not equally justify interference with landed, funded, and commercial property."[19] Late in April 1834, the Government government accepted a motion that would reduce and redistribute the Irish Church revenues. Standing alone against his own party, Edward Geoffrey Stanley resigned his position in the Whig government following the motion.[20]

The Stanleys owned property in Ireland that had been in the family for many years. Despite the terrible troubles that plagued Ireland during the nineteenth century, Edward Geoffrey did not relinquish his Irish property in his lifetime and it remained a Stanley possession until Edward Henry Stanley's reign as Earl of Derby. Partially, this was due to the fact that Edward Geoffrey abhorred absentee landlords and felt morally obliged to spend at least part of the year in Ireland. It was in all likelihood, however, the question of the Irish Church that inspired Edward Geoffrey Stanley to keep a foot in Ireland.

Still, we should *pace* the pro–Irish Church policy that Edward Geoffrey adopted with the important caveat that he was *not* supportive of Orange activities and had himself voted for Catholic Emancipation in 1825, 1827, 1828 and 1829. When Edward Geoffrey Stanley entered politics, the Tories were uniformly against the removal of Roman Catholic disabilities and the Whigs were set on emancipating Catholics. Yet, Edward Geoffrey the Tory was no bigot, and his sons would later demonstrate their father's progressive sense of tolerance and acceptance, at least in terms of nineteenth-century English politics, often acting, as their father had, on their own. Saintsbury said of the Prime Minister, "he was singularly faithful to particular convictions, particular friendships, even particular whims."[21] He was very much his own man.

Moreover, while Edward Geoffrey Stanley was not willing to exempt Catholics from contributing to the Established Church, he also called upon the agricultural interest to attend to the poor and was sincere enough in his aim to better the plight of the under-classes. The 14th Earl did not play into the anti-Catholic sentiment that permeated Protestant Scotland and England, nor did he try to win the Roman Catholic vote with overly sympathetic oratories. Edward was chastised by various groups for one particular unfortunate speech in the middle of the nineteenth century that described previous emancipating measures as the "un-muzzling" of Roman Catholics in Britain. Tory ministers felt that this speech extinguished any chance of the party getting the Catholic vote. Again, Edward Geoffrey was very much his own man.

By no means, however, was the Earl a radical reformer; time and again he proved reluctant on many reform questions. Nevertheless, he was possessed of profound humanitarian impulses which propelled him to, as historian William Devereux Jones contended, "alleviate human misery whenever possible" and eliminate "the 'inveterate abuses' in various British institutions."[22] Saintsbury concurred: "Aristocratic as he was accused of being, he was more liked by his inferiors in station than most democrats."[23] At the risk of sounding cliché, Edward Geoffrey Stanley was very much in touch with the common man.

As a Conservative, Stanley served as Colonial Secretary in Sir Robert Peel's government of 1841. Only three years later, Stanley was summoned by writ of acceleration to the House of Lords, with the title Lord Stanley of Bickerstaffe.

Stanley was heavily principled and did not let party affiliation overly influence his decision as a man. As he had done with the Whig party in 1834 over the disestablishment of the Church of Ireland, so too did he resign from Sir Robert Peel's Tory government in 1845. This time, it was over the repeal of the Corn Laws, and it was rather a less lonely adventure as he took several Tory members with him, including his muse, rival and legendary political partner, Benjamin Disraeli.

With the question of the Corn Laws, Edward Geoffrey began his crusade as a staunch protectionist — a defining hallmark of the modern Conservative party of his and later times. The Corn Laws had been created to protect the British farmer — and, perhaps more significantly, the British landowner — from foreign grain imports.[24] The issue split the Parliament into two groups: on one side, Free Traders were a group comprising such various unlikely bedfellows as the Radicals, most Whigs and several Pro-Peel Tories; on the other side, the Protectionist branch of the Tories, as led by Edward Geoffrey, included Disraeli and Lord George Bentinck, who would greatly contribute to the shape of the Conservative agenda in the near future. Remarkably, Edward Geoffrey Stanley had spoken in favour of emergency corn importation in 1826 to help alleviate the distress of the poor and criticized the agricultural interests for their lack of sympathy toward those in need.[25] Yet the social landscape had changed significantly since then, and Edward Geoffrey now sought measures to protect the interests of the landowners.

As there were no viable foreign rivals to challenge British interests, historians feel that the Corn Laws were a measure to protect the profits of British landowners against cheaper rival British imports. New industrialists (specifically the so-called Cotton Lords) sought to decrease the price of grain, which would allow businesses to lower wages and so increase profit. As far as Edward Geoffrey and the protectionists were concerned, a repeal of the laws would substantially reduce the income generated by the sale of crops and, by extension, reduce the hereditary power so closely linked with land ownership.

The bill repealing the Corn Laws passed in 1846 and greatly altered the complexion of British imports. And, for the second time in his career, Edward Geoffrey resigned from his own party. It is difficult to find a single other nineteenth-century British politician who gave up office rather than change or surrender his personal opinion so as to appease the prevailing sentiment within his own party. Yet Edward Geoffrey Stanley had twice done so.

The future prime minister spoke brilliantly on the protection matter that many felt had the power to change the social structure in England, per-haps even more than Reform did. Edward Geoffrey's speech, as Saintsbury recalled, was:

> by consent of friends and foes, magnificent. Lord Palmerston and others thought it his very finest. It was in a tone more moderate, and also much more stately, than most of his speeches, and the description which it contains of the English squirearchy, and its connection with Protection, is not only a fine piece of oratory; it is an historical document and point de repère.[26]

Edward Geoffrey had drawn his line in the sand and fostered a dramatic change within the Tory party forever.

Following the defeat of the Irish Coercion Bill only a month after the repeal of the Corn Laws had passed, Prime Minister Peel resigned and the Conservative party was splintered in two. Peelites, including William Gladstone and Lord Aberdeen, eventually teamed up with Whigs and Radicals and, within a little more than a decade and a half, would form the modern Liberal party. It was up to Edward Geoffrey Stanley and Disraeli to piece together the remnants of Peel's Conservative party and begin anew.

Still, Stanley, now the 14th Earl of Derby, had to wait until 1852 to form his first minority government, which included the rising political star Disraeli as Chancellor of the Exchequer.

Political figures who had come to Parliament by way of an aristocratic family were often prejudged by other politicians as simple and were often pronounced guilty of underachieving in the political arena. This was not so with Edward Geoffrey Stanley. *The Times* regarded the Prime Minister as the most "brilliant eldest son produced by the British peerage for a hundred years."[27]

Stanley was forced to fill his government with relatively unknown members as many Conservative ministers remained Peelites and were in no way interested in joining forces with the unproven tandem of Derby and Disraeli. To that end, the Duke of Wellington, who was extremely hard of hearing, is reputed to have asked, "Who? Who?" following the introduction of each of Derby's obscure ministers. And so begat one of the most enduring, if humorous, tidbits of the Stanley legacy — a euphemism that can be found in parliamentary language every time rookie ministers fill out the ranks of a new government: the "Who? Who? Ministry."

Certainly, Benjamin Disraeli was the star of all three of Stanley's ministries. Already a literary figure after a fashion, Disraeli would soon be regarded as one of England's most prominent statesmen. It was as a member of Derby's ministries that the future two-time prime minister cut his teeth and honed his legendary oratory skills. Disraeli's skills as an orator would be repeatedly put on trial during his now-famous parliamentary duels with iconic leader of the Liberal party, William Gladstone. Although he would frame the modern Conservative party with Derby, the two did not always see eye to eye. This was partially due to the fact that Disraeli had struggled to reach the high station he commanded, while Derby had been born into a privileged and important family.

Like Stanley, Disraeli had been a member of the protectionist wing of the Tory government from 1846 and, also like Stanley, enjoyed a warm relationship with Queen Victoria. Yet, it wasn't until the 1860s that the relationship between Derby and Disraeli became less strained.

Disraeli had been overlooked by Peel in the 1840s when the latter formed his government. Peel had thus, perhaps unwittingly, created an enemy in Disraeli, and one who would complement the Derby prerogative in no less than three ministries.

Stanley's protectionist philosophy proved highly beneficial for England. Years before Disraeli was free to pursue a policy that engendered the development of Britain's military pre-eminence in Europe, Stanley, alongside his Foreign Secretary Lord Malmesbury and later his son, Frederick's brother Edward Henry Stanley, sought to avoid armed conflict and looked to the "Concert of Europe" to peacefully deal with continental issues that caused concern among various countries. This foreign policy was a signature trait of Stanley's modern Conservative ministry and in no small way anticipated the isolationist policies that later incarnations of the Tory party engaged in.

Despite the ministry's relatively groundbreaking achievements, Derby was unable to achieve a parliamentary majority, and only ten months after it had began, Derby's government fell and gave way to a Peelite-Whig coalition formed by Lord Aberdeen.

In 1858, Derby was once again in the position to form a minority government. Once again, Disraeli was chosen as Chancellor of the Exchequer as well as Leader of the Commons. During this administration, England survived the famous Sepoy Mutiny in India. The British East India Company was made defunct and India, for the first time, came under direct control of the British. In terms of longevity, Derby's second ministry fared only marginally better than his first one. One year and four months after its inception, Derby's government collapsed.

Derby became prime minister for the third and final time in 1866. Perhaps the single greatest achievement of the ministry — and, it may be argued, the greatest achievement of Stanley's career — was the introduction of the Reform Act of 1867. It was indeed the natural "conclusion" to the Great Reform Act of 1832 and actually went further in many areas than Gladstone's defeated Whig Reform Bill of 1866.

For several years, Prime Minister Palmerston had successfully opposed any potential calls for further electoral reform. Still, members from all factions within Parliament had hoped to improve on the measures that had been secured with the first Act in 1832. And with the death of Palmerston in 1865, the path to a second reform act was cleared.

Pragmatically, the Tories put forth a more revolutionary Bill than the Whigs had in an attempt to gain control of the actual reform process itself. Not surprisingly, Disraeli had largely been responsible for engineering the failure of the Whig version of the act in the first place. The successful act put forward by the Conservatives expanded the franchise by an impressive one and a half million voters. Again, rotten boroughs with fewer than ten thousand inhabitants were wiped out, and large towns that had hitherto been under- or unrepresented were now granted constituencies.

Not all members of the Conservative party celebrated the passing of the bill. Lord Cranborne, later the Marquess of Salisbury and the prime minister during Frederick Stanley's reign as Canada's governor general, was very much vocal in his opposition. Still, the bill passed and the Conservative party was able to convert a golden political opportunity to re-establish — and in some respects, reinvent — itself as a modern and viable party. The second bill spoke far more to the idea of democracy than the first one had, though we should pace this optimistic assessment because the days of "one man, one vote" remained but a speck on the distant horizon. Furthermore, historians argue that the bill was far more a product of ego and personal satisfaction than it was an attempt to improve the lot of the great unwashed. Regardless of whether the bill was simply the result of the first of many Gladstone/Disraeli bouts, the second Reform Act revolutionized British politics forever and brought the British people household suffrage.

In assessing a bill that he had been largely responsible for, Edward Geoffrey Stanley humorously claimed that this latest version of reform was "a leap in the dark."[28] Some historians feel that the bill was wholly un-Tory in its character and point to the rash or capricious manner in which Edward Geoffrey sometimes acted. Saintsbury claimed that there was "a great deal of boyishness in Lord Derby: and this boyishness took, among other forms, the form of being ready to act in a sort of 'here goes' and 'in for a penny in for a pound' spirit."[29] Certainly, the Second Reform pushed through measures that were not in concert with the traditional line of Tory philosophy. Yet, once again, Edward Geoffrey did not fit tidily into any one party. If he was periodically rash and reckless, he was never subservient. He was very much his own man.

Edward Geoffrey Stanley was prime minister during 1867, the year Canada became a nation. He had been to Canada in 1824 and felt that the Dominion, at least at the time of his journey, was as languid as it was loyal and paled in comparison to the energetic United States. During his tour of Canada's giant neighbour to the south, Edward Geoffrey Stanley wrote:

If I left the United States without much admiration for the attractive qualities of their citizens, I left them also with feelings which I would fain hope are gaining ground in England of respect for much of solid and sterling merit, and

*with a full persuasion of the firmness of the foundation on
which their political structure is built.*[30]

Nearly forty years prior to Confederation, Edward Geoffrey recommended
that Britain treat Canada with the "most unfettered liberality" and allow
the colony to pursue a liberal course in terms of the shape of its social
structure and the grammar of its economic market.[31] Following the 1837
Rebellion, Upper and Lower Canada were united and the colonists were
given a voice in government in the form of an elective lower chamber, the
Legislative Assembly. Edward Geoffrey acted as an advisor to Sir Charles
Bagot, who had been sent to control the Canadian Assembly. In essence,
Edward Geoffrey walked Bagot through political initiatives that in no small
way placated anxious Canadians. Edward Geoffrey felt that Canadians
could enjoy a form of "Imperial Preference," chiefly in the area of exports.
In short, Corn Laws would be relaxed in the case of Canada, allowing
Canadians to export corn to the mother country. This resolution may seem
odd, coming from a man that would later be considered a devout protectionist; however, the future prime minister sought to strengthen Canadian
loyalties, weaken the chance of future rebellions and assist Bagot, whose
political skills were suspect, through some rather murky waters.

By 1867, Canada was a country. This development, however, was likely
only a small matter for most British politicians, given the enormity of the
Second Reform Act. Nevertheless, while the merits of the new Reform Bill
were being weighed and scrutinized, John A. Macdonald became Canada's
first prime minister. Edward Geoffrey Stanley, Macdonald's counterpart in
Westminster, likely had little idea that his son Frederick would one day embark on a long and dear friendship with Macdonald.

In 1868, only two years after forming his last government, Stanley
retired from politics, leaving Disraeli to lead the Conservative party. Less
than two years later, he would be dead.

Edward Geoffrey's leadership was often criticized by nineteenth-century
historians, who referred to his refusal to form ministries in 1845, 1850 and
1855 as a sign of weakness. Yet he did form governments three times and,
although his terms as prime minister were often brief, Edward Geoffrey was
the leader of the Conservative party for a remarkable twenty-two years, a
record that remains intact. He was in his element whenever there was
fighting to be done, which is one reason Edward Geoffrey Stanley is generally

considered by historians to be the father of the modern Conservative party. Saintsbury declared that for Edward Geoffrey,

> *to be thrice a Tory Prime Minister, to have resigned office even in Whig and unregenerate days rather than injure the Church, to run second for the Derby, and to translate Homer not unacceptably — no well-conducted and healthy undergraduate could possibly add much more as an expression of the chief end of man — though of course it would have been better to run first than second.*[32]

All witty analyses aside, Edward Geoffrey was an able politician and a sound and respected statesman who left exceptionally large shoes for his sons to fill.

Whatever contemporaries may have thought of his political moves, most would have agreed that Prime Minister Stanley was a kind parent, a good husband and a man who possessed a deep reverence for his faith. The Earl was never indifferent to religious questions, and very early in life he had written a children's book entitled Conversations on the Parables.[33] Yet he could hardly have been called a zealot — witness the 14th Earl's progressive step of allowing the British Museum to be open on Sunday afternoons. Nevertheless, while his seemingly sound and rational faith system sometimes worked against him in the political realm, in his private life, Edward Geoffrey imparted his profound reverence for religion onto all three of his children.

Frederick Arthur Stanley's mother, Emma Caroline Bootle-Wilbraham, was the second daughter of Edward Bootle-Wilbraham, the 1st Baron Skelmersdale. She married Edward Geoffrey Stanley in April 1825. Though she may have been plain and uncomplicated in the eyes of English society, Emma Stanley was, as Jones claimed, her husband's "closest, and perhaps only real confidante and partner of the next half-century."[34] All things considered, Frederick could have done much worse.

Edward Geoffrey Stanley loved hunting, horse-racing and other aristocratic sporting pursuits, but also retained a deep reverence for Latin and English literature. As Jones attested, "on quiet evenings nothing pleased Stanley more than to read Shakespeare to his family in that rich tenor with which he regaled the Commons."[35] The Prime Minister spoke many languages and also had a great love of poetry. When he was twenty, the 14th

Earl won the Chancellor's prize for Latin verse at Oxford in 1819 with a poem on Syracuse. Forty-three years later, he published *Translations of Poems Ancient and Modern*, which included Book 1 of Homer's *Iliad*. Between terms as prime minister, the Earl took on the immense task of translating the remainder of the *Iliad* into two volumes in 1864. Professor Gilbert Murray wrote, "I think you can safely say that Lord Derby's translation of Homer was the most successful at the time when Pope had gone out of fashion and the prose translation of Andrew Lang and Leaf, and the verse of William Morris had not yet come in."[36]

Likewise, Edward Geoffrey Stanley's biographer, T. E. Kebbel, wrote that the 14th Earl:

> ... has produced one of the best translations of the Iliad of Homer which our literature can boast, and his other translations ... show that he possessed the literary faculty in no ordinary degree, and that a great English classic may have been lost in him when he devoted himself to politics.[37]

Many years later, when Frederick was in Ottawa, he would not escape his father's shadow. The Royal Society of Canada lamented the achievements of the 14th Earl for the benefit of his son, the governor general, who presided over the meeting.

> All of us remember with the deepest interest that your illustrious father, in youth, won many academic honours in the study of the great poets of ancient days. While the political historian will record his triumphs as the 'Rupert of Debate,' men of letters will like best to linger on his success in rendering the Iliad into matchless English verse.[38]

While Edward Geoffrey might have deprived the literary world of an English classic, the world of politics gained a master orator. And though his decision-making process might not have been so easily understood, Edward Geoffrey Stanley remained one of the key architects of various policies that profoundly affected people living in nineteenth-century Britain.

* * *

In his final political fight, the Earl defended the main, and perhaps only, pillar of what had been his lifelong political philosophy: the question of the Irish Church. The writing was on the wall for the church, and the old man could see it. In his famous last speech, which employed the imagery of Sir Walter Scott's *Guy Mannering* for effect, Edward Geoffrey pointed the finger at those in the House of Lords who either pushed for or passively allowed the disestablishment of the Church of Ireland.

> *My Lords, it is ... with sorrow, but with resentment — that the Protestants of Ireland may look upon you from whom they expected protection — a protection which they repaid with the most faithful loyalty, when they now find you laying upon them the heavy hand of what I must consider an undeserved oppression. There are ... 700,000 hearts, and 700,000 more who have connected themselves with you in loyal attachment to the sovereign for the sake of that Protestant religion ... remember who these men are.*[39]

Edward George Geoffrey Smith-Stanley died on 23 October, 1869, surviving by a few weeks the chuch he fought so long to defend.

On the day the Earl passed away, Lord Malmesbury wrote in his journal, "Lord Derby died this morning at seven o'clock. In him I lose my greatest friend, and the country a most brilliant and accomplished statesman."[40] Saintsbury said of him, "He was indeed altogether a delightfully human person ... a thorough sportsman ... a man original genius ... Lord Derby may be pronounced the most perfect example that we have yet had of the aristocratic type of Minister of a constitutionally-governed country."[41]

* * *

Edward Geoffrey Stanley and his wife, Emma, had six children, although three died at birth. The first-born, Edward Henry Stanley, later the 15th Earl of Derby, was born 21 July, 1826, and died 21 April, 1893. Ferdinand Charles Stanley was born 26 July, 1829, and died the next day. An unnamed child was born and died 3 May, 1832. Emma Charlotte Stanley, so named for her mother, was born 25 December, 1835, and died 23 August, 1928. Charles Stanley was born 6 August, 1838, and died that day. The youngest child, Frederick Arthur Stanley, was born 15 January, 1841, at the family's residence at 10 St. James's Square, Westminster.[42]

When Edward Geoffrey Stanley died, Edward Henry, the eldest, became the 15th Earl of Derby. Edward Henry inherited a massive and seemingly unmanageable family debt in excess of £500,000. His father had, as historian John Vincent explained, "left a muddle, with the estate office and accounts in confusion."[43]

Edward Henry was considered shy, unassuming, generally open-minded and fair, but rather lacking in ambition. Educated at Rugby and later Trinity College, Cambridge, Edward Henry took a high degree and was a member of the Apostles' Society. At Cambridge, Edward Henry took a First in Classics — thanks, no doubt, to the attention paid to the subject by his father. He possessed a terrific memory and was ultimately a great businessman. As such, Edward Henry rather brought Knowsley out of the red.

Still, it wasn't an easy road. Indeed, when Edward Henry Stanley claimed the earldom, his financial responsibilities to numerous family members were onerous. Frederick, for example, had received an inheritance from his father, however, there were other matters to be resolved, including the Irish estate. With some consternation, Edward Henry understood his brother's decision to opt for money over the possession of the estate that Edward Henry wanted desperately relieved of:

> *[Frederick] has decided for the money. I think in his own interest, he is right, but where am I to find £125,000 in addition to existing debts is not easy to see. Probably however he will be content to draw the interest and let the principal lie. He talks sensibly about matters here, and says that the heads under which reduction ought to be made are the stables, the shooting, and perhaps the gardens.*[44]

Edward Henry also recorded in his diary the arrangement that his father had made with Frederick regarding the Witherslack estate. The arrangement called for Frederick to become the tenant of Witherslack. In his journal, Edward Henry said of the matter, "I see no objection to this, as the property is completely detached, and too far from Knowsley to have any residential advantage."[45] As heir to the earldom, Edward Henry would hardly have begrudged his brother becoming the resident at Witherslack.

23

In an attempt to reduce his great burden, Edward Henry eliminated various extravagances at Knowsley, perhaps the most important of which had been the family's horse stable and breeding interests. The 15th Earl sold the race stock for £4,650, and with it, the stud that had cost the 14th Earl over £1,300 a year to maintain. Though it likely broke the hearts of various family members, horse breeding, according to Edward Henry was a, "business I neither understand nor care about."[46]

There was, however, some remorse in the decision, as one entry from Edward Henry's diary has revealed.

> *Talk with Hornby ... especially of the great breeding establishment kept up here, at a heavy loss, and which I shall at once get rid of ... but I am sorry for old Jim Forshaw, who was in charge of it, and served my father over forty years.*[47]

With the help from a windfall generated by sales of land to the railway companies, Edward Henry impressively surmounted the massive debt that he inherited. And though he had aimed to do so over a period of ten to twelve years, Edward Henry repaid £510,000 of debt in only six years.

* * *

The most curious chapter of Edward Henry's life came with, of all things, a revolution in far-off Greece in the early 1860s. With King Otho expelled, the Greeks offered the throne first to Prince Alfred, who refused, and then to Edward Henry Stanley. Although this may have been a case of romance lusting after fact, in a letter dated 7 February, 1863, Benjamin Disraeli wrote, "the Greeks really want to make my friend Lord Stanley their king. This beats any novel, but he will not. Had I his youth, I would not hesitate."[48] There is some reasonable question as to whether the offer was officially made. It is true, however, that the Greeks had a fondness for the Stanley brood.

Although he was a moderate Liberal at heart, this was still the nineteenth century and Edward Henry Stanley was very much a man of his time. He was not interested in the further accumulation of more tropical colonies for the Empire, a conviction that was harshly pronounced when he shared his views on the matter: "We have quite black men enough."[49] While in opposition, Edward Henry vehemently opposed the needless expansion of Empire and fought the government at every angle on the issue, from the conquering of Ashanti to the fortification of Fiji as a protectorate. On balance, however, Edward Henry was fairly progressive by nineteenth-century aristocratic standards. As Vincent declared, Edward Henry Stanley

> *abhorred Anglican sectarianism. He did not wish conservatism to be confined to gentry traditionalism. He looked to a future in which science, including social science, played an honoured part. He cultivated the cooperative movement. He sought to appeal to a non-radical intelligentsia and a satisfied but politically conscious working class. In his version of conservatism, there was room for almost all.*[50]

Edward Henry was also a humanist and keenly interested in the welfare of many organizations and humanitarian initiatives, such as hospital charities, prisoners' aid, tree-planting, the betterment of artisans' dwellings, orphans of seamen, technical education, the mechanics' institutes, and the deaf, to name a few.[51] With respect to philanthropic endeavours, Edward far exceeded most of his Conservative peers.

He unsuccessfully ran for the borough of Lancaster in 1848. Following his defeat, Edward Henry took a tour of the Americas, including Canada, the same country of which his younger brother would be governor general some four decades later.

Edward Henry joined his father's party and made his first speech for the Conservatives in May 1850. Later, in his father's first ministry, Edward was appointed Under-secretary for Foreign Affairs. Like his father, Edward did not fit tidily into any of the existing parties of the day. In this respect, he is considered to be a liberal-leaning Tory, though, also like his father, he would one day cross the floor and join another party.

Long before this, however, Edward Henry had actually been offered the post of Colonial Secretary in Lord Palmerston's government in 1855. In a now-infamous event, Edward Henry hurried over to Knowsley to ask his father's advice on the proposal. When Edward Henry entered the room, his father is reputed to have quipped, "Hallo Stanley! What brings you here? Has Dizzy cut his throat or are you going to be married?" Edward Geoffrey Stanley talked his son out of accepting the post.

Although it took him some time to decide to actually serve with his father again, Edward Henry held two posts in the 14th Earl's second ministry, including the office of Secretary for the Colonies and later the President of the Board of Control. Following the India Bill of 1858, Edward Henry Stanley became the first Secretary of State for India. Later, in his father's third and final ministry, Edward held the important post of Foreign Secretary.

A few years later, in 1870, Edward Henry was himself offered the leadership of the Tory party — an offer he refused. Though he carefully weighed the proposal, he chose not to lead the party for various reasons, which included an acute anxiety around public speaking. In his diary, Edward Henry wrote:

> *Want of readiness in speech is the difficulty which affects me most: but that is lessened by practice: the audience, though cold, is attentive: and I am conscious that without some external inducement I should not easily overcome my dislike to speaking, while such inducement is supplied by a position which makes silence impossible.*[52]

This shyness was a characteristic that he shared with his brother Frederick, who also was not overly fond of public speaking.

After his father's death, the 15th Earl joined Disraeli's government in 1874 in the same capacity as Foreign Secretary and was vaguely involved in the Russo-Turkish squabble, though his exact role — while likely important — was never fully explained, either publicly or in personal memoirs.

Disraeli had been "tethered" and did not have the same free rein he enjoyed in Edward Geoffrey's last ministry.[53] Over time, Edward Henry developed a fondness for and a trust in Disraeli to such an extent, he confessed, that should Disraeli leave the party, "I do not think I can go on with the rest of the party, either as leader or follower."[54] Edward Henry Stanley officially left the Tories in 1880 and joined the Liberal party headed by Gladstone (Disraeli's natural enemy). This move was something he believed he could never have done in his father's lifetime. In an unpublished memorandum curiously written in the third person, Edward Henry confessed that his "own opinions and sympathies were in the main with the Liberal Party of that period." On refusing the famous offer to join Lord Palmerston's government in 1855, Edward Henry lamented that he "felt disappointment whilst he did not wish to be on the other side of the house as against his father, but he would perhaps have felt less keenly had his father seemed to estimate what he had relinquished."[55]

As sons of a man considered by most to be the father of the modern-Conservative party, it would have been extremely difficult for either son — Edward Henry or Frederick — to operate outside of the party, even though Edward Geoffrey Stanley himself had been very much an anomaly within the party he helped to shape.

In 1882, Edward Henry became Secretary for the Colonies in Gladstone's government, a position he held until the fall of the government in 1885. In another party shift, Edward Henry became a key member of the Liberal Unionist Party in 1886, a party he led in the House of Lords until 1891. One year prior to his death, Edward Henry presided over the Labour Commission.

* * *

Knowsley had been, at least in Edward Henry and his father Edward Geoffrey's time, a place that entertained almost exclusively members of the aristocracy. Few members of the new middling classes — mill-owners and the *new* money crowd, were ever entertained at Knowsley.

While Edward Geoffrey took great pains to make his presence felt in Ireland, Edward Henry wanted to sell the family's estate there, believing that the whole of Ireland was "Fenian at heart."[56] Also unlike his father, Edward Henry, bolstered by his love of David Hume and Bishop Butler and his fondness for Disraeli and Charles Darwin, was not a strict churchman and took exception to politicians who were "strong religionists."[57] While Edward Henry emulated his father's sentiments whenever the question of the Irish Church was raised, in general terms he possessed a pronounced distaste for religion — a fact that served him as much as it worked against him.

* * *

Given a father who was not quite a Whig and later became a protectionist Tory with some Liberal sensibilities, and an older brother who was not quite a Tory and later a Liberal with some Tory leanings, Frederick Arthur Stanley's political biases are not easily gauged. Nevertheless, it can be said with some degree of assurance that our Stanley was a Tory — if perhaps one with a predisposition to some liberal creeds.

Having a prime minister for a father certainly helped Stanley get established in political life. Though his father's influence may have got Stanley in the door, it was the son who was able to prove his worthiness and consequently enjoyed a string of political successes and promotions. Following his service with the Grenadier Guards (1858–65), Stanley was successively elected Conservative member of Parliament for Preston (1865–68), Lancashire North (1868–85) and finally Lancashire-Blackpool (1885–86).

In 1886, following two decades of dedicated service as a Tory MP, a second title was bestowed upon Frederick Arthur Stanley: Baron Stanley of Preston. The second son of the 14th Earl was going to enter the House of Lords.

Stanley held various portfolios, including Civil Lord of the Admiralty (1868), Financial Secretary to the War Office (1874–77) and Financial Secretary of the Treasury (1877–78). Stanley's brother was delighted by the news of the Treasury appointment:

> *Heard of my brother's appointment to the vacant post at the Treasury, which I am glad for his sake and that of his family, since it shows that Disraeli & Northcote really think well of him as an administrator. There is too much work in that place, & work of a kind which cannot be neglected or mismanaged without immediate inconvenience, for the appointment to be a job. He has now got a fair start, & if his health lasts, will probably be a secretary of state before he dies.*[58]

One year later, following the resignation of his brother Edward Henry from Cabinet, Stanley became Secretary of State for War (1878–80).

As Secretary of State for the Colonies (1885–86), Stanley was brought into direct contact with Canadian politicians, including, for the first time, John A. Macdonald. Stanley's brief and final posting before he accepted the position as Canada's governor general was as President of the Board of Trade (1886–88).

Beginning in his youth, Stanley had been susceptible to bouts of depression. He remained susceptible throughout his life, as one diary entry from his brother Edward Henry can attest: "Constance says Frederick in subject to fits of depression and low spirits, which lasts for days, and from which it is not easy to rouse him."[59] While he was in the post at the Treasury, Edward Henry spoke of his brother as being "despondent about the prospects of the session," which Edward Henry believed was "rather his habit."[60] Frederick Arthur would habitually measure his success against that of his brother and father. In Canada, Stanley secretly longed for a prestigious post in India — though his brother advised him against this. While there must have existed some degree of competition with his much older brother, Stanley was simultaneously seeking his approval on all important decisions.

If Stanley's father didn't provide the same sort of sounding board that his brother had, he *did* give his youngest son an excellent model after which Stanley was able to model his own political career. If the Prime Minister had championed the Second Reform Bill (after a fashion), opened museums on Sundays and, on balance, enhanced the age of improvement and exemplified the socially reformed consciousness of nineteenth-century Britain, Frederick Arthur and his young family would carry these same cautiously progressive principles with them to Canada.

---

1 Scottish Battles (Newtongrange, Midlothian: Lang Syne Publishing Ltd., 1985), p.108.

2 R. S. Churchill, *Lord Derby: King of Lancashire — The Official Life of Edward, Seventeenth Earl of Derby, 1865-1948* (London: Heinemann, 1959), p.4.

3 Ibid., p.2.

4 G. Saintsbury, *The Earl of Derby* (London: Sampson Low, Martson & Company, 1892), p.6.

5 Ibid.

6 Ibid., pp.6-7.

7 W. D. Jones, *Lord Derby and Victorian Consevatism* (Athens: The University of Georgia Press 1956), pp.1-2.

8 A. Briggs, *The Age of Improvement: 1783–1867* (London: Longman, {1959} 1979), p.236.

9 Ibid., p.238.

10 Saintsbury, *The Earl of Derby*, p.12.

11 Ibid., p.75.

12 Ibid., p.8. The song was also sung at Edward George Stanley's wedding to Lady Alice Montagu in 1889. See, V. Stanley, *Letter to his Mother, Lady Constance Stanley* (6 January, 1889); Churchill, *Lord Derby*, p.28.

13 Saintsbury, *The Earl of Derby*, p.197.

14 'Rotten Boroughs' was a term used to describe county seats that had often been secured by underhanded means or through absurd and trivial technicalities. Some questionable means of securing an election victory included the practice of bringing a large regiment of soldiers into an otherwise sleepy village on the eve of an election and having them cast a vote for the 'chosen' candidate to ensure victory. See, Briggs, *Age of Improvement*, pp.236–85.

[15] *The Leeds Mercury* (8 July, 1841); G. Kitson Clark, 'The Electorate and the Repeal of the Corn Laws', *Transactions of the Royal Historical Society* (London: 1951); Briggs, *Age of Improvement*, p.264.

[16] Saintsbury, *The Earl of Derby*, p.21.

[17] The popularity of the Stanleys in the Preston region experienced a brief nadir when 'radical' reformers singled out individual members of Parliament for special attention. The Wellington government was disposed and Edward George's seat with it in the 1830 election. Waves of reformers, specifically those lobbying for the emancipation of Catholics, became violent in their protests. Edward George Stanley was actually mobbed, beaten and was in genuine danger of losing his life. See, Saintsbury, *The Earl of Derby*, p.22.

[18] Jones, *Lord Derby*, p.8.

[19] Saintsbury, *The Earl of Derby*, p.15–6.

[20] The Church of Ireland was not actually disestablished until 1871 following an 1869 Act of Parliament which all removed the Church's representation in the House of Lords.

[21] Saintsbury, *The Earl of Derby*, p.19.

[22] Jones, *Lord Derby*, p.15. Edward George spoke with contempt regarding, 'Tories of the old school, sticklers for inveterate abuses under the name of the wisdom of our ancestors ... of the spirit which supported the Holy Alliance, the friend of despotism, rather than the advocate of struggling freedom.' Edward George Stanley as quoted in Saintsbury, *The Earl of Derby*, pp.16–7.

[23] Ibid., p.209.

[24] 'Corn' in this case, primarily refers to 'grain' as in the grain crop of a particular nation.

[25] Jones, *Lord Derby*, p.13.

[26] Saintsbury, *The Earl of Derby*, p.54.

[27] *The Times* (London: 25 October, 1869).

[28] Saintsbury, *The Earl of Derby*, p.175.

[29] Ibid., p.178.

[30] E. Stanley, *Journal of a Tour in America: 1824–1825* (London: Privately Printed, 1930), p.336.

[31] *Hansard* (report of debates in the House of Commons – London: New Series, XIX), p.339; Jones, *Lord Derby*, p.13.

[32] Saintsbury, *The Earl of Derby*, p.2.

[33] Ibid., p.213.

[34] Jones, *Lord Derby*, p.10.

[35] Ibid., p.104.

[36] G. Murray, *Letter to R. S. Churchill*; Churchill, *Lord Derby*, p.7.

[37] T. E. Kebbel, *Life of the Earl of Derby, K G.* (London: W. H. Allen & Co., 1890), p.182; Noonan, *Canada's Governors General*, p.163.

[38] 'Meeting of the Royal Society of Canada', *Semi-Weekly Citizen* (Ottawa: 9 May, 1889), p.4; James Noonan, *Canada's Governors General* (Ottawa: Borealis Book Publishers, 2002), p.163. Lord Lytton's famous account of Lord Derby the Prime Minister, 'The brilliant chief, irregularly great — frank, haughty, rash, the *Rupert of Debate*', can be found in Saintsbury, *The Earl of Derby*, p.194.

[39] Edward George Stanley, as quoted in a speech in the House of Lords, 1868. See Saintsbury, *The Earl of Derby*, pp.191-2.

[40] Lord Malmesbury, *Personal Diary* (23 October, 1869); Saintsbury, *The Earl of Derby*, p.194.

[41] Saintsbury, *The Earl of Derby*, p.209-210.

[42] The Peerage.com, is a Genealogical survey of the peerage of Britain as well as the Royal Families of Europe – on Person Page 1276 one finds Edward Geoffrey Stanley, 12755.

[43] J. Vincent, *A Selection From: The Diaries of Edward Henry Stanley, 15th Earl of Derby* (1826-93) (London: Offices of the Royal Historical Society, 1994), p.8.

[44] E. H. Stanley, *Personal Diary* (25 October, 1869); Vincent, *Diaries of Edward Henry Stanley*, p.38.

[45] E. H. Stanley, *Personal Diary* (2 October, 1869); Vincent, *Diaries of Edward Henry Stanley*, p.36.

[46] E. H. Stanley, *Personal Diary* (6 November, 1869); Vincent, *Diaries of Edward Henry Stanley*, p.8.

[47] E. H. Stanley, *Personal Diary* (6 November, 1869); Vincent, *Diaries of Edward Henry Stanley*, p.40.

[48] B. Disraeli, *Personal Letter*; Churchill, *Lord Derby*, p.11.

[49] T. H. Sanderson and E. S. Roscoe (*eds*), *Speeches and Addresses of Edward Henry XVth Earl of Derby K. G.*, (2 Vols., 1894); Vincent, *Diaries of Edward Henry Stanley*, p.25.

[50] Vincent, *Diaries of Edward Henry Stanley*, pp.23–4

[51] Ibid., p.24.

[52] E. H. Stanley, *Personal Diary* (20 February, 1870); Vincent, *Diaries of Edward Henry Stanley*, p.52.

[53] E. Cowper, *K.G. A Memoir* (Printed for Private Circulation, 1913), pp. 254, 265; Vincent, *Diaries of Edward Henry Stanley*, p.14.

[54] E. H. Stanley, *Personal Diary* (6 March, 1875); Vincent, *Diaries of Edward Henry Stanley*, p.20.

[55] E. H. Stanley, *Unpublished Memorandum*; Churchill, Lord Derby, pp.9–10.

[56] E. H. Stanley, *Personal Diary* (11, 15 November, 1871); Vincent, *Diaries of Edward Henry Stanley*, p.9.

[57] Edward Henry Stanley was a pallbearer at both Charles Darwin and Benjamin Disraeli's funerals. See, E. H. Stanley, *Personal Diary* (20 July, 1874); Vincent, *Diaries of Edward Henry Stanley*, p.11.

[58] E. H. Stanley, *Personal Diary* (11 August, 1877); *Vincent, Diaries of Edward Henry Stanley*, p.430.

[59] E. H. Stanley, *Personal Diary* (18 September, 1871); Vincent, *Diaries of Edward Henry Stanley*, p.89.

[60] E. H. Stanley, *Personal Diary* (8 January, 1878); Vincent, *Diaries of Edward Henry Stanley*, p.481.

CHAPTER THREE

Stanley's Youth and the Impact of Sports

Frederick Arthur Stanley was born into his distinguished Lancashire family on a bitter cold day in the first month of 1841. The Stanley family residence was mere steps from Buckingham Palace, Piccadilly Circus and Trafalgar Square, and had been home to the famed British prime minister William Pitt the Elder from 1757 to 1761 while he served as Secretary of State. Between 1837 and 1854, 10 St. James's Square served as both the home and office of the 14th Earl of Derby. At that time, it was not uncommon for ministers to conduct much of their official business from home.

The Stanley children, including young Frederick, were little different than their peers in that an afternoon of running or swimming constituted great entertainment. The Stanley children played stick and ball games like cricket, knur and spell, tip-cat and rounders, as well as marbles and whipping tops.

The youngsters took great delight in visiting their grandparents. Paternal grandfather Edward Smith Stanley, the 13th Earl of Derby, was a politician and landowner who prided himself on his remarkable collection of art. From the time of his father's death on 21 October, 1834, when he retired from politics and succeeded his father as earl, he followed an unbridled passion for natural history. His unrivalled collection, harboured at the family estate of Knowsley on an area better than one hundred acres of property and more than seventy acres of water at an annual cost of more than ten thousand pounds, included twenty thousand specimens of mammals, birds, reptiles, fish and eggs. At the time of his death on 30 June, 1851, the 13th Earl's collection was dispersed. Many of the living animals were sent to the Zoological Society in London's Regent's Park while others were sold off. The museum artefacts were donated as the Derby Collection to the World Museum Liverpool.[1]

The Earl had been president of the Linnean Society of London, a biological organization formed in 1788, and of the Zoological Society of London, founded in 1826. As an adjunct to his menagerie, Stanley also had taxidermists preserve rare animals and birds, several of which are now extinct. These include the long-tailed hopping mouse from Australia, which was last sighted in 1901, the Himalayan mountain quail, last sighted in 1868, and the paradise parrot, last seen in 1927 in Australia.[2]

Following the 13th Earl of Derby's death, his will provided the opportunity for Queen Victoria and the Zoological Society of London to select from his existing menagerie and aviary. The remainder of the animals and birds were subsequently sold at auction. The Earl bequeathed his collection of stuffed animals, reptiles and birds to the town of Liverpool, and this formed the foundation of the Derby Museum, which opened in 1853 on Duke Street, sharing space with the library. The Derby Museum outgrew its surroundings, and in 1860 the renamed World Museum of Liverpool moved into its own building on what would be William Brown Street.

In 1832, Frederick's grandfather became the patron of artist Edward Lear, who was commissioned to draw portraits of the wildlife on the estate. In 1846, Lear published *Gleanings from the Menagerie and Aviary at Knowsley Hall.*

Frederick and his siblings and cousins were all fascinated with their grandfather's collection of animals and birds. But they were equally enthralled with the eccentric Lear, who went to great lengths to entertain the Earl's grandchildren by writing silly rhymes for their enjoyment.[3] The limericks made the children roar with laughter and call out for "just one more." Lear would graciously comply:

> *There was an old person of Cromer,*
> *Who stood on one leg to read Homer.*
> *When he found he grew stiff,*
> *He jumped over the cliff,*
> *Which concluded that person of Cromer.*[4]

There was an old person of Rhodes,
Who strongly objected to toads.
He paid several cousins
To catch them by dozens.
That futile old person of Rhodes.[5]

The same year that he published his wildlife portraits, Lear collected the nonsensical rhymes written for the Stanley grandchildren and published *A Book of Nonsense*. It was convention at that time for children's books to be published anonymously, so when the book was issued in February 1846 Lear used the name Derry Down Derry. His actual name wasn't mentioned until the third edition was published, in 1861. Lear later published arguably his best-known poem, *The Owl and the Pussycat*, in 1871. Suffering from epilepsy and depression for much of his life, the popular Lear died in San Remo, Italy, in January 1888.

* * *

The Stanley family often entertained — Noonan confirmed that there was "no aristocratic family in the country having greater facilities for entertaining royal guests than are possessed by the Earls of Derby."[6] Yet, Frederick's father and his wife, Emma, who was also his personal secretary, held political occasions that were described as "dull and depressing as a London fog."[7]

* * *

As an eleven-year-old, Frederick began to consider a military career. In 1852, the young Stanley corresponded with the famous Henry Hardinge, the commander-in-chief of the British Army. In his correspondence, Stanley informed Hardinge that he liked the good range of the Louis Quatorze gun, although the long-range Warner was a superior rifle.[8]

One year later, Frederick enrolled at Eton, the highly regarded boys-only college on the Thames, twenty miles west of central London. Frederick's father, the 14th Earl of Derby, had been a student there from 1811 to 1817. Curiously, Frederick's brother Edward, the future 15th Earl of Derby, did not attend Eton. The reason was long rumoured to be because he had been caught stealing.[9] The future governor general was a student at Eton only until December 1854, although attending for a brief period of time was quite common in that era.[10]

In order to prepare himself for military training, Stanley then attended Royal Military College, Sandhurst, found in Camberley, Surrey. Like all students attending Sandhurst at that time, Stanley was considered a gentleman cadet, whose parents paid tuition and boarding fees for their son while at the military training school — a philosophy that Stanley later applied to the Canadian militia when he came to the Dominion.

While at Sandhurst in 1857, the sixteen-year-old Stanley received a letter from General Sir Harry G. Smith, a British war hero who had participated in the Battle of Waterloo. Smith told the youngster he was sending him a "milk-white terrier of great tenacity" to keep him company.[11] Perhaps it was here that Stanley began to develop a love of dogs.

After leaving Sandhurst in 1858, Frederick Stanley joined the Grenadier Guards, where he rose through the ranks and was eventually made a captain. Stanley was appointed an Honorary Colonel of the 3rd and 4th Battalions of the King's Own Royal Lancaster Regiment and of the 1st Volunteer Battalion of the Liverpool Regiment. As a result of his military maturation and pedigree, Stanley was selected as supernumerary aide-de-camp to Her Majesty, Queen Victoria. At this time, Stanley was a justice of the peace for Lancashire and Westmoreland.

Stanley resigned his army commission on 11 July, 1865, and decided to follow the political path blazed by both his father and brother. Frederick was unopposed as he won a seat in the House of Commons as the Conservative Member of Parliament from Preston. Now fully committed to a life in politics, Stanley, the youngest of three children of the Earl of Derby (thrice the British prime minister), had much to live up to. If the large shadow cast by his father was hard to evade, so too was that cast by his elder brother Edward, heir to the earldom. The two brothers had a tempestuous relationship at times. While Frederick looked up to Edward and called on him several times for advice, he was also painfully aware that he was, in certain respects at least, dependent on Edward.

After successfully contesting a seat in the general election of 1868, Frederick sat as a member of Parliament for the Blackpool Division of Lancashire North, serving jointly with Colonel Wilson-Patten — later Lord Winmarleigh. Stanley was returned in 1874 after running unopposed and was twice elected through by-elections, once in 1878 and again in 1885. Following the Redistribution Act of 1885, Frederick once again ran unopposed in the general elections of 1885 and 1886.

During his tenure in the House of Commons, Stanley enjoyed several political appointments. From August to November 1868, he was Civil Lord of the Admiralty. From February 1874 until August 1877, Stanley was appointed Financial Secretary to the War Office. In 1878, Frederick was appointed Secretary to the Treasury, then from April 1878 until his party was ousted from office in April 1880, he held the portfolio of Secretary of State for War. It was a popular decision. "No one that I could think of in political life would be equally acceptable to me,"[12] suggested the Duke of Cambridge in a letter to Gathorne-Hardy, who preceded Stanley in that post. In the fall of 1878, Stanley and W.H. Smith, the Lord of the Admiralty, paid an official visit to Cyprus, which Turkey had recently ceded to Great Britain. Frederick succeeded his brother as Secretary of State for the Colonies from June 1885 until February 1886, then was president of the Board of Trade from August 1886 until his appointment as Governor General of the Dominion of Canada.

When offered the peerage in 1886, Frederick sought the advice of his brother Edward, the 15th Earl of Derby, whom he regarded to some extent as a mentor. Edward, fifteen years older than Frederick, advised his younger brother to remain in the House of Commons. Frederick pondered that possibility, but ultimately chose the peerage. "He said he had been over twenty years in the House of Commons, was growing weary of it, felt the work harder than he liked, did not feel sure that he agreed with his intended colleagues on many points, disliked [Randolph] Churchill as a leader and thought he should be more free in the Lords."[13] Stanley was thus created Baron Stanley of Preston.

* * *

Prior to embarking on his career in politics, Frederick Arthur Stanley married Constance Villiers on 31 May, 1864, in St. Paul's Church, Wilton Place, in Knightsbridge. The magnificent Victorian church is located very close to where Lady Stanley was born, on Grosvenor Crescent, Belgravia, just off Hyde Park Corner in central London.

Lady Constance Villiers, born 2 September, 1840, was the elder daughter of George William Frederick Villiers, the 4th Earl of Clarendon, and Lady Katherine Grimston. *The Dominion Illustrated Monthly,* a periodical in which both Frederick and Constance appeared regularly when they arrived in Canada, reported right around the time of the Stanleys' arrival that Lady Stanley was:

> ... *of good Whig stock — a daughter of the late Lord Clarendon; distinguished for his long and important services in the Foreign Office. Her Excellency is highly gifted with mental and physical accomplishments and, as such, will gracefully keep up the traditions of the three ladies who lived before her at Rideau Hall — a countess, a princess and a marchioness.*[14]

Later, that same year, Lady Stanley would grace the cover of the same periodical.[15]

Lady Stanley's father had enjoyed an extremely impressive political career. The Earl's important positions included British Ambassador in Madrid, Lord Privy Seal, Chancellor of the Duchy of Lancaster, Lord Lieutenant of Ireland and, perhaps most importantly, Foreign Secretary — the latter being a position the Earl held three times. Clarendon died only six years after his eldest daughter's marriage.

* * *

In the early years of their marriage, Lord and Lady Stanley lived with Frederick's father and mother, the 14th Earl and Countess Derby, in Derby House at 10 St. James's Square in London. As a wedding gift, the 14th Earl had given Lord and Lady Stanley a choice of properties: part of the family's estate of Witherslack in Westmoreland in England's Lake District, or Ballykisteen in Ireland. The newlyweds chose Witherslack and built a new country residence there.[16] It was an accommodating home that eventually more than allowed for the proper raising of the Stanleys' substantial brood.

Over the course of the next thirteen years, Stanley and Lady Stanley had ten children, of whom eight survived into adulthood. Edward George Villiers Stanley was born within the first year of the couple's marriage. Eddy, as he was known, was born 4 April, 1865, at Derby House in London.

For centuries, the Stanleys had been loyal to, and enjoyed the affection of, the Royal family — many members of the Royal family had been guests at Knowsley. Upon Eddy's birth, the Queen sent her congratulations to the boy's grandfather, who was still the 14th Earl of Derby at the time:

> *The Queen is most truly rejoiced to hear of dear Constance's safety and of the birth of Lord Derby's grandson. She congratulates him on this happy event which she knows must give him and Lady Derby such pleasure and sincerely hopes that the Mother may go on as well as possible and Lord Derby derive much comfort and pleasure from his little grandson.*[17]

The Prince of Wales also congratulated father Frederick on the birth of the future 17th Earl of Derby:

> *My Dear Stanley, I only heard yesterday of the good news, and that you are now a father. Pray accept my most sincere congratulations on this happy event, and I trust that Lady Constance is going on as well as possible, and your little boy also. May I also ask you to congratulate Lord and Lady Derby on having a grandson.*[18]

The future king would remain close with Frederick and his family, and even chose to visit Lord Stanley in Canada while Frederick was governor general. Many years later, Edward George Stanley, the 17th Earl, could call King George V one of his closest friends.

The family kept growing in number. Victor Albert was born on 17 January, 1867, and a daughter, Katherine Mary, shortly after. Twins Arthur and Geoffrey were born 18 November, 1869. Edward George was, according to his mother, "much pleased with his twin brothers who were born on November 18 at The Grove. Eddy was delighted when he was told that he was the eldest of five, and not yet five years old!"[19]

Ferdinand Charles, known within the household as Ferdy, was born 28 January, 1871. Sadly, Lord and Lady Stanley lost two infants later that year. Geoffrey died 16 March, 1871, not yet two years of age, and Katherine died on 21 October, 1871.

George Frederick was born 14 October, 1872. Algernon Francis, called Algy by the family, was born 8 January, 1874. Isobel Constance Mary was born 20 September, 1875. Frederick William, known as Bill to avoid confusion with his father, was born 27 May, 1878.

Speaking to the impressive number of Stanley's offspring, brother Edward affirmed, "there is certainly no present fear of our name dying out in the land."[20] When Frederick and Constance were married, and for some years following that, they were generally at Witherslack with their growing family from July until December, and in London for the rest of the year. And they were happy.

* * *

Frederick Stanley's official duties during the first ten years of his marriage to Constance kept the couple separated from each other for months at a time. With Stanley in London and Constance and the family at Witherslack or at her mother's estate in Hertfordshire, the couple, as Churchill noted, "plainly pined at these separations and the few letters which survive show that both frequently felt lonely."[21] It was likely these separations that compelled Frederick and Constance to be so very close later in life.

While separation may have made their hearts grow fonder, it did little to reduce the family's mounting debt. In the mid-1870s, Stanley's War Office position brought in £7,000 per annum. Although this was a handsome salary, Stanley's growing family incurred many expenses. In an effort to clear an outstanding debt that Stanley had incurred in a neighbouring town, Constance Stanley chose to take measures into her own hands and paid the bill herself. Fearing that her husband was getting a bad name, she later confessed to Frederick, "I hope you won't be angry with me dearest."[22] Frederick, for his part, was also mindful of the family's fiscal reality, a fact that Constance reiterated in a letter to her husband.

> *Thanks so much for you dear letter of today and the financial talk which tells me as I see as well as you do (you make it quite clear) we have only got to live carefully and save when we can on unnecessary outgoings and in time outstanding bills will get paid.*[23]

Financial freedom was a little ways off in the distance for the couple, but when it came, Frederick Stanley would end up one of the richest men in the world.

The financial burden of the 1870s was compounded by a bout of scarlet fever that attacked four of the children. At the same time, eldest son Edward George was fighting mumps while he was away at school and Constance had just given birth to the couple's sixth child Isobel and was suffering from neuralgia at her mother's home. Constance wrote Stanley:

> *This is a dreadful day not hearing anything about all my darlings and I fell so low having been very bad with neuralgia … I thought of you so much my duck yesterday after we parted for I am sure your life is too terribly lonely and dull, but I feel we must only be so thankful that a worse misery was spared to us for how unhappy we were this time last week, and I feel things will brighten and we shall not be so long separated as we now think.*

Still, in the same letter, Constance felt it necessary to raise the matter of the expense:

> *I don't see how you can make out that this illness will cost £500. The doctors' bills can't be very heavy and even if you burnt everything in every room it would not amount to £100, so I hope and think you will find it is not so bad as it looks now. Oh! How nice it would be to have a real nice comfortable talk but as that can't be we must not long for it more than one can help.*[24]

This worry and separation, although taking its toll on the Stanleys early on, was a major reason why, in later years, the family did so many things together. By the time Frederick Arthur Stanley was offered the position of Canada's governor general, he had had enough of being away from his loved ones. Despite their modest financial woes and the nebulous state of the relationship between Frederick and Edward Henry, the Stanleys were a very content family and, as Churchill attested, "all the family letters and records show that they were a happy family, and that the children were united in love and loyalty to their parents."[25]

The Stanley family was very affectionate towards one another, enjoying a relatively normal, albeit privileged, lifestyle. "Edward and the other children had an ideal life at Witherslack," wrote Churchill. The boys indulged in and excelled at a number of sports, while all eight children frolicked with their dogs, Dinah and Jess. Prince George, later King George V, spent a great deal of time with Eddy and wrote, "I think your family was the happiest and most united one I have ever seen."[26]

Because she was modest to a fault, insisting her husband speak on her behalf at any public function, Lady Constance Stanley had far less profile than her husband. And yet, what we know of her is most endearing.

> *Lady Stanley is a charming matron, still upon the sunny side of middle life, whom it is almost impossible to believe can be the mother of so grown up a son as Mr. Edward Stanley and nine others. She has the fresh, beautiful complexion of all her country women, dark blue eyes, perfect teeth and a most charming smile.*[27]

The Stanleys' aide-de-camp, Lord Kilcoursie, recalled that:

> *Lady Stanley was always kind to me and however much she scolded me for forgetfulness in lighting the candles at bedtime and other shortcomings, there was always a twinkle in her eye ... she was certainly one of the 'Grande Dames' of the old school but with the warmest heart and a wealth of devotion to her husband and her children. Eddie, the present Lord of Derby, was too old to be at Rideau Hall, having joined the Grenadiers in 1885, and Victor was at sea, but the younger children, even the irresponsible Ferdy, were clearly in awe of their mother.*[28]

Lady Stanley, like her husband, was born of ancient and distinguished pedigree, yet, according to the *Victoria Daily Colonist*, was "as simple and unaffected in manner as anyone could desire."[29] Constance took great pleasure in her children, and as a result, her benevolent interests involved causes benefiting children, as well as women. In one instance Lady Stanley inspected the arrival of recently arrived immigrants at Quebec to make sure the women and children were treated appropriately.[30]

As a wife, Lady Constance Stanley was dutiful and supportive. As a mother, she was nurturing, warm and caring. Within her community, Lady Stanley was a tireless worker for causes involving hospitals and children, leaving behind a legacy of her own.

* * *

When the 14th Earl of Derby died, Frederick inherited £125,000 — having received £80,000 from the family some time earlier.[31] Shortly after the death of Edward Geoffrey Stanley, a chasm divided the family. Although Edward Henry, now the 15th Earl of Derby, was regarded as a mentor, Frederick and his young family did not visit the family estate at Knowsley from 1870 until the unexpected death of the 15th Earl in 1893. When, some twenty-three years later, Frederick did return to Knowsley, it was as the 16th Earl of Derby.

Edward Henry had very little to do with the extended Stanley family in general. Indeed, from the entire family pool, only his brother Frederick could be regarded as having been somewhat close. This is especially true if one invests any great currency into what Edward Henry had planned for his estate following his death. In his will, written up in 1869, the 15th Earl arranged to leave "£1,000 to my sister, £500 to Smith [his manservant], all the rest to my brother."[32] Seven years later, he updated his will to include fourteen people — though £65,000 was to be divided among thirteen beneficiaries, including his wife, while Edward Henry left "£50,000 to my brother to be invested in land and settled as a part of the family estates … all the rest, with some trifling exceptions, to my brother."[33]

From 1870 onward, the relationship between the brothers was strained. It seems that Lady Constance, Frederick's wife, had got in the way of the relationship. According to Edward Henry, Constance was "full of gossip, and fragments of stories of what she had heard had passed here, none of them well-founded. She makes mischief without meaning it, as all people must do who pass the greater part of their day in discussing their neighbour's affairs."[34]

Later that same week, Edward said of his brother and sister-in-law:

I thought Frederick out of spirits … Frederick has hardly

inhabited Knowsley since the change (the death of the 14th Earl). Constance also appeared to be changed, being irritable, inclined to find fault, and generally out of humour: but her condition may account for disturbed nerves. She, and her sisters also, felt very acutely the loss of social importance which belonged to them as daughters of the foreign secretary, trusted by him with his closest secrets, and acquainted with everything that passed both at home and abroad. It would be unjust not to add that her grief on other grounds has been deep, and is likely to be lasting. To all three sisters their father, while he lived, was the first object of affection: and as a father, he deserved to be so.[35]

Lord Clarendon's death and its ramifications no doubt dictated Lady Constance's mood. Still, one wonders if at least part of the "irritability" was not a result of a growing tension between Edward Henry and his sister-in-law.

Two months later, Frederick had made his choice regarding the estate, as Edward Henry recorded in his diary:

The estates have, practically, cost me £125,000, for that is the sum which Frederick accepted in lieu of them: I ought to be able to obtain, by a little waiting, £150,000 and at that rate the bargain will be a good one. They may be worth more, if Ireland remains quiet: but the political future of the country is not satisfactory, and it is scarcely worth my while to run risks in the hope of getting a little more.[36]

This decision, at least on some level, must have affected the brothers' relationship, but no more than the unsettled relationship between Constance and her brother-in-law. While Edward Henry was still unmarried and serving in the Foreign Office, Lady Constance filled in as a hostess and companion for Edward Henry during the latter's special business and diplomatic events. Enter Mary Gascoyne-Cecil.

On certain occasions, especially when Parliament was in session, Edward left his brother and sister-in-law in charge of the family home and its social affairs, as he noted in his journal:

Munster went down yesterday with his daughter to Knowsley, to shoot, Frederick and Constance being there, and acting hosts in my place: it is probably the first time in the present century that the owner of the Knowsley had passed the winter away from home.[37]

Being away from Knowsley was a prospect that did not give great comfort to Edward. "The more I have of this official life, the less it suits me, and I shall be glad though when an opportunity offers to drop it."

The 15th Earl was a bachelor for the first forty-four years of his life, but on 5 July, 1870, he married Mary Gascoyne-Cecil, the forty-six-year-old widow of the 2nd Marquess of Salisbury. This development, in no uncertain terms, relieved Lady Constance from her brother-in-law's special engagements. This might not have been terribly welcome from Lady Constance's perspective and might have added to her increased haughtiness around Edward.

Unfortunately for the brothers, their wives did not take a great deal of joy being in one another's company. From the outset, Lady Constance disapproved of Mary when she was introduced to the family. The tension between the two set into motion a long-standing rift within the Stanley family. Edward George, Stanley's eldest son, added, "My father and his brother … did not speak, for the most part to my mother's influence." He claimed that his Aunt Mary and his mother "cordially disliked each other, and if there was anything either of them could say against each other, they did so."[38]

Historian John Vincent believed that it was something that Constance had said in 1878 that "proved unforgivable."[39] Yet, the rift may not have been the result of a single event, but rather the consequence of a steady and growing tension that developed following Edward Henry's marriage. When Mary arrived on the scene, Constance had to reconcile her new position and dynamic within the family.

The 15th Earl's diary has offered no real insight into any particular event that permanently damaged the brothers' relationship; most entries are of the nondescript variety. For instance: "Dined with Frederick and Constance. Pleasant evening."[40] What is certain, however, is that after 1878, the brothers met neither often nor openly.

Perhaps catching Edward by surprise, Frederick accepted the post as

Canada's governor general in 1888 and left England for nearly five years. There was a final luncheon given in London by Edward Henry for his departing brother's family.[41] Considering the tension surrounding the family, one might imagine it being a subdued affair. At any rate, it was the last time Frederick would see Edward Henry alive. When Frederick returned to England, he was the 16th Earl of Derby.

* * *

Constance's sister, Alice Villiers, married the Earl of Lathom in 1860. This union brought the House of Lathom, which had in a much earlier time been a Stanley possession, back into the fold. There was, as Churchill described, "much coming and going at this time between Witherslack and Lathom, and also between both these houses and Knowsley."[42] Still, there was a bit of sibling rivalry between the sisters following Frederick's succession to the earldom, as Lady Emily Lytton, a first cousin of Constance Stanley's, recounted in a letter:

> We had a most excellent meal in an hotel, where the Lathom
> party also dined, only in a separate room, as Lady Derby
> was most anxious to be independent and have her own way.
> It is very comic the pride she takes in her new position and
> her delight in lording it over Lady Lathom, who is fearfully
> jealous.[43]

It seems the Lady of "good Whig stock" got under the skin of more than one person.

* * *

Still, the family did manage to operate like a family. When Edward George was engaged to be married, Frederick, Constance and most of their brood were in Canada. It seems that Edward Henry and his wife picked up the slack and became very involved in the preparations of their nephew's marriage, as Frederick's son Victor described the wedding in a letter to his parents: "The Derbys have been everything that's nice about it. Aunt M. [Mary] sends you her love and the normal regrets about your not having been there."[44] Later, when the young couple were struggling with their bills, Edward George chose to ask his uncle Edward Henry for assistance. Constance applauded her son's decision to seek help from her brother-in-law:

> *Dear old boy, we are so very pleased to hear about Uncle Stanley's great kindness. He really is most generous to you and how right you were to go straight to him about your debts. I hope your mind is quite at ease for I know you hate to have unpaid bills.*[45]

Whether the animosity between Constance and Mary had been genuine, there also seems to have been genuine goodwill on both sides as well.

As Edward Henry married so late, an heir to the earldom was not expected, and none was produced. And so, Edward George Villiers Stanley, Frederick's eldest son, became the heir apparent. At the time of his first son's birth and for some time after, Frederick was very much reliant on his brother Edward, both financially and with respect to large family decisions. Edward Henry's wishes were to be observed. With this in mind, Edward Henry implored his brother to have Edward George educated at Wellington College and *not* Eton, where both Edward Henry and his father had studied. This may have had, in no small way, to do with the fact that Edward Henry Stanley had been suspended indefinitely from Eton — a fact that forced him to finish his study at Rugby School.

All but one of Frederick's sons obliged their Uncle Edward by attending Wellington College. Victor was the sole son to choose a career in the Royal Navy and he attended Kempthorne's House. Wellington was not an altogether unnatural choice for the family. While Eton had been the college of choice for the Stanley men, Wellington also had special ties to the family. The 14th Earl — Frederick's father, Edward Geoffrey — had been one of the founders of the college in 1856. Wellington was, as Churchill confirmed, "intended to provide a good but economical education for the sons of Army officers."[46] Later, both Frederick and his son Edward served as vice president of the college's governing body.

* * *

The Stanleys were quite naturally sports-minded long before Frederick, the

16th Earl of Derby, purchased the Cup. Horse racing is synonymous with the Stanley name. In 1780, Edward Smith Stanley, the 12th Earl of Derby and Frederick's great-grandfather, established The Derby, which takes place each June at Epsom Downs in Epsom, Surrey, is the second leg of the British Triple Crown. The annual race for three-year-old thoroughbreds is still considered the most prestigious horse race in the world. History reveals that the race might very well have been called The Bunbury instead of the The Derby, as E. J. Bunbury explained in a letter to R. S. Churchill:

> It has always been the traditional story in my family that Sir Thomas Charles Bunbury, Bt., and Lord Derby invented the Derby Race on Epsom Downs and that they dined together the night before the race (run of May 4th, 1780) and tossed up as to whether it would be called the Derby or the Bunbury. Derby won the toss and it was called the Derby.[47]

Bunbury got his own back, however, as his horse Diomed won the first running of the Derby.

The 12th Earl was also instrumental in founding The Oaks, a mile-and-a-half race for fillies named after his estate. The Oaks instantly became another pivotal date on the world's horse-racing calendar. In 1779, the Earl won the Oaks with his filly, Bridget, and later won his first Derby with Sir Peter Teazle in 1787. Frederick's father, Edward Geoffrey Stanley, was a horse-racing fanatic, but he never won the Derby. He did, however, manage a victory at the Oaks and enough wins that his purses totalled close to £100,000. Edward was, as Churchill has suggested, "happier on the turf than in the House of Commons."[48]

Charles Greville, a contemporary of Edward Geoffrey Stanley's, composed a wonderful sketch on the 14th Earl in his diary:

> It is worthwhile to be at Newmarket to see Stanley. A few weeks ago, he was on the point of being Prime Minister, which only depended on himself. Then, he stood up in the House of Lords and delivered an oration full of gravity and dignity such as became the man who had just undertaken to form an Administration. If any of his vociferous disci-

*ples and admirers, if some grave members of either House
of Parliament or any distinguished foreigner who knew
nothing of Lord Stanley but what he saw, heard of read of
him could have suddenly found himself in the betting
room at Newmarket on Tuesday evening and seen Stanley
there, I think they would have been in a pretty state of astonishment. There he was in the midst of a crowd of
blacklegs, betting men and loose characters of every description in uproarious spirits, chaffing, rowing and
shouting with laughter and joking. His amusement was to
lay Lord Glasgow a wager that he did not sneeze in a given
time, for which purpose he (Glasgow) took pinch after
pinch of snuff while Stanley jeered at him and quizzed him
with such noise that he drew the whole mob around him
to partake of the coarse merriment he excited. It really was
a sight and a wonder to see any man playing such different
parts so naturally and caring what anybody might think
of the minister and statesman as long as he could have
his fun.*[49]

While Frederick's brother Edward, the 15th Earl of Derby, put the family's
horse-racing tradition on hold to help clear the family's debt, his nephew
Edward George successfully persuaded his father, Frederick, to revive the
family's time-honoured love of the turf at Knowsley after the latter became
the 16th Earl. With the help of the Honourable George Lambton, Edward
found a horse trainer that would return the Stanley family to the very top
of the horse-racing world. In Churchill's opinion, "Lambton was one of the
greatest trainers of the century."[50] The Stanleys also rejuvenated the stud
farm at Knowsley under the Griffiths' father-and-son stud groom team.
Frederick Stanley enjoyed two classic victories with his own homegrown
stock: Canterbury Pilgrim, a filly Edward had purchased for his father and
was one of the best fillies of her year, captured the 1896 running of the
Oaks, while Keystone II won the same race a decade later in 1906. Stanley's
son, on the other hand, enjoyed upwards of twenty important victories, including three Derbys (1924 with Sansovino, 1933 with Hyperion and 1942
with Watling Street), the Oaks twice, the St. Leger six times, the 1,000
Guineas seven times and the 2,000 Guineas twice. As Churchill explained,

"[Edward George Stanley] won nearly every famous weight-for-age race in the Calendar, and over twenty Liverpool Cups."[51] Edward, who succeeded his father as the Earl of Derby on Frederick's death in 1908, won over a thousand races and accumulated over £800,000 in winnings. The bloodline of the Stanleys' exceptionally talented stallions entered many important pedigrees throughout the world, and the family's race-horse reputation is not out of place alongside such other renowned twentieth-century owner-breeders as Lord Woolavington and the Aga Khan.

Apart from horse racing, which was dear to most of the Derbys, Stanley's family shared a strong tradition in sports with decidedly aristocratic taste. Shooting was a great passion of the Earls of Derby. Edward Henry, for example, was reputed to possess a "great shot" in game shooting.[52] Frederick, too, enjoyed the hunt. By extension, Frederick took a keen interest in sharpshooting, an interest that continued in Canada.

Cricket, too, featured prominently in the family's sporting agenda, the Governor General's XI being an example of a Stanley-centric club. The Stanley boys played their share of the game growing up and at Wellington College. As Edward Henry reported to his mother, "I think I shall find plenty to do in London and I might go down on Saturday afternoons to Perceval House and play cricket there."[53] These traditions were certainly hallmarks of the quintessential aristocratic British family. Yet it was a Canadian sport that the Stanley name would be forever linked with.

* * *

Historian James Noonan has questioned why Frederick was so interested in the sporting side of his father's life and not at all in the cultural side. Certainly, Stanley followed an honoured family tradition in possessing a love for horse racing, a deep interest in shooting and a general enthusiasm for the outdoors, including fishing, but he stops short, in Noonan's opinion, in taking part in any of his father's "higher" aims.

Stanley was not known to be overly fascinated with art. When considering the artistic pursuits of other families at Rideau Hall — especially the Lansdownes and the Aberdeens — the Stanleys' collection and publicly displayed interest in art seems comparatively negligible. The same is true when one considers the Stanleys' modest participation in theatrical productions, both at Rideau Hall and in Ottawa.

While it is true that other governors general demonstrated a keener interest in high-brow pursuits — if, of course, we are keeping score of theatrical productions and gala costume balls presented by several governors general — it is, however, a bit imprudent to suggest that Stanley was culturally bankrupt. Lord and Lady Stanley were regular attendees at theatrical and musical presentations in Ottawa during their stay, and the Governor General lent his name as patron to a number of cultural organizations.

Whether it was the vice regal's avid interest in the Canadian educational system or his ability when, having been addressed in Latin by a student while on a visit to Toronto, he was able to perfectly form an answer in the same dead language, Stanley proved many times over that he possessed a formidable and imaginative mind. What might confuse his few biographers is that he *chose* to live simply and expressed himself through sporting endeavours — a fact that no doubt bemuses some cultural historians, but one that nevertheless has significant cultural implications for Canadians.

In fact, Stanley's endorsement of hockey may have contributed more to cultural identity in Canada than any other figurehead, never mind governor general, in Canadian history. Sports historian Alan Metcalfe confirmed that "few Canadian historians have regarded sport as an integral part of the social history of Canada."[54] This failing, insofar as it pertains to Canada, has not yet been fully remedied. If, as Burns once slyly pondered, we were able to see ourselves as others see us, would we not see a people who not only conquered winter but embraced it? Would we not see, on balance, a hockey-loving nation? One could submit that far more Canadians are interested in Stanley Cup playoff contests than they are in arguing over the most reliable translation of Homer's *Iliad*. This rationale does not equal lowering the bar of high culture, nor does it mean that "culture" should be exclusively determined by the lowest common denominator; rather, it is in support of raising the profile of hockey specifically, and sport in general, and their collective impact on Canadian culture.

Other countries have long recognized the significance of how sport is uniquely able to reflect cultural patterns and how, beyond the final results of a given game, sport informs the larger narrative of a nation's history. In this respect, Canada is lagging behind slightly. Indeed, when the vice regal party gave its endorsement to hockey, Canadians took notice. With the blessing of the Queen's representative, hockey rose from a child's game to an essential pastime that transcends every community of the entire nation. This, in and of itself, is of great historical and cultural significance.

---

1 C.H. Keeling *Marvel by the Mersey: The First Book to be Devoted to the Knowsley Menagerie, the Remarkable Zoological Collection Owned by the 13th Earl of Derby* (Shalford, Knowsley Estate: Clam Publications, publication date unknown).

2 *The Earl and the Pussycat, the 13th Earl of Derby's Life and Legacy* (Liverpool: Walker Art Gallery, June-Sept. 2002). <*exhibit*> See also, *www.liverpoolmuseums.org.uk/about/news/archive02.asp*.

3 The 13th Earl and his wife Charlotte Hornby had three children and, eventually, fifteen grandchildren. Edward Geoffrey Stanley and wife Emma Bootle-Wilbraham had three children, including their youngest, Frederick. Henry Thomas Stanley and his wife Anne Woodhouse had four children, although only three survived childhood. Charles James Fox and his wife Frances Campbell were parents to eight children.

4 According to the Oxford English Dictionary, the word "limerick" did not enter the language until 1898. See, Edward Lear, *A Book of Nonsense*, third edition, (London: Routledge, Warne & Routledge, 1861), p.63.

5 Ibid., p.51.

6 Noonan, *Canada's Governors General at Play*, p.162; W. Pollard, *The Stanleys of Knowsley: A History of That Noble Family including a Sketch of the Political and Public Lives of the Rt. Hon. The Earl of Derby, K.G. and the Rt. Hon. Lord Stanley, M.P.* (Liverpool: Edward Howell, 1868).

7 The Earl of Derby 1852, 1858–9 and 1866–8, Conservative, *www.direct.gov.uk*

8 Noonan, *Canada's Governors General at Play*, p.161.

9 K. Shea, *Interview with Penny Hatfield*, College Archivist, Eton College (February 2006).

10 Ibid.

11 Noonan, *Canada's Governors General at Play*, p.161.

12 *Gathorne-Hardy Papers*, National Archives of Canada.

13 J. Vincent (ed), *Later Derby Diaries: Home Rule, Liberal Unionism and Aristocratic Life in Late Victorian England*, (Bristol: University of Bristol, 1981).

14 *The Dominion Illustrated Monthly* (7 July, 1888), p.7.

15 *The Dominion Illustrated Monthly* (10 November, 1888), *edition cover page*. Lord Stanley also appeared on the cover of the same periodical. See, *The Dominion Illustrated Monthly* (14 July, 1888), *edition cover page*.

16 Noonan, *Canada's Governors General at Play*, p.166.

17 Queen Victoria, *Letter to Lord Derby, 14th Earl* (14 April, 1865); Churchill, *Lord Derby*, p.12.

18 Prince Albert Edward, *Letter to Frederick Arthur Stanley* (6 April, 1865); Churchill, *Lord Derby*, p.12.

19 Lady Constance as quoted in Churchill, *Lord Derby*, p.15.

20 E. H. Stanley on the birth of F. A. Stanley's 5th son. See, E. H. Stanley, *Personal Diary* (29 January, 1871); Vincent, *Diaries of Edward Henry Stanley*, p.73.

21 Churchill, *Lord Derby*, p.17.

22 Lady Constance Stanley, *Letter to F. A. Stanley* (c.1873); Churchill, *Lord Derby*, p.17.

23 Lady Constance Stanley, *Letter to F. A. Stanley* (c.1875); Churchill, *Lord Derby*, p.17.

24 Lady Constance Stanley, *Letter to F. A. Stanley* (17 October, 1875); Churchill, *Lord Derby*, pp.17–8.

25 Ibid.

26 J. J. Bagley, *The Earls of Derby, 1485–1985* (London: Didgwick & Jackson, 1985), p.207.

27 'Progress', *Exhibition Daily* (3 October, 1888).

28 Lord Kilcoursie, *Recollections Hazy But Happy* (Churchill College Cambridge: unpublished memoirs of Lord Kilcoursie, Earl of Cavan), p.4.

29 *Victoria Daily Colonist* (1 November, 1883), *edition cover page*.

30 Ibid.

[31] J. Vincent, *Disraeli* (London: Oxford Paperbacks, 1990).

[32] E. H. Stanley, *Personal Diary* (15 December, 1869); Vincent, *Diaries of Edward Henry Stanley*, p.43.

[33] E. H. Stanley, *Personal Diary* (14 June, 1877); Vincent, *Diaries of Edward Henry Stanley*, p.408.

[34] E. H. Stanley, *Personal Diary* (24 October, 1870); Vincent, *Diaries of Edward Henry Stanley*, p.69.

[35] E. H. Stanley, *Personal Diary* (28 October, 1870); Vincent, *Diaries of Edward Henry Stanley*, pp.69–70.

[36] E. H. Stanley, *Personal Diary* (12 December, 1870); Vincent, *Diaries of Edward Henry Stanley*, p.71.

[37] E. H. Stanley, *Personal Diary* (13 December, 1876); Vincent, *Diaries of Edward Henry Stanley*, p.351.

[38] E. G. Stanley, as quoted in, Vincent, *Later Derby Diaries*; Noonan, *Canada's Governors General*, p.170.

[39] Vincent, *Later Derby Diaries*.

[40] E. H. Stanley, *Personal Diary* (27 January, 1878); Vincent, *Diaries of Edward Henry Stanley*, p.494.

[41] Vincent, *Later Derby Diaries*.

[42] Churchill, *Lord Derby*, p.16.

[43] Lady Emily Lytton, *Letter to Reverend Whitwell Elwin* (18 October, 1893); Churchill, *Lord Derby*, p.42.

[44] V. Stanley, *Letter to his Mother, Lady Constance Stanley* (6 January, 1889); Churchill, *Lord Derby*, p.29.

[45] Lady Constance Stanley, *Letter to Edward George Stanley* (10 December, 1891); Churchill, *Lord Derby*, p.32.

[46] Churchill, *Lord Derby*, p.18.

[47] E. J. Bunbury, *Letter to R. S. Churchill*; Churchill, *Lord Derby*, p.46.

[48] Churchill, *Lord Derby*, p.8.

[49] C. Greville, *Diary* (10 April, 1851); Churchill, *Lord Derby*, p.8.

[50] Churchill, *Lord Derby*, p.49.

[51] Churchill, *Lord Derby*, p.50

[52] Vincent, *Diaries of Edward Henry Stanley*, p.7.

[53] Churchill, *Lord Derby*, p.21.

[54] A. Metcalfe, *Canada Learns to Play: The Emergence of Organized Sport*, 1807–1914 (Toronto: McClelland & Stewart Inc., 1987), p.9.

CHAPTER FOUR

Arrival in Canada

On Thursday, 31 May, 1888, in Liverpool, Lord Stanley and his suite boarded the *S.S. Sarmatian*, a former troop vessel. Accompanying Lord and Lady Stanley, both forty-seven years of age, were four of their children: the twenty-three-year-old Edward, who would later serve as an aide-de-camp to his father; Victor, twenty-one; twelve-year-old Isobel; and William, having just turned ten years of age, the youngest Stanley child. The four other Stanley children remained in England: nineteen-year-old Arthur, sixteen-year-old Ferdinand, fifteen-year-old George, and Algernon, who was fourteen years of age. Arthur was serving in the military, while the three younger boys were attending boarding school at Wellington College in Crowthorne, Berkshire, and would come to Canada for their holidays.[1] In the summer, they would enjoy wonderful excursions fishing on the Cascapedia River with the family and in the winter, as Lord Kilcoursie recounted, "great and glorious were the games of ice hockey on the Rideau Rink."[2]

Also travelling to Canada with Lord and Lady Stanley were several members of the Governor General's new staff. Eight servants as well as Miss Lister, Lady Stanley's relative, also made the transatlantic trip.

The *Sarmatian* was built by R. Steele and Company of Greenock, Scotland, in 1871 for the Allan Line, owned by Hugh Allan, who was one of Canada's wealthiest entrepreneurs.[3] The 370-foot *Sarmation* was a 3,647-gross-ton vessel that could accommodate two hundred first-class passengers, seventy-five second-class and eight hundred and fifty third-class passengers while cruising at a speed of thirteen knots. The ship was primarily employed to transport emigrants from the British Isles to Canada. A brochure published by the Allan Lines in the mid-1880's read,

"The *Sarmatian*, a favourite steamer of the Line, was the vessel selected for conveyance of H.R.H. Princess Louise and the Marquis of Lorne to Canada in November 1878 on His Excellency assuming the post of Governor General of Canada."[4]

After a brief stop in Londonderry, Ireland, the *Sarmatian* continued its voyage. The Stanley entourage was "a very cheery party" and, as *The Montreal Gazette* reported, was the "life of all on board, taking part in all the activities presented on board the vessel."[5] The Stanley suite was made most comfortable in spite of rough seas experienced during the ten-day trip. The vice regal guests were lodged in lavish staterooms upholstered in crimson satin and featuring special mahogany beds that ensured that seasickness was all but impossible, "the bed adjusting itself to every motion of the vessel so that its pitch and roll cannot be felt."[6] Lord Stanley had experience on the water, having been commodore of the Royal Mersey Yacht Club in Liverpool, so he was the least affected of his party. Each room had its own en suite bathroom and an adjoining sitting room.

As the ship reached Cape Race on the southern tip of the Avalon Peninsula of Newfoundland, the crew pointed out three icebergs to Lord and Lady Stanley. The ship arrived in Lévis, Quebec, just opposite Quebec City, on 9 June.

A grand reception was planned in Quebec City but the party was spoiled when an aide-de-camp telegraphed committee organizers that Lord Stanley had decided to proceed immediately to Ottawa upon his arrival in Quebec. Nonetheless, a large crowd began gathering on a night described as "dark and disagreeable" to welcome Stanley and his party at the expected arrival time of eleven in the morning; however, the *Sarmatian* had docked three hours earlier, catching everyone by surprise. As *The Montreal Daily Witness* confirmed, "Lord Stanley arrived quite unexpectedly about eight o'clock this morning and drove at once to Rideau Hall."[7] As the rain fell, the *Sarmatian* sailed up unnoticed and moored along the wharf at the Grand Trunk depot. The ship announced its arrival by discharging military bombs.

A nineteen-gun salute was immediately afforded the pending vice regal, welcoming him to Canada. Stanley telegraphed his safe arrival to Queen Victoria and the Prince of Wales. Upon his arrival, he spoke readily on general subjects but carefully avoided political questions. He expressed the sincere wish that friendship between Canada and the United States be firm and enduring. Then, he and Lady Stanley proceeded to Ottawa by special train in order to be sworn in. The rest of the party was left in Quebec City, awaiting the return of the newly-installed Governor General.

* * *

Once in Ottawa, on Monday, 11 June, Lord Stanley was sworn in as the sixth Governor General of the Dominion of Canada by Chief Justice Sir William Ritchie. The swearing-in ceremony was to have taken place in the Scarlet Chamber of the Senate at three o'clock in the afternoon, but Lord and Lady Stanley arrived twenty minutes early, escorted by the Princess Louise Dragoon Guards. Lord Stanley's arrival caught the Guard of Honour of the Governor General's Foot Guards off guard, as they were at the corner of Sparks and Elgin streets, outside the grounds of the Parliament Buildings, at the time. The ceremony, when it finally got underway, included Ottawa Mayor McLeod Stewart, Sheriff John Sweetland and several other prominent government officials.

Stanley shared his thoughts with those present:

> *I shall well and truly execute the office and trust of Governor General of Canada and the territories depending thereon and duly and impartially administer justice therein, so help me God … I shall well and truly execute the office of the great seal of Her Majesty's Dominion of Canada, according to the best of my knowledge and ability, so help me God.*[8]

Lord Stanley then signed the book in which the oaths were recorded by the Supreme Court judge:

> *The foregoing oaths were taken and subscribed by His Excellency, Sir Frederick Arthur Stanley, Baron Stanley of Preston, as Governor General of Canada, before us being duly empowered to administer the said oaths at the city of Ottawa this eleventh day of June, 1888.*[9]

His Excellency, the Right Honourable Sir Frederick Arthur Stanley, GCB, Baron Stanley of Preston, was now Governor General of Canada and

Commander-in-Chief of Prince Edward Island. Having seen both his brother and his father attain such high-ranking posts throughout his political career, Stanley was no longer watching from the sidelines — now, the future Earl of Derby administered one of the Empire's greatest possessions.

* * *

Canada's new governor general took a moment to speak to the citizens of the country over which he had now been made vice regal.

> *Although I have been here but a few hours amongst you, I think I can say that I have already experienced, even before my arrival, that hospitality, that kindness, that cordiality, which has made the name of every citizen of this Dominion proverbial, and I have fallen, even now, under a certain amount of the charm which, after riper experience, seems to have settled upon my predecessors.*

His Excellency concluded:

> *I trust that, be my career long or short, I may feel when my period of office comes to an end, that I have endeavoured, God willing, to devote to the utmost, my abilities to the cause, to the interests and to the welfare of your great Dominion.*[10]

The Citizen added:

> *Judging by the complimentary references made by all classes of citizens who witnessed the installation of the new Governor General yesterday afternoon in the Senate Chamber, it is quite evident that Lord Stanley has made a favourable impression on the people of Ottawa.*[11]

Prime Minister Macdonald further described Stanley's address: "his reply was so hearty in manner, so simple in expression and so natural in every respect that those who had the pleasure of hearing it felt that they were listening to words which sprang from the heart."[12] If their correspondence was cordial, Stanley's eloquence had pleasantly arrested the Prime Minister — ordinary goodwill between the two men began to give way to an extraordinary relationship.

Following the investiture of Stanley, Mayor Stewart delivered an address on behalf of Canada's capital city. Then, at four o'clock, Prime Minister Sir John A. called upon Lord and Lady Stanley with an official welcome. His Excellency, Lord Stanley, and his wife returned to Quebec on Tuesday, 12 June, where they were the subjects of another civic address — the one that had first been slated for delivery upon the new vice regal's arrival in Canada.

* * *

"Lord Stanley is in the prime of life, medium height, a strong, well-built frame, a graceful carriage with something of the look and air of the Prince of Wales when the heir apparent was not quite so stout as he is now," suggested the *Toronto World*. "He is fair, with full beard which is just slightly streaked with grey, has a ruddy complexion, blue eyes, clearly cut features with aquiline nose. He has a fine, broad forehead upon which the hair is becoming thin; a genial, winning and frank expression of countenance. His manner is affable."[13] Montreal's *Daily Witness* described Canada's newest vice regal as "a tall, powerfully-built man of about five feet ten inches, of soldier-like appearance and wears a short iron grey beard and moustache."[14] "His beard and hair are liberally streaked with grey and his voice and accent are unmistakably English," wrote *The Globe*.[15] According to the *Toronto Evening News*, Lord Frederick Stanley was "a plain man and looks more like a quite well-to-do gentleman farmer than a Governor General of Canada. He is of medium stature with a short, full brown beard of scant growth and hair to match."[16]

The "well-to-do gentleman" was well-suited as the choice for governor general, as historian John Cowan confirmed:

> *Of a retiring disposition and without any pretensions to oratory, there lay behind his natural modesty a firm mind and strong common sense. His patrician lineage gave him an instinctive habit of command and his manner had a peculiar charm.*[17]

In short order, Stanley began to win much popularity and encouraged the continuation of imperial sentiment that permeated the entire Dominion.

* * *

As governor general, Stanley had rather enormous shoes to fill. His predecessor, Lord Lansdowne, was a most popular vice regal, even though much of the thirty-eight-year-old's tenure took in some harrowing times in Canada's storied history. *The Ottawa Citizen* wrote:

> *His period of service, though short, has been fruitful of many important and remarkable events. The completion of the Canadian Pacific Railway from ocean to ocean, opening up a new pathway over British territory to the East; the rebellion in the North-West Territories, which, however much to be deplored for the causes of its origin and the loss of life involved in its suppression, was not devoid of public advantages; the final settlement of the Atlantic fisheries dispute, a matter of long standing contention between two of the great powers, and one which might at any moment, develop into a serious international complication; and the initial step towards securing the admission of the ancient colony of Newfoundland into the Canadian Union, thus ensuring the complete political unification of British North America are some of the matters of the weightiest import which have engaged the attention of Lord Lansdowne, and with respect to which, as in his general administrative course, he has displayed consummate ability, tact and judgement.*[18]

Yet Lansdowne proved to be much loved by Canadians during his five years as the Queen's representative, as *The Ottawa Citizen* testified:

> *His Lordship's general services to Canada — on his warm interest in Education, particularly Higher Education, in Literature, in the Fine Arts, and in Science; on his efforts to promote among the youth and manhood of the country,*

healthful out-door Sports and Amusements; and on his
sympathetic encouragement of the Volunteer Militia Force.
Let it suffice that he has devoted his time and his means to
the promotion of all good and deserving works.[19]

Nonetheless, Lansdowne travelled extensively during his time in Canada and discovered a magnificent country whose pleasures greatly appealed to him. In 1885, in spite of the railway not yet having been completed, Lansdowne ventured through the Rocky Mountains by a combination of boat and horseback. He returned to western Canada a second time during his term as governor general. While in Canada, Lansdowne developed a great love of the country's vast wilderness. He discovered a passion for salmon fishing that led to the purchase of a summer residence on Quebec's Cascapedia River. When fishing rights were at the centre of a serious dispute between Canada and the United States, Lansdowne played an integral role in beginning the delicate negotiations that would ultimately and amicably settle the dispute.

Without a doubt, Lord Stanley continued many good works that had been the initiative of Lord Lansdowne, but the new governor general was faced with a growing and intense complication in the nation's relationship with the United Sates. While the Atlantic fisheries had been seen to, the Pacific remained a huge question, one that had Canadians pondering the prospect of war with their neighbour to the south. There would also be, in very short order, a domestic issue that set religion against religion, one that called upon Stanley to act with the utmost care and deliberation. These times were not as uninteresting as some historians have claimed.

Certainly, there were many mundane responsibilities for the governor general to undertake. A great deal of Lord Frederick Stanley's correspondence, found in the Stanley Papers at the National Archives of Canada in Ottawa, dealt with day-to-day tasks and the tedious business of conferring titles and knighthoods. Stanley received letter after letter from Canadian politicians of various orders, all applying on behalf of some person or another for a knighthood to be conferred on them. Among the petitioners was Prime Minister Macdonald:

I enclose you a letter sent me sometime ago from all the
Judges of the Supreme Court of the Province of New

Brunswick requesting the honour of Knighthood for the
Chief Justice of that Court. As I mentioned to Your
Excellency when you visited Dalhousie, I desire strongly to
recommend Chief Justice Allen for the mark of Her Majesty's
favour prayed for by his Brother Judges.[20]

These sorts of tasks took up the better part of Stanley's administrative
energies.

But not all tasks were mundane. Much larger duties, like the prorogation of Parliament, fell to Stanley as governor general. At the end of April
1889, Macdonald unofficially informed Stanley:

I think that we shall finish in the Commons our work
tonight, but must give the Senate tomorrow to consider or
reject our measures. It will be safe however to fix Thursday
at 3 pm for the prorogation. I send you a draft of the speech.
Will your Excellency kindly look over and criticize it?[21]

* * *

Stanley had a strong staff to assist him in his duties. Replacing Captain
Josceline Bagot as the governor general's military secretary was Captain
Charles Colville, the eldest son of Lord Colville of Culross. Born on 26
April, 1854, Colville was educated at Harrow and joined the Grenadier
Guards in October 1871. Between March 1881 and April 1883, Colville was
an aide-de-camp to the Commander-in-Chief to Bombay. He was gazetted
to captain in June 1884 and was appointed to his position with the new
Governor General in August 1888.

Lieutenant Aubrey Hope McMahon, born on 26 August, 1862, fol-
lowed a similar path to his new supervisor, having been educated at Eton
before entering the Grenadier Guards in 1882. Several others served as
ADCs in a lesser capacity, including John Armstrong, Hewit Bernard,
Arthur Cobren, George Dawson, Phillipe Landry, James MacPherson,
Hector Prevost, Edward Prior, Charles Short and Henry Smith. The
Governor General would appoint additional aides-de-camp to his staff
over the course of his five-year term in Canada, including his eldest son,
Lieutenant Edward George Villiers Stanley, who joined his father's staff in

January 1889. Edward had travelled to Canada with his parents in 1888 but returned to England to do duty with his regiment, returning — newly married — to serve as an aide to his father.[22]

Constance Stanley had three ladies to assist with her duties: Mrs. Colville, wife of Captain Charles Colville and sister of Captain Streatfeild, who had been military secretary to Lord Lansdowne; Mrs. Bagot, wife of Captain Bagot; and Miss Lister, who was described variously as either Constance's cousin or niece.

* * *

While his aides-de-camp earned a salary of three thousand dollars per year, the Governor General was paid an annual salary of ten thousand dollars[23], a sizable amount of money for the era. The annual income of production workers at approximately the same time was three hundred seventy-five dollars. For supervisory or office employment, the annual earnings averaged eight hundred forty-six dollars. It was also estimated that Canadian citizens would spend approximately one hundred fifty thousand dollars a year for the salaries of the vice regal, his staff, housing, travel and general expenses.[24]

* * *

The official residence of the Governor General, Rideau Hall, is situated on seventy-nine acres of property at One Sussex Drive, some three and a half kilometres from the Parliament Buildings on a historic street referred to as the "Mile of History." The street is on a cliff that rises from, and runs parallel to, the Ottawa River. Today, Sussex Drive is home not only to Rideau Hall, but to the embassies of South Africa (at number 15), France (42), Saudi Arabia (201), Japan (255), Kuwait (333) and the United States (490). Canada's High Commissioner resides at Earnscliffe at 140 Sussex, the former home of Canada's first prime minister, Sir John A. Macdonald. Other Sussex addresses of note include the Royal Canadian Mint, the National Gallery of Canada, Old Ottawa City Hall and Notre-Dame Cathedral. Rideau Hall, or Government House, faces the Prime Minister's residence at 24 Sussex Drive.

Although held in great regard today, Rideau Hall was not always looked upon with particular fondness. Neither Lord nor Lady Stanley was enamoured with the official residence of the Governor General:

> *It is understood that Parliament will be asked next session to make an appropriation for the erection of a new residence for the Governor General, as Lord Stanley is thoroughly disgusted with the unsightly and unhealthy patchwork building known as Rideau Hall, in which he has to spend his time while in Ottawa. Lord Dufferin, Lord Lorne and Lord Lansdowne have all, in their turn, protested against living in Rideau Hall and spent all the time they possibly could away from the capital.*[25]

Discussions concerning the construction of a new Government House have long since evaporated. "Every government since Confederation has been sworn in here," explained John Ralston Saul, husband of Her Excellency Adrienne Clarkson. "Every one of Canada's great initiatives, as well as every one of our deepest crises, has been discussed in private between governor general and prime minister."[26] Inductions into the Order of Canada are traditionally held in the ballroom, the same place where prime ministers and Cabinet ministers swear their oaths.

The two-storey, rectangular stone villa was built in 1838 by Thomas MacKay, a stonemason who had emigrated from Scotland and found work as a contractor in his adopted home before helping in the construction of the Rideau Canal.

Queen Victoria designated Ottawa, formerly known as Bytown, as the new capital of Canada in 1857. Construction began on the Parliament Buildings and plans were made to build an appropriate residence for the governor general. But by 1864, no Government House had yet been built, so the MacKay house was leased to the government of the Dominion of Canada as a temporary residence for Viscount Charles Stanley Monck, then Governor General of British North America and later, Canada's first governor general. In 1868, the government purchased the house and grounds from the MacKay family for eighty-two thousand dollars. Thomas himself had died in 1855.

Although the Department of Public Works had made great strides in adapting the "miserable little house," as George Brown, the leader of the Opposition referred to the former MacKay house, none of its residents found it adequate. "Rideau Hall is a long, low, unpretentious building, exceedingly comfortable as a dwelling-house, if somewhat inadequate as an official residence for the Governor General of Canada," wrote Lord Frederick Hamilton following a visit to Lord and Lady Lansdowne.[27] Hamilton, a member of Parliament for South-West Manchester in Great Britain between 1884 and 1886, was also Lady Lansdowne's brother. "After 1867, they couldn't make up their mind as to whether they should build," explained Adrienne Clarkson. "They had rented it, then they thought they might build something. I don't think governments are different at any time."[28]

Each governor general, in turn, made alterations to Rideau Hall. In 1865, Lord Monck had a cricket ground and pavilion built when Prime Minister Macdonald declared cricket Canada's national sport.[29] In 1872, the Earl of Dufferin added a ballroom, complete with a stage at one end, as well as an indoor tennis court, which could be ingeniously converted within a few hours into a reception room or large dining room. It became known as the Tent Room, as a red-and-white-striped canvas could be lowered from the roof for official functions, giving it a decided resemblance to a tent. But any and all changes were regarded as temporary measures until a proper Government House could be built.

The Honourable Adrienne Clarkson further elucidated:

> The British were governors general here and they were usually British aristocrats. They would arrive on ships at Quebec City from Britain and they would have a container full of furniture and other things for their five years in office. It became a place where people lived for just five years and there was no feeling that it was part of the Canadian fabric, even though it was so historic.
>
> It is the oldest continually inhabited house in Canada. Everybody has visited Rideau Hall. John A. Macdonald drank there, Wilfrid Laurier danced there and every head of state that has ever visited Canada has been there for a state dinner. That's what gives it a patina of work. It isn't an architectural jewel by any means. It's very odd. Lord Minto built a wing. The Duke of Connaught built new offices. Lord Dufferin built a ballroom. "Let's have the indoor

*tennis court made into a tented room." Madame Sauvé did
in 1985. So right up until the very present, this house has
been ad hoc. Whatever it is one needs, you do it, but it is
quite exciting because it isn't a standard kind of palace.*

*Everybody who works at Rideau Hall works in that
building. The habitable quarters have seven bedrooms on
the second floor and a lovely chapel that was made out of
one of the bedrooms. It has its own charm. We found that
when we lived there. We tried to make it as homey as possible. You have to keep it up attractively so that people feel
welcomed and warm there.*[30]

Because of the dryness of the Canadian winter climate, Lady Lansdowne
discovered a remarkable trick that was quickly adopted by her children,
much to the amazement and amusement of their friends. Her Excellency
discovered that it was possible to light the gaslights through the static electricity generated within her body. She would shuffle over the carpet
wearing thin shoes and then touch the metal of the lamp, creating a spark
half an inch long that would zap out of her finger. But although Lady
Lansdowne used her new-found powers to light the gas lamps, the children
were somewhat more mischievous, as Lord Hamilton recalled:

*They loved, after shuffling their feet on the carpet, to creep
up to any adult relation and touch them lightly on the ear,
a most sensitive spot. There would be a little spark, a little
shock, and a little exclamation of surprise.*[31]

Most of the early residents of One Sussex Drive — all of them British-born
until 1952, when Vincent Massey was named governor general — adapted
quickly to Canadian winters, embracing the various sports that could be
played outdoors. "A beautiful ideal winter day: the ground and trees white
with snow, blue sky and sun. The children were unable to resist some of the
pleasures of a first day of snow, and tumbled about in it as though it were
sand," Lady Dufferin entered in her journal of 1872.[32]

Rideau Hall boasted two imposing toboggan slides, which were used
with great regularity during Ottawa winters. As writers MacMillan, Harris
and Desjardins humorously instructed, "put a toboggan and two or three

beaux at her disposal and a pretty Canadian girl never looks prettier."[33] Both Lord and Lady Aberdeen took their turns going down the toboggan run, but Lady Aberdeen didn't care to repeat the adventure and claimed, "it leaves too much of one's inside behind one to be comfortable for such folk as me — still, it wasn't bad." But, along with "merry, romping company" on the renowned toboggan runs, there was occasionally reason for concern. Lord Frederick Hamilton offered his thoughts on his time at Rideau:

> *We had a serious toboggan accident one night owing to the stupidity of an old Senator, who insisted on standing in the middle of the track. The aides-de-camps room was converted into an operating theatre, and reeked with the fumes of chloroform. The young man had bad concussion, and was obliged to remain a week at Rideau Hall, whilst the poor girl was disfigured for life.*[34]

These events, however, did not put a freeze on further winter fun.

The first ice rink at Rideau Hall was built in 1878. Shortly afterwards, Rideau Hall began hosting skating at two open-air rinks. Hamilton declared that by skating every day, "most of the Government House party became very expert, and could perform every kind of trick upon skates." Hamilton added that "Lord and Lady Lansdowne and their two daughters, now Duchess of Devonshire and Lady Osborne Beauclerk, could execute the most complicated Quadrilles and Lancers on skates, and could do the most elaborate figures."[35]

The rink is still in operation today and, as Adrienne Clarkson explained, the Rideau Hall Rink

> *is the oldest outdoor skating rink in the same place in continuous existence. It started in 1878 and it has never not been a rink in the winter. When I got to Rideau Hall and I learned that they were planning to have to build an administration building where the rink was, I fought that like crazy. I thought that this was a rink that was historic, skating is historic to Canadians, this rink is open to the public and indeed the public has a good deal of fun with it in the winter. It was also nice for the staff because there was*

a pick-up shinny game every Wednesday. There were a number of women who played along with the men. I think that our obsession with hockey is one of the symbols of Canadian winters that is really very important.[36]

The former governor general took her own turns around the rink at Rideau like everyone else, but confessed, "I just wasn't very good." Despite her love of skating, Clarkson's weak ankles hindered her development in the grand Rideau tradition.[37]

Twice each winter, in a tradition begun by Lord and Lady Lansdowne, the citizens of Ottawa were invited to visit Rideau Hall for elaborate evening winter parties called Arctic Cremornes — after the then recently defunct gardens in London. The rinks were lit with coloured fairy-lamps and the curling rink and tearoom above it were outlined with hundreds of coloured electric light bulbs and Japanese lanterns stretched between the trees. Powerful arc lamps were placed at the top of the toboggan slides and a massive bonfire roared by the skating rink. The spectacle was remarkable.

The parties reflected the resolute nature of the governor general and the people of the capital at large, who were committed to making the very best of the harsh Canadian winter. Hamilton described how beauty could be found in an Ottawa winter:

> *The effect was indescribably pretty, and it was pleasant to reflect how man had triumphed over nature in being able to give an outdoor evening party in mid-winter with the thermometer below zero. The gleaming crystals of snow reflecting the coloured lamps; the Bengal lights staining the white expanse crimson and green and silhouetting the outlines of the fir trees in dead black against the burnished steel of the sky; the crowd of guests in their many-coloured blanket-suits, made a singularly attractive picture, with a note of absolute novelty in it; and the crash of the military band, the merry whirr of the skates, and the roar of the descending toboggans had something extraordinarily exhilarating about them in the keen, pure air.*[38]

While skaters rounded the Rideau Rink and the toboggan runs echoed with shouts of sheer delight, the Governor General's Foot Guard band performed in a palace constructed entirely of ice. Once again, Hamilton described the scene:

> *Once given a design, ice-architecture is most fascinating and very easy. Instead of mortar, all that is required is a stream of water from a hose to freeze the ice-blocks together, and as ice can be easily chipped into any shape, the most fantastic pinnacles and ornaments can be contrived. Our ice-palace was usually built in what I may call a free adaptation of the Canado-Moresque style.*[39]

But because the ice palace was the band's home for the evening, it was essential that it contain a large stove so that the brass musical instruments could be protected from the Canadian cold; should the moisture that accumulates in a brass instrument freeze, it would render the instrument useless. The musicians were forced to perform wearing woollen gloves.

Lord and Lady Dufferin had a covered rink for curling built at their own expense in 1873, and the sheet of ice was used enthusiastically by subsequent governors general. The Hall's curling foursome of 1887 consisted of Lord Lansdowne himself, along with General Sir Henry Streatfeild and one of Lansdowne's footmen, who seemed to have a natural flair for curling. A long-distance telephone was used for the first time in Canada during an 1887 curling match between the Rideau Hall team and a team from Montreal. A line was specially installed so that each end could be telephoned from Rideau Hall to Montreal, where the result was shown on a board. On that day, it was Montreal that won the match.

Staff at Rideau Hall, wearing fur coats, served dinner to guests in the curling rink. Gazing around the grounds, both men and women wore knickerbockers with bright-coloured stockings, long coats, and knitted toques. "A collection of three hundred people in blanket-suits gave the effect of a peripatetic rainbow against the white snow," punctuated Lord Hamilton.[40]

On special occasions, the ice of the curling rink was decorated elaborately in multiple colours. Stencils were laid on the ice, and coloured inks mixed with water were poured through the stencil holes. The inks froze almost immediately onto the ice. Complicated designs of maple leaves, thistles and roses could be made quickly and effectively. When Lord Lansdowne's term as governor general concluded in 1888, the curlers of Canada bade him farewell before he left for a post in India. Hamilton was on hand to describe the evening:

> *Speaking of the regret he felt at leaving Ottawa, and at severing his many links of connection with Canada, [Lansdowne] added that, bearing in view the climate of Bengal, he did not anticipate much curling in India, and that he would miss the 'roaring game'. In fact, the only 'roaring game' he was likely to come in contact with would probably take the unpleasant form of a Bengal tiger springing out at him!*[41]

Lansdowne's post in India was one that his successor had coveted — even during his early tenure in the Dominion. But soon, Stanley's desire waned and he settled into life in Canada.

* * *

A sizable portion of early Canadian history can be found at the governor general's second official residence. La Citadelle, anglicized to The Citadel, is an imposing heritage structure poised on a cliff overlooking the St. Lawrence River. In 1820, the British army, under the direction of Lieutenant-Colonel Elias W. Durnford of the Royal Engineers, built a massive citadel in the shape of a four-pointed polygon atop Cap Diamant, with each point forming a bastion, encompassing thirty-seven acres in all. Durnford incorporated into the structure parts of the 1693 redoubt fortress of New France's Governor General Frontenac as well as a 1750 powder magazine. In 1872, the Marquess of Dufferin, Canada's third governor general, established the former officers' quarters as an official vice regal residence, inaugurating the tradition of using this edifice for several weeks each year.

Former Governor General Adrienne Clarkson described the vice regal's Quebec home:

> *La Citadelle is something that Lord and Lady Dufferin brought into being. They loved Quebec and they had a*

summer house built at Tadoussac at the mouth of the Saguenay on the St. Lawrence. It was a great big, old-fashioned cottage. Personally, I'm eternally grateful to him, because this is not only a beautiful place but a magical one, with the great river flowing beneath us and what I believe to be the most beautiful urban view in the world. We look out on the city of Quebec with its meaningful history for all of us as Canadians and its modern dynamism for the present.[42]

Clarkson added, "While it is still a grand house, it is much smaller and therefore more homey than Rideau Hall."[43]

Over a century ago, Stanley's aide-de-camp Lord Kilcoursie documented the family's shift to Quebec: "in the autumn, we moved to The Citadel at Quebec, an old-fashioned and very dirty building but extremely lovable." Kilcoursie recalled the joy of cricket matches that took place on the most unusual pitch of the Plains of Abraham and added, "although I found the Canadian French very difficult to follow, I liked the people enormously and the less rigid atmosphere of the official dinners."[44]

Lord Hamilton also had a favourable opinion of The Citadel:

There are few finer views in the world than that from the terrace of The Citadel of Quebec over the mighty expanse of the St. Lawrence, with ocean-going steamers lying so close below that it would be possible to drop a stone from The Citadel onto their decks; and the view from the Dufferin Terrace, two hundred feet lower down, is just as fine.[45]

"It's a wonderful place and it has the most wonderful view over the St. Lawrence," added Ms. Clarkson. "You're right within the 1812 fortifications that were built to keep the Americans away from us."[46] Although this possibility may seem ridiculous to us today, it had been a real consideration during Stanley's term as governor general.

Shortly after her arrival in Canada, Lady Stanley wrote a letter to her sister expressing delight in the accommodations and the reception afforded the Governor General and his family:

We are, up to now, very much pleased with our new homes

and all the people in Ontario and Quebec are most cordial
and charming to us. [Frederick] has made a very great and
good impression by his French.

Stanley would need these skills to help the Dominion through the Jesuit
Estates Act crisis which was lurking on the horizon.

* * *

That summer, Lord Stanley purchased property on which to build a vacation
residence. Dubbed Stanley House, the summer retreat on the Cascapedia
River in Quebec provided many of the most satisfying personal moments for
Stanley, who enjoyed being away from many of the official duties that being
governor general entailed, and it allowed him and his frequent guests to
indulge in their passion for fishing. Stanley spent his first summer in Canada
on the Cascapedia, fishing for the plentiful salmon and working from
Stanley House.

During the summer months when Parliament was not in session, the
governors general had begun the annual tradition of leaving Rideau Hall
for the cooler temperatures and more relaxed atmosphere of The Citadel in
Quebec City. Word of the magnificent Cascapedia and its fat, spawning
salmon had been spread since the 1840s. Lord Lorne first discovered the
pleasures of the Gaspé Peninsula of eastern Quebec in 1879. From The
Citadel, with railway service having opened up much of eastern Canada,
Lorne followed the St. Lawrence River to the north shore of the Baie des
Chaleurs or Chaleur Bay.

The fast-flowing Cascapedia, which runs some one hundred twenty
kilometres before emptying into the Bay, required Aboriginal navigators to
assist the vice regal party. As writer James Whalen recently explained, "by
virtue of their skills with the birch bark canoe and their knowledge of rivers
and forests, native people served as guides from the earliest days of recreational sporting in the North American colonies."[47] Kilcoursie recalled his
summers with the Governor General on the Cascapedia:

Louis Jerome, the Indian canoe man who looked after me,
was a genius. He could spot where fish were lying in the
pools as we poled up stream so that one was never flogging

empty water, and he took such an interest in England that he never could get over his astonishment when I told him that the Thames was 'settled right up to the source' and that there was no more virgin country to be explored in the British Isles. He never really quite believed me.[48]

The Dominion Government originally granted the Cascapedia's fishing rights to the office of the Governor General during the term of the Marquess of Lorne, who was governor general between 1878 and 1883. Lorne had fallen in love with the country. "I should like to stay here all my days," he told Sir John A. Macdonald in a letter.[49] Lorne, who was married to Queen Victoria's fourth daughter, Princess Louise, had discovered the extraordinary bounty of large Atlantic salmon in the river's chilly waters. His biographer, W. S. MacNutt, said of Lorne, "his patronage and that of his successors established the reputation of the stream as queen of all Canadian salmon fisheries with the record of the heaviest weight of fish."[50] Lorne had a camp built at a spot six miles from the waters of the Cascapedia. He called his summer home 'Lorne Cottage'. Although referred to as a camp, there was little hardship to endure. Lorne Cottage had a staff that included cooks, servers, cleaners, guides and smokers, who cleaned and filleted the daily catch of fish and then hung them in smokehouses to cure."[51]

Although the fishing was splendid, the early conditions were not, as Hamilton described:

> *My brother-in-law, Lord Lansdowne, had been appointed Governor General in 1883, and I well remember my first arrival in Quebec. We had been living for five weeks in the backwoods of the Cascapedia, the famous salmon river, under the most primitive conditions imaginable (in Lord Lansdowne's summer camp, which was named 'New Derreen' after his Irish estate). I had come there straight from the Argentine Republic on a tramp steamer, and we lived on the Cascapedia coatless and flannel-shirted, with our legs encased in 'beef moccasins' as a protection against the hordes of voracious flies that battened ravenously on us from morning to night. It was a considerable change from a tent on the banks of the rushing, foaming Cascapedia to*

> The Citadel of Quebec, which was then appointed like a
> comfortable English country house, and gave one a thor-
> oughly home-like feeling at once.[52]

Lord Lorne caught such a surfeit of fish during his angling excursions that
he gave away much of his catch to those in the area, and astonishingly, even
shipped some of the finest salmon, packed carefully on ice, back to England
for the enjoyment of Queen Victoria, where they arrived "cold, pink and
perfect."[53] Like his immediate predecessors Lorne and Lansdowne, Lord
Stanley was another British aristocrat, now seated in the governor general's
role, who fell in love with fishing the Cascapedia.

Stanley purchased sixty-eight acres of land nine miles from the
Cascapedia during the summer of 1888. The property had originally
belonged to John and George Duthie, who had occupied the land since the
late eighteenth century. The Duthies later sold it to John Robertson. In 1888
it was purchased by Andrew Fairservice, who subsequently sold it to Stanley
that same year.[54] Stanley hired a carpenter named Reid to help build Stanley
House, although the Governor General took an active role in the design and
construction of his new summer home. With eighteen bedrooms and a large
octagonal drawing room that included an open fireplace and brick hearth,
unpretentious Stanley House, nestled among the cedars on a bluff just west
of what is now New Richmond, Quebec, was certainly more than a camp or
even a large cottage. There was clearly plenty of room for the Stanley family,
staff, friends and guests. The furniture in the wood-framed house was, as
Emma Tate of the Stanley Estates newsletter illustrated, "so rustic it belied
the persons initially using it. Tables utilized plain boards with legs made of
the unbarked trunks of small trees. Wardrobes were simple wooden shelves
with modest curtains hanging from them."[55] The Stanley family traditionally spent June and July at Stanley House, then moved to The Citadel until
October, when they returned to Rideau Hall.

Insects plagued the summer retreats on the Cascapedia of both
Stanley's predecessors. Both Lorne Cottage and New Derreen faced seem-
ingly endless onslaughts of blackflies, mooseflies, sandflies and mosquitoes.
But, much to the satisfaction of Lady Stanley, the breeze from the Bay of
Chaleur substantially reduced the numbers of pests around Stanley House.
A relieved Lady Aberdeen, a later resident of Stanley House, added:

The former Governors lived at fishing lodges which they re-
spectively built on the river, but they were very small and
infested with the mosquitoes, black flies and sand flies for
which the river is famous. So the site of this house was
chosen nine miles away from the beginning of the fishing.
However hot it is, there is always some breeze and the
evenings and nights are always cool.[56]

The Stanley family kept copious records of their fishing successes during
the days spent at Stanley House. The charts included the number of days
fished, the number of fish caught and the weight of each fish. Through the
summer of 1888, the best year for the vice regal family and guests, three
hundred salmon, each weighing an average of twenty-five pounds, were
caught. Over a five-year period, the Stanley family, staff and guests hooked
894 salmon with an average weight of 23.7 pounds. Victor landed the
largest salmon recorded — a fifty-three-pound specimen caught during
the summer of 1892.

In many ways, Stanley was happiest fishing on the Cascapedia —
though he would be accused by some for being overly fond of fishing and
less so to any real commitment to the task at hand. Although several guests
visited Stanley House during Lord Stanley's term as governor general,
including Auguste Réal Angers, the Lieutenant Governor of Quebec in
1889, and His Royal Highness, Prince George, who visited in 1891, Lord
Stanley's most frequent fishing companions were his sons Victor and
Ferdy, daughter Isobel and aides-de-camp Aubrey McMahon, Josceline
Bagot and Willie Walsh. For her part, Lady Stanley was an infrequent
angling partner.

Stanley often sent colleagues the gift of a salmon caught on the
Cascapedia. During the summer of 1890, Honoré Mercier, the Premier of
Quebec, was sent a forty-six-pound specimen,[57] though one wonders if
Mercier would have received the token of appreciation in the years to come,
given the heated Jesuit Estates Act crisis. Quebec City Mayor Jules-Joseph
Fremont also received a "superb salmon" from the Governor General.[58]

Yet Stanley House was not merely a summer retreat for the governor
general; a good amount of government business was also conducted from
New Richmond. The residence was equipped with both telephone and telegraph lines so that Lord Stanley could remain in touch with Ottawa,

although he also used the telephone to call upriver to find out how the salmon were rising.[59]

In his journal, Kilcoursie retold a harrowing story involving communicating with Stanley House:

> *In 1892, some very delicate negotiations were in progress between the Colonial Office, Canada and the USA regarding fishing rights. I was left behind in Ottawa for three weeks in July when the vice-regal party had gone up to the Cascapedia for salmon fishing. My instructions were to decipher the telegrams and send them on a bi-weekly messenger, but that a certain cable marked 'urgent' might arrive asking if the Canadian government would agree to a certain word or clause being inserted in a draft. I was given the draft and the answer to be sent which was, roughly, as follows: 'The Canadian government cannot agree to the words suggested but we have sent a revised draft by mail which left yesterday.'*
>
> *Sure enough, a few hours after Their Excellencies' departure, the cable arrived, but not quite worded as expected. I hesitated for some time whether I should send the draft answer or not but finally decided I had better ask for further instructions. Meanwhile, I sent to the Colonial Office a cipher message saying: 'Cable received and forwarded to His Excellency at Bay of Gaspé.' Three days later, I got a message from the Canadian Government that they had heard from His Excellency and that the draft message left in my hands was to be destroyed. I then forgot the whole matter.*
>
> *Three weeks later, it was my turn to go up to the fishing lodge and His Excellency said to me, 'If you had sent the draft reply, nothing could have prevented war between the United States and Canada.' As it was, I believe it took another four or five months to arrive at a 'modus vivendi.'*[60]

Kilcoursie added that "the weeks spent [on the Cascapedia] in the July of 1892 are among my happiest memories."[61]

* * *

Between 1878 and Lord Stanley's departure from Canada in 1893, the Cascapedia was the exclusive domain of the Queen's Canadian representative. Yet in 1882, under a judgement by the Supreme Court of Canada, the fishing rights of the Cascapedia passed from federal jurisdiction to provincial. In a letter to Prime Minister Macdonald, Quebec Premier Joseph-Alfred Mousseau asked for the vice regal fishing privilege to come to an end. "It is cruel to deprive us of the income for the sake of furnishing a few days of fishing to the Governor General."[62] Still, those days were precious to Stanley.

Little changed until 1893, when Quebec auctioned off the fishing rights on the Cascapedia. By then, Stanley had announced his resignation and was packing to return home to the country seat at Knowsley. Lord Aberdeen replaced Stanley as governor general and purchased Stanley House from his predecessor. Aberdeen's representative was instructed to bid as high as five thousand dollars per year for the fishing rights to the Cascapedia, but an American consortium of ten millionaires, including Henry DeForest of the Southern Pacific Railroad, R.G. Dun, later of Dun and Bradstreet, stockbroker H.B. Hollins, neurologist Dr. S. Weir Mitchell and railroad tycoon William K. Vanderbilt, outbid the vice regal by offering six thousand a year for a ten-year period.[63] The syndicate, calling itself the Cascapedia Salmon Club, retained the lease until the 1970s. The Earl of Minto, who succeeded Lord Aberdeen as governor general, blamed Lord Stanley for not taking the appropriate steps to secure the exclusive fishing rights when the provincial government was trying to open up the rights to bids.[64]

Stanley House remained the summer home of governors general until 1904. Lord Aberdeen, who purchased the home from Lord Stanley in 1893, had intended to sell the residence. Lady Aberdeen exclaimed, "we are very glad now that we have not succeeded in finding a purchaser for this place as we have been trying to do."[65] The Earl of Minto bought Stanley House from his predecessor in 1894.

But without the river's exclusive salmon fishing rights, both Aberdeen and Minto spent less time at Stanley House, and it was sold by the Earl of Minto in 1904 to John E. Reyburn, the congressman from Pennsylvania. As Minto's contemporary John Buchan remembered, "it was great grief to Minto that the fishing on the Cascapedia was no longer the perquisite of the Governor General."[66]

Stanley House changed hands several times through the century, although continued to be the summer playground of the wealthy. Roméo and Estelle Lanctôt from Montreal eventually took possession of Stanley House. Their stepdaughter, Olivia Terrell, inherited Stanley House in 1957, and in 1962 she donated it to the Canada Council for the Arts.[67]

The Canada Council used the estate until 1984, when budget cuts forced it to board up the building. Although not in use, the building was maintained by a guardian for several years. Then, in 1991, two local groups vied to resurrect Stanley House. Roch Boissonnault, a local florist, made a proposal that would turn Stanley House into a botanical garden. At the same time, the Gaspesian British Heritage Centre exhibited plans to restore the home to its original state and turn a barn on the grounds into a theatre, featuring videos of Lord Stanley and his hockey legacy. "We'd definitely give it a hockey vocation," stated Michel Larrivée, co-chairman of the heritage centre.[68]

Finally, in 1996, local residents Lucille and J. Edgar LeBlanc purchased the property and have transformed the estate into the Stanley House Inn, maintaining much of its flavour and most of its history.

* * *

From the very outset of their time in Canada, the Stanleys chose to embrace the Canadian experience rather than fight it. From those splendid summer fishing trips on the Cascapedia to making the best of the long cold winters by snowshoeing and playing hockey, Frederick and company gave the country a fair trial.

One periodical described Lady Stanley's adjustment to her new home:

> *The hostess of Rideau Hall seems to enter thoroughly into every phase of Canadian life, and to make herself quite at home amongst all classes of Canadians. She has accompanied her husband wherever he has been since their arrival in the Dominion, and has worked indefatigably to make herself acquainted with all the institutions and features of our great Dominion.*[69]

Stanley would be beaten by neither the onerous duties that fell to his high-ranking position nor to the often harsh winter conditions that characterized the Dominion in the nineteenth century.

* * *

The Governor General's sound but relatively quiet political career had rendered the characteristics of the man himself rather obscure — he was largely unknown outside of his association to his famous brother and father. Certainly, there was neither the glamour nor pomp about Frederick that other governors general elicited, but he would be no less loved by Canadians. Frederick was not the most engaging orator the Dominion would ever witness, yet his speeches were measured and purposeful. While he stole far fewer headlines than his father, brother and even his son later would, Lord Stanley would prove no less useful and diligent in public service.

What is missing from the accounts of the scarce number of historians that have bothered to review his career and life is the kindness, even-handedness and generosity of Frederick Arthur Stanley. Like his father before him, Stanley put his family first, chose to involve his great number of children in his busy public life, was devoted to his wife and could be relied upon to act as a fair judge in both personal and public matters. There exist but few glimpses into the "personal" side of Stanley, but those that do exist speak to a gentle, quintessentially refined man with a general love of life. Writing to her eldest, Lady Stanley informed Edward that his father was "now quite devoted to 'Dinah', a large black retriever that belongs to Canada and that Victor asked to leave here because she could not stand the heat of the West Indies. [Frederick] is quite a slave to her."[70]

Stanley was, by all accounts, a supportive father as well. When Edward George began addressing meetings in Lancashire with a view towards winning a seat in his first election, Stanley wrote to offer his praise:

> *I have been reading your speech in the Bolton paper, and can honestly congratulate you upon it. You chose your topics judiciously and handled them skilfully. You said nothing that would have been better let alone, and your treatment of the labour question showed tact. You were a little 'flabby' on the free trade question as connected with*

the colonies; but something must be forgiven to the son of a colonial governor. Altogether the speech is a success, and does you credit.

Stanley even took care to warn his son that, although Edward George would receive the telegram on "All Fools' Day," he need not consider it a "*poisson d'avril.*"[71] The Governor General's first spring in Canada, however, would be punctuated by a growing resentment among the Dominion's Protestant community following the passing of a very controversial Act of Parliament.

[1] Wellington College received its Royal charter in 1853 as the 'Royal and Religious Foundation of The Wellington College'.

[2] Kilcoursie, *Recollections Hazy But Happy*.

[3] Besides shipping lines, Allan was involved in banking, insurance companies and the burgeoning railway industry. In fact, it was the accusation that Sir John A. Macdonald's government accepted illicit funds for involvement in a transcontinental railway in 1873 that ultimately brought down the Conservative government. Macdonald ultimately rebounded from the Pacific Scandal, but it left his legacy forever tarnished.

[4] Brochure published by the Allan Lines in the mid-1880s.

[5] *Montreal Gazette* (10 June, 1888).

[6] Ibid.

[7] *Montreal Daily Witness* (11 June, 1888), *edition cover page*.

[8] *Stanley Papers* National Archives of Canada

[9] *Ottawa Daily Citizen* (12 June, 1888), *edition cover page*.

[10] *The Life of Sir John A. Macdonald* (Toronto: Morang & Company, 1908), p.376.

[11] Ibid.

[12] Ibid., p.375.

[13] *Toronto World* (11 September, 1888), *edition cover page*.

[14] *Montreal Daily Witness* (11 June, 1888), *edition cover page*.

[15] *Toronto Globe* (11 September, 1888), *edition cover page*.

[16] *Toronto Evening News* (10 September, 1888), p.4.

[17] J. Cowan, *Canada's Governors General: 1867–1952* (Toronto: York Publishing Toronto), p.52.

[18] 'Lord Lansdowne's Departure From Ottawa: His Administrative Record in Canada', *Ottawa Citizen* (14 April, 1888).

[19] Ibid.

[20] J. A. Macdonald, *Letter to F. A. Stanley, from Lord Stanley of Preston Papers*, The Public Archive of Canada in London, (Dalhousie: 2 August, 1888).

[21] Ibid.

[22] J. A. Gemmill (*ed*), *The Canadian Parliamentary Companion* (Ottawa: J. Durie & Son, 1889).

[23] Ibid.

[24] F. H. Leacy (*ed*), *Historical statistics of Canada* (Ottawa: Statistics Canada in joint sponsorship with the Social Science Federation of Canada, c.1983).

[25] *Qu'Appelle Vidette* (Fort Qu'Appelle: 10 October, 1889), p.3.

[26] M. MacMillan, M. Harris & A. Desjardins, *Canada's House: Rideau Hall and the Invention of a Canadian Home* (Toronto: Alfred A. Knopf Canada, 2004), p.43.

[27] F. S. Hamilton, *The Days Before Yesterday* (New York: Doran, 1920).

[28] Adrienne Clarkson interview with Kevin Shea 28 April, 2006.

[29] D. Birley, *A Social History of Cricket* (London: Aurum Press, 1999

[30] K. Shea, *Interview with Adrienne Clarkson* (28 April, 2006).

[31] Hamilton, *The Days Before Yesterday*.

[32] MacMillan (*et al.*), *Canada's House*, p.33.

[33] Ibid., p.34.

[34] Hamilton, *The Days Before Yesterday*.

[35] Ibid.

[36] Shea, *Interview with Adrienne Clarkson*.

[37] Ibid.

[38] Hamilton, *The Days Before Yesterday*.

[39] Ibid.

[40] Ibid.

[41] Ibid.

[42] Shea, *Interview with Adrienne Clarkson*.

[43] MacMillan (*et al.*), *Canada's House*, p.40.

[44] Kilcoursie, *Recollections Hazy But Happy*.

[45] Hamilton, *The Days Before Yesterday*.

[46] Shea, *Interview with Adrienne Clarkson*.

[47] J. M. Whalen, 'A Vice Regal Kettle of Fish,' *Legion Magazine* (March-April 1999).

[48] Kilcoursie, *Recollections Hazy But Happy*.

[49] W. S. MacNutt, *Days of Lorne: from the private papers of the Marquis of Lorne, 1878–1883*, in the possession of the Duke of Argyll at Inveraray Castle, Scotland, (Fredericton, 1955); P. B. Waite, *Dictionary of Canadian Biograhy On-Line*.

[50] Ibid.

[51] A. Shoumatoff, 'Mystic River', *Travel and Leisure on-line* (July 2005).

[52] Hamilton, *The Days Before Yesterday*.

[53] J. E. Collins, *Canada under the Administration of Lord Lorne* (Toronto: Rose Publishing Company, 1884).

[54] Whalen, 'A Vice Regal Kettle of Fish'.

[55] E. Tate, *Stanley Estates Newsletter* (August 2005), p10

[56] *The Canadian Journal of Lady Aberdeen: 1893-1898* (Toronto: The Champlain Society, 1960).

[57] *Le Canada*, (26 June, 1890), p.3.

[58] *Le Canada*, (2 August, 1892), p.3.

[59] Whalen, 'A Vice Regal Kettle of Fish'.

[60] Kilcoursie, *Recollections Hazy But Happy*.

[61] Ibid.

[62] Whalen, 'A Vice Regal Kettle of Fish'.

[63] *The Canadian Journal of Lady Aberdeen*.

[64] Shoumatoff, 'Mystic River'.

[65] *The Canadian Journal of Lady Aberdeen*.

[66] Whalen, 'A Vice Regal Kettle of Fish'; Buchan, *Lord Minto: A Memoir*.

[67] Shoumatoff, 'Mystic River'.

[68] *Peterborough Examiner* (16 May, 1991)

[69] *The Dominion Illustrated Monthly* (10 November, 1888), p.294.

[70] Lady Constance Stanley, *Letter to Edward George Stanley*, (10 December, 1891); Churchill, *Lord Derby*, p.33.

[71] Lord Stanley, *Letter to Edward George Stanley*, (30 March, 1891); Churchill, *Lord Derby*, p.34.

CHAPTER FIVE

Agitation

The Canada that Lord Stanley was assigned to oversee was, by many accounts, a recently improved country. Crop prices were strong and there was, as Macdonald wrote, "quite a revival of a spirit of enterprise in Canada."[1] And while the transcontinental railway was still experiencing teething pains, the question of the North-West Rebellion, at least, had been largely put to rest, even if fragments of its fallout would resonate during Stanley's tenure.

One fragment, an "extremist politician" named Honoré Mercier, would put into motion perhaps the most controversial domestic issue of Stanley's time as governor general. Mercier, seeking a resolution of an existing dispute over the estates of the Jesuits, had effectively procured a constitutional attack on the unity of the Dominion.[2] The Jesuit Estates Act would prove to be an extremely volatile matter that caused terrific political hardship for the government, and actual violence and agitation for the people of Canada.

The Jesuit Estates matter managed to once again pit race and religion against one another — French-speaking Roman Catholics at cultural odds with English-speaking Protestants — as they had been prior to Confederation, and as they would be time and again in the country's young history.

At the core of the matter was the final settlement of large estates that the original Society of Jesus had been granted in New France prior to the British conquest of 1763. The society was suppressed by Papal brief in 1773, and when the last Jesuit in Canada had died at the turn of the nineteenth century, the Crown confiscated the estates. By 1775, one-seventh of the Crown land in the Quebec was reserved for the Protestant clergy. In 1831, the estates were transferred to the legislature of Lower Canada as an endowment in support of education. By the 1850s, Canadian opinion was squarely opposed to the clergy reserves, and the Canadian Legislature sought to control the reserves and divide them among the various churches in Lower Canada.

Stanley's father had strongly defended the clergy reserves, a fact that might not surprise in light of his strong views against the disestablishment of the Church of Ireland. Edward Geoffrey Stanley felt that the Canadian plans to divide and secularize the reserves was a violation of property rights and warned that the measure mimicked the dangerous "voluntary" system that had been established regarding churches in the United States.[3]

By the 1860s, however, the Jesuits were re-established in Canada and had begun to insist on some form of compensation for their lost estates. This claim was met with a counter-claim by Roman Catholic bishops who, as historian Donald Creighton explained, "argued that the property of religious houses suppressed by papal brief reverted to the hierarchy of the diocese in which they were situated."[4]

Enter Honoré Mercier. Opposed to Confederation from the beginning, Mercier was the primary founder of the Parti National in 1871 and had won the popular support of French-speaking Quebec for his anti-federal sensibility. As a Quebec nationalist, Mercier opposed the execution of Louis Riel, defended the notion of "provincial autonomy" and would take the lead, and much of the headlines, in the Jesuit Estates matter.

The Quebec premier sought to resolve the matter through the passing of a bill in the provincial legislature, one that had been approved by the Pope.5 The Jesuit Estates Act was passed in the summer of 1888 and provided the following terms: four hundred thousand dollars to be divided among the claimants, and sixty thousand dollars for the Protestant Committee of Public Instruction for Quebec.

The same year the Act was passed, Stanley, also in his first year as governor general, reminded French-Canadians of the benefits of living under the Canadian system of government.

No doubt French Canadians were tempted to throw aside loyalty in the troublesome times of 1775 and 1812. Similar difficulties might be met with in the 19th century in the

> *shape of annexation and other cries, but the spirit that pre-*
> *served the loyalty of French Canadians in those years is still*
> *alive. Here we enjoy all the freedom of the republic with the*
> *safeguards that a monarchical form of government sur-*
> *rounds it. Canadians of all classes enjoy more substantial*
> *liberty than the people to the south of us, while free from*
> *the violent agitations that occasionally occur there.*[6]

Yet as one might expect, more radical elements in French Canada were hardly interested in what a British governor general had to say.

Opposition to the Act began to gather strength in the Dominion's Protestant-run newspapers after the bill was passed, and by 1889 the matter was reaching a fever pitch. The questions were fair: why were the Jesuits — or the Roman Catholic bishops, for that matter — to be compensated at all? And how could a Papal brief confer property rights in a British country? The *nouveau* Society of Jesus, it seemed to many, had only revived the name in order to petition for the old claims of the defunct corpora-tion.[7] A great many people also felt that the question of public endowment of religious bodies had already been settled through the secularization of the clergy reserves. As Creighton added:

> *It was unfair and unwise to depart from this decision for*
> *the benefit of one religious communion only; and it was*
> *particularly objectionable to waive the rule in respect of*
> *property which had been transferred in trust to the*
> *province for the support of education.*[8]

Still, education was not the focal point for those who objected to the Act. The most contentious element was the Pope's involvement.

Mercier invoked the authority of the Papacy in order to settle the ques-tion, and the written correspondence between Mercier and the Pope was reprinted *in extenso* in the bill's preamble. It was here that Orange Canada, among other voices, found the Act to be reprehensible. And so, in January 1889, the first petition requesting the disallowance of the Act was presented to Macdonald's government.

Macdonald and his colleagues carefully considered the mounting re-quests to disallow the Act. Yet, as it was a provincial act, and therefore affected change only in Quebec, Macdonald and company saw no reason to intervene. Macdonald resolved to take no action, in the hope that the growing agitation would wane.

Unfortunately for Macdonald, the tensions continued to spread, and the issue did indeed become one with national repercussions. In a letter to Stanley, Macdonald expressed the opinions of Captain Charles Colville, who had been reporting on the growing number of incidents relating to the Act: "the agitation is so great in Ontario that a refusal would add fuel to the flame."[9] This "flame" was not only burning in the hearts of Protestant Canada, it was also very much alight in Parliament.

Dalton McCarthy, who had often been at loggerheads with Sir John A. Macdonald, his own party leader, pressed the issue of disallowance and rallied a small number of Conservative members around his mission. McCarthy, along with Colonel W. E. O'Brien and their small band of Conservatives who espoused the idea of a unified English-speaking Canada under the British Crown, chose to raise the matter in Parliament in March 1889.

Although Sir John Tupper, Macdonald's Minister of Justice, stood toe to toe with McCarthy in defence of the government's position, it was Sir John A.'s solitary but impassioned speech that may have won the day. In warning, Macdonald gave account of the religious quarrels that had existed before Confederation and asked the House, "What would be the consequences of a disallowance? Agitation, a quarrel — a racial and religious war would be aroused. The best interests of the country would be prejudiced, our credit would be ruined abroad, and our social relations destroyed at home."[10]

The speech worked, and was supported by other speeches in favour of the government's policy from notable members including Laurier, Cartwright and Colby. Only thirteen members (later known as either the "devil's dozen" or the "Noble 13," depending on one's political persuasion) voted in favour of disallowance, while one hundred and eighty-eight voted against it.[11] The thirteen members that voted for disallowance were: Barron, Bell, Charlton, Cockburn, Denison, Macdonald (of Huron), McCarthy, McNeill, Scriver, Sutherland, Tyrwhitt, Wallace and Colonel O'Brien himself.[12] Sensibly, the Governor General declined to intervene.

Where the matter may have, for a time at least, been settled in Parliament, the people of the nation were not done having their voices heard. There were rallies across Ontario, and the "drum ecclesiastic" beat throughout the province. Protestant Canada was incensed. Opposition did not only take the form of demonstrations: the Orange Order even took legal action against a newspaper for libel, as *The Dominion Illustrated Monthly* reported:

> *The anti-Jesuit agitation in Ontario has reached an acute stage, of which the chief incident is the entering by the Order, through its lawyers, of an action for libel against the Toronto* Mail, *based on the imputation of a disloyal oath, which is distinctly disavowed. The outcome of trial will be awaited with no small interest.*[13]

The Equal Rights Association, headed by McCarthy, held raucous demonstrations in Toronto. It seemed that the people of the Dominion were less worried with annexation to the United States than they were with the question, as McCarthy exclaimed, of "whether this country was to be French or English!"[14]

Mercier and company let their views be known in Quebec on the feast day of St-Jean Baptiste and, as Creighton described, "thundered a defiant rejoinder" to the ultra-Protestants.[15] There was, however, some finger-pointing within French Canada. An article in *Le Canadien* described the anti-Catholic agitation as a result of the actions of the Jesuits themselves and of Mercier's own aggressive course of action.[16] In every camp, the country was aflame with politico-religious fervour, and by late summer everyone anxiously awaited news from Ottawa and the final say of one man.

From the beginning of the Jesuit Estates question, Lord Stanley had been set on a steep learning curve. He first had to understand exactly how the rarely-used power of disallowance might be employed. Then, of course, there were the petitions from various parts of the Dominion, mostly Ontario, that called upon Stanley to use his unique power in the situation. Yet, by the summer of 1889, Stanley knew well his role in the Estates matter — namely that, since the Act had come into effect, the Governor General was the only person in the country who still had the power to disallow it. The limitation to Stanley's power of disallowance was fixed one year from the date of the passage of the bill. That date was 8 August, 1889.

As the date drew nearer, the agitation and mudslinging grew louder and uglier. The main members of the Equal Rights Association requested and were granted an interview with Lord Stanley so that they could implore the Governor General to disallow the controversial act. At the same time, Macdonald's government reached out to the mother country and enjoined the services of British law officers to review the constitutionality of the legislation.

While Stanley heard the Equal Righters' appeal, he remained steadfast in his prerogative, choosing *not* to disallow the Act, an opinion that was strengthened by the British law officers' review of the bill. Sir Charles Tupper cabled Macdonald to advise him on the English lawyers' conclusions, specifically that "the Law Officers of the Crown are prepared to give opinion that decision arrived at by Governor General not to interfere … was right and constitutional."[17]

Macdonald had got the support he felt he needed to assuage the call for disallowance. Stanley's judgement, now shored up by constitutional advisers, had been correct.

Macdonald had earlier explained to Stanley his belief that the desired effect might be obtained by involving the English lawyers. "The importance of an early answer is obvious. The statement of the Law Officers affirming the validity of the Provincial Act will I think put an end to the unwholesome agitation from going on."[18] At the same time, Macdonald chose to delay releasing the officers' conclusion to Canadian newspapers, as he advised Stanley:

> *I don't think anything has been lost by the delay in sending Your Excellency's dispatch. The time for disallowance — that is to day the statutory year will expire on 8th August and it would not be well to publish the [Law Officers'] opinion before that date.*[19]

The findings were finally published in Canadian newspapers in September. The brief report from the Law Officers of the Colonial Office read as follows:

> *We have taken the matter into our consideration and, in obedience to Your Lordship's commands, have the honour to report that, in our opinion, the decision arrived at by the Governor General not to interfere with the operation of the Provincial Act in question was right and constitutional.*[20]

But by the time this news was published in the Dominion, Protestant Canada already knew that the Jesuit Estates Act was here to stay.

Although the greater part of the agitation subsided over time, it left an indelible mark on the Dominion's cultural landscape. The agitation also did much to renew suspicion between Protestant and Catholic and, as Macdonald confessed, "It has revived the hostile feeling that time had nearly extinguished between English and French, and which may lead to disastrous results."[21]

In and of itself, the Jesuit Estates Act was an altogether brief affair in Canadian history, but the ill feeling it engendered was not sucked up in the vacuum of time. Indeed, it was an evolution of ancient misgivings between Canada's two main cultures and stood as a harbinger of things to come.

Almost immediately following the Act, Manitoba, a province still dealing with the fallout from a major rebellion, was thrust into a French-language and separate-school debate that further irritated French-English relations. *The Dominion Illustrated Monthly* reviewed the debate in a tone that can only be described as rather wishful thinking on the part of the editorialist.

> *A vexed question in Ontario just now is whether, in any circumstances, French should be the teaching language in any of the provincial schools. The arguments used pro and con are not new, but the discussion has been attended with considerable animosity. Good sense and mutual forbearance should settle all such questions, especially as each section is convinced of the importance of learning the language of the other.*[22]

Yet "good sense" and "mutual forbearance" was an oversimplification of the measures that would be needed to resolve the problem at a time when political winds emanating from the Jesuit Estates Act fanned the already aggravated flame of the language debate.

The central issue remained unchanged: the privileges and legal power of the Roman Catholic Church. Manitoba, as it was then and as it remained for decades, had not become the imagined French Canada of the west that Riel and company had tried to establish through the Manitoba Act of 1870. The timing of the Jesuit Estates issue fit perfectly with the prevailing sentiment of most Manitobans who sought to reclaim the legal standing of their Britishness in the province. This reclamation began with the French-language debate, and the movement spread to the North-West Territories, which were still under the exclusive jurisdiction of the federal government.

The fallout from the debate was ugly, and the subsequent proposed legislation pitted culture against culture in the House of Commons. Only through a last-minute amendment and a stirring speech was Macdonald able to reconcile the House. He implored his colleagues:

> *Let us forget this cry and we shall have our reward in seeing this unfortunate fire, which has been kindled from so small a spark, extinguished forever, and we shall go on, as we have been going on since 1867, as one people, with one object, looking to one future, and expecting to lay the foundation of one great country.*[23]

And with this, Macdonald was able to rally enough French and English support to subdue the "spark." Stanley regarded Macdonald's work as a "brilliant division" — but was it enough?

Less than a generation later, the "spark" was reignited against the backdrop of the First World War, with the hotly contested Conscription Crisis of 1917. Although the Jesuit Estates Act is only one in a long list of cultural grievances between English and French Canada, it was significant in its timing; though it should not be oversold, French-English relations had improved in the wake of the North-West Rebellion, and the young Dominion did not need such an irritating setback as the agitation delivered.

History has applauded Stanley's decision not to disallow the Act. It was the sort of decision that one might expect from Stanley: measured, fair and politically sound. It ignored the raging and radical Orange voice and solidified the non-political role that had been envisioned for the office of the governor general from the first.

---

[1] Mowat to Macdonald, 'Pope', *Sir John A. Macdonald Papers*, (17 November, 1888).

[2] D. Creighton, *John A. Macdonald: The Old Chieftain*, (Toronto: Macmillan Company of Canada Ltd., 1955), p.513.

[3] Jones, *Lord Derby*, p.189.

[4] Creighton, *John A. Macdonald*, p.514.

[5] The Pope decided that $100,000 be given to Laval University in Quebec; $40,000 to the Montreal branch of Laval; $20,000 to the Apostolic Prefect of Labrador; $10,000 to each of the eight bishops of the ecclesiastical Province of Quebec — and the remaining $160,000 to the Society of Jesus itself. See, *The Dominion Illustrated Monthly* (March 30, 1889), p.194.

[6] F. A. Stanley, *Speech*, reprinted in, *Qu'Appelle Vidette* (Fort Qu'Appelle: 22 November, 1888), *edition cover page*.

[7] Creighton, *John A. Macdonald*, p.515.

[8] Ibid.

[9] J. A. Macdonald, *Letter to F. A. Stanley, Lord Stanley of Preston Papers*, from the Public Archives of Canada in London (Ottawa: 6 July, 1889).

[10] John A. Macdonald, *House of Commons Debates*, 2, (1889), p.908.

[11] Creighton, *John A. Macdonald*, p.517. Interestingly enough, John Augustus Barron MP for North Victoria, was one of the few to vote in favour of disallowance. Barron had played hockey with the Governor General's son, Arthur Stanley, on the Rideau Rebels.

[12] *The Dominion Illustrated Monthly* (6 April, 1889), p.210.

[13] *The Dominion Illustrated Monthly* (16 March, 1889), p.162.

[14] McCarthy to Macdonald, 'Pope', *Sir John A. Macdonald Papers*, (17 April, 1889).

[15] Creighton, *John A. Macdonald*, p.518.

[16] For a review of French-Canadian newspapers' reaction to the agitation, see, *The Dominion Illustrated Monthly* (13 April, 1889), p.226.

[17] C. Tupper, *Cable to Macdonald*, as retold to Stanley in, J. A. Macdonald, *Letter to F. A. Stanley, Lord Stanley of Preston Papers*, from the Public Archives of Canada in London (Riviere Du Loup: 12 July, 1889).

[18] J. A. Macdonald, *Letter to F. A. Stanley, Lord Stanley of Preston Papers*, from the Public Archives of Canada in London (Ottawa: 31 May, 1889).

[19] J. A. Macdonald, *Letter to F. A. Stanley, Lord Stanley of Preston Papers*, from the Public Archives of Canada in London (Riviere Du Loup: 17 July, 1889).

[20] R. E. Webster and E. Clarke, care of The Right Honourable Lord Knutsford, *Report from the Royal Courts of Justice, Lord Stanley of Preston Papers*, from the Public Archives of Canada in London (London: 9 July, 1889).

[21] Macdonald to Lansdowne, 'Lansdowne Papers', *Macdonald Letters*, (National Archives of Canada: 28 September, 1889).

[22] *The Dominion Illustrated Monthly* (23 March, 1889), p.178.

[23] Macdonald, *House of Commons Debates*. (February, 1890).

CHAPTER SIX

Crisis in Masculinity

In 1871, the British Garrison left Canada to defend itself. This development, along with the quickening pace of industrialization and subsequent urbanization, gave pause to influential Canadians who feared that the nation was now left in the hands of an inexperienced and vastly outnumbered militia.

It was also thought that, with men leaving their traditional rural environs to go to work in urban factories or offices, young boys would be reared mostly by their mothers. As peculiar as it may seem to our twenty-first-century sensibilities, Victorian Canadians were convinced that these boys would turn out effeminate.

With war against the United States a real possibility, various Canadians — and even members of the vice regal circle — sought to remedy the apparent weaklings of the home forces. What was demanded was a program of "manliness and militarism" that was systematically enforced in nearly every aspect of Canadian life. From schools to libraries, boys' clubs to toy shops — and of course, team sports throughout the nation — a doctrine of manliness was imposed to meet the responsibility of raising a standing army in Canada.[1] Nineteenth-century military life and organized sport of the same era are so inextricably tied that it is hard to determine where one stops and the other begins.

* * *

Prior to Stanley's arrival, Canada's modest military strength had been tested in the North-West Rebellion of 1885. While it can be argued that the various militia units passed the test, Canadian military authorities anticipated an increase in participation in conflicts around the globe, not to mention the growing tension with the United States. A more experienced standing army was required, and the various social and government agencies continued to endorse manly behaviour, insisting that the nation's young men aspire to the robust model of the British Imperial man. This was especially true during the alleged "crisis in masculinity" that followed Confederation.

It was no secret that a large portion of Britain's dominant classes used organized sport in the late nineteenth century in order to provide a regimen that brought physical fitness to the individual, toughening him against the debilities of city life and maintaining his readiness for armed service.[2] Social theorists, church leaders, politicians, the aristocracy and even the Queen perceived a strong link between sport and war, and enthused about how useful sport could be in preparing a young man for military life. Dr. Thomas Arnold at Rugby School in England explored the notion of "muscular Christianity," whose tenets linked physical exertion and sportsmanship with the utmost in virtue and loyalty to Monarch and God.

English-speaking people of the Dominion saw themselves as people of the Empire. The British influence was paramount, and that which "was in vogue in the mother country was steadfastly followed in the Dominion."[3] Historian Scott Young assured readers that Canada in the 1890s, and especially Ontario, was effectively British,

> *... to an extent that today's Canadian could scarcely imagine. Speeches from public platforms were afloat with almost religious fervour for British fair play, British common law, British educational standards.*[4]

Therefore, Canadian team sports mirrored the evolution of their British counterparts. Canadian social agents organized and gave order to team sports as a means of fostering imperial and national allegiance.[5] As if out of a Kipling poem, the British ideals of "fair play, civilized conduct and equality on the playing field" were adapted to a colonial context. The *Renfrew Journal* declared that fair play:

> *... must be made dominant in our Canadian life. It must rule in the school yards.... We must call them to cherish*

and develop the spirit of fair play that should be our her-
itage as a child of the British Empire. It should rule in our
sports as it does in those of the motherland.[6]

As leisure time increased for average Canadians, many citizens sought out "rational" forms of recreation for their children. Vigorous sport was a purposeful form of recreation in most Canadians' eyes as it was also a means of manufacturing a prospective military.

* * *

Ice hockey took most of its early rules from field hockey, and was originally played by the professional and middle classes of Montreal, Kingston and Halifax.[7] By the 1890s, hockey had captured the imagination of most Canadians, and the game eventually managed to transcend the social spectrum and began to find favour outside of the Anglo-Protestant hegemony. Ice hockey was one of the first sports to establish a governing body in Canada with the formation of the Amateur Hockey Association of Canada (AHAC), established in 1886. Remarkably, the AHAC preceded the Canadian Rugby Football Union (1887), the Canadian Cricket Association (1892) and even the Canadian Amateur Lacrosse Association (1914).[8]

Perhaps the most important proponent of the early game could be found at Rideau Hall. It was the vice regal stamp of approval that accelerated the breathtaking growth and development of hockey over other team sports of the day. Stanley possessed that invincible attitude that one might expect to find in an aristocratic nineteenth-century Brit in his position: an important custodian of the Royal prerogative, proud servant of the world's biggest empire, defender of a seemingly indestructible Queen, proud beneficiary of a navy that ruled the waves and an appreciative and subservient audience in Canada ready to help him advance the Imperial cause. With Stanley at the helm, most Canadians would have needed little convincing that hockey was a worthy endeavour for young boys and men alike. If games like hockey could keep the sun from setting on the Empire, then the loyal people of Canada were only too willing to assist their new liaison to the Queen in achieving his aims.

Stanley must have recognized that hockey was considered especially "manly" because it tested so many laudable qualities.[9] Arthur Farrell, a star forward for the Montreal Shamrocks, wrote in 1899 that "hockey is a game for men, strong, full-blooded men. Weaklings can not play in it."[10] Early leagues had always endeavoured, as *The Dominion Illustrated Monthly* reported in 1892, "to preserve all foul and unmanly methods."[11] Yet it was a thin line between manly and violent, and only a decade after the Stanley Cup was awarded for the first time, the game took on a sanguinary tone, as outright violence was not merely tolerated, but even encouraged. The overtly aggressive side of the game was even celebrated in children's literature, as one journalist in *Harper's Young People* magazine explained in 1891:

> Hockey is a violent game, and tests both wind and muscle to the utmost. The player must make up his mind to many falls, and no lack of hard knocking on shins and knuckles, for such things will happen however faithfully the contestants try to keep to the rules.[12]

This glorification of sanctioned violence was, however, exactly what many thought necessary to ready a nation for war while instilling the perceived British ideals of "fair play" and "gamesmanship."

During Lord Frederick Stanley's term as governor general, R. Tait McKenzie said of the game:

> Its whole tendency is to encourage and develop in boys that love of fair play and manly sport so characteristic of the British gentleman. With so many advantages, both intrinsic and extrinsic, one of the most potent influences in building up a race of men, hardy and self-reliant, will, throughout the future, be by Canada's national winter game.[13]

And so, the physical game of hockey was advanced mostly towards Canada's young male population.[14] Montreal, Ottawa, Toronto, Winnipeg, Regina, Calgary and Vancouver would all, over the course of the next decade or so, establish either a public school hockey league or a high school hockey league. Hockey, thanks to the high profile the vice regal circle afforded it, became the Dominion's winter game of choice. As for the nation's young men, the game was seen as the ideal safeguard of masculinity.[15] The fraternity of the dominant classes in Canadian society sought to reclaim manliness and Canadian boys at the end of the nineteenth-century were soon circumscribed by the game and all of its social urgency.[16]

Hockey would, in short order, ascend to its position as the nation's winter game. It has never looked back.

* * *

Canadians knew that they had to improve the country's army and militia. With poor Canadian-American relations and the British Garrison just a memory, most people endorsed any and all means that would strengthen Canadian's line of defence. J.C. Hopkins echoed the popular sentiment:

> *To Canadians it must be obvious that the existing system of Imperial defence is not satisfactory. The Behring Sea seizures; the long drawn out Atlantic fishery disputes; the danger to our commerce in case of a great war, over the declaration or termination of which we should have no control; even the French shore question of to-day in Newfoundland, all prove that our present position in that respect is not and cannot be a permanent one.*[17]

Mounting aggression from American policy makers caused great concern among Canadian journalists:

> *Let us suppose, for instance, that the aspirations of Young Canada had been fulfilled and we were to-day face to face with hostile neighbours, are we in a position to defend our frontier from Halifax to Victoria against all comers? This question, never irrelevant has a peculiar opportuneness at the present time.*[18]

In the editorial sections of newspapers across the Dominion, in the drawing rooms, in the markets, even in the taverns, Canadians were asking the valid question: Are we able to fight if we need to? Most Canadians were cautiously optimistic about the army proper. And the establishment of the Royal Military College and various other schools of Cavalry, Artillery and

Infantry, along with the raising of the North-West Mounted Police added efficient, if small, branches of Canada's permanent force. The militia, on the other hand, was in most minds woefully undermanned, ill-equipped and poorly instructed. *The Dominion Illustrated Monthly* lamented the state of the militia:

> *If our war-lords have not the wishes and means to en-deavour to increase the number of men put under military training each year — to arm the force with a weapon on some sort of a par with that used by other nations — or to have an active service equipment in accordance with the ideas of modern civilization — a few minor measures might well be adopted which would not involve an alarm-ingly serious addition to the estimates, and might even add a few more rays of brilliancy to the lofty military position we now occupy.*[19]

If the average Canadian was worried about the nation's defence capabilities, Stanley was nothing short of horrified. "Brilliant" and "lofty" were probably not been two words Stanley would have used to describe Canada's permanent force. Still, he would have agreed that it was plainly in better shape than the militia.

When applicants were put forward for the vacant post of general, Stanley confided in Macdonald regarding who, in his opinion, might be eligible for the job. "I believe that you agree with me that the time has not yet come for limiting the appointment in question to officers who are Canadian by birth or settlement." Furthermore, Stanley earnestly hoped that "whoever may be appointed will be allowed to do his best to make the Militia a reality as a defensible force."[20]

Stanley's criticism of the Canadian military was based less on the tenor of the country's leading newspapers than from first-hand experience. The military's personnel was good on balance, according to the former Grenadier Guard, but in areas such as equipment and discipline Stanley felt that "there seems to me to be very much to be desired." He knew that it was in no party's interest to have Canada as a leading military strength — that would have been impossible even if it had been the desire of some. Yet he believed that the Dominion's military should improve on its existing state and, at the very least, aspire to some basic level of defence. In a letter to Macdonald, Lord Stanley asked the Prime Minister to allow him "to impress on you how strongly I feel that if [the Canadian Military] were capable of development, even a smaller force than you have would be preferable, if it could be made efficient, to what you have now."

Recalling his days in the Treasury, Stanley knew full well the difficulty in allotting monies for defence, and he afforded the Prime Minister some understanding on the matter. At the same time, he took the Prime Minister to task on military spending and the general state of the militia.

> *I do not vouch for the statement for I don't possess the requisite knowledge — but you must be aware that it is openly said that the disposal of the money voted for the militia, is not always that for which it is voted, nor is it influenced only by considerations of the well being of the force, or of its proper equipment. I have reason to believe that there is a widespread feeling of distrust amongst the militia, on this point. The arms are worn out, and though I asked the Imperial Authorities ... and received reply that for a comparatively small cost they could be replaced, no move has been made, and the men are firing with arms which are barely safe themselves and others.*

Stanley did not conceal his keen interest in the development of the militia, and he punctuated his letter to Macdonald with the assertion "I have set, and always will set, my face against the Dominion Government being asked for too much, but I should be grievously wanting in my duty if I were to pretend that things are satisfactory at present."[21]

Then the Cassandra alluded to the volatile times: "If we do not keep our eyes open, and our hands fairly ready, we may have a bitter awakening some day."[22] For their part, Canadians did want to improve the military and did not need to be made aware of the potential threat from the south, but it seems as though they wanted to go about matters in their own way. In a letter to Salisbury, Stanley explained his understanding of the situation: "Canada is just at the stage when she cannot walk alone, and yet rather resents being led."[23]

In a letter to Lord Knutsford, British Secretary of State for the

Colonies, Lord Stanley complained bitterly about the uselessness of the Defence Committee:

I very soon learnt from General Middleton, who was then commanding the Militia here, that it was utterly useless to expect any good result from the Committee as it has been constituted. I have made repeated efforts to get them to meet, and to do some work but it was clear to me that the Minister of Militia, Sir Adolphe Caron, did not intend anything to be done, and I am sorry to say that our late friend, Macdonald, forcibly backed him up in this neglect.[24]

Stanley added:

Now that Parliament is over, Mr. Abbott will have to reconstruct his Cabinet, and I believe that the change in the Ministry of Militia will be one of the first that will be made, but it depends somewhat on matters affecting Provincial as well as Dominion politics, and it is possible that Sir A. Caron may go for some little time.

Caron, accused by many as being sadly underqualified for the position, was not the only factor that stood in the way of an improved militia. Stanley also faced the challenge of convincing Canadian politicians, including the new Prime Minister, that Britain took some interest in the Dominion's military future. Writing to Knutsford, Stanley suggested "it would be advisable that I should be able to show Mr. Abbott some evidence that the Home Government really do care about the Defence Question,"[25] though Britain's sometimes nebulous course of action during the Behring Sea crisis did little to assure Canadian politicians that their backs were covered.

* * *

From very early on, the martial spirit of military training had inveigled its way into hockey culture. The strict discipline of military life could be found in the way hockey teams trained. As it was in the military, the hockey world had a rank system, with generals (coaches) and captains leading the other soldiers. It was understood that sport was simply a reflection of war. By the First World War, the two concepts were interchangeable and "war as sport" analogies abound in military histories: "When Captain W. P. Nevill of the 8th East Surreys led his company over the top at the start of the Somme offensive, he just had time to kick a football towards the German lines before he was shot dead."[26]

The same sentiment could be found in the memoirs of many soldiers of that same war, including Conn Smythe's metaphor: "Under the topsoil was white chalk that showed up clearly to the Germans on the slope beyond Courcelette. It felt like being at centre ice with no clothes on."[27]

The converse analogy, sport as war, is one that is perhaps more prevalent and recognizable to us today. Even Wayne Gretzky, known for his non-violent and gentlemanly conduct, has said, "hockey is war on ice."[28] Hockey players of the early twentieth century joyfully carried the warrior tradition of their game into actual war and, having been indoctrinated with the manly principles of late-nineteenth-century Canada, were resolved to "Play up! Play up! And win the war!"[29]

People of great influence were able to use hockey to help raise a domestic militia and a permanent army. Their efforts, developed over time, were hugely successful, and one only needs to point to Canada's hockey-playing soldiers of the First World War — just one generation after Lord Frederick Stanley's term as governor general — to see how frightfully effective the effort was.

Prophetically, Stanley and his contemporaries had envisioned the day when the Dominion might be required to mass a sizable army in defence of the British Empire against a foe, though few would have predicted Germany as the eventual enemy — the United States being, at least for a time, a far more plausible adversary. Still, Edward Henry Stanley had been fearful of an Anglo-German clash as early as 1875. "There can never be entire cordiality between a military despotism, such as Germany is now, and a peaceable constitutional community like England."[30]

The Stanleys were not, however, warlords spoiling for a fight — quite the contrary. As a rule, Edward Henry — and Edward Geoffrey before him — sought to give any European conflicts a miss, relying heavily instead on diplomatic methods and The Concert of Europe. Reviewing the prevailing sentiment in England during the late nineteenth century, Edward Henry Stanley entered in his diary:

> *There is in England a curious desire, when war is going on*
> *anywhere, to take part in it, and a doubt whether to look*
> *on without siding with either combatant be not a cowardly*
> *proceeding. This disposition to fight, without well knowing*
> *with whom or for what, is manifest just now.*[31]

Indeed, while Financial Secretary of the Treasury, Frederick complained to his brother that every time he thought he had settled on firm budgetary numbers with the War Office, the estimates would be subsequently raised by three-quarters of a million pounds.[32] It was a peacetime characterized by an emphasis on military spending and preparedness.

In 1878, Britain was on the verge of war with Russia over Turkey. Edward Henry, as Churchill declared, "strove incessantly for a peaceful solution of the dispute, and after one abortive resignation, left the Government."[33] Even the Queen complained more than once to Disraeli about the 15th Earl's "weak attitude."[34]

As far as Canada was concerned, there was a feeling at the time that, had England entered into any European conflagration, the Americans would have been upon the British, by way of Canada, before the European fighting was done. Preparation, at least in the minds of many Canadians, was vital to the survival of the Dominion. Assessment and improvement were the order of the day.

If anyone possessed the proper credentials by which to plainly evaluate the effectiveness of Canada's defences, it was Stanley. When he was still Financial Secretary to the War Office in 1877, he presented a memorandum that detailed the strength of the British forces, both the permanent army and the militia. His memorandum received high praise from within Cabinet and demonstrated Stanley's ability to appraise an army, even the size of the British one.35 This, coupled with a solid career in the Grenadier Guards, did much to persuade those listening to pay special attention to Stanley when it came to military matters and their complex administration.

The Stanleys had forged a tradition with the Grenadier Guards. Frederick put in seven years before opting for a career in politics. Likewise, his son Edward George received his commission in the Guards in 1885 and served in Ireland before opting for a political career himself. Frederick's uncle Charles Stanley was a lieutenant-colonel of the Grenadiers, as was his cousin Charles Edward. Edward George's son Edward (Frederick's grandson) served in the First World War, while his son, John Stanley, was awarded the Military Cross in the Second World War with his heroic efforts at Anzio.36 Frederick Stanley's brother-in-law, George Villiers, was a colonel in the Grenadiers.

In one of the earliest pieces on the new Governor General of Canada, *The Dominion Illustrated Monthly* called on its readers to behold the military pedigree of Stanley of Preston:

> *The military bearing of our new Governor General has been noticed at once. He was a Grenadier Guardsman for years, and his son belongs to his father's regiment. His Excellency is a solid man, like his father, the late Earl of Derby, but not so fluent. What he says, however, is to the point, as coming from a full mind.*[37]

Stanley himself confessed to Macdonald that he had been "brought up as a soldier, and not as a diplomatist."[38] The nation would call upon this soldier with the "full mind" more than once to help deliver it from danger.

* * *

When the British Garrison left in 1871, the Canadian government organized Canadian troops to garrison The Citadel in Quebec and Fort Henry in Kingston. On 20 October, 1871, "A" and "B" Batteries of the Canadian Artillery were born, consisting of two divisions: Field and Garrison. The onerous responsibility of schooling militia enlistees also fell to these batteries. This process quickly proved itself to be highly inefficient and in 1883 the Militia Act was amended to mandate the organization of three companies of infantry to "provide for the care and protection of forts, magazines, armaments, warlike stores and such like service, also to secure the establishment of schools for military instruction."[39] In effect, three schools of infantry also came into existence, which altogether formed the Infantry School Corps. Various stations were opened throughout the Dominion: "A" Company was placed at Fredericton, New Brunswick, "B" Company at Saint John and "C" Company at Toronto. Subsequently, "D" Company was stationed at London, Ontario. In 1883, the Cavalry School Corps was organized and stationed in Quebec City. In 1885, a company of mounted infantry was organized and stationed in Winnipeg. Two years later, the "C" Battery of Victoria, British Columbia, came into existence. *The Dominion Illustrated Monthly* described the life of students of these various military schools:

> *The course of instruction lasts three months, and there are three courses in the year. The officers attached for instruction live and mess in barracks and receive one dollar a day pay. The instruction is carried on by the permanent or regular officers and non-commissioned officers under the direction of the commandant. In addition to militia officers, militia non-commissioned officers and men can also be attached. They receive fifty cents a day pay. The pay of the regular Canadian private soldier is forty cents a day and a full kit. The only stoppages are fifteen cents a day when in hospital and a trifling monthly stoppage for hair-cutting.*[40]

The earnest efforts on the part of Canadian military officials to build a military-instruction infrastructure across the nation garnered at least some degree of success. Canada's own equivalent to the Grenadier Guards, the Royal Military College in Kingston, Ontario, was one place that gave the Canadian Army a great number of hockey-playing soldiers. The College was considered a place where "sturdy Canadianism" was the happy result of strict military training.[41] Shortly after the school opened, *The Dominion Illustrated Monthly* chronicled the benefits of having such an institution in the heart of the nation:

> *The advantage to Canada of having such a centre of military education and tradition can hardly be over-estimated. The years spent at Kingston are not only likely to be recalled as the most pleasant in the lives of those favoured with cadetships, but cannot fail to be most fruitful in the formation of character and habits. The association of young men of lofty aspirations with veterans of the English army, rich in its best traditions and masters in military lore, is itself an education. The moral effect of the training is invaluable, whether the cadet chooses an army career or turns his gathered knowledge to account in the furtherance of the great public works*

of his native Canada. He is, though professionally civilian, a soldier by discipline and ready for the soldier's patriotic task should ever danger threaten our borders.... The Royal Military College is the best link that could have been devised between Canada and the motherland. The presences of native Canadians in the Imperial service tends to perpetuate the sentiment of enthusiasm in our national glories and to make the prestige of connection with them a real thing to every province in the Dominion.[42]

It seems that having a good professional standing army was *nearly* as important as celebrating the union of Canada and the motherland.

However, French-Canadians were, on balance, less enthusiastic about committing its young manhood to the cause of the Empire, especially during Stanley's reign, when the people of Canada were considering various directions that the nation might take, including "Imperial Federation" — a step that would have brought Canada, if it were at all possible, into an even closer relationship with Britain. A strong opponent of Imperial Federation, Honoré Mercier, let his feelings be known about the growing importance of having a standing army and militia in Canada during a speech in Montreal:

... to seek to expose us to the vicissitudes of peace and war against the great powers of the world, to the rigorous exigencies of military service as practised in Europe; to disperse our sons from the frozen regions of the North Pole to the burning sands of the desert Sahara, an odious regime which will condemn us to the forced export of blood and money and wrest from our arms our sons, the hope of our country, to perish in foreign wars.[43]

These ominous warning not only spoke to approaching conflicts in the near future in South Africa and sometime later in France and Belgium, but to the popular sentiment that pervaded French Canada when war did finally come. The fallout from the Jesuit Estates Act set English and French Canada on a collision course — again.

Still, in the 1890s, war with the United States was far more likely, and efforts to bolster the nation's defence could be found at every turn of Canadian life. A report lauding the "moderate" increase in Canadian permanent troops and militia appeared in *The Dominion Illustrated Monthly* in February 1891.

> *… our Canadian Regular Infantry will thus form a brigade with the very moderate establishment of three thousand men. Such an increase would do wonders for the active militia at large by the ability of the permanent troops to then furnish adjutants and sergeant-majors to every volunteer regiment in the Dominion, besides furnishing ample detachments to keep occupied and in repair the various forts and military buildings bequeathed to us by the Imperial authorities, and which are at present rapidly falling into decay and utter ruin. In case of war the very points, now neglected, would be of vital importance in the defence of Canada, and their preservation should be of deep interest to the people at large as on them might depend the security of our homes from an invader.*

These positive spins on the depleted force did not fool Stanley or other more experienced critics of military matters. In fact, the same journal wrote only one month later that "the Canadian volunteer militia is in a more or less chaotic state, under-drilled, under-paid, and, practically under the management of a civilian."[44] And one month later:

> *Compared to the population, the actual number of militiamen is absurdly small; and when nearly one-half of these drill but once in three years, and all have only obsolete equipment, the situation becomes a disgrace to the country.*[45]

It was a disgrace that a few good men set about to remedy.

Stanley had garnered an intimate understanding of Canada's military prowess and, of course, the nation's many weaknesses. While not every recommendation would be observed, the Governor General worked with Macdonald to help repair some areas that were in urgent need. In April 1891, they created a highly confidential and detailed appraisal of the militia and the defence of the nation at large:

> *It appears to be very desirable that there should be a better definition than now exists of the duties assigned in time of war or disturbance to the Imperial and the Dominion Military Officers respectively.*
>
> *Before the Imperial Troops were withdrawn from Canada in 1871, the Chief Military Command of all troops in British North America was vested both in theory and practice in the Imperial General Officer. He commanded all troops north of the American Boundary Line — the Queen's Troops at all times and the Militia if called out for active service.*
>
> *In 1871, the military posts in Canada were taken over from the Imperial Troops by the Militia Department and the whole Imperial Force in British North America was concentrated at Halifax which continues to be the only place it now occupies. At this period, British Columbia was still a separate Colony. It was entirely cut off from the rest of Canada. There was a small naval yard at Esquimalt on Vancouver Island and although a few blocs of land were kept on the coast as naval reserves, they were and still are wholly in a state of nature. The recital of these facts shows how the present anomalous position of affairs has grown up:*
>
> *The present position is this: The G.O.C. British North America is still theoretically answerable for the whole Dominion in time of war and for Imperial Military Stations as distinguished from those of the Dominion. British Columbia having joined the Confederation comes under his command in time of war, and Esquimalt is one of the fortified stations which it has been decided is to be held for Imperial purposes.*
>
> *If there are Imperial Troops there, of whatever arm, they cannot be under the command of the G.O.C. Militia of Canada, even in the time of peace and even if a Corporal's Guard of the Regular Troops were at Esquimalt they would have to report to and look for orders from the*

General Officer who is stationed at Halifax four thousand miles away.

If a war were to break out the G.O.C. British North America would be answerable for two Imperial Garrisons separated by the whole breadth of the North American Continent.

Again if the border Line between the Dominion and the United States were menaced by and armed force and if it were necessary in consequence to take military measures short of actual war for the protection of our frontier by concentrating Militia and otherwise, the Imperial General Officer though responsible for what might happen the moment war broke out, has absolutely no power to intervene in a precautionary measure.

To put it shortly, he commands two important Imperial points, one on the east and one on the west 4000 miles apart, connected for the most apart by a single break line and in regards the intermediate frontier and territory he has in time of peace no authority whatever.

It may of course be said that under the general powers of the Militia Act, Section III et al., the Governor General has it in his power in time of emergency to exercise such command as may be necessary as the Queen's representative: but that is in fact leaving arrangements of the most vital importance to be dealt with at the last moment — not improbably a time of confusion.

Having regard to altered circumstances which time has brought about in the Dominion since the year 1870, we think that the Imperial and Dominion authorities should be severally approached with a view of better arrangements being made for the distribution of the Military defence of the Dominion. It is suggested in the first place that Esquimalt should be considered wholly as an Imperial station held like Halifax for an Imperial Officer. The Dominion of Canada is in process of such material development that its finances are strained to the utmost in providing railways, canals and other public works. The Government have not the means, even if they had the will, to incur the expense necessary for placing and maintaining Esquimalt in such a state of defence as its importance from an Imperial point of view appears to demand. It is wholly improbably that the works laid down by the Defence Committee will be carried out as they should be — nor is it probable that they could raise and keep up a sufficient garrison even for the works now contemplated. The sole permanent garrison is a battery of Militia numerically weak and kept up with difficulty. There are not the men upon the spot to keep its ranks full and even if there were wages are so high and the demand for labour so great that local recruiting would be almost an impossibility.

We recommend therefore that is should be created a separate Imperial command and that it should be garrisoned in the first instance with a detachment of Imperial forces.

It would be a matter of secondary consideration whether the Battery at present there should not be with drawn to the mainland.

We further recommend that the responsibility of the Imperial G.O.C. now stationed at Halifax should be recognized in theory as well as in practice to be limited to that command.

The G.O.C. Militia of Canada should have his commission enlarged if necessary so as to give him the fullest authority over all the Forces of the Dominion exclusive of Halifax and Esquimalt. Of course this would not be held necessarily to give him any command over any Imperial Officers senior to himself who might be sent out in the event of a force of Imperial Troops being sent to the Dominion on active service or otherwise.

The General Officers Commanding at Halifax and Esquimalt respectively should have authority to indent, so to speak, upon the Dominion Government for a specified number of Militia Battalions or other troops so as to complete the garrison of their fortresses.

The G.O.C. Militia who would presumably have his Headquarters at Ottawa should be expressly responsible for

all such duties as are involved in the preparation of schemes
of defence of the frontier and such other work as is performed by the Intelligence at home.

We think that the alterations suggested above would
afford the best means for defining the best distribution of
duties and command within the Dominion and of avoiding
the confusion which must occur under the present system in
the event of any grave emergency.[46]

Lord Stanley knew how important his role as governor general was in case
of a "grave emergency" — he was not willing to accept the state of the
Canadian defence system while he was at Rideau Hall. And with the
Behring Sea issue graduating from nuisance to full-scale crisis, the future
Earl of Derby was not wrong in his aim to improve the Dominion's readi-
ness.

---

[1] M. Moss, *Manliness and Militarism: Educating Young Boys in Ontario for War* (Toronto: Oxford
University Press, 2001), pp.90–109, 131–4.

[2] P. Bailey, *Leisure and Class in Victorian England: Rational Recreation and the Contest for Control,
1830–1855* (London: Routledge & Kegan Paul, 1978), p.129.

[3] F. Cosentino, *The Renfrew Millionaires: The Valley Boys of Winter 1910* (Burnstown: General Store
Publishing House, 1990), p.11; Moss, *Manliness and Militarism*, pp.23–5.

[4] S. Young, *100 Years of Dropping the Puck* (Toronto: McClelland and Stewart, 1989), p.37.

[5] C. Howell, *Blood, Sweat and Cheers: Sport and The Making of Modern Canada* (Toronto: Univesity of
Toronto Press, 2001), p.50. Dr. Arnold's 'muscular Christianity' is a concept that would not be foreign to
the early amateur hockey player. See, Moss, *Manliness and Militarism*, p. 77; R. Gruneau and D.Whitson,
Hockey Night in Canada: Sport, Identities and Cultural Politics (Toronto: Garamond Press, 1993), p.64;
Bailey, *Leisure and Class in Victorian England*, p.129.

[6] *The Renfrew Journal* (15 January, 1909).

[7] R. C. Watson and G. D. Rickwood, 'Steward of Ice Hockey: A Historical Review of Safety Rules in
Canadian Amateur Ice Hockey', *Sports History Review 30* (1999), pp.28–9; D. Guay, *L'Histoire du Hockey
au Quebec* (Quebec: G. Morin, 1980), pp.42, 65, 91.

[8] B. Kidd, *The Struggle for Canadian Sport* (Toronto: University of Toronto Press, 1996), p.22.

[9] M. Mott, 'Inferior Exhibitions, Superior Ceremonies: The Nature and Meaning of the Hockey Games
of the Winnipeg Victorias, 1890-1903', *5th Canadian Symposium on the History of Sport and Physical
Education* (Toronto: 1982), p.11.

[10] A. Farrell, *Hockey: Canada's Royal Winter Game* (Montreal: 1899).

[11] R. T. McKenzie, 'Hockey in Eastern Canada', *The Dominion Illustrated Monthly* (February 1893), p.62.

[12] J. Macdonald Oxley, *Harpers Young People* reprinted in *The Montreal Star* (26 February,1891).

[13] R. T. McKenzie, 'Hockey in Eastern Canada', *The Dominion Illustrated Monthly* (February 1893), p.64.

[14] D. A. G. Seglins, *Just Part of the Game: Violence, Hockey and Masculinity in Central Canada, 1890-1910*
(Kingston: Queen's University, 1995), p.24.

[15] Ibid, pp.27-8.

[16] J. J. Wilson, 'Skating to Armageddon: Of Canada, Hockey and The First World War', *The International Journal of the History of Sport*, 22, 3, (Oxford: Routledge, May 2005), p.318.

[17] J. C. Hopkins, The Britannic Empire, *The Dominion Illustrated Monthly* (Montreal: 3 May, 1890), p.287.

[18] *The Dominion Illustrated Monthly* (2 August, 1890), p.66.

[19] *The Dominion Illustrated Monthly* (13 September, 1890), p.187.

[20] F. A. Stanley, *Letter to J. A. Macdonald, Lord Stanley of Preston Papers*, from the Public Archives of Canada in London (New Richmond: 21 July, 1890).

[21] F. A. Stanley, *Letter to J. A. Macdonald, Lord Stanley of Preston Papers*, from the Public Archives of Canada in London (New Richmond: 21 July, 1890).

[22] F. A. Stanley, *Letter to J. A. Macdonald, Lord Stanley of Preston Papers*, from the Public Archives of Canada in London (New Richmond: 21 July, 1890).

[23] F. A. Stanley, *Letter to Lord Salisbury, Lord Stanley of Preston Papers*, from the Public Archives of Canada in London (Ottawa, 11 October, 1891).

[24] F. A. Stanley, *Letter to Lord Knutsford, Lord Stanley of Preston Papers*, from the Public Archives of Canada in London (Ottawa, 9 October, 1891).

[25] F. A. Stanley, *Letter to Lord Knutsford, Lord Stanley of Preston Papers*, from the Public Archives of Canada in London (Ottawa, 9 October, 1891).

[26] See, P. Fussell, *The Great War and Modern Memory* (Oxford: Oxford University Press, 1975), p.27; N. Ferguson, *The Pity of War: Explaining World War I* (New York: Basic Books, 1999), p.360.

[27] C. Smythe and S. Young, *If You Can't Beat 'Em in the Alley: The Memoirs of the Late Conn Smythe* (Toronto: McClelland and Stewart, 1981), p.48.

[28] Apart from owning fifty NHL records, Gretzky was a five-time winner of the Lady Byng Trophy, awarded for most gentlemanly conduct on the ice. D. Diamond, J. Duplacey, R. Dinger, E. Fitzsimmons, I. Kuperman & E. Zweig (eds) *Total Hockey: The Official Encyclopaedia of the National Hockey League Second Edition* (Toronto: Dan Diamond and Associates, 2000), pp.188, 1132–3; A & E's Biography, *Wayne Gretzky: The Great One* (United States: 2002). <film>

[29] C. Veitch, 'Play Up! Play Up! And Win The War! Football, The Nation and The First World War', *The Journal of Contemporary History 20* (Great Britain, 1985), pp.426-51.

[30] E. H. Stanley, *Personal Diary* (1 September, 1875); Vincent, *Diaries of Edward Henry Stanley*, p.17.

[31] E. H. Stanley, *Personal Diary* (27 December, 1870); Vincent, *Diaries of Edward Henry Stanley*, pp.71–2.

[32] E. H. Stanley, *Personal Diary* (20 January, 1878); Vincent, *Diaries of Edward Henry Stanley*, p.487.

[33] Churchill, *Lord Derby*, p.10.

[34] Churchill, *Lord Derby*, p.10.

[35] See, E. H. Stanley, *Personal Diary* (11 July, 1877); Vincent, *Diaries of Edward Henry Stanley*, p.417.

[36] Churchill, *Lord Derby*, pp.23-4.

[37] *The Dominion Illustrated Monthly* (Montreal: 7 July, 1888), p.3.

[38] F. A. Stanley, *Letter to J. A. Macdonald, Lord Stanley of Preston Papers*, from the Public Archives of Canada in London (Ottawa: 6 May, 1891).

[39] *The Militia Act of 1883*, as reprinted in, *The Dominion Illustrated Monthly* (Montreal: 1 November, 1890), p.303.

[40] *The Dominion Illustrated Monthly* (1 November, 1890), p.303.

[41] C. J. Morris, 'Where Sturdy Canadianism is Built of Military Training: A Review of the Work that is being done at the Royal Military College of Canada', *Macleans Magazine* (April, 1914), p.38–40.

[42] *The Dominion Illustrated Monthly* (10 August, 1889), p.82.

[43] H. Mercier, 'Excerpt from a Speech in Montreal', *The Dominion Illustrated Monthly* (3 May, 1890), p.286.

[44] *The Dominion Illustrated Monthly* (14 March, 1891), p.242.

[45] *The Dominion Illustrated Monthly* (25 April, 1891), p.386.

[46] F. A. Stanley, *Review of the State of the Canadian Military, Sir John A. Macdonald Papers* Vol. 90, (Ottawa: 2 April, 1891).

CHAPTER SEVEN

1888

As Lord and Lady Stanley attempted to settle into their new Canadian life, they made every attempt to embrace the young country. Still, they found the country and its traditions similar, yet very different, from the life they had enjoyed in England.

Ottawa had grown haphazardly from its birth as a military site. Through its incarnation as a lumber town, most were astonished when Ottawa (formerly Bytown) was selected as Canada's capital by Queen Victoria in 1857. But the town embraced its role and developed quickly during the five years Stanley served as governor general.

In Ottawa, the Stanleys witnessed the world's changing technology. Arc lights, the predecessors of the incandescent light bulb, began to be used to light up the city in 1885. A spark jumping from one electrode to another created a burst of light, and although it was both inconsistent and dangerous, the arc light proved highly effective. By the time of Lord Stanley's arrival in 1888, most of the city's streets and main buildings were illuminated by arc lights. Hundreds of residents strolled through the streets, astounded by the sputtering lamps that now lit the way.

The advent of electric streetcars featured prominently in one of Lady Stanley's letters to her son, Edward:

> *The electric cars in Ottawa are an enormous success and*
> *though they were only started in July, have already paid.*
> *They add to the dangers of driving very much as they come*
> *along at an awful pace and as for overhead, the whole space*
> *as far as you can see is one network of wires. The great*

question is will they be able to run when the winter really comes. A heavy fall of snow and icicles form on the wires.

This technological development, albeit fraught with danger, clearly fascinated Constance and her family.

* * *

During the period of Lord Stanley's term, there was an escalated growth in social societies in cities right across Canada, but Ottawa certainly saw a proliferation of benevolent societies. The Home for the Blind, a Home for Friendless Women, the Perley Home for Incurables, the Society of the Friends of the Poor, the Union Mission for Men, the Victorian Order of Nurses and the YMCA were all established during these years. In January of 1888, a group of Ottawa women established an organization to help protect neglected children and animals. That summer, shortly after her arrival, Lady Stanley became involved with the group, which was going by the name of the Women's Humane Society. The society eventually divided into two streams, although not until 1896: the Children's Aid Society, offering foster homes to neglected children, and the Ottawa Humane Society, overseeing the welfare of animals. This would be but the first of many organizations with which Lady Stanley would find herself associated while in Canada.

* * *

On 10 September, 1888, *The Globe* announced:

> *Today, his Excellency, Lord Stanley, and party will arrive at North Toronto station at 7:23 a.m. … They will be met by the Reception Committee and accompanied to Union Station and thence to the Queen's Hotel.*[1]

The Toronto daily added:

> *Lord Stanley of Preston, ever since he arrived in Canada, has conducted himself in the traditional fashion of Governors General and will, of course, obtain from Torontonians*

without distinction of party or sect, the warm welcome al-
ways hitherto given to the representative of the Crown.[2]

This was to be Stanley's first visit to Toronto, and the city was delirious with
excitement at the prospect. The invitation had been extended by Mayor
Edward Frederick Clarke shortly after the Governor General's arrival in
Canada. When Stanley accepted, Clarke was able to inform the Toronto
Industrial Exhibition Association (organizers of the forerunner to today's
Canadian National Exhibition) on 10 July that "there was very little doubt
but that Lord Stanley, the new Governor General, would open the
Exhibition."[3]

Although the principal reason for the visit to Toronto was to enable
Stanley to officially open the Toronto Industrial Exhibition, there were
other opportunities for several civic organizations to meet and address the
Governor General.

The train, pulling the government car *Cumberland*, pulled into the station modestly tardy at 7:40 a.m. and was greeted by about two hundred
people who were assembled on the platform. The delegation from the City
of Toronto included Mayor Clarke and several aldermen.[4] Several Toronto
newspaper reporters were also on hand. *The Globe* offered:

> *Lord Stanley is easily recognizable from his pictures. He*
> *was dressed in a plain dark suit with turn-down collar and*
> *black tie. In manner, he is affable and unassuming and in*
> *a few minutes, his Aldermanic visitors felt quite at home*
> *with him.*[5]

The World described the Governor General thusly:

> *His Excellency was dressed and looked well in a black Prince*
> *Albert frock, with striped pants of exact fit. On his head was*
> *a shiny plug, while beneath the frock coat could be seen the*
> *broad crimson sash of the K.C.M.G. order. Beside the star of*
> *the same order on the left breast was a badge of the Brock,*
> *Simcoe and York Pioneers. The only other jewellery visible on*
> *His Excellency was a double-switched gold chain strung*
> *across the front of his waistcoat.*[6]

But there were far more than well-wishers and journalists present for the occasion. Politicians crowded into the smoking compartment of the car and engaged Lord Stanley in conversation while the train proceeded towards Union Station. As the train approached West Toronto Junction, the mayor and aldermen were introduced to Lady Stanley and her associate, Miss Lister. *The Globe's* detailed description continued:

> *Everybody stood up and offered the ladies a seat and, while standing, a sudden stoppage of the train telescoped the whole party into a corner … Lady Stanley laughed very heartily and said, 'I am afraid we shall have to sit down whether we will or not!'*[7]

At 8:40 a.m., the train pulled into Union Station, which at that time was located on Front Street West, between York and Simcoe streets. The large, boisterous crowd of dignitaries and well-wishers greeted the vice regal party's arrival. *The Telegram* reported:

> *A row of cabs stretched in an unbroken line along the north side from York to Simcoe streets. Inside, the platforms were thronged with an eager, expectant crowd, who pushed and jostled each other in a frantic endeavour to get somewhere near the spot they expected the car bearing His Excellency, Lord Stanley of Preston, Governor General of Canada, would come to a stop.*[8]

Lieutenant-Colonel William Otter led the crowd in a "right royal shout of hip hip hurrah" as the Governor General stepped down from the train onto the platform.[9] According to *The Telegram*, "the cheering became deafening as all pressed forward to obtain a glimpse of the Queen's representative in Canada."[10] The vice regal party, consisting of Lord and Lady Stanley, three of their children — twenty-one-year-old Victor, eighteen-year-old Arthur and seventeen-year-old Ferdinand — the Governor General's aides-de-camp Captain Charles Colville and the Honourable Aubrey McMahon, Miss Lister and G.J. Hawley, immediately climbed into carriages and were driven to the Queen's Hotel, located at Front and York where the Fairmont Royal York stands today.

"During all the years that Toronto has been the capital and the metropolis of the greatest province in the Dominion," *The Telegram* pronounced, "she has never honoured the coming of a distinguished guest with a more enthusiastic welcome than that which Lord Stanley has received from the citizens."[11]

The first class welcome spilled over to the Queen's Hotel. Lord and Lady Stanley were escorted to their Red Parlour suite, where they relaxed over breakfast. This "Royal Suite" at the Queen's consisted of eight bedrooms, two sitting rooms and two parlours, and easily accommodated the twelve-person Stanley party. The façade of the hotel was decorated with gas jets that formed a crown and spelled out *VR*, for Vice Regal.

The Queen's Hotel was considered the city's most fashionable and was favoured by dignified guests from around the globe. Known as the Sword's Hotel when it was built in 1853, it was renamed Revere's Hotel after a change in ownership. In 1862, it was expanded and refurbished and named the Queen's, and it remained one of Toronto's finest hotels until it closed in 1927.[12] The four-storey inn contained 210 guest rooms, each heated by hot-air furnaces rather than the more pedestrian fireplaces used by other hotels, and it was the first hotel in Canada to offer bathtubs as well as hot and cold running water in each room. The Queen's was also the first to offer a passenger elevator and was the first business in Toronto to install a telephone.[13]

Lord Stanley faced a busy afternoon of addresses while in Toronto. At two o'clock, Mayor Clarke and the Civic Reception Committee met Lord and Lady Stanley and Miss Lister in the parlour of the west wing.

At half past two, a large delegation from the Synod of Toronto arrived to meet with the Governor General. The Synod, made up of licensed clergy of the Church of England in the diocese of Toronto, was led by Venerable Archdeacon Samuel Boddy in the absence of Bishop Arthur Sweatman.

Stanley replied to the Synod's address:

> *Whether it be in civil life or in the Church, we recognize alike that doctrines of toleration have their advantages over perhaps the most forcible methods which prevailed at an earlier period of the world's history. We know that by a spirit of conciliation, without in the slightest degree departing from those principles which we hold dear ... may*

> *ensure that peace which we desire, and ... ensure that pros-*
> *perity to which you have also made reference.... Let me*
> *hope that those lessons ... to which we all alike look ... may*
> *guide me safely in the true principles of a just and righteous*
> *administration and that they may be blessed by those*
> *hands to which we all alike look for recompense.*

If his brother had become suspicious of church life, Frederick still retained the great reverence for the Anglican faith that his father had instilled in him.

At three o'clock, the St. George's Society visited Lord Stanley and pledged its loyalty. The Society began in the middle of the nineteenth century as a benevolent organization to help people of English origin, but never limited itself in providing help to those in need, offering assistance to anyone who qualified. The Governor General stated:

> *I gather that you hold true to the principle that a friend in*
> *need is a friend indeed and that amongst many other desir-*
> *able objects of your society, is that of being able to afford*
> *relief and encouragement to our fellow countrymen who*
> *are continually arriving amongst us. You aim to help him*
> *by teaching him to help himself and this affords the best*
> *guarantee that he will become a useful and thriving citizen*
> *of the new land.*

Giving a nod to the utilitarian message of the St. George's Society, Stanley may simply have been anticipating his next appointment. Members of the Toronto Methodist Conference arrived for their three-thirty meeting, with their address presented in book form by Reverend Hugh Johnston. The Methodist Church, which made up a third of the population of Ontario at that time, was continuing its missionary work in bringing a religious foundation to Native Canadians. Lord Stanley spoke passionately about his affection for the work being done by the Methodist Church:

> *It is a source of satisfaction to those who occupy the posi-*
> *tion which I hold to feel there are such influences at work*
> *tending without the hope of reward to break down the bar-*
> *rier which divides civilization and uncivilization and to*

carry into the very utmost parts of the Dominion these principles of religion, of truth and of godliness, which you hold in common with other communions.

As progressive as Stanley may have been, he was, nevertheless, aristocratic and very much a product of his age — and while the Methodist faith better represented a class of people that the family had little contact with in Britain, the social order became far more relaxed on the other side of the Atlantic.

The Toronto Board of Trade was next. Addressing the vice regal at four that afternoon in his parlour at the Queen's Hotel, member of the Board desired to:

… extend to Your Excellency and to Lady Stanley, the most cordial and loyal welcome to our city, and we desire to join with all classes of the community in expressing our gratification at the appointment of Your Excellency to the exalted position of that of Governor General of the Dominion of Canada.

The spokesman for the Board of Trade continued, thanking the vice regal for his role in preparing a Canadian-made fishing treaty that was to be considered by the United States:

And while we greatly regret that for the moment our treaty has failed to secure the endorsement of the Senate of the United States, we are nevertheless of the opinion that nothing will arise to disturb those relations which ought ever to exist between nations so closely identified by blood, language and commercial interests as are Canada and the United States.

Lord Stanley responded:

The natural advantages of this country, the vast resources which abound everywhere in this young country, are indeed being turned to the fullest account by the energy and enterprise of its people. Nothing, of course, tends more di-

rectly to that end, under the free institutions in which you live, than the promotion of an honest commerce which is winning its way and gaining strength every day. The last office which I held in the Government at home, and which I surrendered to assume my present position, was the place of president of the Board of Trade, which deals with all Parliamentary questions connected with the trade and commerce of the Mother Country. I can claim almost as well as yourselves, though perhaps not with the same practical interest, to know something of the difficulties which beset commerce in these days — something of the remedies, good and bad, which are suggested whenever a crisis arises and on whole, to have learnt the lesson that our commercial friends, perhaps wiser than our political ones, are generally able to take care of themselves. I know at the present moment nothing of politics; my whole duty, my true pleasure, is to do all that in me lies to the best of my humble power to advance the prosperity of the Dominion in every way I can.

Still, economic issues — and indeed, fishing rights — were scarcely settled by the time the Governor General had returned to Knowsley.

The Sons of England were next to see Lord Stanley, arriving for their appointment at four-thirty. The Sons of England Benefit Society, founded in Toronto in 1874, organized receptions for newcomers and provided co-operative insurance, medical services, unemployment and disability benefits, as well as burial plots, to British immigrants to Canada. The benevolent society was organized into local lodges, usually led by affluent Englishmen, and as one Canadian encyclopedia claimed, "The largest and most important English cultural society was the Sons of England, which in 1913 had forty thousand Canadian members." The most important vehicle for maintaining traditions was the social evening, or the "at home," modelled on the English music hall. Members were, on these occasions, "expected to thrill to jingoistic songs, weep at evocations of England, savour warm, dark ale and revert to regional dialects." The Sons of England pledged their allegiance to Her Majesty, Queen Victoria, and vowed to "uphold the integrity of the British Empire, the Constitution which guarantees the liberties secured to us by our forefathers, and to maintain intact the proud status of the Dominion as an integral part of the glorious Empire upon which the sun never sets."[14] The sun did set, however, on the society — in 1971, when it ceased operations.

His Excellency, having thanked the attendees warmly, urged the Society to "treat all others as Sons of England so long as they were true to the Empire." Stanley was at all times mindful of his chief duties in one of the Empire's most prestigious posts.

Next to visit Lord Stanley were fifty members of the Army and Navy Veterans' Society, "mostly grey-headed and bent in figure." Many wore the medals they had earned on the battlefield as they marched into the lounge with military precision. "The association is composed of men of all ranks who have … fought for Queen and country in almost every battle in which her Majesty's forces have been engaged during the present century."

The Governor General, during the five o'clock meeting, informed the veterans that he, too, had served in the army and thanked them for their loyalty, adding, "Her Majesty would be delighted to know that those who had served Her were well and happy in their colonial home."

The final visitors in the string of appointments were members of the St. Andrew's Society, another benevolent society, this time one that oversaw the well-being of immigrants to Canada with ties to Scotland.

There is the knowledge that the few dollars given each year may, wisely spent as they are, rescue some Scots laddie from despair or reassure some anxious heart in the Old Land.

President Donald Clark read the society's address, and the members ended with "A *richt guid nicht* to the noble Scots o' Glengarry!"[15]

Lord Stanley's response alluded to the fact that in every corner of the globe, the pioneers of civilization were usually found to be Scots, which elicited a warm cheer from the St. Andrew's Society members in attendance.

The afternoon concluded just before six. Stanley showed no evidence of weariness from the afternoon of addresses, although "the ladies, especially, were getting tired-looking after the long afternoon of speech-making."[16] Earlier in the week, reporters predicted that the afternoon of 10 September would prove to be tedious and suggested that His Excellency might prefer "working in a quarry."[17] "Our Governor General must be a very pleasant, good natured man," intoned *The Evening Telegram*. "There is not the least doubt in the world that he was nearly bored to death yesterday by reason of the many addresses which he had to reply to."[18]

The vice regal party retired briefly before descending to the street to climb into carriages that would take them to the next stop on their busy itinerary. Thousands lined the streets hoping to catch a glimpse of Lord and Lady Stanley and the remainder of the vice regal party as it snaked its way north from the hotel along York to King, then east to Yonge Street. Their route would take them north to Gerrard, ending at the Horticultural Pavilion in expansive Allan Gardens.

The mild September weather brought many out to observe Canada's new vice regal, and Yonge Street, from King to Gerrard was blocked for a substantial length of time by the throngs of people. *The Telegram* reported that "Lord Stanley's carriage was caught in the bustle of activity for twenty minutes and the Governor General smiled broadly at the Toronto citizens. He seemed particularly pleased when he was motioned to look up at the banner on Walker House. 'On Stanley On' drew a satisfied grin."[19] (The Walker House Hotel adjoined the Cyclorama on the south side of Front Street just west of York.[20] Old Union Station was just south of Walker House.)

At approximately 8 p.m., a number of mounted police led the torchlight procession, followed by Heintzman's band and three hook-and-ladder wagons strung with Chinese lanterns preceding eighty firemen marching two abreast. As *The Globe* described the spectacle, "they were dressed in their fanciful costume of red tunic, dark pantaloons and tin helmets and appeared as handsome and athletic a body of men as could be selected anywhere."[21] Nearly one hundred Sons of England followed, riding on horseback and bearing torches. Lord and Lady Stanley and the vice regal party were next in the procession, riding in two carriages, followed by Mayor Edward Clarke and several aldermen.

Once at Allan Gardens, the Sons of England, holding their torches, lined either side of the path as the vice regal carriages drove through. Chinese lanterns draped the building and were scattered throughout the gardens. Fireworks were set off from the roof to greet His Excellency as the excited crowd mounted cheers of welcome.

Many in the crowd had been waiting over an hour for the arrival of the Governor General and his party. Among those shoehorned into the pavilion were Mayor Clarke, members of the City Council, Premier Oliver

Mowat and officers of the garrison. A concert was provided for those unable to squeeze into the pavilion.

Lady Stanley and Miss Lister, the latter celebrating her twentieth
birthday, were presented with beautiful bouquets of roses. Then Mayor
Clarke addressed the guests of honour and those assembled in the gardens:

> To his Excellency, the Right Honourable Sir Frederick
> Arthur Stanley, Governor General of Canada. The Mayor
> and the Corporation of the City of Toronto desire, on behalf
> of its citizens, to express the gratification it affords them to
> welcome your Excellency and Lady Stanley to the capital of
> the Province of Ontario. We desire through your Excellency
> to express our unalterable devotion to the person and
> Crown of our beloved Sovereign, our loyalty to the Empire
> and our firm attachment to those institutions under which
> we have been so happily governed. We recognize your
> Excellency's appointment as the representative of our
> Sovereign, the choice of a statesman whose name is not
> alone historically illustrious in the annals of the realm, but
> who brings to Canada a personal prestige of experience in
> Colonial administration.

The murmurs from the crowd increased, partly in response to the Mayor's
lengthy address, in part due to the excitement of the vice regal visit and also
in response to the sheer size of the crowd. Although the hubbub subsided
as Lord Stanley rose to speak, most still found the Governor General's address all but lost in the buzz from the thousands in attendance:

> Mr. Mayor, aldermen, ladies and gentlemen. It is no form of
> words to say that I find it impossible, adequately, to express
> my deep sense of the kindness of your welcome and the mag-
> nificent reception which you have been good enough to give
> me this evening as the representative of our beloved
> Sovereign. I feel certain that nowhere in Her Majesty's
> Dominions could her name be recognized with greater pride
> and patriotism, nowhere would it be received with greater
> warmth and fervor or with more sincere attachment and

devotion, both to her person and to her crown.

It is solely in an official capacity that I can venture to claim the smallest part of your indulgence tonight. I shall never forget the grand sight which your crowded and wealthy streets have afforded this evening, the universal signs of joyousness and the cordial welcome which has been extended to me here. I have never felt in a happier position than when the youngest member of that family has been able to hold the high position which I now have the honour to fill and to complete that acquaintance with Her Majesty's great colonial dominions, which my predecessors could only look at afar. I can only hope that on another occasion we may be able to prolong our visit and to thank you in person for the many kindnesses which we have received.[22]

Later, Lord and Lady Stanley hosted a supper for the Civic Reception Committee back at the Queen's Hotel.

A special treat provided by Toronto's firefighters was intended for the vice regal party at midnight. At the stroke of twelve, as had been well-planned, a general alarm sounded all through the city. Two hook-and-ladder wagons with a number of firefighters demonstrated how they would respond to a fire. An alarm was sounded and the brigade rushed from the fire hall on Lombard Street, down Church to King, then west to a location close to Lord Stanley's hotel. Within five minutes, eight streams of water were pouring onto the buildings on the north side of King Street. Lord and Lady Stanley were greatly interested and clapped heartily during the fifteen-minute demonstration. But best-laid plans at times go awry: as one of the wagons swept wide to turn from Church onto King, the horse pulling the wagon of hoses suddenly veered and the wheels were caught on the rails, sending out a cascade of sparks as the wagon and reels slid about forty feet. The wagon overturned and the firemen were thrown to the pavement. Two of the men broke their legs, and a third suffered painful injuries. *The Evening Telegram* offered, "the truck horses, mad with fright, reared and plunged. The reel horse lay struggling on the pavement."[23] Lord and Lady Stanley were oblivious to the accident.

Two ambulances, the only ones in the city at that time, rushed to the accident scene and were joined by a police wagon. *The Telegram* reported, somewhat ironically, that:

> *Apart from this, the display was quite a success and wit-*
> *nessed by the Vice Regal party from the hotel balcony.... To*
> *set all the reels and ladder trucks racing at midnight to-*
> *wards one central point when neither lives nor property is*
> *endangered is a needless imperilling of men whose lives are*
> *already full of risk.*[24]

The Stanleys were horrified to discover two days later that while they were enjoying the firefighters' display, several men were being attended to by hospital staff. Captain Colville sent word back to the city on behalf of Lord and Lady Stanley:

> *I am directed by Their Excellencies, the Governor General*
> *and Lady Stanley of Preston, to say that they have heard*
> *with deep concern of the unfortunate accident which hap-*
> *pened on Tuesday night and they hope that you will express*
> *to the injured men how deeply they sympathize with them.*[25]

* * *

Tuesday, 11 September was no less busy for Lord Stanley. The day began at 9:45 a.m. with an address from the Irish Protestant Benevolent Society at the Queen's Hotel. Shortly after ten o'clock, six carriages took the vice regal party from the hotel to University College, the teaching arm of the University of Toronto. When they arrived at ten-thirty a sizable crowd, made up mostly of women, was awaiting them. They were greeted by the school's president, Sir Daniel Wilson, as well as the chancellor of the university, Edward Blake. No stranger to politics, Blake had been Premier of Ontario in 1871 and 1872 and was leader of the Liberal party from 1880 to 1887 before joining the university. The current Premier, Oliver Mowat, was also on hand to welcome the honoured guests.

Wilson led the way along the echoing corridors to Convocation Hall, where a crowd had already gathered to witness the Governor General's remarks. Wilson gave an address on behalf of the university, to which Lord Stanley replied, commenting on the high standards of Canadian education and on the university building itself and offering congratulations to the university president on his recent knighthood.

> *The speech was received with much applause, gentlemen clapped their hands, ladies smiled and the score of sad-eyed university students who wore their gowns and lined themselves along the walls, tried desperately hard to look intelligent.*

Stanley took time to meet each faculty member and graduate in turn. After a brief stop at the mathematics department, which was of great interest to the Governor General, the allotted hour had elapsed and it was time to move on to the next stop.

At 11:30 a.m., the vice regal party was taken by carriage to Osgoode Hall, the home of the Law Society of Upper Canada. Osgoode had moved into a six-acre location on Toronto's northwest boundary at Queen Street West and College (now University) Avenue in 1829. What was then considered a remote location is today at the heart of the city's bustling downtown. At the time of the vice regal visit, Toronto architect Kivas Tully was completing work on the ornate Courtroom Number 2.

Receiving the group were several prominent hosts, including George W. Ross, Ontario's Minister of Education, and lawyer Dalton McCarthy, who escorted Lord Stanley through the building. Samuel Hume Blake, who had founded a law firm with his brother and was Vice Chancellor of the Ontario Court of the Chancery, was host for Lady Stanley.[26] Premier Mowat accompanied Miss Lister. According to *The Evening Telegram*, "the usual crowd of hungry sightseers surged up the stairs, and almost blocked the entrance to the library."[27] The courtrooms were inspected, the massive shelves of books noted and the mosaic floors admired. Cheers were given "by lusty-lunged loungers and stub-toed urchins" as the Governor General's suite was driven away to make a stop at Toronto's Normal School (teacher's college).[28] After a visit to the Education Department at the University of Toronto, Lord Stanley and his group returned to the Queen's Hotel for luncheon.

* * *

Already, the media was growing uncomfortable with the platitudes being lavished upon Stanley with each of the countless addresses:

> *Lord Stanley of Preston, ever since he arrived in Canada, has conducted himself in the traditional fashion of Governors General, and will of course, obtain from Torontonians, without distinction of party or sect, the warm welcome always hitherto given to representatives of the Crown. We sincerely hope that he may be able to submit as cheerfully to all the afflictions of his position — for instance, to the shower of addresses that inconsiderate enthusiasts will insist on pouring over him. There are in every town, a certain number of otherwise amiable men who cannot refrain from the cruelty of requiring a Governor General to stand up like a man and look like a listener and respond to the wearisome sentences in which they set forth loyalty and goodwill he would doubtless be glad to take for granted.*[29]

At 2:30 p.m. on 11 September, Lord and Lady Stanley and their party were escorted by a cavalry detachment from the Governor General's Foot Guards from the Queen's Hotel to the eastern gate of the Toronto Industrial Exhibition, which His Excellency was to formally open.

The exhibition was in its tenth year, having been first held on 5 September, 1879. Since then, visitors had witnessed some of the most modern innovations found anywhere in the world. Outdoor lighting was introduced in 1882 and experiments with electric streetcars a few years later.

But not everything had gone smoothly in preparing for the ceremonial opening in 1888. *The Globe* explained that, "from an early hour till late in the evening, heavily-laden teams were entering the grounds, every one of them carrying exhibits of one kind or another…. It seemed impossible to have the exhibits in order and properly arranged for the official opening."[30]

Amidst the chaos of last-minute preparations, and punctual to the moment, Lord Stanley and his suite were driven to the horse ring, escorted by the Governor General's Foot Guards, where a band from "C" Company greeted the vice regal party with "God Save the Queen" — a moment recorded by *The Globe*: "Cheer after cheer went up as the distinguished visitors stood on the platform and looked at the sea of faces in the grandstand."[31]

The exhibition's president, John J. Withrow, then proceeded to read his address, which had been printed and beautifully bound in a red morocco case that was later given to the Governor General. Stanley replied warmly and concluded, "and now, in the exercise of my duty, I declare this Exhibition open." Then, one Erastus Wiman offered some remarks that were "ground out" on the cutting-edge technology of the day, the phonograph.[32]

William Lea of the York Pioneer and Historical Society then read an address dedicated to the Reverend Dr. Henry Scadding, who had chronicled much of Toronto's early history in his book *Toronto of Old*, published in 1873. In failing health, suffering from "obstruction in the organ of speech,"[33] Reverend Scadding responded feebly. Lord Stanley presented a life-sized oil portrait to Toronto's beloved historian on behalf of the York pioneers. Scadding was born in 1813, and after retiring from the ministry, was president of the York Pioneer and Historical Society between 1880 and 1898. Scadding's cabin, which was originally on the east bank of the Don River just north of Queen Street, was moved log by log and reassembled on the grounds of the Toronto Industrial Exhibition by the Society in 1879.[34]

Withrow, aided by Mayor Clarke, Alderman Garrett Frankland and several members of the reception committee, ushered Lord Stanley and his party through the exhibition. For two hours, as confirmed by *The Globe*, the group "took His Excellency in hand and showed every nook and corner in the fairgrounds."[35]

Visitors entering the main building were greeted by a huge glass case filled with electroplated goods on the left, while on the right, there were ornamental pampas grass and peacock plumes.

The Daily Telegram recounted the wonders of the exhibition: "the fountain plays in the middle and the three floors are crowded with exhibits and present are all the brilliancy and intricacy of an Oriental bazaar."[36]

The gallery drew the particular attention of Lord and Lady Stanley. Under a management committee that included the mayor and the founder of the Toronto Electric Light Company, Henry Pellatt,[37] featured works included Renaissance painter Titian's *Mary Magdalene*, created in 1560; an extremely valuable painting from seventeenth-century Dutch artist Jan Steen; and Baron Juokovsky's 1882 painting *The Late Abbé Liszt c.1832*. The exhibition also showcased several paintings from exciting young Canadian artists, with special emphasis on Homer Watson, a young man from Upper

Doon, near modern-day Kitchener. Watson, just thirty-three at the time of the exhibition, was one of Canada's first internationally recognized artists. In 1880, Lord Lorne, Canada's governor general at the time, purchased Watson's *The Pioneer Mill* for Queen Victoria, who was not only the reigning monarch but also his mother-in-law.[38] The Sovereign loved Watson's painting so much that she purchased two more for herself.[39]

Thomas Mower Martin's *Sunrise, Muskoka*, which had been exhibited at the Colonial and Indian Exhibition at South Kensington, England, in 1886, was another of the works exhibited in Toronto. Martin was the director of the Ontario School of Art, which he had helped establish. Lady Stanley commented that "she had no idea that Canada possessed such good landscape and portrait painters."[40]

Another highlight for visitors was *The Fathers of Confederation*, painted by Robert Harris in 1884. Property of the Dominion Government and lent by Prime Minister Macdonald, the painting cost the exhibition an exorbitant five hundred dollars in shipping alone.

Among the amusements at the exhibition were Professor F. A. Thomas's national dances of the world and tableaux by sixteen little girls in costume, the Wonderful $10,000 Dog, Professor Burton's Dog Circus — with the tagline "It is enough to make the old feel young again to see and hear the children as they watch the dogs going through their performances." The Chinese monkey acrobats and the Zanfretta Family's trapeze and high-wire act were also on view. Professor Hartt's Viennese Lady Fencers put on a demonstration of "Neopolitan" [sic] while elsewhere, Monsieur Valjean's spinning and juggling, Mr. Williams's balloon ascensions and three-thousand-foot parachute drops, and the female International Bicycle Contest were favoured exhibits.

Among the displays in the main building were exhibits from Manitoba, the North-West and Alberta. The Horticultural and Floral Hall, which featured a gargantuan pumpkin weighing one hundred and five pounds and a twenty-two-pound cabbage, was also housed in the main building. Elsewhere, Lord Stanley was walked through the Massey manufacturing exhibit in the Machinery Hall and the Natural History exhibit, which included live alligators on one side and fish from Lake Ontario in tanks on the other — these included a huge sturgeon from Georgian Bay, pike, pickerel, perch, trout and black bass. "Any one would make a splendid breakfast for three or four hungry men," indicated the sign. "No visitor to the exhibition should fail to see it."

As he passed Houlgraves' Mammoth Restaurant, which expected to feed three thousand visitors each day of the exhibition, Lord Stanley explored the Zoological Garden, the birds' nests and eggs of the Dairy and Apiary Hall, the Poultry Hall, the Carriage Annex, an exhibit of stove, machinery and agricultural implements, the Temple of Mysteries and Automatical Wonders, concerts by Professor Toulmin's Exhibition Band, the "C" Company Band, the Massey Band, and Archduke Joseph's Hungarian Gypsy Band. Organ and piano recitals took place in the main building, and the Governor General stopped for several minutes to listen to "Boulanger's March: The Return From the Review," which was played with "a glittering brilliancy of rendition from a score of pianos all at once at different parts of the building."

The Governor General and Lady Stanley spent nearly half an hour at the zoo, finding the greatest pleasure in watching the lions. *The Globe* reported that before leaving the zoo, Stanley "informed Alderman Piper that while he had seen much larger collections of animals, he had never seen animals that were better kept and cared for or that looked so well."[41] Stanley must have been reminded of his grandfather's famous zoological collection at Knowsley. The Stanleys were continuously astonished and delighted at the exhibition and paid close attention to almost all of the many exhibits.

While Stanley was inside enjoying the displays, word quickly spread that a steamer from Hamilton had run into the exhibition's wharf, although on inspection, the ship had sustained only minor damage.

Lady Stanley told Alderman Dodds that their reception in Toronto surpassed their expectations. The Governor General thanked Chairman Withrow and wished him much success with the year's exhibition.

Alderman John Hallam, who led the campaign to establish a free Toronto library and was the first chairman of the Toronto Public Library's board, led the vice regal suite from the exhibition to the Mechanics' Institute at Church and Adelaide streets at four-fifty that afternoon. After they quickly perused the library, which was established in 1884, Hallam hosted Lord and Lady Stanley at his home, where at 5:30 p.m. they received an address from the Lancashire Lads and Lasses. The Governor General and his party then proceeded to Government House for supper.

That night, and each evening of the exhibition, an elaborate pyrotechnic display entitled "The Siege of Sebastopol" was mounted. The display was intended to approximate the final battle of the Crimean War on 15 December, 1854. Nearly four decades later, Stanley must have been reminded of his father and his insistence on keeping Britain out of war and instead relying on the "Concert of Europe" to settle disputes diplomatically. The Crimean War had been the beginning of the end for the Concert of Europe — now, Stanley must have wondered how Britain, and of course, Canada, would manage to avert a similar conflagration with the U.S. given the seemingly insurmountable fishing rights and trade issues.

* * *

There are indications that Lord Frederick Stanley's voice was recorded by Thomas Edison's phonograph on 11 September, 1888, while attending the Toronto Industrial Exhibition. If a 1935 copy of a wax-cylinder recording is authentic, it would almost certainly be one of the oldest surviving recordings.[42]

Edison was no stranger to Toronto when he arrived for his public demonstration of the phonograph. In 1863, at only sixteen years of age, Edison had moved to Toronto to take a job as a telegraph assistant. The tedium of reporting to Toronto each hour via telegraph prompted Edison's first invention, an automatic telegraph transmitter that emitted a signal at the appointed timeeven if the operator was asleep.

Through his remarkable life and his plethora of patents, Thomas Edison maintained that the phonograph was his favourite invention. While working at his Menlo Park, New Jersey, laboratory to improve the efficiency of telegraph transmissions, Edison accidentally discovered the basic elements of a "talking machine."

Edison experimented by attaching a needle to the diaphragm of a telephone receiver. He deduced that the needle could etch vibrations into a malleable material like tinfoil, allowing him to record a short message. To his great surprise and amusement, one of his early experiments played back the short message he recorded: the nursery rhyme "Mary Had a Little Lamb." Edison used the trade name "phonograph" for his apparatus, which he refined so that two needles, one for recording and one for playing the message back, would be employed on a cylinder wrapped in tinfoil. Edison earned international fame for producing an apparatus that could record and accurately reproduce sound.

By December 1877, Edison had filed an application with the United States patent office for an "Improvement in Phonograph or Speaking Machines," which was granted the following February. The Canadian patent was granted in October 1878. The device, as the *Canadian Antique Phonograph Society* elucidated, involved "a ribbon of paper with a raised V-shaped boss that was moved past a diaphragm-activated embossing point by a clockwork drum."[43]

The Edison Speaking Phonograph Company was set up in January 1878 and immediately began demonstrating the tin-foil apparatus. Astonished onlookers were incredulous. *Harper's Weekly* wrote that "the phonograph never speaks until it has first been spoken to … it has no original ideas to advance, or else is possessed of that spirit of modesty which precludes the possibility of annoying the public with unripe fantasies and crude speculations."[44]

Edison proposed a multitude of uses for his phonograph, including a connection with the telephone so that conversations could be recorded, letter writing, phonographic books for the blind, preserving the voices of family members recollecting family histories, clocks that announce the time, music boxes and toys.

Agents booked demonstrations of the phonograph across the United States and Canada. These took place in theatres, and spectators paid twenty-five cents admission. The device consistently amazed onlookers. In April 1878, Edison visited U.S. President Rutherford B. Hayes, and on 17 May the phonograph was taken to Rideau Hall and demonstrated for Governor General Lord Dufferin and his guests. Lady Dufferin described the scene on a page in her diary:

> *This morning, we had an exhibition of the phonograph. Two men brought this wonderful invention for us to see. It is quite a small thing; a cylinder which you turn with a handle and which you place on a common table. We were so amazed when we first heard this bit of iron speak that it was hard to believe there was no trick! But we all tried it. Fred sang 'Old Obadiah,' [Lord Dufferin] made it talk Greek, the Colonel sang a French song and all our vocal efforts were repeated. As long as the same piece of tinfoil is kept on the instrument, you can hear all you have said over*

and over again. The last performance was for D. to say
something which should be repeated by the machine to a
public exhibition in Ottawa in the evening. When D. had
finished, it was repeated to us by the machine and was, we
hope, again delivered with good effect in the evening.[45]

The next day, *The Daily Citizen* reported that "His Excellency made a brief speech (recorded earlier by the phonograph at Rideau Hall) which was ground out in his voice last night to the intense satisfaction of those who visited St. James Hall."[46]

Regrettably, those recordings no longer exist, but the 1935 copy of the recording purportedly made by Lord Stanley does exist. Although there is some question as to the authenticity, the unidentified voice on the recording says:

Mr. President and gentlemen. The best use that I can make
of this wonder of the age, the phonograph, is to bid you, on
behalf of the citizens of the Dominion of Canada, the most
hearty welcome and to assure you that we are, at all times,
most happy to meet our friends from the United States in
the pursuit of song, of art, and all that may embellish the
human life. We bid you a hearty welcome.[47]

For many years the recording was thought to be of the voice of Sir Henry Morton Stanley, the explorer who in 1871 found Dr. Livingstone in East Africa. But Leo Laclaré, the former head of the Historical Sound Recording Department at what is now the National Archives of Canada, was quite certain that the recording was made at the opening of the 1888 Toronto Industrial Exhibition by Lord Frederick Arthur Stanley of Preston.[48]

In 1970, while visiting the Edison Laboratory National Monument at West Orange, New Jersey, Laclaré discovered a catalogue card that mysteriously labelled a disc, "Lord (Henry M.) Stanley. Greetings from Canada to the United States, 1888? Probably 1890 as it was then that he made his trip to this country."[49] The original container was simply labelled, "Lord Stanley, 1888" when the cylinder was copied to disc in 1935. The reference to "Henry M." reference was later added by a curator. The original cylinder has since disappeared.

Upon discovering that Lord Stanley had appeared at the opening of the exhibition in 1888, Laclaré concluded that the recorded voice was that of the Governor General. He also compared the voice found on the disc with a recording of Sir Henry Stanley produced by the British Broadcasting Corporation and discovered the voices to be substantially different. On the other hand, Arthur Zimmerman, in a series of brilliantly researched and written articles for the Canadian Antique Phonograph Society, argues strenuously that the recording could not have been made by Lord Frederick Arthur Stanley on 11 September, 1888.[50] Zimmerman notes that he was unable to find any corroborating evidence that the Governor General encountered Edison's phonograph on this visit. "If the recording year was indeed 1888, it was likely not made at the Toronto Industrial Exhibition," states Zimmerman. "Lord Stanley spent only a few hours at the T.I.E. after opening the fair that afternoon of 11 September, left Toronto at nine a.m. the next day and did not return that year. When the cylinder was dubbed in 1935, neither the speaker's identity nor the recording date, 11 September, 1888, was realized. Both were later deduced by Laclaré, based upon 'Lord Stanley, 1888' inscribed thereon."[51]

* * *

The new invention was the topic of much discussion within North American society, and its presentation at the exhibition was eagerly anticipated. But there was concern that, due to overwhelming demand, it would not be possible to supply a Perfected Phonograph for Toronto's Exhibition. John J. Withrow, president of the Exhibition board, contacted Erastus Wiman, a longtime friend then living in New York, to determine what could be done. Wiman managed to secure not only a phonograph for the exhibition, but also an expert to manage the apparatus.

Wiman was an expatriate Canadian who started his journalistic career with *The Globe* in Toronto. In 1856, he joined a mercantile agency, later becoming a partner and moving to New York, where he held several positions, including president of the Staten Island Rapid Transit Railway company. He was also involved in establishing the Canadian Club of New York, and in 1885 he was named its first president. Wiman was a tireless supporter of his native country. In 1881, he donated two "free floating swimming baths" to be built on what is now Ward's Island, part of the

Toronto Islands. The Wiman Baths were, essentially, floating enclosed swimming pools docked by the water's edge. Openings in the sides of the pool allowed lake water to circulate through.[52] The baths, in tandem with Ward's Hotel, built the following year, proved to be a popular destination for visitors to Toronto. Through the 1890s, Wiman lent financial support to the Montreal Winter Carnival. He was also a relentless advocate of Commercial Union, today known as free trade, with the United States.

Wiman consented to record four short speeches that would later be played for audiences on the phonograph once it was displayed in Toronto at the exhibition. But in September 1888, Canadian sentiment towards the United States and the free trade that Wiman championed were strained. Toronto Mayor Edward Clarke, who was also a member of provincial Parliament at the time, was vocal in his insistence that Wiman be denied the opportunity to "inflict his views on Commercial Union upon the Canadian public through the medium of Edison's phonograph" on the grounds that "it might cause division and mar the success" of the exhibition. Mayor Clarke insisted that "there will be no political matter of any kind in the speech."[53]

The four wax cylinders were shipped along with the phonograph from New York in time for the exhibition's 10 September opening. On one of the cylinders, Wiman proudly espouses the benefits of Edison's wonderful new invention:

> *The voice, expression and emphasis, and the precise modulation of each tone, can be transmitted for thousands of miles. I look upon the uses of the phonograph as almost unlimited. For my own purpose, I shall want one in my own house so that in a sleepless night, I may get up and speak a word or two to some friend, to whom I shall transmit it perhaps thousands of miles away. Some neglected duty, some unperformed service that should have been rendered during the day can be supplemented by a memorandum of precise directions and, better than all, a good letter may be delivered in the silent hours of the night. The children can delight the old grandfather hundreds of miles away, and thousands of other uses will develop as the machine gets into common and everyday use. It seems to have a dazzling future, and I wish it every success.*[54]

The Globe related, with no small measure of incredulity, how stunning it was to witness the new invention:

> *To give some idea of how perfect the phonograph is, it is only necessary to state the modulation of Mr. Wiman's voice, his exact tone and his exact words are reproduced. In one of the speeches, Mr. Wiman coughed a couple of times while speaking into the instrument. His coughing is reproduced just as naturally as if he himself was in the phonograph and not many hundred miles away. The perfection that has been attained is simply marvelous, and as every speech can now be produced and reproduced, as long as the wax cylinders last, and as those cylinders can be mailed to any part of the world and put into any phonograph, some idea of the marvelous perfection of the instrument and its ultimate use to humanity can be gathered.*[55]

In a small building near the grandstand sat Ajeeb, the astonishing chess- and checker-playing automaton, a predecessor of the computerized robot. Brought to Toronto from London, England, at great expense in order to bewilder spectators, hundreds lined up to challenge Ajeeb at ten cents per game of checkers and twenty-five cents for a game of chess. Each, in turn, was defeated by the mechanical technology. But what appeared to be a most miraculous invention was later found to be a hoax. Although positioned as entirely automated, a human was tucked inside, and a champion chess-playing human at that.[56]

Ajeeb shared its pavilion with another technological wonder, although this one was much more authentic. Visitors were able to experience the Edison Perfected Phonograph, the first of its kind ever introduced into Canada, for free. "The phonograph will be in working order today and the long-expected speech of Erastus Wiman will be given to the world," reported *The Globe.*[57]

Such was the popularity of Edison's phonograph at the exhibition that it was moved on 13 September to the annex of the main building to give spectators more room to witness the miraculous invention. George Dunham, the host for the phonograph's Toronto visit, was exhausted after describing the attributes of the invention, without a break, between eight each morning and ten each night. Dunham illustrated how the membrane and stylus operated, noted that the wax cylinder normally spun at one hundred revolutions per minute, pointed out that "a speech or song or musical instrument could be repeated five hundred times by the phonograph before its specially-prepared wax cylinders wore out. The battery would run without renewal for twelve consecutive hours."[58] Dunham then gave a program of songs, duets, violin solos and other instrumental music, each piece being tolerably heard in every part of the room when perfect quiet prevailed.[59] Astonished visitors were able to hear "the duet by two coloured gentlemen which was sung in the South a couple of months ago. The 'plunk plunk' of the banjo could be heard distinctly." *The Empire* noted that "visitors at the great Exhibition should not miss the opportunity of seeing what, in the superstitious days of our grandfathers, would have scared them night unto death."[60]

* * *

Stanley's visit to Toronto had been an overwhelming success. *The Globe* declared that:

> *The Governor General stayed long enough to allow authors of addresses to unload their platitudes upon him. The popular welcome extended to Lord Stanley was flattering to him and creditable to the citizens. The enthusiasm that greeted our visitors was spontaneous.*[61]

The carriages met the Governor General's party at the Queen's Hotel just before nine o'clock on Wednesday, 12 September, as hundreds of Torontonians stood by to bid goodbye to the vice regal party. *The Evening Telegram* reported that G. F. Frankland, the 425-pound alderman, called on the crowd to "give [Stanley] a good British sendoff."[62] This was greeted by a roar from the crowd, most of whom followed the carriages to Union Station.

The resounding voice of the station constable bellowed, "All aboard!" As Lord and Lady Stanley were helped onto the railway car, Alderman Dobbs cried, "Three cheers and a tiger for Lord Stanley," to which the crowd replied, "Hurrah! Hurrah! Hurrah!" and followed with a rising growl.

"Three more for Lady Stanley," added Alderman Frankland, who started the cheer "by emitting a bass roar that seemed to come up from his boots."[63]

"Another for luck," piped Alderman Swait. Lord Stanley stood on the rear platform while Lady Stanley waved from the doorway. With that, the engine belched out a cloud of smoke and slowly pulled away from the platform.

According to *The Evening Telegram*, "the party had been bidden a right royal and loyal farewell. And now that it is over, it must be acknowledged that the different events connected with the visits have come out most elegantly and harmoniously."[64]

* * *

The next stop for the Governor General and his party was Kingston, where they attended the Ontario Agricultural and Arts Association Provincial Fair on the afternoon of 12 September. The fair had been officially opened the day before by Sir John A. Macdonald. While thousands of visitors, in the words of *The Globe*, spent the morning "catching glimpses of the varied exhibits or listening to the music of bands, the candy butchers, the menageries and sideshow managers," Lord and Lady Stanley enjoyed luncheon at Annandale, the magnificent residence of local shipbuilder John Carruthers.[65] At four o'clock sharp, the Stanleys and their suite arrived and were escorted to the grandstand amidst thunderous applause.

"A" Battery performed the national anthem, after which Kingston's mayor, J. D. Thompson, delivered an address on behalf of the town. Lord Stanley reciprocated, stating that "he hoped for great prosperity in the future and that during his term of office, there would be a continual increase in the wealth and growth of the country."[66] While the rest of the party retired, the Governor General toured the fairgrounds and was highly interested in what he observed.

Stanley and his suite stayed in Kingston for two days. On 13 September, he was entertained at a luncheon attended by many of Kingston's leading citizens. A carriage then took a coterie that included Lord and Lady Stanley, Mayor Thompson and several of the aldermen for a drive along Front Road, so that the couple could view the harbour and islands. At two-thirty, the vice regal inspected the Rockwood Asylum, escorted by medical staff. *The Globe* explained that "the patients, not disturbed by the visitors, kept quietly on making brushes…. His Excellency asked about treatment given the pay and charity patients and was well pleased to hear that there was little or no difference shown."[67] The Governor General asked a number of pointed questions upon his arrival at the Kingston Penitentiary, but discovered that discipline for prisoners was more humane in Canada than in England.

A visit to Kingston's well-recognized Queen's University was most interesting to Lord Stanley, who upon returning to Great Britain in 1893 would be a chancellor of Liverpool University. Sir Sandford Fleming, Chancellor of Queen's, presented the address to His Excellency in front of the student body seated in Convocation Hall. Fleming later stated that Stanley "talked as a wise man who had the interests of higher education at heart."

The thirty minutes spent at Kingston General Hospital was time very well spent, especially in the eyes of Lady Stanley, who was "very much affected by the sufferings of the patients and to several, especially the young, spoke tenderly." The hospital had launched a nurses' training program in 1886, and that same year was the first hospital in Canada to purchase x-ray equipment for medical use. The party was then escorted to Hôtel-Dieu Hospital, which included an orphanage that tugged at the heartstrings of the vice regal couple. "The little folks sang sweetly and wound up the meeting by promising to pray for His Excellency."

Luncheon was served and the afternoon was spent visiting the military institution. "A" Battery went through various drills under Major General Cameron. Refreshments were served after a gymnastic performance. The vice regal party then retired once again to the home of John Carruthers.

* * *

On 14 September, 1888, Lord and Lady Stanley and their travelling suite left Kingston for Montreal on the Richelieu and Ontario Navigation Company's steamboat, *Passport*.[68] Once in Montreal, the party boarded a steamer and sailed for Quebec, where they would spend their first appreciable time at The Citadel before returning to Ottawa later in the month.

While in Quebec City, the vice regal couple hosted their first state ball, which was described by *The Dominion Illustrated Monthly* as "a brilliant and successful opening of the fall entertainment."[69] The Stanleys were scoring huge points with the socialites, dignitaries and even the nation's underprivileged.

* * *

Back in Ottawa on 24 September, Stanley participated in the opening of the inaugural Central Canada Exhibition. This annual fair grew out of a quadrennial provincial exhibition that had faltered, leaving Ottawa residents concerned that they would be left without an exhibition. In an interview at the time, Exhibition President Charles Magee recounted that:

> *A number of us talked things over informally and the upshot was a public meeting of citizens, which was held at City Hall…. At this meeting, the unanimous feeling was that a new and better exhibition — one worthy of Ottawa — should be built out of the old one.*[70]

Then as now, the exhibition was held at Lansdowne Park, which was then on the southernmost outskirts of Ottawa, but which today is in part of the core of the Canadian capital.

At two o'clock, on a platform opposite the grandstand, the Governor General's Foot Guards band played "God Save the Queen" as Lord and Lady Stanley, Prime Minister Macdonald, MP Hector-Louis Langevin and vice regal physician Sir James Grant, as well as other prominent citizens, listened.

Magee provided an opening address:

> *The Central Canada Exhibition has very great gratification in welcoming Your Excellency and Lady Stanley to the exhibition, which Your Excellency has kindly consented to open. It is with pleasure we associate your name with the first annual exhibition, which it is our hope to make permanent.*[71]

Lord Stanley witnessed many marvels of the age as he was escorted around Lansdowne Park. The park and Elgin Street were illuminated by electric light every night of the week, an astonishing feat for the era. The exhibits of cattle, horses and poultry were said to be among the best features of the fair, as were the North-West and Manitoba dairy exhibits. The telephone company had an office opened on the exhibition grounds, while the Women's Christian Temperance Union provided refreshments in the main lobby.

In the afternoon, the Zanfretta Family performed a series of trapeze and high-wire manoeuvres. In the evening, two chariots, pulled by eight horses each, raced in a Ben Hur-type race. Each day ended with a pyrotechnic demonstration.

With Lord and Lady Stanley, as well as twenty thousand others visitors looking on, a horrific accident marred the opening day of the Central Canada Exhibition. A parachutist who needed volunteers to hold down the hot-air balloon to be used for his jump enlisted twenty-two-year-old Thomas Wensley for support. Stepping forward from the crowd, Wensley volunteered to hold onto the ropes until the parachutist hollered, "Let go!" But Wensley held on instead and the balloon carried him some three hundred metres above the crowd, which was hushed in a combination of awe and fear. "Straight as a bolt he came," *The Ottawa Citizen* reported, "feet down for a couple of feet, then with a wild wave of his hands and feet, the body turned horizontal to earth."[72] Wensley fell to his death, landing west of Bank Street, just outside the park.

In spite of the tragic accident, the Central Canada Exhibition was a resounding success and the decision was made to ensure that it become an annual event.

* * *

Prior to Lord Stanley's arrival in Canada in 1888, Prime Minister Macdonald wrote to the departing Governor General, Lord Lansdowne:

> *I'm afraid that Lady Lansdowne and you have rather spoiled both my wife and myself, and that that it will be some time before we become reconciled to the newcomers.*[73]

In short order, however, Macdonald managed to become a close friend and dear confidant of Lord Stanley.

As early as 1870, Frederick Stanley's brother Edward had come to some crude understanding of Macdonald's inexplicable character and at times humorous behaviour:

> *Read, with much amusement, a letter from Northcote to Disraeli in which [Northcote] relates how during the Canadian difficulty at Red River, matters were unpleasantly complicated by the news that 'Sir John has broken out again.' Sir John being the Canadian premier, Macdonald, and his breaking-out the indulgence of a periodical fit of intoxication, which lasts over many days. It seems that he breaks out in this fashion once or twice in the year, and the habit is so well understood that no especial notice is taken of it — the grievance in the present instance being not that the minister should be drunk for a week together, but that he should not have waited till the urgent business on hand was disposed of.*[74]

Where Edward had been amused, Frederick would be moved and, after a short time in the Dominion, the Governor General was inspired by the legendary Prime Minister and his passion for the country he helped create.

* * *

While Macdonald and the new Governor General might have been getting along, the same could not be said about the Dominion and its massive neighbour to the south. Forged in a tradition of distrust and suspicion, Canadian-American relations were, to say the very least, strained in the late nineteenth century. This was especially so when it came to the matter of fisheries.

When the United States purchased Alaska and the adjacent islands from Russia in 1867, a problem manifested itself: where did American territory end, and where exactly might British, Russian and Canadian vessels freely fish and seal? Following the Alaska purchase, Russia and the United States divided the Behring Sea in two, cutting through the Komandorski and Aleutian Islands. But it was the Pribilof Islands, which fell in Alaskan, or American, territory, that proved to be the problematic area in the dispute as they were home to one of the main breeding grounds for fur seals.

American Acts of Congress in the 1860s and early 1870s prohibited the killing of seals upon the Pribilof group of islands and "the waters adjacent thereto." This vague reference plagued all parties who had to wrestle with its meaning. It was, of course, a matter of interpretation. The U.S. maintained that all waters east of the boundary line drawn up with the Russians were to be considered within American jurisdiction. Moreover, with a mind to global perception, Americans claimed that the killing that British and Canadian sealers had been conducting "on the open sea" was destructive to the fur seals' way of life. These were convenient moral grounds to stand behind because, at the same time, the United States government had given exclusive "killing rights" to the American-owned Alaska Commercial Company in 1870. The company therefore enjoyed a monopoly on the fur seal industry; British and Canadian sealers who had previously enjoyed access to pelagic sealing in the Behring Sea were now officially shut out.

And so began a long list of failed negotiations, treaties and resolutions. The untenable Chamberlain-Bayard Treaty of 1888, signed by Britain and the U.S., was essentially a way to open up a free market for Canadian fish. Yet the treaty was rejected by the U.S. Senate, and American fishermen were forced to obtain fishing licences to conduct their business in Canadian waters. The failure of the treaty was an ominous harbinger of the era, which was marked by vessel seizures, political grandstanding and, ultimately, third-party arbitration some five years later. This series of poor relations with the United States had politicians, lawyers, businessmen and Lord Stanley himself fearing the worst — war with America was not wholly out of the question.

From the beginning of the republic, American policies were openly hostile to British interests and Canada, as an extension of the motherland, suffered by association. In 1883, the United States notified the Canadian government that it would abrogate the fishery clauses of the Washington Treaty of 1818, which had allowed for free trade in Canadian fish in exchange for American fishing privileges on Canadian coasts. This reversal of the established understanding between the two nations only echoed a pattern that had emerged over the previous twenty years; in the 1860s, American-based Irish groups led the violent Fenian Raids into Canada, resulting in the assassination one of the Fathers of Confederation, Thomas D'Arcy McGee.[75] In 1866, the United States also chose to abrogate the Reciprocity Treaty, a reversal whose implications would come to a head during Stanley's tenure.

These American policies greatly affected Canadians. It may be argued that then, more than today, American presidential elections were more important to Canadians for the simple reason that Canada was still very much a young country, and the threat of annexation by the United States, or indeed war with America, were tangible scenarios that few Canadians wished to explore. For their part, American politicians gave no visible quarter to Canadian considerations. President Grover Cleveland, for instance, allowed little or no concession when it came to Canadian interests. This was especially true during election campaigns.

Cleveland, among other politicians and political hopefuls of his time, was acutely aware of the profound impact that the Irish vote had on the outcome of an American election. Anglophobic Irish-Americans harboured a profound resentment towards Britain and all things British. Canada, the satellite of the mother country, was emblematic of the John Bull that many Irish-American voters had grown to hate. An American president had to position himself opposite British interests were he to gain the bulk of the substantial Irish vote. As Macdonald himself wrote, "Cleveland, I fancy, had ascertained that the Irish vote would carry New York against him, and so in desperation took an extra twist at the tail of the British lion."[76]

The American Senate comprehensively rejected the Chamberlain-Bayard Treaty. For his part, President Cleveland issued a message to Congress that requested the power to proclaim "a state of complete commercial non-intercourse with Canada."[77] Following the repudiation of the Treaty in 1888, Cleveland issued a statement, which Canadians came to know as the "Retaliation Message":

> *I fully believe the treaty just rejected by the Senate was well suited to the exigency, and that its provisions were adequate for our security in the future from vexatious incidents and for the promotion of friendly neighbourhood and intimacy without sacrificing in the least our national pride or dignity.*[78]

Was this a prelude to war?

Certainly the most contentious issue between the two countries was the dispute over the fur-seal fisheries of the Behring Sea. As early as 1886, Canadian sealing vessels had been arrested and seized by American ships on the high seas. American claims clearly violated at least two treaties regarding the area. In 1824, the United States signed a treaty with Russia that allowed for unmolested fishing on the Pacific, free navigation of all rivers flowing into the Pacific and a system of "free commerce" for the resulting yields. The Russians then signed an identical treaty with the British one year later. In 1841, Russian authorities were compelled to observe the 1824 treaty when American vessels began whaling on the Pacific. It was, of course, well within their rights.

By the 1880s, these rights were rendered somewhat more obscure as American cruisers began to seize Canadian whaling vessels. Meanwhile, in Washington, the government tabled a proposal for a "close season" (April to November) calling for no pelagic fishing for seals on ecological grounds. The rationale was that the fur-seal nurseries only existed on the Komandorski Islands, which were owned by Russia, and the American-owned Pribilof Islands. Though most experts felt that the extermination of seals had been caused by on-land sealing, the United States government insisted that it was pelagic sealing that was to blame for the disruption in seal life.

Americans tabled various proposals for a close season, all of them in the guise of humanitarian considerations for the well-being of the seals themselves. This spin on the close season issue found favour around the world, as Sir Julian Pauncefote explained to Stanley: "the Americans have certainly got the sympathy of all nations on the Close Season question — which, rightly or wrongly, is believed to be a condition *sine qua non* of the preservation of the fur seal fisheries."[79] These American proposals for a close season, however, would find little currency among Canadian politicians.

Canadian representatives reasoned that the United States' proposal benefited American fur-seal fisherman rather than setting any clear ecological boundaries for the seals themselves. First, Canadian vessels were not the only ones who sealed out of season. Moreover, the British government had already begun to consider the ecological cost of the hunt and was, if sluggishly, seeking an arrangement to safeguard the migration of seals to their breeding grounds in the spring.

Commercially, a close-season prohibition of Canadian pelagic fishing in and of itself would have greatly tipped the scales in favour of the American Alaska Fur Company, which, had the Canadians acquiesced, would have been in the envious position of undertaking the wholesale slaughter of seals on the Pribilof Islands.[80] This, coupled with America's policy regarding fishing rights on Canada's eastern seaboard, was worthy of criticism, as one journalist happily offered:

> *The whole question of the United States in these fisheries disputes has been marked by one-sidedness and self-contradiction. While seeking privileges in our Atlantic fishing-grounds, to which they do not hesitate to set up a monopoly in the North Pacific, which is clearly preposterous.*[81]

Preposterous or not, the U.S. government was willing to follow through with this "one-sided" policy — even if it required force.

The British did not want to rock the boat with the United States, and they implored the Dominion government to try and negotiate a friendly resolution to the situation. Robert Gascoyne-Cecil, the 3rd Marquess of Salisbury, had long been associated with the Stanleys. Indeed, Salisbury had replaced Edward Henry Stanley as Foreign Secretary. He had earlier been Secretary of State for India in Edward Geoffrey Stanley's third term as British Prime Minister and was one of the key architects of the "Splendid Isolation" philosophy of the new Tories. In 1885, Salisbury had the unusual distinction of being both Foreign Secretary and Prime Minister of Britain concurrently.[82] Salisbury and Sir Frederick Stanley were close, and Stanley often used his friend as a sounding board.

After consulting Salisbury, Stanley, mindful of the Canadian prerogative, wrote to Macdonald in the summer of 1888:

> *In my conversation with Lord Salisbury, I thought it right to mention to him the special circumstances which tend to make the United States proposal a one-sided arrangement; but he apparently retained the belief that it would be possible to arrive at some such understanding with modifications, which would effect all that the Dominion Government could reasonably claim. On the other hand, he impressed upon me the importance of removing, by amicable negotiations, a cause of friction between ourselves and the United States with respect to which public opinion at home and indeed in Europe would hardly sustain us in adopting an extreme view of our rights.*[83]

These thoughts, however, were expressed early in Stanley's tenure as governor general, and as relations with American policy makers deteriorated,

Stanley's opinion more resembled those in Canada who had tired of U.S. aggression towards the Dominion.

Only weeks later, Stanley was beginning to more clearly see the frustrating position the United States had adopted in the fishery question and the obvious dangers that such a line of reasoning presented. Once again, Stanley informed Macdonald:

> *I am entirely of your mind about the aspect of the seal fishing question, and for that reason, I need to save Lord Salisbury from coming to a nasty conclusion instead of waiting for the U.S. to be in their right minds after the election is over.... I think there may be danger. If there can be some opening left for further negotiations, he may be trusted to take due advantage of it.*

Still, U.S. politicians had already made up their minds on the matter. And while American representatives called for a close season, they concurrently flexed their muscles in the vicinity of the Behring Sea, as *The Dominion Illustrated Monthly* testified:

> *The President and his Cabinet do not come out boldly and assert their exclusive sovereignty over the waters of Behring's Sea, but they make dark speeches and circulate documents that seem to take their right to such monopoly for granted. There is not a power in either hemisphere that would more promptly or more obstinately refuse to acknowledge so unreasonable a claim, if preferred by another Government, than the United States.*[84]

With no real choice, Stanley, Macdonald and the rest of Canada awaited the next "dark speech."

* * *

In the autumn of 1888, Lord Stanley was named a patron of the Royal Canadian Yacht Club. The club, devoted to the interests of yachting, was established in Toronto in 1854, although it did not receive its Admiralty warrant until 1878. This warrant allowed the club to use the designation "Royal" within its charter, allowed members the use of the Royal blue or red ensign on their vessels, and usually allowed free harbour dues to members. Joining the Governor General as a patron of the Royal Canadian Yacht Club was His Royal Highness the Prince of Wales. The club's commodore was George Gooderham, the president of Gooderham and Worts Distillery, the Bank of Toronto, the Canada Permanent Mortgage Corporation and the newly created Dominion of Canada General Insurance Company.

* * *

The vice regal couple and two sons visited Niagara Falls, Ontario, on the morning of 17 October, 1888. After a civic luncheon, the Stanley family visited a number of sites on the Canadian side, including Queen Victoria Park, directly across from the American Falls and just north of the Horseshoe Falls. The next day, the Stanleys visited places of interest on the American side.[85]

* * *

During the North-West Rebellion led by Louis Riel, military authorities in Ottawa had ordered the formation of a volunteer militia corps. So many volunteers from the Ottawa area answered the call that a lottery was instituted. Chosen from the Governor General's Foot Guards and the 43rd Regiment, these soldiers served at the Battle of Cut Knife Hill in Manitoba on 2 May, 1885. Although the uprising was quelled and Riel was eventually hung for his actions, two Ottawa men were killed in the action, the first of the Governor General's Foot Guards to lose their lives. The "Sharpshooters Monument," a seven-foot bronze statue of a rifleman capping a ten-foot pedestal made of grey granite, was designed by British sculptor Percy Wood to honour Privates William Osgoode and John Rodgers. The monument was erected at the entrance to Ottawa's Major's Hill Park, within view of the Parliament Buildings and on the site now occupied by the Château Laurier. It was also the site where Ottawa's founding father, Colonel By, originally had his home.

Lord Frederick Stanley presided over the unveiling of the monument on 1 November, 1888 — an event that was recounted in *The Dominion Illustrated Monthly*:

The Governor General arrived sharp on time, and was led to the platform, where were the Right Reverend Bishop of Ontario and Reverend Messrs. Pollard and Bogert, Sir Adolphe Caron, Major General Sir Fred. Middleton, Mr. Percy Wood, the sculptor, and several members of the press. Prayer was offered by Bishop Lewis. The Benediction followed, and the Guards' Band played a verse of the hymn, 'All People That on Earth Do Dwell'.[86]

The affair was well attended and included many distinguished military guests.

* * *

The Rideau Curling Club was founded on 10 November 1888, with Sir Sandford Fleming as the first president and Lord Stanley of Preston, the Governor General, as its patron. The club began with one hundred and twenty members from the Ottawa area, renting three sheets of natural ice in the modest quarters of the Rideau Skating Club. Curling was not new to the area; in fact, the Bytown Curling Club had existed prior to 1855 and was renamed the Ottawa Curling Club when the town changed its name. In 1875, the Earl of Dufferin presented the club with a new trophy, the Governor General's Trophy, on behalf of his office. Lord Stanley was on hand in 1889 to award the trophy to the team from the Ottawa Curling Club. That same night, he awarded the team a silver medal dated 1888. The tradition of inviting the appointed Governor General to be a patron of the Rideau Curling Club, which began with Lord Stanley, exists to this day.[87] Stanley also participated in the occasional curling match with the Rideau Curling Club during his five years in Canada.

* * *

"*Ceud mile failte*" was the greeting proffered by the St. Andrew's Society of Ottawa to Lord Frederick Stanley on 12 November, 1888. The Society, made up of members of Scottish descent already settled in the Ottawa area and assisting newly arrived immigrant Scots, decided to present an address of welcome to Lord Stanley, the new Governor General. Stanley was invited to their meeting that evening and greeted appropriately. The secretary of the Ottawa chapter was Philip Dansken Ross, who would become a close friend of the Governor General and would be named a Stanley Cup trustee in 1893, by which time he had become the chapter's second vice president. Later that month, Lord Stanley visited the St. Andrew's Society of Toronto.[88]

After visiting Toronto early in September 1888, Lord Stanley returned to the provincial capital on Friday, 30 November. It was on this day that the Governor General called upon the St. Andrew's Society of Toronto, who, led by President D. R. Wilkie, were careful not to "spill their mercies" as they repeatedly toasted His Excellency.[89] Major A. M. Cosby, who later served as president of the Ontario Hockey Association, was a member of the Toronto order.

That evening, Lord and Lady Stanley were guests of honour at a "brilliant gathering of fair ladies and fine-hearted men." The ball was held at the Pavilion Music Hall.

* * *

The following day, 1 December, the city of Hamilton was most excited to have a visit from the Governor General. Preparations were quite elaborate, as *The Hamilton Spectator* affirmed, "easily eclipsing the decorations put up by Torontonians for the Governor General's appearance there the day before."[90] The city created the first triumphal arch ever erected in honour of the Governor General, an idea borrowed by most cities and towns as Lord Stanley travelled across the country.

* * *

For the first time since their arrival in Canada, Lord and Lady Stanley had their entire family surrounding them when Victor, George and Ferdy took time from school in England for a visit and to see the new country over which their father presided. The vice regal family met in Ottawa, where they planned to spend that winter.[91]

Both Frederick and Constance seemed quite content, having spent their first few months in Canada busily attending to vice regal matters, but now able to witness the end of their first year in Canada with no official duties remaining on the itinerary and with their children around them.

Belying the aristocratic pose of a Governor General, Lord Stanley took great delight in spending the last few weeks of 1888 simply as Fred or Father. The Stanley children roared with laughter in the snow around Rideau Hall on Christmas Eve as their father bravely took his first-ever toboggan ride.[92]

A small group of family and friends gathered at Rideau Hall on New Year's Eve to enjoy two short performances that included members of the Stanley family as well as staff. "Cut Off with a Shilling" featured military secretary Captain Josceline Bagot as Colonel Berners, while his wife played Mrs. Gaythorne and George Stanley performed as Sam Gaythorne. That play was followed, after a twenty-minute intermission, by "Dearest Mama," which included nineteen-year-old Arthur Stanley as Nettie Croker, seventeen-year-old Ferdy as Browser, fourteen-year-old Algernon as Harry Clinton, thirteen-year-old Isobel as Mary, ten-year-old Freddy Stanley as Jones, Mrs. Bagot as Breezely Fussell, Mrs. Colville as Edith Clinton and Miss Lister as Mrs. Honeywood. *The Daily Citizen* reported that, "after the performances, their Excellencies entertained the guests at supper and at midnight, the gong sounded out the old year and in the new year. Everybody wished everybody else a Happy New Year, and the gathering broke up."[93]

---

[1] *The Globe* (Toronto: 10 September, 1888), *edition cover page.*

[2] *The Globe* (Toronto: 11 September, 1888), *edition cover page.*

[3] CNE Archives Industrial Exhibition Association of Toronto, Minute Book, p.286.

[4] *The Empire* (Toronto: 10 September, 1888), p.3.

[5] *The Globe* (Toronto: 11 September, 1888), *edition cover page.*

[6] *The World* (Toronto: 12 September, 1888), *edition cover page.*

[7] Ibid.

[8] *Toronto Evening Telegram,* (10 September, 1888), *edition cover page.*

[9] Ibid.

[10] Ibid.

[11] *Toronto Evening Telegram,* (11 September, 1888), p.4.

[12] *Lost Toronto,* William Dendy, p33

[13] M. Filey, 'Hotel Fit for Royals', *Toronto Sketches–The Way We Were* (Toronto: Dundurn Press, 2000), p.117.

[14] *Canadian Encyclopaedia* (Edmonton: Hertig Publishers, 1988), p.709.

[15] J. A. MacIntosh, P. D. McIntosh, J. McLaverty & R. Fleming (*eds*), *One Hundred Years History of the St. Andrew's Society of Toronto: 1836–1936* (Toronto: Murray Printing Company, 1936), p.34.

[16] *The Globe* (Toronto: 11 September, 1888), *edition cover page.*

[17] *Toronto Evening Telegram* (8 September, 1888), p.4.

[18] *Toronto Evening Telegram* (11 September, 1888), p.4.

19 *Toronto Evening Telegram* (10 September, 1888), *edition cover page.*

20 The Cyclorama was a circular building constructed in 1887 by the Toronto Art Company as a showroom for panoramic religious murals.

21 *The Globe* (Toronto: 11 September, 1888).

22 Ibid.

23 *Toronto Evening Telegram* (11 September, 1888), p.4.

24 Ibid.

25 *Toronto Evening Telegram* (14 September, 1888), p.4.

26 The law firm begun by the brothers Blake is now Blake, Cassels and Graydon.

27 *Toronto Evening Telegram* (12 September, 1888).

28 Ibid.

29 *The Globe* (Toronto: 11 September, 1888).

30 *The Globe* (Toronto: 12 September, 1888).

31 Ibid.

32 *Toronto Evening Telegram*, (11 September, 1888).

33 E. Firth & C. Fahey, *Dictionary of Canadian Biography On-Line.*

34 Filey, 'The Ubiquitous Reverend Scadding', *Toronto Sketches*, p.35.

35 *The Globe* (Toronto: 12 September, 1888), pp. 1, 3.

36 *Toronto Evening Telegram*, (12 September, 1888), p.4.

37 In 1911, Pellatt would start plans on building the incredible Casa Loma in Toronto, which he stocked with outstanding art once it was completed three years later.

38 Lord Lorne had married Queen Victoria's daughter, Louise.

39 M. Miller, *Homer Watson: The Man of Doon* (Toronto: Summerhill Press Ltd., 1988).

40 *The Globe* (Toronto: 12 September, 1888).

41 Ibid.

42 Older recordings do, in fact, exist. The Edison Archive includes several wax cylinders sent from England by Edison's European agent, Colonel George E. Gouraud. The cylinders were recorded 29 June, 1888 during a performance of 'Israel in Egypt' at the Handel Festival in the Crystal Palace in London.

43 A. E. Zimmerman, 'Lord Stanley and Edison's Perfected Phonograph at the Toronto Industrial Exhibition', *Canadian Antique Phonograph Society* (Toronto: November, 1888).

44 *Harper's Weekly* (30 March, 1878), p.45.

45 The Marchioness of Dufferin & H. G. Ava (Hamilton), Marchioness of Hamilton-Temple-Blackwood, *My Canadian journal, 1872–8: Extracts from my letters home written while Lord Dufferin was Governor-General* (Toronto: Coles Publishing Company, {1891} 1969), p.292.

46 *Ottawa Daily Citizen* (17 May, 1878), p.4.

47 From CNE Archives, Sound and Moving Image Collection.

48 L. Laclaré, *Lord Stanley and the Demonstration of the Edison Perfected Phonograph in Canada, 1888* (British Institute of Recorded Sound: April–July, 1973), p.198.

49 Ibid.; Zimmerman, 'Lord Stanley and Edison's Perfected Phonograph'.

50 *Antique Phonograph News* (Canadian Antique Phonograph Society: September–October 2005 & November–December 2005).

51 Ibid.

52 S. Gibson, *More Than an Island: A History of the Toronto Island* (Toronto: Irwin, 1984), pp.90–91.

53 *Toronto Daily News* (10 September, 1888), p.4.

54 *The Globe* (13 September, 1888), p.4.

55 Ibid.

56 Ajeeb spent its final years as an attraction at New York's Coney Island.

57 *The Globe* (Toronto: 12 September, 1888), p.4.

58 *The World* (Toronto: 24 September, 1888), p.1.

59 Zimmerman, 'Lord Stanley and Edison's Perfected Phonograph'.

60 *The Empire* (Toronto: 14 September, 1888), p.2.

61 *Toronto Evening Telegram* (12 September, 1888), p.4.

62 *Toronto Evening Telegram* (12 September, 1888), p.4.

63 Ibid.

64 Ibid.

65 *The Globe* (Toronto: 13 September, 1888), p.1.

66 Ibid.

67 *The Globe* (Toronto: 14 September, 1888).

68 *Brandon Mail* (14 September, 1888), p.3.

69 *The Dominion Illustrated* (15 September, 1888), p.174.

70 *Ottawa Evening Journal* (25 September, 1888).

71 Ibid.

72 *Ottawa Citizen* (13 August, 1988 — from an article originally published in September 1888).

73 J. A. Macdonald, *Letter to Lansdowne, Lansdowne Papers* (1 February, 1888).

74 E. H. Stanley, *Personal Diary* (14 May, 1870); Vincent, *Diaries of Edward Henry Stanley*, p.58–9.

75 'One-Eyed' Frank McGee, hockey legend of the Ottawa Silver Seven who perished in the First World War, was Thomas D'Arcy McGee's nephew.

76 Macdonald to Lansdowne, 'Macdonald Letters', *Lansdowne Papers* (6 September, 1888).

77 Creighton, *John A. Macdonald: The Old Chieftain*, p.508.

78 President G. Cleveland, as reprinted in, J. C. Hopkins, 'Canada and American Aggression', *The Dominion Illustrated Monthly* (Montreal: December 1892), p.701.

79 J. Pauncefote, *Letter to F. A. Stanley, Lord Stanley of Preston Papers*, from the Public Archives of Canada in London (Washington: 24 November, 1889).

80 Creighton, *John A. Macdonald*, p.507.

81 *The Dominion Illustrated Monthly* (Montreal: 19 July, 1890), p.34.

82 It was far more common for the British Prime Minister to be the 1st Lord of the Treasury.

83 F. A. Stanley, *Letter to J. A. Macdonald, Lord Stanley of Preston Papers*, from the Public Archives of Canada in London (New Richmond, Quebec: 5 July, 1888).

84 *The Dominion Illustrated Monthly* (Montreal: 22 June, 1889), p.386.

85 *Qu'Appelle Progress* (22 October, 1888), p.2.

86 *The Dominion Illustrated Monthly* (Montreal: 24 November, 1888), p.326.

87 K. Shea, *Interview with Jackie Carberry*, Club Historian of the Rideau Curling Club, (23 June, 2006); C. H. Little, *A Short History of the Rideau Curling Club: 1888–1978* (Ottawa: The Club, 1979).

88 J. Thorburn & A. E. Cameron, *History of the First Century of the St. Andrew's Society of Ottawa: 1846–1946* (Ottawa: published privately, 1946), p.75.

89 J. A. MacIntosh (et al.), *One Hundred Years History of the St. Andrew's Society of Toronto*, p.34.

90 *Hamilton Spectator* (Hamilton: 3 December, 1888), edition cover page.

91 *The Dominion Illustrated Monthly* (Montreal: 13 October, 1888), p.39.

92 *MacLeod Gazette* (3 January 1889).

93 *Ottawa Daily Citizen* (3 January, 1889), p.2.

CHAPTER EIGHT

1889

Lord and Lady Stanley's son Edward may have accompanied his parents to Canada during the summer of 1888, but he didn't stay in the colonies long. Instead, Edward George Villiers Stanley returned to England to marry Lady Alice Maude Olivia Montagu, the youngest daughter of the Duke of Manchester, on 5 January, 1889. The Stanleys were disappointed not to be able to part of the vetting process, which, despite any animosity, was left to Edward Henry and his wife. Curiously, neither Lord nor Lady Stanley attended the wedding itself.

The wedding took place at the Guards' Chapel in Wellington Barracks in London. Modelled after a Grecian temple, the chapel was called a "military Valhalla" when it was restored in the 1870s.[1]

The ceremony was documented for Canadians by *The Dominion Illustrated Monthly*:

> *The marriage of the Hon. Edward Stanley is specially interesting because he is the eldest son of our esteemed Governor General, and is to take up his dwelling at the Capital as A.D.C. to his father. He was wedded on the 5th inst. to Lady Alice Montagu, daughter of the Duke of Manchester, in the Guards' chapel. The Prince of Wales and family, the Duke of Cambridge, the Duke and Duchess of Teck, and an aristocratic company present. The Rector of Hatfield, who is a son of the Marquis of Salisbury, officiated. Beautiful presents were received from Queen Victoria, Empress Frederick of Germany, and other royal personages.[2]*

Colourful and detailed reports were sent to Canada by several family members, including one account to Lady Stanley from her son Victor:

> *Tum [the family's nickname for Edward, The Prince of Wales] was very gracious to me, came up and asked if I was Edward's brother and talked to me for a long time. He told me to tell you how much he and everybody else wished you had been there, and so they did dear Mamma, on all sides and from everyone you heard 'Oh wasn't a pity dear Constance isn't here'.*[3]

The Honourable Edward and Lady Alice Stanley sailed for Canada six weeks after their wedding, arriving in Canada in late February 1889. For the next two years, Edward served as his father's aide-de-camp. "[Edward] Stanley greatly enjoyed his time in Canada, particularly the summer months, which were passed in The Citadel at Quebec. In the winter they played ice hockey and in the summer they would go off for weeks at a time to the Cascopedia [*sic*] for fishing."[4]

* * *

Arguably, amateur sport had reached its zenith in Canada during the late 1800s. As cities sprang forth across the country during that era, winter sports were being embraced — snowshoeing, tobogganing, curling, skating and hockey were finding enthusiastic participants. For the most part, these activities were hobbies for the wealthy, who had the time and resources to expend on them.

Casually at first, like-minded sportsmen began to congregate, and clubs devoted to favoured sports were formed. In 1881, for example, the Montreal Amateur Athletic Association was founded as an umbrella organization that unified the city's existing cycling, lacrosse and snowshoe clubs with a mandate to provide rational recreation for members. Within a few years, the M.A.A.A. added curling, cycling, football, hockey, skating and tobogganing to its curriculum.

Yet, as carefree as these activities sounded, Dr. David Morrison, the Director of Archaeology and History at the Canadian Museum of Civilization in Gatineau, Quebec, recently told *The Globe and Mail,*

"Spontaneous fun was not something people of the middle class were supposed to engage in…. The Victorians were always formal and over-organized."[5]

At the annual meeting of the Montreal Snowshoe Club in 1882, Vice President R.D. McGibbon introduced the idea of staging a winter sports festival.[6] The proposal was embraced and shared with local merchants, who declared that some sort of winter attraction for the city, a series of events that would attract visitors from hundreds of miles around, would not only result in sizable sums of money being left behind in the city, but would shatter the image of Canada as a frozen tomb come wintertime. The Montreal Winter Carnival was the outgrowth of the enthusiasm for winter sports. *Harper's Bazaar* said of the city, "Montreal, perhaps more than any of our cities by virtue of its situation and surroundings, its pure air and healthy outdoor sports, possesses attractions which have made it the one place in Canada where a winter carnival may be most fully carried out."[7]

Various clubs from across the city joined the effort. In late January 1883, the weather was ideal as the first Montreal Winter Carnival was staged over five days. Events were held at various locations within the city, including the frozen St. Lawrence River, the Victoria Rink, the grounds of McGill University and various public parks. Events included "fancy dress" skating parties, fancy sleigh rides, parades and parties galore, as well as elite sporting competitions including curling, snowshoe races, tobogganing down thousand-foot *glissoires* and "the novel game of hockey."[8]

The city spent large sums of money to both construct and promote its Winter Carnival, which attracted thousands of visitors, specifically the American tourists at which the carnival was primarily aimed:

> *To all a Canadian welcome, and the grasp of a hearty hand.*
> *Though our clime be rude, it serves us well, in our hardy northern land.*
> *Our sons are brave and stalwart, our daughters blooming and fair.*
> *And more than wealth is the glow of health, which they draw from the wintry air.*[9]

Among the visitors, and adding an immediate legitimacy to the carnival, was Governor General, the Marquess of Lorne, along with his wife, Princess Louise, who was Queen Victoria's daughter.

The focal point of the carnival was a magnificent ice castle built in Dominion Square, across from the Windsor Hotel in downtown Montreal, by brothers A. C. and J. H. Hutchison. The blocks of ice used for the bricks were hauled from the Lachine Canal; each of the bricks measured three feet, four inches square and was fifteen inches thick, and sixteen thousand of them were used to construct a Gothic castle covering an area 160 feet by 120 feet and rising 44 feet into the frigid Montreal sky. The castle was complete with arches, barbicans and a drawbridge, plus a main tower that reached a height of a hundred feet. The roof was constructed of tree boughs frozen solid from having water sprayed upon them.

Harper's Bazaar described the ice castle: "viewed in the daytime, every block emitting its prismatic ray, dazzling and sparkling with crystal brilliancy as the sun lights on it, it presents an appearance which is completely fascinating."[10] At night, the transparent blocks of ice glistened with the novelty of electric lights that illuminated the interior of the palace.

A highlight of the carnival was the storming of the ice castle by the various snowshoe clubs of Montreal, followed by a pyrotechnic display. Snowshoeing, the senior event at the carnival, was immensely popular: in 1883, there were twenty-five snowshoe clubs in Montreal alone. Sixteen hundred snowshoers, each dressed in blanket coats along with toques, stockings and sashes in their respective club colours, advanced on the castle and, for half an hour, fired thousands of Roman candles at their target, which returned fire at the assailants. Red, blue and green Bengal lights were burned at intervals, each offering a brilliant effect. "It really was a gorgeous feast of colour for the eye," Lord Hamilton confirmed, "a most entrancing spectacle, with all this polychrome glow seen against the dead-white field of snow in the crystal clearness of a Canadian winter night."[11]

Amidst shouts and cheers, the climax of the castle's capture was reached when the snowshoers took possession. A burst of fireworks and booming cannon blasts let the thousands of assembled spectators know that victory had been achieved, as *Harper's Bazaar* affirmed:

> *After the capitulation, victors and vanquished alike joined in one long line and, with torches high in air, marched toward the Mountain. Taking a zigzag course, they reached*

the summit where they again sent off fireworks and turning, wended their serpentine way back, looking in, the distance like a thread of gold.[12]

A skating party was held each year at the Victoria Skating Rink. Although not the first covered rink in the city, at ten thousand square feet it was certainly the largest. Located in the heart of downtown, between Stanley and Drummond streets just below St. Catherine, the Victoria Rink was ideally suited for the carnival's skating party. The rink was elaborately decorated with flags, wreaths of foliage and coloured lights that danced off mirror balls and threw beams of light over the skaters. Guests dressed in costumes circled the downtown rink and participants followed the "gay music from the band, roll and double roll, figures eight and three, grapevine, waltzing backward and forward (all impressive skating techniques) — the merry bladers skated round in seemingly unending streams, making the whole place one moving mass of ever-changing form and color."[13] Although hockey had been played at the Victoria Rink, there was an ice grotto in the middle, making it perfect for pleasure skating but all but unusable for hockey games.

A sculptor created six massive statues out of wet snow, and these were arranged along opposite sides of the rink. As they froze, they began to resemble white marble.

Hockey, still very much a fledgling sport, was organized into a three-team series in 1883 — the first-ever hockey tournament. The Montreal Victorias iced a squad, as did McGill University and a team from Quebec City. Games were played on the St. Lawrence in an area designated for curling. The winning team was to be presented with badges and a "solid silver cup."

Using the Halifax Rules first introduced to Montreal for an historic game on 3 March, 1875, the teams played contests comprising two thirty-minute periods with a ten-minute intermission squeezed in between. The puck was square and made of wood. Teams were to play what was a reasonably traditional game with nine players per side, except the Quebec team arrived with only seven players. The Quebecers pleaded with carnival organizers to let the tournament go on; the perplexed organizers finally decided that McGill and the Victorias would each drop two players from their respective rosters to make the competition fair to all. From that point, and for several decades thereafter, hockey was a seven-player game.

Montreal's *Daily Star* described the action in the final match:

> *Owing to the narrowness of the rink, there was not much room for skating, and as a natural result, the game was more one of shinny than hockey. The play was very close throughout, the bully [puck] flying from one end of the rink to the other with the speed of lightning. The match was begun at 11:30 [in the morning], McGill going off with a rush for Quebec's goal. [Quebec's] Scott, however, was on hand and sent the rubber flying back when it was for a moment dangerously near McGill's sticks [goal]. [McGill's] Elder scoured the bully and sent it flying up when [team-mate] Murray captured it from Vallance [of Quebec], who recaptured it but only to lose it to [McGill's] Foster. A scrimmage took place, when Foster again secured it and made a shot goal, passing the ball through (the goalposts). Time, 9 minutes.*[14]

No goals were scored in the second half, giving McGill a 1-0 win and the carnival championship.

McGill's win over Quebec allowed the university squad to claim the first-ever hockey championship. Team members earned a silver clasp, and as the winning club, McGill earned the newly minted Birks Carnival Cup, also called the Bedouin Cup, an ornate oval cup balanced on a tripod of hockey sticks and purchased at a cost of $750. A replica of the square wooden puck used in the games was placed under the Cup, but it has been lost through the years.[15] The trophy, which was considered symbolic of world championship, was inscribed with the names of each winning player, including captain Jack Kinloch, J. M. Elder, P. L. Foster, T. D. Green, goal-keeper Albert Low, W. L. Murray and Richard F. Smith. Curiously, referee N. T. Rielle also had his name engraved on the cup.[16] Today, the Birks Carnival Cup is exhibited at the McCord Museum of Canadian History, located on the McGill campus in Montreal.

* * *

That initial hockey championship, like the carnival in which it was held, was deemed a great success and was staged again in 1884. Newly appointed Governor General Sir Henry Petty-Fitzmaurice, the Marquess of Lansdowne, and his wife, Lady Maud Lansdowne, attended the Montreal Winter Carnival that year.

> *They have been present at every ball, every masquerade, every tobogganing hill; visited colleges, convents and schools; received and replied to addresses; attended organ recitals, skated, been photographed and, in fact, done everything graciously and pleasantly that an exacting people have desired.*[17]

Snowshoeing remained so popular that on February 6, 1884, the *Montreal Daily Star* devoted four full pages to the sport.

In the 1884 hockey tournament, the Montreal Victorias and the reigning champion McGill squad appeared for a second straight year, joined by the Montreal Crystals, the Montreal Wanderers and the newly formed Ottawa Hockey Club. Quebec declined to take part after having been snubbed by a Montreal team that missed a scheduled game earlier in the year in Quebec City. Organizers officially made the tournament a seven-player-per-side series, with most games played on the rink at McGill.

Heavy rains hampered the entire carnival, including the hockey tournament. Games played on the outdoor rink were challenging for the players and uncomfortable for fans. One fan ranted about having to pay the outrageous sum of fifty cents "to sit on the soft side of a pine plank."[18] There was great disappointment when Governor General Lansdowne failed to show for one of the games, but attended another one. One game was played indoors at the Victoria Rink, in spite of the ice grotto — and a snow sculpture — that rendered the rink ill suited to hockey. Several others were cancelled due to the weather. At the McGill Rink on 21 February, Ottawa ended up defeating the Victorias 3-0 to capture the world championship for 1884.

* * *

Although it wasn't the expected financial windfall, the Montreal Winter

Carnival of 1884 had been truly enjoyable, garnered positive media reaction and generated enough revenue to be held again in 1885.

The carnival had become so large that it was divided amongst two administrative groups. But whereas the first two carnivals had been largely geared towards English Montreal and Americans, the Montreal Winter Carnival of 1885 was staged by an Anglophone committee from the West End and a French-speaking group from the East End. The 1885 carnival was launched on 26 January.

The Governor General and his wife attended the carnival for a second straight winter. The Victoria Rink was bustling with excitement. At precisely nine o'clock on 27 January, the band of the Victoria Rifles began playing "God Save the Queen." The Governor General unveiled a bust of Queen Victoria, with images of snowshoers on either side. A fleet Father Time led a procession of costumed skaters in circles around the ice surface of the Victoria Rink. Montreal's daily *Gazette* described the activities:

> *Around the course this kaleidoscopic gathering revolved, imbued with the spirit of Puck, flashing with smiles, glittering with tinsel, grotesque with all manners and shapes of absurdities, charming with varied types of grace and beauty.*[19]

Although the ice castle maintained its presence as the central icon of the Winter Carnival, the East End committee introduced an exciting new idea. In the Champs-de-Mars, a public park that had been a military parade ground, the "Condora" was built from ice blocks. This structure was a cone fifty feet in diameter and rising to a height of a hundred feet, topped with a snow statue of a snowshoer that added an extra twenty-four feet to the height. During celebrations, hundreds of members of the snowshoe club, bearing torches, stood on the tiers that surrounded the Condora.

A third ice sculpture was that of a lion, perched on a pedestal twenty feet high and located in the Place d'Armes, adjacent to Notre-Dame Cathedral. The main portion of the sculpture was hollow and illuminated by electric lights, creating a magnificent effect for visitors to the Montreal Carnival.

Heavy snow fell on Montreal on 28 January, and the wind bit right through the blanket coats and furs worn by the revellers. The hockey tournament had been well regarded and was repeated, but this time, wisely, games were played indoors at the Crystal Rink, located on Dorchester near Dominion Square. Six teams entered this year: McGill, the Montreal Victorias, the Montreal Crystals, Ottawa, and two new additions, the Montreal Football Club and the Montreal Hockey Club, the latter of which was associated with the Montreal Amateur Athletic Association. R. F. Smith — ironically, a McGill graduate who had helped the Victorias win the championship the previous year — had helped form the Montreal A.A.A. in 1881 by merging the Montreal Bicycle Club, the Montreal Lacrosse Club and the Montreal Snowshoe Club. The 1-0 semifinal win for the Montreal Hockey Club against McGill took nine periods to decide. Then, it took twenty-five minutes of overtime before a "scoop shot" by Bill Aird of the Montreal Hockey Club scored to beat Ottawa 1-0 for the world title.

* * *

The Montreal Winter Carnival was not held in 1886. Bickering between English and French organizers had created conflict; the carnival had not made as much money as had been hoped. But there was one other, far more significant, reason: Montreal was in the midst of a raging smallpox epidemic.

Although it is believed that smallpox arrived in Montreal by way of an infected train porter from Chicago, then travelled through the hospital in which he was treated, sanitary conditions in Montreal were, sadly, conducive to the rapid spread of the contagious and often fatal disease characterized by a fever and a progressive skin rash that gives smallpox its nickname, the Red Death.

Sanitation in the city of two hundred thousand was deplorable. Because automobiles had not yet been introduced, most transportation was by horse-drawn carriage, leaving abundant piles of manure in the city's streets. In the poorer districts of the city, refuse was routinely thrown into the street. Dead animals floated in the harbour. Few residents had indoor plumbing, so human waste from shared outhouses often flowed into the streets. As the seasons changed and the snow melted away, it exposed the tremendous amount of filth that had been left behind. Most homes had piped-in water by now, but the water that flowed through the taps was entirely untreated. On some days, especially in the spring and fall, it was dangerous to drink water out of the tap. Germs and bacteria were extensive. Living quarters were cramped and filthy. The heat of a torrid summer added to the tensions, and stench, experienced in the city.

There was no specific treatment for smallpox, and the only prevention was vaccination. Vaccines, which had been successfully developed in England in 1796, were believed capable of eradicating the disease. But a theological debate on vaccination divided Protestants and Catholics, preventing the disease from being curtailed and isolated. English-speaking Protestants widely regarded vaccinations as a necessity and were inoculated, escaping almost entirely from the ravages of smallpox in 1885; on the other hand, a large percentage of Roman Catholic francophones clung to the hoary idea that smallpox was a judgement of God on the sins of His people, and that to avert it was to actually provoke Him further. Vaccinations were derided as "an encroachment on the prerogatives of Jehovah, whose right it is to wound and smite."[20] Many Roman Catholics lived in crowded, shabby quarters that were most susceptible to the spread of disease; by clinging to ancient theological fears and refusing inoculation, much of the community stayed firmly on a path that ended in death.

Public health officials tried to enforce vaccination, isolate those infected and even remove corpses; they were greeted not only with resistance but, in many cases, rioting. Falsehoods abounded: opponents insisted that vaccines propagated smallpox, or even introduced syphilis. Vaccinators were called charlatans bent on poisoning the children. Confusion reigned and resistance became hostile.

In an interview with *The Witness*, a sanitary inspector reported:

> *I passed a [Francophone household] recently in which there was smallpox and found quite a number of women and children 'round the door talking to the resident of the house. When I remonstrated with them, they replied that it was the 'good God' who sent the disease, that there was no use in fighting against it, and if not, they wouldn't. There is no use in reasoning with them. English-speaking people will do what you tell them, as they appreciate the necessity for precaution.*[21]

The Gazette reported that the French-speaking population was "singularly callous to the deadly character of the disease" and demanded compulsory vaccination, isolation and better conditions for the entire population of Montreal.

The Abbé Filiatrault, a priest at St. James the Apostle Church in Montreal, proselytized about the epidemic from the pulpit:

> *If we are afflicted with smallpox, it is because we had a carnival last winter, feasting the flesh, which has offended the Lord. It is to punish our pride that God has sent us smallpox.*

Many Roman Catholic parishes denounced the evils of Montreal's hedonistic Winter Carnival. The idea of young women promiscuously circling rinks on ice skates or fearlessly enjoying slides down toboggan glissoires, their long skirts swirling and exposing lower limbs, was too much for the clergy to bear.

An editorial in *l'Etendard* stated:

> *What is the real basis of our carnival? Only a folly invented by the devil. Everyone remembers the throngs of lost souls who have come here seeking death in the pleasures of the carnival. These accursed toboggan slides, the meeting place of depraved men and women! These altars where so many young girls have gone to dishonour themselves for life. We have trod a false path in choosing the revelry of carnival; we have taken a false way in building toboggan slides. We must no longer hesitate; we must make a full sacrifice and this sacrifice must be made to a merciful God who cannot fail to end this plague, the fruit of the disorders of carnival.*[22]

Visitors avoided visiting Montreal at all costs, and commerce fell off drastically. The Montreal Board of Trade held an emergency meeting on the first day of September 1885 to discuss the damage to their city's reputation. Indeed, every product manufactured in Montreal, from clothing to cigars, was suspect.

An effort was made to enforce compulsory vaccinations. The working-class poor living in the largely French neighbourhoods were encouraged to resist and take up arms as necessary rather than submit to vaccination. Police from all over the city were called upon to disperse angry mobs who hurled rocks and denounced the practice in the streets. The Oblate Fathers reinforced the anger, denouncing vaccination in spite of the fact most of their parishioners lived in the heart of the most infected district. The congregation was exhorted to rely on devotional exercises for divine intervention, praying to the Virgin Mary to save their infected city.

Between February 1885 and May 1886, 3,234 lives were lost to smallpox in Montreal. Of that total, an astonishing 91.2 percent were French-Canadian and 85.9 percent were children under the age of ten; 3.08 percent of the Roman Catholic population had died of smallpox, while 0.38 percent of the Protestant community was lost. Finally, humanity, reason and science won out and the horrific smallpox epidemic suffered by Montreal in 1885 and 1886 was brought to an end. The reason: better and more widespread treatments and a stricter observance of isolation meant that the disease had run out of unvaccinated targets.[23]

* * *

But while Montreal had more important things to worry about in 1886 than a Winter Carnival, just across the border, the town Burlington, Vermont, decided to adopt a similar idea, hosting "a week of winter sports, to which all the world should be welcome."[24] Burlington relied on assistance from Montrealers in presenting a carnival which, delayed a week by mild weather, took place between 22 and 26 February, 1886. One hundred fifty members of the Montreal Snowshoe Club, an arm of the Montreal Amateur Athletic Association, accepted an invitation from the Coasting Club of Burlington to help the Vermont city stage its carnival.[25]

As in previous years, a hockey tournament was also organized. Two Montreal teams, the Crystals and the Montreal Hockey Club from the M.A.A.A., agreed to participate in a tournament, as did the Ottawa Hockey Club, although the latter was forced to withdraw when the date of the carnival changed. The two Montreal squads played in the series along with a hastily formed local team from the Van Ness House, a hotel in Burlington. The three-team tournament was played on the sheltered Central Vermont Railway slip on Lake Champlain, and gold medals were awarded to the winning team and silver to the runners-up. In the first contest, the Montreal Hockey Club defeated the Crystals 1-0 in overtime. They then met Van Ness House in what can be regarded as the first international hockey game. In the late morning of 26 February, amidst gale-force winds whipping across Lake Champlain, the Montreal club prevailed over the locals, 3-0, to claim the gold medal. Van Ness then met the Crystals in the afternoon to decide the silver medal. The foul weather forced the reduction of the contest to two ten-minute periods, after which the Crystals had earned a 1-0 victory. "Hockey on the ice is one of the prettiest of carnival sports, with the coloured costumes of the players, their rapid movements and the feats of skill accomplished,"[26] reported the *Burlington Free Press*. "Hockey at once leaped into popularity on the part of those Burlingtonians who witnessed the game."[27]

* * *

After missing a year, the Montreal Winter Carnival was staged once again in 1887, although scheduling concerns with the rinks forced the hockey tournament to take place after the carnival had concluded. On 21 February, 1887, M.A.A.A. edged the Crystals, 1-0; two days later, the Victorias dumped McGill 5-1, and on 25 February, M.A.A.A. defeated the Victorias 1-0 to win the series. Members of the Montreal Amateur Athletic Association were recipients of diamond carnival pins.[28]

The carnival skipped 1888 and was held for a final time in 1889. But the festivities never enjoyed the same lustre associated with the first two carnivals. The Winter Carnivals were growing more and more expensive to produce, and they generated fierce arguments between the organizers. And while American interest increased substantially, local interest had waned.

* * *

During their first winter in Canada, the Stanley family were invited to be the special guests at Montreal's Winter Carnival. Lord Stanley was accompanied by his wife, Lady Constance; his eldest son, Captain Edward Stanley; daughter Isobel; military secretary Captain Charles Colville and his wife; aide-de-camp Captain Aubrey McMahon; and Miss Lister, Lady Stanley's assistant.

It may have been his vice regal duty to do so, but Stanley was nevertheless anxious to witness all the winter sporting activities his new homeland had to offer. He attended the carnival of 4-9 February, 1889, in its entirety.

The Dominion Illustrated Monthly commented:

Lord Stanley and his family will open their eyes on the glittering spectacle, and will doubtless not miss a single one of the events. Perhaps nothing will so impress the inmates of Rideau Hall with the winter pleasures of Montreal.[29]

While watching the snowshoeing, Lord Stanley was summoned by the Montreal Snowshoe Club, an arm of the Montreal A.A.A., and was, somewhat begrudgingly, tossed in the air by members in a custom known as "the bounce." It was a custom for special guests, winners of snowshoe races, or new members to the club to be tossed high into the air by a dozen or so members, and then caught in their arms as they fell. "Bouncing was a favourite amusement during carnival week," wrote *Outing*. "The distinction was one that was thrust upon one — not sought."[30] "The bounce" was a tradition performed with great enthusiasm by most snowshoe clubs at that time.

But the widespread popularity of snowshoeing was clearly waning in favour of ice skating and hockey. Historian Don Morrow offered this analysis: "Tobogganing and an old snowshoe nemesis, ice-skating and its rapidly emerging derivative, ice-hockey, popularized by the carnivals, captured public interest more fervently than walking or racing 'on three-feet long sieves.'"[31]

* * *

Lord Stanley and the vice regal suite witnessed their first-ever hockey game on 4 February, 1889, at the Victoria Skating Rink. The Montreal Hockey Club (M.A.A.A.), wearing the design of a white winged wheel on the fronts of their royal blue sweaters, protected one goal while the other was guarded by the Montreal Victorias, sporting maroon sweaters embellished with white Vs. Both teams were members of the recently organized Amateur Hockey Association of Canada.

While the contest progressed, play was interrupted by a herald of trumpets and the arrival of Lord Stanley and his party. Wearing fur coats and boots, the entourage shuffled down the length of the rink and took their seats alongside the ice surface. Jack Arnton, the captain of the Victorias, led all players in three cheers and a tiger for the distinguished visitor.

The Gazette described the game as "one of the finest exhibitions of Canada's national winter game." The Victorias won the contest by edging the Montreal Hockey Club, 2-1, after which "Lord Stanley expressed his great delight with the game of hockey and the expertise of the players." Stanley would have had but a passing awareness of hockey during that first winter in Canada. It is amusing to think that a name tied so inextricably to the modern sport would have witnessed his first game on that cold February day in 1889.

* * *

The Montreal Winter Carnival ceased to be held after 1889. The *Outing* sounded the carnival's death knell:

> *Though distinguished by the presence of thousands of visitors, the home spirit was gone. A reaction had set in, and Canadians began to feel that their cities and country were being looked upon as an abode of ice and snow.*[32]

Outing also lamented, "Although the Carnival and ice palace are a thing of the past, the memory of their brilliant and meteoric existence will be cherished by the thousands who were permitted to share in their glories."[33]

* * *

The Montreal Winter Carnival had done a tremendous amount to help catapult hockey to public prominence. Snowshoeing and tobogganing, although immensely popular during each of the five Winter Carnivals, never rose beyond amateur status. Skating certainly increased in popularity, but it was hockey that earned the greatest measure of favour from the thousands who attended the carnivals. "The winter carnivals at Montreal, beginning in 1883, gave the game its first great impetus, it gained rapidly in popular estimation and, to the visitors who thronged to the city, the hockey matches in the Victoria Rink were soon among the chief attractions," wrote Robert Tait Mackenzie, an elite athlete who attended McGill University beginning in 1885 and later became a celebrated sculptor. Spectators took enthusiasm for hockey back to their communities throughout Canada and the United States, helping expose the game to a broader, very receptive, audience.

As much as Lord Stanley had enjoyed witnessing his first hockey game, it was his son, his daughter and his ADC Aubrey McMahon who fell in love with the sport even more. Their enthusiasm for the fast-paced game elicited a desire to play hockey themselves, and informal games on the rink back in Ottawa at Rideau Hall gradually evolved into the formation of a team, the Rideau Rebels; the first women's hockey games; the formation of the Ontario Hockey Association; and, most astounding of all, the gift of hockey's most cherished prize — the Stanley Cup.

* * *

Canadian boys of the final decade of the nineteenth century became men in a worrisome time. The idea of manliness had been promoted by those Canadians who had a hand in organizing the nascent sport of ice hockey. By the outbreak of the First World War, many players who had been influenced, directly or indirectly, by the legacy of Frederick Arthur Stanley had already skated its dress rehearsal on the frozen ponds and new indoor rinks of Canada.

* * *

Soon after the Stanleys' arrival in Canada, *The Dominion Illustrated Monthly*, a periodical in which both Frederick and Constance appeared regularly, reported that Lady Stanley was:

> … *of good Whig stock — a daughter of the late Lord Clarendon; distinguished for his long and important services in the Foreign Office. Her Excellency is highly gifted with mental and physical accomplishments and, as such, will gracefully keep up the traditions of the three ladies who lived before her at Rideau Hall — a countess, a princess and a marchioness.*[34]

Later that same year, Lady Stanley would grace the cover of the same periodical.[35] While she may have possessed many of the same enviable characteristics of her three predecessors, Lady Stanley did not strictly follow the traditions at Rideau Hall insofar as keeping the status quo.

Lady Stanley's time in Canada was defined by her significant contribution to the state of hospitals in Ottawa. In 1888, she was elected president of the Ministering Children's League of Ottawa, which purchased property on which to build a hospital to accommodate forty-seven children. But her goodwill was met with resistance. "Lady Stanley made the mistake, in those fiercely sectarian days, of recommending that the hospital be non-denominational. The Protestant community, and especially the Anglican bishop, were furious, and Lady Stanley was forced to resign from the presidency and from the Ministering Children's League itself."[36]

Angry and embarrassed to suffer such humiliation, but unwavering in her devotion to the advancement of the treatment of illness, Lady Stanley led a campaign to build a facility in Ottawa in which to train nurses. She proposed the idea at a well-attended meeting held at City Hall on 18 February, 1890.

The idea was embraced, and the first step taken by the committee was to confirm that the proposed institution be called The Lady Stanley Institution for Trained Nurses, "in this way, certifying permanently with the name of Her Excellency, and to appoint her the Honorary President."[37] Lady Macdonald, the wife of the Prime Minister, was named honorary vice-president.

The Free Press continued:

> *On the twenty-first of May, 1891, the Institute, a seemly and substantial structure completed at a cost of $15,830 and well within the estimate, thoroughly equipped in every way and paid for in full to the utmost farthing, was formally opened by His Excellency, the Governor General, Lord Stanley of Preston, in the presence of a large and representative gathering of citizens of Ottawa, including most of the prominent clergymen.*[38]

Located immediately next to the Protestant Hospital, the Lady Stanley Institute was opened on May 21, 1891, with Lady Stanley as its honorary president. Lady Stanley was lauded for her "untiring efforts towards making it a success."[39] Lord Stanley spoke on behalf of his wife, and said that he felt "so proud that one so near and dear to him had been associated with such a movement."[40]

If Frederick's father, Edward Geoffrey Stanley, had been a Tory with a heart, and his brother Edward Henry a relatively liberal-minded aristocrat, Governor General Stanley had a comparatively modern sensibility culled from a lifetime spent in one of Britain's leading families at a time when that nation was making terrific social advances in a short period of time. Considering Lady Stanley's express wish that a new Ottawa hospital be nondenominational, coupled with Lord Stanley's varied social initiatives, Canada could be assured that the family residing at Rideau Hall would be rather progressive for the nineteenth century.

Nevertheless, early on in Stanley's term in Canada, he discovered that the Governor General had, on more than one occasion, to set clear limits as to how far the vice regal party could extend its hospitality. On one such occasion, Stanley's secretary had to explain the details of Stanley's rejection of a charitable institution to the Prime Minister's Office:

> *On the 14th of January, the Governor General went to the Convent of the Good Shepherd along with Lady Stanley and Lady Macdonald, the Prime Minister's wife. While there, he was asked by Madame de Bonald for the use of the Ballroom at Rideau Hall to be used for a performance which would provide funding for the institution. His Excellency himself would be disposed to say that he regrets that he could not allow the use of the Ballroom, and he feels, moreover, that the Institution, being one principally for fallen women, does not itself possess quite that character for which an exception should be made.*[41]

The request had fallen on the wrong side of the boundary in 1889, a fact of which Stanley was acutely mindful.

* * *

On January 31, 1889, the Governor General, along with military secretary Captain Charles Colville and an aide-de-camp, was driven by carriage from Rideau Hall in the company of a mounted escort from the Princess Louise Dragoon Guards. In front of the Parliament Buildings, waiting to greet His Excellency, was a detachment from the Governor General's Foot Guards. Lord Stanley acknowledged the throng waiting on Parliament Hill to catch a glimpse of him as he arrived at the Senate Chamber to open the 1889 session of the Dominion Parliament. The Governor General's remarks were as follows:

> *In addressing the Parliament of Canada for the first time, in fulfillment of the important trust which has been committed to me as Her Majesty's Representative, I desire to express the satisfaction with which I resort to you for advice and assistance.*
>
> *I am conscious of the honour which attends my association with your labours for the welfare of the Dominion and it will be my earnest endeavour to co-operate with you, to the utmost of my power, in all that may promote the prosperity of the people of this country, the development of her material resources and the maintenance of the constitutional ties which unite her provinces.*
>
> *It is to be regretted that the treaty concluded between Her Majesty and the President of the United States for the adjustment of the questions which have arisen with reference to 'The Fisheries' has not been sanctioned by the United States Senate, in whom the power of ratification is vested; and that out legislation of last year on the subject is therefore in a great measure inoperative.*
>
> *It now only remains for Canada to continue to maintain her rights as prescribed by the Convention of 1818, until some satisfactory re-adjustment is arranged by treaty between the two nations.*
>
> *During the recess, my Government has carefully considered the subject of Ocean Steam Service, and you will be asked to provide subsidies for the improvement of the Atlantic Mail Service, and for the establishment, in concert with Her Majesty's Government, of a line of fast steamers between British Columbia and China and Japan. Your attention will also be invited to the best mode of developing our trade and securing direct communication by steam with Australasia, the West Indies and South America.*
>
> *Several measures will also be presented to you for*

improving the law of procedure in criminal cases. Among these will be a Bill to permit the release on probation of persons convicted of first offences, a Bill authorizing regulations to be made for the practice in cases partaking of the nature of criminal proceedings, and a Bill to make the Speedy Trial Act applicable throughout Canada.

Bills relating to the inspection of timber and lumber, for the improvement of the Postal System, and for increasing the efficiency of the North-West Mounted Police, will also be submitted for your consideration.[42]

* * *

Before departing for England in 1893, Lady Stanley wrote to Lady Aberdeen, her successor that "the walls are absolutely bare — we brought out a large collection of old prints we happened to have."[43] And although neither Lord nor Lady Stanley seemed to take any particular interest in art — unlike the 14th Earl of Derby, who had amassed an extraordinary collection at the family estate in Knowsley — Lord Stanley attended at least one exhibition of the Royal Canadian Academy of Art. The Academy, under the patronage of Queen Victoria's daughter, Princess Louise, and her husband, the Marquis of Lorne, Governor General of Canada between 1878 and 1882, had been created in 1880 and included the works of painters, sculptors, architects and designers. During March 1889, Lord Stanley congratulated the members of the association for their impressive exhibits arranged around the hall. "He expressed the hope that the young artists of Canada would persevere in their noble calling and made a mark for themselves and be a credit to their country."[44]

* * *

Lord Stanley hosted a luncheon in early May, 1889, at Rideau Hall for the Royal Society of Canada, of which he was a patron. Founded in 1882 by Governor General Lorne, the Royal Society of Canada is a national body of distinguished Canadian scientists and scholars intent on promoting research in the arts and sciences by making its members' knowledge available for the good of all Canadians.

Sir Sandford Fleming, the Society's president, stated:

> *We feel that a Society that has the cultivation of literature as one of its principal objects has a special claim on Your Excellency's attention. All of us remember with the deepest interest that your illustrious father, in his youth, won many academic honours in the study of the great poets of ancient days. In the noted oratorical efforts of his brilliant career, he displayed that fire and energy which were characteristic of the heroes of the immortal epic he had mastered so well. While the political historian will record his triumphs as the 'Rupert of Debate,' men of letters will like best to linger on his success in rendering the* Iliad *into matchless English verse.*[45]

In 1865, the 14th Earl used profits from the *Iliad*'s translation for an endowment to Wellington College, Berkshire. The award is known as the Earl of Derby's Gift.

Lord Stanley didn't share his father's passion for literature.

---

[1] Guards' Chapel, *Royal Military Chapel: Wellington Barracks* (London: Hatchards, 1882).

[2] *Dominion Monthly Illustrated* (12 January, 1889), p.18.

[3] V. Stanley, *Letter to his Mother, Lady Constance Stanley*, (6 January, 1889); Churchill, *Lord Derby*, p.28.

[4] Churchill, *Lord Derby: King of Lancashire*, p.30.

[5] *Globe and Mail* (2 November, 2006).

[6] *Montreal Gazette* (13 February, 1882).

[7] *Harper's Bazaar* (8 March, 1884).

[8] J. W. Fitsell, *Hockey's Captains, Colonels and Kings* (Erin: Boston Mills Press, 1987), p.44.

[9] M. Bliss, *Plague: A Story of Smallpox in Montreal* (Toronto: Harper Collins, 1991), p.4.

[10] *Harper's Bazaar* (March 8, 1884).

[11] Hamilton, *The Days Before Yesterday*.

[12] *Harper's Bazaar* (8 March, 1884).

[13] Ibid.

[14] *Montreal Daily Star* (27 January, 1883), p.7.

[15] K. Shea, *Interview with Bill Fitsell*, founding President of the Society for International Hockey Research (8 January, 2006).

[16] *Montreal Daily Star* (27 January, 1883), p.7.

[17] *Harper's Bazaar* (8 March, 1884).

[18] Fitsell, *Hockey's Captains, Colonels & Kings*, p.47.

[19] *Montreal Gazette* (28 January, 1885).

[20] A. D. White, *A History of the Warfare of Science with Theology in Christendom* (New York: D. Appleton & Company, New York, 1896), p.63.

21 Bliss, *Plague*, p.95.

22 Ibid.

23 Ibid.

24 P. Kitchen, 'Hockey on the Lake', D. Diamond, J. Duplacey, R. Dinger, E. Fitzsimmons, I. Kuperman & E. Zweig (eds) *Total Hockey: The Official Encyclopaedia of the National Hockey League, Second Edition*, (Toronto: Dan Diamond & Associates, 2000), pp.20–1.

25 W. Whyte, 'Montreal Amateur Athletic Association', *Outing* (New York: April, 1888).

26 *Burlington Free Press* (February 1886).

27 Kitchen, 'Hockey on the Lake', p.20.

28 E. Zukerman, 'McGill University', D. Diamond, J. Duplacey, R. Dinger, E. Fitzsimmons, I. Kuperman & E. Zweig (eds) *Total Hockey: The Official Encyclopaedia of the National Hockey League*, Second Edition, (Toronto: Dan Diamond & Associates, 2000), pp.16-9.

29 *Dominion Monthly Illustrated* (9 February, 1889), p.83.

30 'The Passing of the Ice Carnival', *Outing* (New York: January 1889), p.362.

31 D. Morrow, 'The Knights of the Snowshoe', *Journal of Sports History* (Spring 1988).

32 'The Passing of the Ice Carnival', pp.360-363.

33 Ibid.

34 *Dominion Monthly Illustrated* (7 July, 1888), p.7.

35 *Dominion Monthly Illustrated* (10 November, 1888), *edition cover page*. Lord Stanley also appeared on the cover of the same periodical. See, *The Dominion Monthly Illustrated* (14 July, 1888), *edition cover page*.

36 Canada's Governors General At Play, James Noonan, Borealis Press, Nepean, 2002, p181

37 The Lady Stanley Institute for Trained Nurses, (Ottawa: Free Press Office, 1892), p.6.

38 Ibid

39 Ibid.

40 *Ottawa Daily Citizen* (22 May, 1891).

41 Cpt. Charles Colville, *Letter to Mr. Pope, the Prime Minister's secretary, Sir John A. Macdonald Papers* (National Archives of Canada).

42 Library of Parliament, Parliament of Canada website, *www.parl.gc.ca*.

43 R. H. Hubbard, *Rideau Hall: An Illustrated History of Government House, Ottawa, from Victorian Times to the Present Day* (Montreal: McGill-Queen's, Montreal, 1977), p.71.

44 *Ottawa Daily Citizen* (Ottawa: 14 March, 1889), p.4.

45 *Ottawa Daily Citizen* (Ottawa: 9 May, 1889), p.4.

CHAPTER NINE

1889 — The Behring Sea Question

In the summer of 1889, the United States Senate rejected Canada's proposed Fisheries Treaty, leaving in its wake an increasing ripple in Canadian–American relations.

Prime Minister Macdonald often took John Thompson, the Minister of Justice and chief Canadian negotiator with the United States on fishing rights, as well as a future prime minister, into his confidence. Macdonald wrote Thompson for advice:

> From [Sir Julian] Pauncefote's note to the Governor General, it is clear that Lord Salisbury won't move, but shall wait for a move from the United States. And they won't move. Now shall we? And if yes, in what mode or direction? The modus vivendi will expire next February and our troubles will recommence. We must not like so many foolish virgins sit with our lamps untrimmed.

It was true that the *modus vivendi* was an ephemeral repair to the question of the fisheries and that it was to soon expire.

James G. Blaine, the U.S. Secretary of State during Grover Cleveland's tenure as president, was plainly contrary to Canadian interests. Macdonald feared Blaine's political rise and had privately expressed his fears to Lord Lansdowne before Blaine's appointment as Secretary of State, "[Blaine] would do everything disagreeable short of war, and perhaps if England had trouble elsewhere, go further."[1] Upon Pauncefote's appointment as the British minister at Washington, Blaine immediately called for a renewal of fur-seal negotiations.

Through Stanley, Macdonald accepted the proposal, provided that the Americans abandon their "claim to jurisdiction" in the Behring Sea and that Canada be represented directly during the negotiations and on any proposed joint commissions that might result.[2] Macdonald's conditions were flatly refused; moreover, the Americans continued to take a most exasperating line of reasoning — namely that they had never asserted the *mare clausum* and, as such, had no reason to abandon a claim that never had taken place. This was, of course, completely contradictory to American action, as officers on American patrol ships were consistently seizing Canadian vessels in mid-ocean. There were other issues with the American reply. Blaine opted for the less formal "diplomatic conference" rather than any formal commission.

The United States had consistently opted to dealing with Great Britain in issues regarding the Dominion. It was a clever strategy, but it was becoming less manageable as the Canadian contingent, rightly, wanted to be more involved in matters that directly affected them. Initial discourse called for experts and opinions of American, British and Russian — and not Canadian — representatives. This meagre attempt at a joint convention, like those that came before, also failed and was judged by some to be simply a waiting game for the United States, which was keen to avoid arbitration.

And still there was talk of aggressive action. For their part, Macdonald and the Canadians considered sending a British man-of-war to the Behring Sea so as to support Canadian sealers and protect them against the police authority under which the Americans had been operating. In a telegram from Sir Charles Tupper in August 1889, Macdonald was presented with the true gravity of the situation:

> *… had long interview with Lords Salisbury and Knutsford and Sir John [Julian] Pauncefote yesterday, which I will communicate by letter. Foreign minister annoyed by reported seizure which he says is violation of engagement made by United States not to seize vessels pending settlement question. I think if Government presses strongly at*

present moment for Ship of War to be sent immediately charged to prevent any further seizures in open waters of Behring's Sea, it would be granted.[3]

Macdonald knew full well just what this meant and said as much to Stanley: "This would be a serious step and before offering Your Excellency any advise on the subject, I should like very much to have the advantage of your opinion."[4] For his part, Stanley knew that any hasty muscle-flexing would help neither diplomatic nor commercial interests in the Dominion. In his response, Stanley told Macdonald:

> *I think that the proposal to send a Ship of War to Behring Sea (or North Pacific) is not one which the Dominion Government should undertake the responsibility of making. I do not necessarily mean that we should oppose it if the Home Government should so decide, but the initiative should be with them for the Foreign Office has the duty of maintaining international rights and they should be settled, in principle, through the usual diplomatic channels.*[5]

Although Stanley had given Macdonald a cautious and measured response, he had by no means ruled out the possibility of an aggressive course of action in the Pacific, and Macdonald agreed to let Westminster lead the way.

The position of British minister at Washington was an extremely important one, and in these times of national uncertainty in Canada, it was an engagement that one might consider the most important calling next to the Prime Minister of Canada himself. Still, it was a British minister at Washington and not a Canadian one, a reality that John A. Macdonald endorsed. Macdonald wrote to Tupper, soon to be Canada's Minister of Marine and Fisheries and an eventual successor to Macdonald:

> *I greatly doubt the expediency of having a Canadian permanent minister at Washington. The present system of uniting the British minister ordinarily appointed with a Canadian whenever a question affecting Canada arises works more satisfactorily than the proposed change.*[6]

Over time, however, Macdonald might have reconsidered this declaration, given the Behring Sea debacle and Canada's constant struggle to have its voice heard, independent of the mother country.

* * *

In the presidential elections of November 1888, Benjamin Harrison defeated the incumbent Grover Cleveland. Prime Minister Macdonald was initially encouraged by the character sketch of Harrison; in a letter to Stanley, he wrote that Harrison "is a firm man who will think for himself and not be dominated by Blaine."[7] Lord Salisbury, in a letter to Stanley, echoed Macdonald's impression that Harrison might be friendlier to Canadian interests: "I think it is very likely we shall get on better with Harrison than with Cleveland."[8]

In the summer of 1889, the *Black Diamond*, a British sealer was captured by the United States for violating one of the statutes that President Harrison had incorporated into his proclamation regarding the seal fisheries. The particular statute that was allegedly violated was one that forbade the "killing by unauthorized persons of seal and other fur-bearing animals within the limits of Alaska or in the water thereof."[9] The statute called for the forfeiture of the offending vessel and either a fine of between two hundred and a thousand dollars or imprisonment for a period of up to six months, or both. Surprisingly, the *Black Diamond* "escaped" to Victoria with neither forfeiture nor fine. This puzzled the Canadian press:

> *If an understanding exists with Great Britain by which the latter power permits such capture and search ... it ought to be duly proclaimed to all commanders of vessels, so that they might be on their guard against infringing the international law or convention.*[10]

Many Canadians expected more from the mother country. Still, the seizure of the *Black Diamond*, on some level, alerted the British to the seriousness of America's policy regarding the waters "thereof"; there had been a lull in the seizure of British vessels since 1886, when three vessels, the *Carolena*, the *Onward* and the *Thornton*, were charged with sealing in the Alaska Territory.

Sir Julian Pauncefote, a rather distinguished British minister, replaced Sackville at Washington in the autumn of 1889. Tupper, however, felt that Pauncefote, in the interest of good diplomatic relations between the United States and Great Britain, sold matters of Canadian interest too cheaply to the Americans. The British position in the matter was somewhat vague, and it perplexed Canadians throughout the Dominion.

American fishers and sealers had enjoyed a *modus vivendi* that allowed them to fish and hunt off the coasts of the Dominion. As American actions grew more hostile towards its neighbour, Canadian politicians began to push to renege on this understanding and supported the refusal of licenses to American vessels. Stanley, however, was able to implore Canada and the colony of Newfoundland to continue to grant such licences for the upcoming fishing season of 1889.[11]

Because of the U.S.'s new policy regarding the Behring Sea, however, it was decidedly not business as usual for Canadian sealers. As Prime Minister Macdonald related to Stanley, the seizure and confiscation of Canadian vessels "paralyzes our seal fisheries. They [Canadian sealers], as a rule, will not proceed to the fishing grounds for fear of capture."[12] Macdonald added that only a "few bold men" were risking the consequences as to continue their work.

By the fall of 1889, Stanley began to recognize more and more that the Canadian voice was not being heard in Washington. In a letter to Macdonald, he showed a hint of frustration with Salisbury and his dealings with Washington, an opinion Stanley had been developing in Britain before taking the vice regal appointment, "Before I left England … the Russian Ambassador had backed up the American claim and I think that the joint pressure of Russian and the U.S. had had rather more effect on [Salisbury] than we should quite like out here."[13]

Indeed, the Russian minister in Washington was, in Pauncefote's opinion, Blaine's alter ego.[14] At the same time, Stanley recognized Salisbury's predicament and knew that, in order for the British representative to secure any favourable outcome as far as Canadian interests were concerned, he would need some direction. As Stanley explained:

> *How far could we go, for instance, as to a close time for seals? The American proposal was of course inadmissible being wholly one-sided. But have we no counter proposi-*

*tion to make? I don't mean that we should make it now, but
I want to answer Lord Salisbury if he says — 'this is all very
well but what do you propose beyond a simple negative?'*[15]

But the counter-proposal was doomed to meet the same fate that earlier
Canadian proposals had met with in a Congress set on creating a nuisance
for Britain by driving the Dominion of Canada to distraction.

---

[1] J. A. Macdonald, *Letter to Lansdowne, Lansdowne Papers* (Ottawa: 28 September, 1889).

[2] Creighton, *John A. Macdonald*, p.532.

[3] C. Tupper, *Telegram to J. A. Macdonald*, reprinted in, J. A. Macdonald, *Letter to F. A. Stanley, Lord Stanley of Preston Papers*, from the Public Archives of Canada in London (Riviere Du Loup: 3 August, 1889).

[4] J. A. Macdonald, *Letter to F. A. Stanley, Lord Stanley of Preston Papers*, from the Public Archives of Canada in London (Riviere Du Loup: 3 August, 1889).

[5] F. A. Stanley, *Letter to J. A. Macdonald, Lord Stanley of Preston Papers*, from the Public Archives of Canada in London (Quebec: 4 August, 1888).

[6] J. A. Macdonald, *Letter to Tupper, Macdonald Papers* (Ottawa: 16 November, 1888).

[7] J. A. Macdonald, *Letter to F. A. Stanley, Lord Stanley of Preston Papers*, from the Public Archives of Canada in London (Ottawa: 15 November, 1888).

[8] Lord Salisbury, *Letter to F. A. Stanley, Lord Stanley of Preston Papers*, from the Public Archives of Canada in London (London: 5 December, 1888).

[9] *The Dominion Monthly Illustrated* (Montreal: 10 August, 1889), p.82.

[10] Ibid.

[11] J. A. Macdonald, *Letter to F. A. Stanley, Lord Stanley of Preston Papers*, from the Public Archives of Canada in London (Ottawa: 30 March, 1889).

[12] J. A. Macdonald, *Letter to F. A. Stanley, Lord Stanley of Preston Papers*, from the Public Archives of Canada in London (Ottawa: 21 June, 1889).

[13] F. A. Stanley, *Letter to J. A. Macdonald, Lord Stanley of Preston Papers*, from the Public Archives of Canada in London (Quebec: 6 September, 1889).

[14] J. Pauncefote, *Letter to F. A. Stanley, Lord Stanley of Preston Papers*, from the Public Archives of Canada in London (Washington: 17 March, 1890).

[15] F. A. Stanley, *Letter to J. A. Macdonald, Lord Stanley of Preston Papers*, from the Public Archives of Canada in London (Quebec: 6 September, 1889).

CHAPTER TEN

The Son of Love — Stanley's Western Canadian Trip

The Dominion of Canada that Lord Stanley encountered upon his investiture as governor general in 1888 was vastly different than the nation we know today. At that time, the country was made up of seven provinces — Nova Scotia, Prince Edward Island, New Brunswick, Quebec, Ontario, Manitoba and British Columbia — as well as eight districts. The Northwest Territories were created in 1870 when the Hudson's Bay Company transferred its holdings (Rupert's Land and the North-West Territory) to the government of the Dominion of Canada. Portions of the vast region were carved out to form provinces, while the remainder was divided into a series of districts. At the time of Lord Stanley's arrival in Canada, the North-West Territory comprised the District of Franklin (including the modern-day Arctic islands and Boothia and Melville Peninsula), the District of Ungava (made up of what we today know as northern Quebec, inland Labrador and an area of land within Hudson Bay), the District of Mackenzie (today's mainland Northwest Territories and western Nunavut), the District of Athabasca (northern Alberta and northern Saskatchewan), the District of Saskatchewan (central Saskatchewan), the District of Assiniboia (modern-day southern Saskatchewan) the District of Alberta (southern Alberta) and the District of Keewatin, (comprising modern-era northern Manitoba, northwestern

Ontario and southern Nunavut). Yukon was administered as part of the North-West Territory. Newfoundland and the coastal portion of Labrador were British possessions but not yet part of Canada; instead, they formed the separate Dominion of Newfoundland.

According to the federal census, the Dominion of Canada had a population of 4,800,000 spread across 3,559,294 square miles of land in 1891. As it is today, the vast majority of that population lived within 185 miles of the 5,525-mile-long border between Canada and the United States.[1] It was a top priority for the government of Canada to populate the vast areas of Canada, specifically in the west, with settlers who would clear the land and form communities which, it was hoped, would someday grow into cities.

During Lord Stanley's tenure as Governor General, farming was far and away Canada's main industry. In 1886, just prior to Lord Stanley's arrival, Parliament authorized the Department of Agriculture to build five research stations across the country to determine the best livestock breeds, plant varieties and farming methods for the different regions in Canada. Four hundred and sixty-six acres of land on the western periphery of Ottawa were purchased for the Experimental Farm which would act as headquarters. Towns and cities were just beginning to flourish, aided by the development and application of electricity and transportation systems that included railways and streetcars.

As it laid its tracks across the continent in the 1880s, the Canadian Pacific Railway became involved in the sale and settlement of land. Under the franchise granted to it by Sir John A. Macdonald's government, the company received twenty-five million acres of land in a belt that paralleled the CPR right of way. This property was disbursed under the auspices of the company's Land Department in Winnipeg until 1912, when the responsibility was transferred to the federal Department of Natural Resources.

When the *Toronto Star* listed its "New Seven Wonders of the World" in 2006, the paper included the Canadian Pacific Railway along with the Code of Hammurabi, the Ford Model T and the British Empire.[2]

The CPR was hailed for its role in helping build the fledgling Dominion of Canada, including the settlement of the Canadian west at a time when the United States coveted the vast territory. In 1887, future United States President Theodore Roosevelt stated that:

It would have been well for all America if we had insisted even more than we did upon the extension northward of our boundaries. British Columbia, Saskatchewan and Manitoba would, as states of the American Union, hold positions incomparably more important, grander and more dignified than they ever hope to reach either as independent communities or as provincial dependencies of a foreign power that regards them with a kindly tolerance somewhat akin to contemptuous indifference.[3]

In 2006, the *Toronto Star* wrote:

The CPR created an east-west commercial corridor to diminish the southward pull of an immensely larger neighbouring economy, and fed central Canadian manufacturers with the prodigious raw materials of the west. The CPR was the first Canadian mega-project, and set the pattern of corporate welfare and government-private sector partnerships — and the scandals that have sometimes arisen from them — that lingers to this day.[4]

* * *

In the mid-1800s, approximately fifty thousand people, almost all of them aboriginal, occupied the area we today know as British Columbia. But with the discovery of gold in the Fraser River valley in 1858, the complexion of the region changed drastically. Between April and September of 1858, thirty thousand people flooded into the area, hoping to benefit from the gold rush.

Britain had established the colony of Vancouver Island in 1849, and at that time fewer than five hundred British settlers lived in the area, almost all of them employees of the Hudson's Bay Company at Fort Victoria. But with the gold rush less than a decade later, the population ballooned to five thousand. In order to strengthen its hold on the area, Britain established the colony of British Columbia on the mainland.

The gold rush brought a flood of settlers to the area, including many from the United States. Although British culture dominated the area, ties to the United States were strong. The two western colonies combined into one in 1866, and Victoria was chosen as the seat of government. But the exorbitant costs incurred in building roads and other infrastructure proved staggering. And in 1867, when the United States purchased Alaska, there were legitimate fears that the U.S. would try to link its western territories by annexing British Columbia.

As Ontario, Quebec, New Brunswick and Nova Scotia negotiated their entry into Confederation in 1867, British Columbia asked the Colonial Office in England for appropriate provisions that would allow its entry as well. The Colonial Office cited a major stumbling block: the vast expanse of Hudson's Bay Company land, several thousand miles wide, which separated British Columbia from Canada. Although there was substantial interest in the proposal, the newly born Dominion of Canada would need to acquire the North-Western Territory and Rupert's Land before its reach could truly extend "from sea to sea."

The Canadian government's purchase of the two territories from the Hudson's Bay Company paved the way for British Columbia to join Confederation. Three delegates were sent from British Columbia to Ottawa in June 1870 to open negotiations. Canada agreed to each of the provisions they brought up, including assumption of the colonial debt and construction of a railway link, to be started within two years and completed in ten.

British Columbia entered Confederation on 19 July, 1871. Crowds gathered in Victoria to celebrate the new beginning. Roman candles were set off, and at midnight, bells rang throughout the town. A twenty-one-gun salute was fired by the frigate *HMS Zealous*, which was anchored in the port at nearby Esquimalt.

The next day, the *British Colonist* wrote:

> *Today, British Columbia passed peacefully and, let us add, gracefully, into the confederated empire of British North America. Perhaps it would be more proper to put it thus: today, the confederated empire of British North America stretches to the shores of the Pacific, 'whose limpid waters,' to quote the poetic language of Mr. J. Spencer Thompson, 'leave in baptismal welcome the brow of the newborn Province which forms the last link in the transcontinental chain — the last star in the constellation which is destined hereafter to shine so brightly in the northern hemisphere.*[5]

The next year, charges were made in Parliament that Prime Minister Sir John A. Macdonald's Conservative government had accepted campaign funds totalling $360,000 from shipping magnate Sir Hugh Allan, the wealthiest man in Canada, in return for the contract to build the transcontinental railway. The Prime Minister argued that the contributions and the railway contract were mutually exclusive, but his argument was met with scepticism, and on 5 November, 1873, he was forced to resign in disgrace. The Liberals, under new Prime Minister Alexander Mackenzie, were opposed to the idea of a railway stretching to the west coast, in spite of the fact it was one of the promises made when British Columbia became a province.

George Walkem, British Columbia's premier, travelled to London that year to discuss the situation with Lord Carnarvon, the Colonial Secretary, and he was prepared to pull British Columbia out of Confederation. Carnarvon recommended that Canada increase its financial commitment to the railway and that the deadline for its completion be extended to 1890. Premier Walkem returned to Victoria, where the battle cry "Carnarvon or Separation" raged — either the Canadian government lived up to the promises made to British Columbians, or the province was prepared to withdraw from the confederacy.

With no progress made, Walkem made a desperate personal appeal to Queen Victoria in 1876. An intractable Prime Minister Mackenzie replied, "Columbians were a selfish aggregation of persons taking advantage of an improvident bargain." Second and third appeals were made to the Queen in 1878. In September of that year, Premier Walkem even went so far as to formally ask for his province's withdrawal from the Dominion of Canada.

But a month later, on 16 October, the Conservatives defeated Mackenzie's Liberals and returned Sir John A. MacDonald to the prime ministerial position. "Until a railway is completed," stated Macdonald, "our Dominion is little more than a geographical expression. With the railway, once finished, we become one great united country with a large interprovincial trade and a common interest."[6]

With a new mandate, Macdonald attacked the railway project with renewed vigour. A new syndicate, unrelated to that of Hugh Allan, was awarded the contract to build the Pacific railway on 21 October, 1880. The consortium consisted of Richard Angus, James Hill, John Kennedy, Duncan McIntyre and George Stephen, with Donald Smith and Norman Kittson as significant but silent partners. They asked for, and received, twenty-five million dollars and a grant of twenty-five million acres. On 15 February, 1881, the contract received Royal assent, and the Canadian Pacific Railway Corporation was incorporated the next day. The government transferred the sections of railway already built as a public-works project under Mackenzie's direction and exempted the CPR from property taxes for twenty years.

Besides the geographic obstacles that stood in the way of completing the railway, there were political stumbling blocks. For instance, much of the central route needed to traverse land controlled by the Blackfoot Nation, a collection of distinct tribes — the Siksika (Blackfoot), Akainawa (Blood) and Pikanii (Piegan), as well as allies the Tsuu T'ina (Sarcee) and Nakosa (Stoney). Father Albert Lacombe, an Oblate priest and missionary who had served as a mediator between the feuding Cree and Blackfoot tribes, was secured by the CPR to negotiate a land agreement between the government of Canada and the Blackfoot Nation, an agreement that came to be known as Treaty 7. Father Lacombe persuaded Siksika chief Issap'mahkikaaw, better known as Crowfoot, to accept a pittance in exchange for approximately thirty-five thousand square miles of land. Each man, woman and child would receive a one-time payment of twelve dollars. Each chief would receive a medal, a flag, a Winchester rifle, an annual payment of twenty-five dollars and a new suit of clothing every three years. Each tribe member would receive five dollars each year. Each tribe would also receive teachers, ten axes, five handsaws, five augers and a grindstone. Every family, depending on size, would receive either cattle or farming implements — a plough, spade, hoes, scythe plus potatoes, wheat, barley and oats.

Treaty 7 was signed on 22 September, 1877, at So-yo-pow-ahx-ko, also known as Blackfoot Crossing, located on the Siksika Reserve in Gleichen, east of Calgary. David Laird, Lieutenant Governor and Indian Superintendent of the North-West Territory, and James F. MacLeod, Commissioner of the North-West Mounted Police, signed on behalf of Queen Victoria, while fifty-one head chiefs, minor chiefs and councillors from the various tribes were involved.

Construction began, slowly, in 1881 — so slowly, in fact, that the CPR hired American railway executive William Cornelius Van Horne to oversee construction. He was promised a generous bonus on top of an already handsome salary if the project was finished on time. By 1883, tracks were laid as far as the Rocky Mountains, while 1884 and much of 1885 were spent crossing the mountains of British Columbia.

Thousands of "navvies" — slang for navigators — were hired to construct the railway. Many were immigrant men lured by the promise of steady work and reasonable pay. Chinese navvies, disparagingly referred to as "coolies," were paid less than their counterparts and were often relegated to the more dangerous jobs, such as deploying explosives to clear rock. Safety was secondary to progress and profit — instead of dynamite, the crews used nitro-glycerine, a less expensive but more volatile explosive. Of the fifteen thousand navvies employed to build tracks over the treacherous terrain of the Fraser Valley, an estimated seven to eight hundred lost their lives. Most of the dead were Chinese.[7]

Some sections of the railway through the Rockies cost almost half a million dollars a mile to build. By the beginning of 1884, the railway was on the verge of bankruptcy. On 31 January, 1884, the government passed the Railway Relief Bill, providing a further $22.5 million in loans to the CPR. The bill received Royal assent on 6 March, 1884.

In March 1885, the North-West Rebellion broke out in Saskatchewan. Van Horne vowed to the government that the CPR could transport troops to Fort Qu'Appelle within eleven days — the trip was made in nine. The feat was particularly astonishing given that sections of the track had not yet been completed or had not yet been used. The rebellion was quelled, and in gratitude, the CPR's debt to the Government of Canada was reorganized and another five million dollars was extended.

* * *

Donald Smith, later Lord Strathcona, had immigrated to Canada from his native Scotland in 1838 and, after acquiring a position with the Hudson's Bay Company, rose quickly through the ranks, eventually becoming the powerful company's governor, a position he held from 1889 until 1914.

The company had evolved from a fur-trading concern into a land and colonization company, and with Smith as its executive officer in Canada, the company made considerable strides in helping develop western Canada. He was appointed president of the HBC's Council of the Northern Department and briefly served as governor of Assiniboia, which later was to become part of the province of Saskatchewan. In his role, Smith played a leading role in reorganizing his company's operations in Canada's northwest.

In attempting to find methods of improving the Hudson's Bay Company's transportation requirements, Smith entered into discussions that led to his involvement in the creation of a transcontinental railway. Although originally a silent but important shareholder in the fledgling Canadian Pacific Railway, Smith was made a director of the corporation in 1883. On 7 November, 1885, in a ceremony at Craigellachie, British Columbia, Smith was chosen to drive the ceremonial last spike. Immortalized in what author Pierre Berton called "the great Canadian photograph," the event is one of the most important in Canada's history. The railway stretched thirty-seven hundred miles to unite the seven provinces and eight districts that were included within the boundaries of the Dominion of Canada.

It has also been suggested that the CPR played an even more significant role than simply bridging the continent: it saved Canada for the Empire. The United States had taken a very serious interest in Canada's western geography, and the steel rails that now crossed that land solidified Canada as a country, rather than a series of disparate regions.

Smith was involved in a number of other areas as well. In 1872, he was appointed to the board of the Bank of Montreal and was named president in 1887. That same year, he was elected as a member of Parliament as an independent Conservative for Montreal West.

Smith's accomplishments earned him many accolades and honours. In April 1886, acknowledging his role in helping build the CPR, Smith was made a Knight Commander of the Order of St. Michael and St. George, an honour bestowed for "services rendered to the Crown in relation to the foreign affairs of the Empire." Eleven years later, Donald Smith was made a peer by Colonial Secretary Joseph Chamberlain, and he chose the title Lord Strathcona.[8]

Although the transcontinental railway was completed four years after the original 1881 deadline, it was five years ahead of the 1890 date suggested by Lord Carnarvon. The successful completion of the extraordinary undertaking had been troubled by scandal, financing and troublesome terrain, yet was widely regarded as one of the most impressive feats of engineering.

For his role in helping unite the country, Donald A. Smith was knighted in 1886 and created Baron Strathcona and Mount Royal.

George Stephen was made a baronet in 1886 and took the title Sir

George Stephen of Dufftown, Banffshire and Grand-Métis, Quebec. He was raised to Lord Mount Stephen of Mount Stephen, British Columbia, and Brocket Hall, Hertfordshire, in 1891. In 1905, he was appointed Knight Grand Cross of the Royal Victorian Order.

For his role in executing the construction of the CPR, William Cornelius Van Horne was knighted in 1894.

For his part in resolving the territorial dispute through Blackfoot territory, Crowfoot was presented with a lifetime pass on the CPR by President William Cornelius Van Horne.

* * *

The 14th and 15th Earls of Derby, Lord Frederick Stanley's father and brother respectively, had both been connected to Canada through their political postings, as had Frederick even before being named Governor General. The 14th Earl had travelled to Canada in 1824, visiting several eastern Canadian locations. In fact, Port Stanley, on the north shore of Lake Erie, was named to honour the 14th Earl, having been known as Kettle Creek prior to his visit. Frederick Stanley, now governor general, expressed great confidence in Canada, specifically with one of the most important events within Canadian history. According to historian John Cowan, "The completion of that magnificent line, the Canadian Pacific Railway, which, completing more communication through the great Dominion, enabled her to open her arms in commerce to the Eastern and Western hemispheres alike."[9]

Through September and October 1889, Lord and Lady Stanley and their suite travelled across Canada, starting in Ottawa and following the route of the Canadian Pacific Railway to the Pacific Ocean in order to view the breadth of the country the Governor General felt honoured to serve. By the end of his term, Stanley had completely crossed Canada by railway from the Atlantic to the Pacific.

Eleven persons travelled to western Canada as members of the vice regal party: Stanley and his wife, Lady Constance; their son Edward and his wife, Lady Alice; Lord and Lady Stanley's daughter Isobel; Miss Lister, Lady Stanley's assistant; Lord Stanley's military secretary, Captain Charles Colville, along with his wife Ruby; aide-de-camp Aubrey H. McMahon; physician Sir James Grant; and Frederic Villiers, an artist/reporter for *The Daily Graphic*, a British current-events magazine. The party was assisted by two maids, a French chef, Lord Stanley's valet Clint, two footmen, Edward's servant Hardy, several other servants and the train conductor. The Stanleys also travelled with their dogs Chump and Nolly.

Edward, the eldest son of Lord and Lady Stanley, was twenty-four years of age when he married Alice Montagu in the social event of London earlier that year. The young couple was enjoying the trip, both as members of the vice regal party and as honeymooners.

Lady Alice had embraced a relatively new hobby: photography. Although the technology had existed for decades, the equipment had long been large and cumbersome and the processes to develop film exhaustive and expensive. But Rochester, New York, native George Eastman set to work to make the camera "as convenient as the pencil," and he succeeded: in 1888, Eastman introduced the Kodak box camera to the masses with the slogan, "You press the button — we do the rest." Thanks to Eastman, anyone could take photographs simply and economically. As a Kodak advertisement assured in 1888:

> *Anybody can use the Kodak without learning anything about photography, further than the mere operation of pointing the camera and pressing a button. No dark rooms or chemicals necessary. The camera is loaded for one hundred pictures. The Kodak System is a division of labour whereby all the work of finishing the pictures is done at the factory, where the camera is sent by mail to be reloaded and is available for those who have no time, inclination or facilities for learning photography.*[10]

Lady Alice took her camera with her on the western Canadian trip. Without grasping the significance at the time, Lord Stanley's daughter-in-law chronicled a slice of Canada's early history.

Isobel Constance Mary Stanley, the second-youngest of the Stanley children, was to celebrate her fourteenth birthday on the journey. Miss Lister, a young relative of Lady Stanley's, attended to Lady Constance's needs.

The Governor General's Military Secretary was Captain Charles Colville, the eldest son of Lord Colville of Culross. The forty-five-year-old Colville, like the man he served, had been a member of the Grenadier Guards and was gazetted to captain in 1884. Colville was appointed to his position with Lord Stanley in August 1888, shortly after Stanley assumed the post of governor general. Colville had been granted permission to bring his wife of four years, the former Ruby Streatfeild, with him across Canada. Ruby was found to be a most amiable travelling companion for Lady Stanley while their husbands attended to vice regal business during the historic trip.[11]

Lieutenant Aubrey Hope McMahon, like Stanley and Colville, was a member of the Grenadier Guards and was appointed an aide-de-camp to the Governor General on the announcement of Stanley's appointment. Coming from a long line of military personnel, the twenty-seven-year-old McMahon was a friend of Edward Stanley but came with peerless credentials and proved to be an excellent ADC.

Sir James Alexander Grant was president and chief of staff at Ottawa General Hospital and was selected as official physician and surgeon to each of the eight governors general from Viscount Monck in 1867 until Earl Grey in 1905. As a student at Montreal's McGill University, Grant had lived as a guest of Allan McDonald, the retired Chief Factor of the Hudson's Bay Company, who was a relative through marriage. Discussions at the McDonald home frequently involved the territory under control of the Hudson's Bay Company. Later, when Allan McDonald lost his eyesight, Grant was placed in charge of his correspondence and gained an intimate knowledge of the North-West Territory, something few others had as the company revealed little about its business or its holdings. In 1862, Grant delivered an astounding lecture at the Ottawa Mechanics' Institute entitled "The Union of the Different Parts of Canada by an Iron Splint." The crowd was mesmerized by Grant's passion for Canada, his insistence on admitting British Columbia, Alberta and Saskatchewan into Confederation, the bounteous resources in the territories controlled by the Hudson's Bay Company, the necessity of a transcontinental railway and subsequent trade possibilities with India, China, Japan, Australia and New Zealand. Word filtered back to Sir John A. MacDonald, who was so impressed that he invited Dr. Grant to stand for election as a member of Parliament for the constituency of Russell. After Grant was elected, Macdonald tapped him to introduce the Canadian Pacific Railway Bill in the House of Commons in 1872. Grant's address on that occasion was described as "the most scholarly and practical exposition of the project in the whole memorable debate."

The western Canadian trip afforded the fifty-eight-year-old physician the opportunity to see firsthand the portions of the country for which he had so passionately argued in Parliament. He had visited western Canada seven years prior, but on his return he would witness substantial progress.

Frederic Villiers accompanied the vice regal tour as an artist and correspondent for *The Graphic*, a large-sized British magazine heavy on illustrative content. Villiers had covered several wars and skirmishes for the magazine. Readers throughout the Commonwealth were well acquainted with Villiers' work at a time when it was customary for magazines and newspapers to print hand-drawn illustrations of news events, rather than employing photographs. There is conjecture that he, too, was related to Lady Stanley, although his work purpose and stature would certainly have justified his inclusion on the vice regal excursion.[12]

* * *

The vice regal party was afforded great comfort while travelling to Canada's west coast. Just behind the locomotive was a Pullman car named *Nagasaki* that served as living quarters for Captain and Mrs. Colville, Lieutenant McMahon, Sir James Grant and Frederic Villiers.

Next was the baggage car, which also housed two orderlies and ten servants, including the chef. The kitchen and dining car was third in the procession. This car contained an elaborate dining room, able to comfortably seat twelve guests. Next to the polished-wood dining room table was a sideboard and a large settee. Beside the dining room was, of course, the well-appointed kitchen, which, in spite of needing to be efficient due to the length of the trip, featured a stove, icebox and larder.

Lord and Lady Stanley, Edward and Alice, Isobel and Miss Lister, as well as the family dogs, travelled in the final carriage, a specially built car named *Victoria*. Called "the most perfect and luxurious car in Canada" by the *Ottawa Citizen*, the *Victoria* provided the living quarters for the Governor General and his family on the two-month excursion.

At the front of the *Victoria* was the large apartment designated for Lord and Lady Stanley. It was elegantly furnished with plush dark-blue velvet seats and thick carpets. The furniture included lace edgings for a visual warmth appreciated by Lady Stanley. There were also two small bedrooms: one for Edward and his wife, Lady Alice, the other shared by Isobel and Miss Lister. The car was also equipped with a large bathroom that featured hot and cold running water, a large bathtub and a shower.

Towards the back of the *Victoria* was a small drawing room where Lady Stanley enjoyed spending much of her time when not required to accompany her husband. In the rear was a small lobby with armchairs and basket chairs for the relaxation of the vice regal party.

On 17 September, Ottawa's *Daily Citizen* commented on the Governor General's trip across the Canadian west:

> *His experience during his journeyings will, we have no doubt, prove novel, agreeable and instructive. He will be impressed with the vast extent and the inexhaustible resources of the 'new Canada' lying beyond the western limits of the Province of Ontario. He will see for himself portions of the great unoccupied country which invites the labour of the husbandman to become richly productive. He will see prosperous towns and sites where up to a few years ago, mankind had never trod. He will visit the aborigines of the plains on their reserves and in not a few cases, will see the fruits of the civilizing influences exercised by a paternal Government. He will revel amidst the world-renowned scenery of the Rockies and the Selkirks and as the train proceeds, he will have time to reflect upon the prodigious character of the work of constructing the greatest railway enterprise of our time. Wherever he goes, he will see evidences of progress and he will return to the Capital more than ever impressed with the greatness of the country in which he has the honour to represent the Queen, and with convictions deepened in regard to its incalculable possibilities.*[13]

* * *

The vice regal suite departed from Quebec City at eight-thirty on the morning of Monday, 16 September. "We are most comfortably lodged and made an easy run to Ottawa, arriving at two-thirty," wrote Lady Stanley in her journal. "We went to do some shopping and to Government House and fetch some things and then to the Colvilles for dinner, returning to the car at nine-thirty." The Prime Minister visited Lord Stanley for one last briefing before the trip began in earnest.

Lord Stanley dropped into his office in the Parliament Buildings at nine o'clock on Tuesday morning. Just before he could leave, Charles Kelleher, a member of Parliament for Lunenburg, insisted that he should be allowed to join the vice regal party on their transcontinental trip. He was told, in no uncertain terms, that he would not be a member of the travelling party. "A most persistent Eastern MP wished to join our party," wrote a cheeky Lady Stanley in her journal. "But he was politely told to go to a 'hot place.'" Then, with officials briefed, the train packed, and both the vice regal party and western Canada excited, the trip was initiated.

* * *

Oliver Mowat, Premier of Ontario from 1872 to 1896, fought long and hard with the Dominion government to extend the power of the provinces, much to the consternation of Prime Minister Macdonald. Mowat battled to ensure that the District of Keewatin, the substantial region to the north and west of the Lake Superior-Hudson Bay watershed, would be included as part of Ontario. The Judicial Committee of the Privy Council sided with the persuasive Mowat, whose victory settled a long-simmering dispute between Manitoba and Ontario over who would govern the region. Both coveted the region's timber as well as the ports of Lake Superior. The Ontario boundary was extended west to Lake of the Woods and north to the Albany River and was embodied in the Canada (Ontario Boundary) Act of 1889.[14]

* * *

The vice regal party departed from Ottawa for their transcontinental goodwill tour on Tuesday, 17 September, 1889. The participants were in good spirits as the locomotive pulled out of the station. The day was exceptionally warm, although not uncomfortable. "The heat was very great," wrote Lady Stanley in her journal, "the thermometer in my room breaking 80."[15]

The first stop on the historic journey was in North Bay, Ontario, described by the CPR as "a bright new town on Lake Nipissing with a very good hotel."[16] At seven o'clock that evening, the Stanley entourage were welcomed by a band of musicians who performed "God Save the Queen." North Bay became a strategic point on the CPR's route. In the era of steam, locomotives needed to take on fuel every 120 miles. Chalk River, located on the Ottawa River, was one fuel stop, and North Bay was established 120 miles west. The CPR chose this location as a divisional point on the transcontinental line, constructing a roundhouse, a coal depot and a repair station to complement the log railway station already there.

After the first of many nights spent sleeping in the *Victoria*, the entourage left North Bay, which at the time a population of eleven hundred. The temperature had plunged by the time the engine pulled out at eight that morning. Lady Stanley's journal entry detailed one of the less public events of the day: "Sir J. Grant lost a tooth and asked every one to help him in looking for it. Eddy found it and nearly made Captain Colville sick by throwing it to him."[17]

The vice regal train bypassed expanses of wild yet beautiful territory as it sped along the tracks. The CPR said of the territory, "The large, clear, rock-bound lakes are, in places, so numerous that, with their connecting arms, they form a labyrinth of waters covering great areas."[18] Forests dotted the scenery as the train passed Sturgeon Falls and Sudbury, pulling into Missanabie at 5:50 p.m. "Very lovely place. Only about two inhabitants. We went for a charming walk," wrote Lady Stanley.[19] Missanabie, just west of Chapleau, sits at the dividing line between waters flowing northward into Hudson's Bay and those that drain southward into Lake Superior and is where the party remained for the night.

The Stanleys left Missanabie at eight o'clock, marvelling at the sights. As the CPR claimed, "From Heron Bay for sixty miles, the line is carried through and around the bold and harsh promontories of the north shore of Lake Superior, with deep rock cuttings, viaducts and tunnels constantly recurring, and at intervals, where the railway is built in the face of the cliffs, the lake comes into full view."[20] But the train was delayed at the village of Peninsula, now Marathon, by a train accident that preceded them. "Mr. Kelleher (MP) again turned up and asked Captain Colville if their train might not go on in front of the [Governor General's] to which again he received a warm answer," wrote Lady Stanley, smugly. "We passed through some lovely country. The line of railway going by the side and round a bend of Lake Superior, which said lake is 'a sea' with real waves breaking against the rocks. The country is wild and sad, for one sees nothing living. No houses, only very wild Indian camp."[21] For Lord and Lady Stanley and the vice regal party, it was their first glimpse of "Gitchee Gumee," or "big sea water," as the First Nations peoples called Lake Superior.

At eight o'clock that evening, the vice regal train stopped at Port Arthur, the principal port on Lake Superior, which boasted a population of five thousand. Up until 1883, the town had been known as Prince Arthur's Landing, named to honour Queen Victoria's son Prince Arthur, the Duke of Connaught, who would serve as Governor General of Canada from 1911 to 1916. Prince Arthur didn't visit his namesake town until 1890, by which time the railway had renamed the town Port Arthur.

Lady Stanley, continually amazed at the size of the country, reported that "there is now an hour difference between the time here and at Quebec." A civic address was presented at the station by the mayor, who then hosted Lord and Lady Stanley and their party at a dinner at the hotel, which was followed by a gala reception, "presents of flowers, photos and some Indian work, the latter given to us by Mrs. George Marks, a nice woman who must have been pretty."[22] Mrs. Marks's husband owned a general store called W.C. Dobie & Companie. Dobie, a former Liverpudlian, was a justice of the peace and the federal fisheries inspector for Western Lake Superior.

Lord and Lady Stanley's daughter Isobel celebrated her fourteenth birthday in Port Arthur on Friday, 20 September, 1889. Lady Stanley's entry spoke to her husband's love of dogs:

> *Chump very quietly walked off the train and in an opposite direction ... The crowd at the station much amused. The [Governor General] lost his dignity and chased the dog but required the train to stop. Chump was fetched by two ADC's and given biscuits on his return in safety to the car."[23]*

The party was taken by carriage to the Beaver Silver Mines, one of the richest mines in Canada at that time. As Lady Stanley recalled:

> *All the leading men of the place had come with us. Very rough drive through rather pretty, wild, desolate country. We had such a bad driver that we were nearly upset twice over. At the mines, we saw something very bright but only in places could one see a sparkle. Also, the amethyst found with the silver. We also were shown many beautiful specimens.[24]*

After returning and eating lunch on the train, Lord and Lady Stanley were driven to Kakebeka Falls, just over thirty kilometres west of Port Arthur. Constance and company felt that the falls, as seen in a "most lovely sunset," were "more beautiful than Niagara."[25]

While eating dinner with their hosts at the hotel, Lord and Lady Stanley were informed of a devastating landslide adjacent to The Citadel, their official second home. On 19 September, torrential rains had caused a massive slab of rock to fall away from the face of Cap Diamant and plummet ninety-one metres, crushing houses on ancient Champlain Street below and killing forty-five people, many of them children.[26] "We heard of the terrible landslide at Quebec," Lady Stanley wrote. "Many lives were lost. Fears are entertained for the safety of Dufferin Terrace. We were very glad to get to bed for we had a long but most interesting day."[27]

Saturday, 21 September was spent in nearby Fort William, which at a population of fourteen hundred was smaller than its neighbour. A Hudson's Bay Company post for more than a century, the burgeoning town was growing into a modern and efficient location.

The Governor General's aides, son Edward and Captain Colville, had preceded the vice regal party and arrived by ship. "A most uneventful day," sighed Lady Stanley in her diary. "Went for the first time on the cowcatcher. Thought it quite delightful. More like flying than anything else."[28]

The locomotive arrived in Rat Portage just after seven o'clock on Saturday evening. Rat Portage, now known as Kenora, had a population of seven hundred in 1889 and was an important lumbering centre, boasting several large sawmills. An address was presented at the railway station upon the vice regal arrival. Lady Alice tried to photograph at night, but the results were "nothing very successful."[29]

Sunday, as tradition dictated, was a day of rest, and Lord and Lady Stanley spent a quiet but rainy morning attending a local church service.

The drizzle continued through into Monday, 23 September. In spite of the cold and rain, Lord Frederick and his son Edward were taken on an excursion on the steamer *Empress*. Lady Stanley, daughter Isobel and daughter-in-law Alice declined the invitation. When the Stanley men returned, the vice regal party departed Rat Portage at two o'clock. Lady Stanley recounted the departure: "Made a stop at some waterfalls. Alice took a photo. I took one of a moose."[30]

Postmaster John Mather, the reeve of Keewatin, guided Lord Stanley through the Keewatin Flour Mills and the Lake of the Woods Milling Company. The Governor General was then addressed by Chief Shashagense, after which His Excellency gave the Hudson's Bay Company an order for flour, pork and other goods to be distributed among the tribe. The visit was brief, and the train left for Winnipeg at four that afternoon, sent off with a rousing cheer.

* * *

The train crossed the border dividing Ontario from Manitoba, turning southward at East Selkirk and following the Red River to Winnipeg. There had been concern that the Governor General's visit to Winnipeg would be boycotted on account of his decision in the controversial Jesuit Estates Act of 1888,[31] but the reception accorded him was extraordinarily warm:

> *No Governor General has had greater demonstrations of loyalty and affection than were shown to Lord and Lady Stanley in this great western centre. Though it was pouring with rain and the streets were a foot thick with the tenacious Winnipeg mud, the cheering crowds plodded on a full two miles to Governor Schultz's residence, where His Excellency and Lady Stanley remained during the few days of their stay in the capital of Manitoba.*[32]

Situated at the confluence of the Red and Assiniboine rivers, Winnipeg's growth had been extraordinary. In 1871, when it was still called Fort Garry, only one hundred people resided in the village. Just eighteen years later, Winnipeg was at the centre of a vast trading region, a gateway to the west and north. Although incorporated as a city in 1873, it wasn't until three years later that the name Winnipeg was officially adopted.

Residents began to congregate at the railway depot at seven o'clock that evening, and by the time Lord Stanley and his guests arrived a half-hour later, the platform was crowded with well-wishers who greeted the special train with prolonged cheering. Hundreds of torpedoes were laid on the tracks so that, as the train passed over them, it created a fusillade.

The vice regal train pulled into Winnipeg at seven-thirty on the evening of 23 September. *The Free Press* said of the affair:

> *The clear sky and bracing atmosphere which Winnipeg cit-*
> *izens like their distinguished visitors to enjoy, were*
> *disappointingly absent.... Instead, there was drizzling rain*
> *which no doubt was a novelty, and may have reminded the*
> *party of their native island.*[33]

There to greet the honoured guests were Lieutenant Governor John Schultz, Manitoba Premier Thomas Greenway, Mayor Thomas Ryan, several aldermen and members of the Legislature. They walked the specially laid carpet from the depot to the vice regal train to be presented to the Governor General, Lady Stanley and the rest of the party. As Stanley and the group disembarked from the train, the infantry band played "God Save the Queen," after which Lord Stanley passed through the station and climbed into the waiting coach. "The Governor General's carriage was drawn by four grey horses, but owing to the flare of the torches and the smoke of the rockets, the driver was compelled to take the front team off," reported the *Free Press*.[34]

A thousand residents, roughly half of them carrying torches in the drizzle, marched behind a procession led by the marshal, Chief Constable John McRae and his local police force, followed by a marching band and the fire brigade. Lord Stanley's carriage brought up the rear. As the procession moved up Main Street, the *Free Press* explained,

> *... it was greeted all along the line by cheers, and at several*
> *places, coloured fires were blazing. While the procession was*
> *passing the city hall, rockets were set off from the cupola.*
> *Little attempt was made at decorating but almost all the*
> *stores along the line of march were brilliantly illuminated.*
> *The Provincial Immigrant office was decorated with bunting*
> *and across the windows was hung cotton of different colours.*
> *With a light behind, it presented a very pretty appearance.*
> *The Rossin House was similarly decorated with window cov-*
> *erings, while on the dining room windows were the*
> *inscriptions, 'Welcome to Stanley' and 'Welcome'.*[35]

Other buildings went to even further extremes to welcome Lord Stanley on his first visit to the Manitoba capital. The Winnipeg Street Car Company's building, for example, was illuminated by decorative flags while a bonfire of calcium lights burned continuously.[36]

The parade route wound past the Legislative Building, which shone like a beacon by way of ten thousand lights placed in its windows. It took twelve men three days each to prepare the lights, and twenty to complete the job the evening before Stanley's arrival. As the entourage neared Government House, a Royal salute was fired from the grounds of the Legislative Building.

Upon arrival at the Lieutenant Governor's residence, Lord Stanley was again honoured with a civic address. An editorial in the *MacLeod Gazette* shuddered at the thought of yet another address to the Governor General:

> *Some very wonderful addresses were presented to His Excellency during his stay in Winnipeg. A sample sentence, taken at random from one of them, reads as follows: 'Your gracious condescendence has crossed our pathway like sunlight, opening our lips to smiles and our hearts to grateful emotions.' We don't know what this means, but expect that it is all right and that Lord Stanley was sufficiently impressed. We should fancy that Lord Stanley would have a very warm place in his heart for those places which neglect to inflict the nuisance upon him. His Excellency may be credited with sense enough to know that the feeling for Her Majesty's representative may be just as warm, and the welcome just as sincere, even if the much dreaded address is omitted.*[37]

Lord Stanley offered his thanks for the magnificent welcome, which he claimed neither he nor Lady Stanley had expected. He remarked that Her Majesty, Queen Victoria, would be gratified to hear of the manner in which her representative was received. With that, the party retired for the night and the hundreds who had hoped to catch a glimpse of their Governor General went home happy.

Lady Stanley's journal entry for the day described the excitement of arriving in Winnipeg:

> *Arrive at Winnipeg at 7 o'clock. Unfortunately raining. Very good reception! Town illuminated. Torch light proces-*

sion. Rockets lit off under the noses of our leaders [the horses]. They did not like it for they turned around and looked into our windows. The coachman wisely had them taken and we were less dignified but more safe. Stay at Government House ourselves and Mr. McMahon. Our host, Mr. Schultz, looks like a corpse. Our hostess a nice kind little woman but who would call us 'Your Excellency' at every other word.[38]

A full itinerary was prepared for the Governor General's first full day in Winnipeg. The rain poured down throughout the day, but nevertheless, at noon, Lord Stanley was the guest of honour at a civic address presented at Government House. At one o'clock, the party left to visit the university.

The 5 September, 1889, edition of the *Winnipeg Free Press* had reported that the Winnipeg Rowing Club's regatta would be postponed "until September 24 when it could be held under the watchful eyes of Lord and Lady Stanley during their transcontinental trip."[39] As promised, at 3 p.m. on the twenty-fourth, the Governor General was joined by son Edward, Frederick Villiers of *The Graphic*, Premier Greenway and the warden of the Stony Mountain Penitentiary, Colonel Samuel Bedson.[40] The ladies, meanwhile, remained at Government House, where they were treated to one Mrs. Cowley, who, according to Lady Stanley:

… played beautifully. She is the daughter of a missionary who has been working amongst the Indians for forty years. He came out with a bride of 19. It is interesting to hear about all her difficulties. Poor woman, with only Indian girls as servants.[41]

Lady Stanley had, of course, had only known an aristocratic life and was very much representative of the era.

The regatta was hampered by cold and rain but proceeded nonetheless. Lord Stanley and the Honourable Edward Stanley were seated on the veranda of the Rowing Club, away from the elements but with a clear view of the Red River. All things considered, the attendance was very strong. There were a large number of trophies to be won through the afternoon, all presented in the clubhouse after the afternoon of races. *The Winnipeg Free*

Press reviewed the day:

> *The prizes were given out by His Excellency, to whom the*
> *successful oarsmen were introduced by President Howell.*
> *After commenting on the magnificence of the cup which*
> *the Lieutenant Governor had given, His Excellency ob-*
> *served to President Howell that among the trophies of next*
> *year, they could put down one from the guest of the day —*
> *an announcement which promptly caused an outburst of*
> *enthusiasm on the part of the club's members.*[42]

A state dinner was held at Government House that evening, followed immediately by a "drawing room" at the Legislative Assembly. Lady Stanley was not impressed:

> *Rather dreadful State Dinner. Awfully dull ... Drawing*
> *Room afterwards a failure owing to a mistake. 'Full dress'*
> *having been said was necessary. The mud of Winnipeg sur-*
> *passes anything I have never seen of the kind and there are*
> *very few cabs. The ladies did not come to dress up.*[43]

Lady Stanley succinctly described the events of Wednesday the twenty-fifth: "Colleges. Convents. Hospitals all day long starting at ten with an inspection of the mounted infantry. The most bitter wind blowing."[44]

After the inspection, Lieutenant Governor Schultz, Mrs. Schultz and Sir James Grant drove with Lord Stanley to St. Boniface, where they were joined by Archbishop Alexandre-Antonin Taché. Taché had been made an archbishop in 1871, in the midst of a lengthy career as a pioneering Oblate missionary. His time in Manitoba coincided with several of the most significant events in Canada's early history, including the Riel Rebellion, the Red River Insurrection and the Manitoba Schools Question. Prior to 1870, Bishop Taché had conducted an effective campaign to discourage French settlements in the Canadian west, claiming to protect the aboriginals and Métis from being seduced by white French society. But he later reversed his stance and worked equally strenuously to encourage Catholic immigrants to populate the vast Canadian west, and to found new parishes within his own diocese. Towards that end, Taché negotiated treaties with the aboriginal tribes whose land was usurped in the process of encouraging settlement. But as importantly, Taché worked diligently to protect French Catholic rights in the territory. At that time, deep divisions existed in Canada concerning the extent of bilingualism — and indeed, biculturalism — in western Canada.[45]

Archbishop Taché welcomed the Governor General to St. Boniface in French. Senator Marc-Amable Girard then welcomed the party: "In this vast territory where so many nationalities are represented, none are more loyal to the Queen than the French-Canadian population."

Stanley was taken to St. Boniface College where he visited a boarding school of two hundred and two pupils, fifty-nine of them boarders. Upstairs in the music hall, a welcome march was played on the piano and the children sang a song composed for the occasion. The Governor General was then toured through St. Boniface Hospital. Founded by the Grey Nuns in 1871, the four-bed hospital was the first in western Canada. The Grey Nuns, who had arrived in St. Boniface in 1844, dedicated their lives to caring for those in need.

The party returned to Government House from St. Boniface at six o'clock and readied themselves for dinner at the Manitoba Club on Garry Street. Lady Stanley confirmed that all were delighted at the dinner:

> *They said it was excellent. Ditto the wine, which they were glad I left at Government House. At dinner, we got nothing but ginger beer or ginger ale to drink but we heard champagne was always pouring where no one could see. We had our private drink in my bedroom. Frederick and I and Mr. McMahon got it when we could. The ladies all dined with Mrs. Schultz, Mrs. Cowley and another female friend and we had really good fun as they taught us the Indian Red River dance[46] and made us answer impossible questions in a dreadful book. Mrs. Schultz was hurt that we did not take it seriously. I had hoped to get to bed when they all returned to the car but these females kept us talking till quarter to one. Oh dear. Such talking. Wanting to know every sort of thing about 'our dear and noble Queen'.[47]*

Whether or not there was a tone of irritation in Constance's voice, the Stanleys were of course representatives of Victoria and must have anticipated the incessant querying about the woman on the penny.

The vice regal couple awoke on the morning of the twenty-sixth of September to another cold, rain-drizzled day. At eleven, they were taken by train twenty-five kilometres north, to Stonewall. Arriving before noon, the vice regal couple was greeted by a novel arch erected on the main street constructed of sheaves of wheat, oats and barley and monster root vegetables and bookended by ploughs and other agricultural tools. In her journal, Lady Stanley commented on their entrance to the town. "Arch made of wheat sheaves. A dove was let down into our carriage as we passed."[48] The Governor General was greeted by a civic address. Then, Lord Stanley officially opened the Rockwood Exhibition and was given a unique memento of his visit: a bronze case containing jars of local produce, including both red and white Fife wheat, black oats, barley, field peas, China beans (small red lima beans), butter beans (lima beans) and Red River corn. Carriages took the Governor General a half-mile out of town for a brief tour of the limestone quarries of which the town was so proud. Much of the stone quarried in Stonewall was used for buildings in the quickly-growing city of Winnipeg.

Boarding the train again for Stony Mountain, where luncheon was awaiting, Lord and Lady Stanley were quite amused to see wolves running alongside the train. Lord and Lady Stanley were later led through the penitentiary of which Bedson was warden and they viewed an exhibition from a First Nations group. Lady Stanley harshly recounted, "Saw some Indian woman dance a war dance. Didn't think much of that. The poor thing had been so long in captivity that it seemed unreal." The entourage also saw Colonel Bedson's buffalo herd, which was driven close to the train tracks for their benefit. Lady Stanley remarked that she thought this "very beautiful." Throughout the course of the day, Lord Stanley looked on, smiled and commented to Colonel Bedson on his great enjoyment. Lady Stanley smiled approvingly, but her journal tells the real tale: "Should have enjoyed the day very much but I got a chill and felt so ill."[49]

The couple was returned to Winnipeg, where that evening they were guests of honour at a well-attended reception at Government House. Lord Stanley stayed for the dinner, while Lady Stanley returned to the vice regal car Victoria. "[Frederick] remained for main dinner which he said was awful. We are struck very much with Winnipeg considering that it is only the growth of about eighteen years. It is quite wonderful and has such an appearance of 'go aheadness.'"[50]

The Governor General's destination on Friday, 27 September was Portage la Prairie. The town of three thousand was one of the principal grain markets in the province, boasting flour mills, a brewery, a biscuit factory and several grain elevators. Welcomed to the town by an explosion of railway torpedoes as the *Victoria* pulled into the station, the party was greeted by Mayor John James Garland, who delivered an address on behalf of the town. As the Portage band played, Lord Stanley was escorted through exhibits of local produce. Lady Stanley's journal entry for the day illustrated that the party had free time that afternoon. "Mr. McMahon and all the other men went down the line to try to shoot something, then returned having seen nothing. [Frederick] went for a walk and saw lots of Indians."[51] Lady Alice Stanley was ill that day, so the ladies stayed behind while the men were taken to the new Portage train station, described by Constance as "a dingy little combination of country tavern and freight shed."[52] Lady Isobel spent some time taking photographs.

Saturday, 28 September was a lovely, warm day, and several in the vice regal party decided to take advantage of a light official itinerary to go hunting. "Alice and Isobel and Mr. McMahon went out quite early to try to shoot something. They returned at 2:30 very dirty and with one bird," reported Lady Stanley, adding:

> I went for a drive with Dr. Haggerty and his wife Ruby. Mr. J. Grant and Mr. McMahon came also. We went to see an Indian burial ground which was curious. They build sort of little houses over the graves and once a year, they come and visit the place and lay upon the lips of 'medicine herbs'. Saw a gopher. Such a pretty little animal rather like a squirrel striped all over. It does a great deal of damage to the crops.[53]

The entourage remained in Portage la Prairie on Sunday. Lady Stanley continued to display her nineteenth-century sensibilities: "Church in the morning with an odd-looking clergyman, a half-breed."[54] After the Governor General went for a walk with his daughter-in-law Alice, he addressed a group of children at three in the afternoon. The entire vice regal party visited a farm and then went hunting. Lady Stanley proudly reported that "F was the only successful one … he got three birds."[55]

In the evening, Lady Stanley and the Colvilles attended a second church service. "When we came out, we found that it was pitch dark. Not a light anywhere. We got into the middle of the road and were all but run over and we could not find our way back to the sidewalk. We laughed so much we could hardly stand. I have never heard Captain Colville laugh so heartily."[56]

As the transcontinental expedition continued west, the train carrying the vice regal party left Portage La Prairie at nine on the morning of Monday, 30 September and arrived in Brandon at noon. With a population of forty-five hundred, Brandon was a divisional point for the railway and the largest grain market in Manitoba. As the CPR explained, "The town is situated on high ground and although only six years old, has well-made streets and many substantial buildings."[57] After spending the night in Brandon, the Governor General's party departed at eight o'clock on the first day of October, with the tracks pulling away from the Assiniboine River and reaching an extended prairie area. The *Victoria* passed Virden and Elkhorn and, a mile east of Fleming, entered the District of Assiniboia.

* * *

The Northwest Territories during Lord Stanley's term in office comprised four distinct districts: Athabasca (which encompasses northern Alberta and northern Saskatchewan today), Alberta (today's southern Alberta), Saskatchewan (central Saskatchewan) and Assiniboia (modern-day southern Saskatchewan). This vast region had a population of only sixty-seven thousand in 1891, and the Dominion of Canada was determined to increase those numbers. By 1901, one hundred fifty-nine thousand had settled in the Northwest Territories.

To encourage western settlement, Ottawa offered settlers a homestead of one hundred sixty acres for a ten-dollar registration fee. In order to receive the land, the settler had to be a male of at least twenty-one years of age or a woman who was the sole support for her family. Before being granted the acreage, each settler had to reside on the homestead for a period of time — usually six months of the year for three years — had to cultivate at least thirty of the acres and had to erect a house worth at least three hundred dollars.[58]

Although most heavily populated by settlers of British origin, the attractive land offer attracted good numbers of settlers of French, German, Hungarian, Russian and Scandinavian background, as well as a strong contingent of Métis.[59] It was of prime importance to Lord Stanley to address and encourage the settlement of what would become, in 1905, the provinces of Saskatchewan and Alberta.

* * *

Through the vast, flat Prairies, the train would routinely hit speeds in excess of ninety kilometres per hour. Steam locomotives didn't have speedometers, so there was no manner in which to accurately measure speed other than counting the time between mileage markers. Sustained high speeds taxed the locomotives, so the train would stop at each divisional point, located approximately every two hundred kilometres. As the engine squealed to a halt, a "car man" would squirt some lube oil into each journal box. When the stops were for visits or layovers, the engine would be watered, greased and oiled and a fresh supply of fuel added.

A new month and a new territory — the *Victoria* stopped briefly in Moosomin, the first town reached in Assiniboia, on Tuesday, 1 October, arriving at 10:30 a.m. The train pulled into the station and its passengers noted a sign that read, "Welcome to the North-West Territories." The local band played "God Save the Queen" while Lord and Lady Stanley were greeted by Major Charles E. Phipps, a former page to Queen Victoria. Earlier that year, the Dominion government had opened a land titles office in nearby Cannington Manor and appointed Major Phipps its agent. Cannington Manor had been quite a site on the Prairies in the late 1880s. In 1882, Captain Edward Pierce planned to develop an aristocratic community based on Victorian society in this sparsely populated area of southeast Saskatchewan. Pierce advertised in Britain and among the expatriate Brits already living in Canada. His campaign attracted three Manchester brothers, the Becktons, who, although the oldest was only twenty, used a portion of their sizable inheritance to buy twenty-six hundred acres of land and build a mansion they called Didsbury. Cannington Manor included an agricultural college used to train wealthy young English bachelors in the fine art of farming. The community failed miserably, and within twenty years, one of the most curious experiments in the development of western Canada had come to an end.[60]

After a civic address was read by Mayor Joseph Daniel, followed by the Governor General's suitable reply, Lord Stanley was driven to Academy

Hall. All the children from the town's public school were assembled there and fidgeted with excitement, in spite of stern looks and warnings from the schoolmaster, as they awaited the arrival of the Governor General. As instructed, when Lord Stanley's carriage pulled up in front, the children marched into the hall, accompanied on the piano. Seven young girls each carried a small ceremonial banner that, when placed side-by-side, spelled out "S-T-A-N-L-E-Y." Behind the girls, thirty boys carried Union Jack flags and waved them enthusiastically as they spied the Governor General. Lord Stanley commented on how pleased he was with the appearance of the "Gateway Town" of Assiniboia.

In the afternoon, the party drove into the country to the crofter settlement near Saltcoats. Forty-nine families (two hundred and eighty people in all) had arrived in the area as small-scale tenant farmers the previous spring, sent as an experiment by the British government. Some contend that the farmers were *forced* to emigrate from the United Kingdom, victims of a larger plan that would allow wealthy landowners to consolidate their holdings into larger, more profitable farms. The crofters' buildings, small and constructed for sixty-six dollars apiece, "are a marvel of accommodation at that price."[61] The crofters often banded together in the new land, finding strength in numbers and bringing their language and culture (many were of Scottish descent and they introduced *ceilidh* parties to the area), religion and work ethic. *The Dominion Illustrated Monthly* reported, "His Excellency asked the Crofters many questions as to their condition and evinced the liveliest interest in their success."[62] Lady Stanley was not terribly enamoured of western living. "We go to see the schools then went off to see the crofters and to shoot … we sit with [Mrs. Phipps]. Oh! Such a dirty miserable house and making Prairie life not appear at all attractive."[63]

While the remainder of the party proceeded on to Broadview, Lord and Lady Stanley arrived in Whitewood on a separate train. Three addresses greeted Lord Stanley, and one was also intended for Lady Stanley. The first was a civic address from the citizens of Whitewood. The second, delivered by a Mr. Ohlen, was made on behalf of the Scandinavians residing in the area. The *Regina Leader* recounted the rest of the proceedings:

> *Then, Mr. F. Morrison came forward and read a long address from the Agricultural Society, to which His Excellency made a suitable reply. The address of the ladies*

*of Whitewood had to be sent on by mail as Lady Stanley
had not time to hear it read, the train being already
behind time.*[64]

The CPR described the area thus: "All the way from Brandon to Broadview,
the frequent ponds and copses[65] afford excellent opportunities for sport —
waterfowl and 'prairie chickens' being especially abundant."[66]

Crossing the Qu'Appelle River, Lord and Lady Stanley arrived in
Broadview at half past three. They were greeted on the CPR platform by a
number of civic dignitaries, including Sam Steele, the head of the North-
West Mounted Police's "D" Division. Steele had participated in some of
the Dominion of Canada's most historic events, including the North-West
Rebellion of 1885, the construction of the Canadian Pacific Railway and
the Yukon Gold Rush. The village of Broadview, with a population of six
hundred, was prettily situated at the head of Weed Lake.[67] Lord and Lady
Stanley visited the town during evening, spending the night in their
railway car.

The Stanleys left Broadview early the next morning for a visit to the
Crooked Lake Agency, made up of the Cowessess, Kahkewistahaw,
Ochalace and Sakimay reserves. Edward and Alice, along with Isobel and
Mrs. McMahon, were on horseback while Lord and Lady Stanley and the
remaining members of the vice regal suite were driven the nine miles in
carriages belonging to the Chief Commissioner of Police, escorted by a detachment of the North-West Mounted Police. Also present was
Lieutenant-Colonel Alan McDonald, who had been appointed the local
Indian agent by the Dominion government. McDonald wielded considerable power as justice of the peace for the reservation and the man in charge
of ensuring the effective application of Canadian Indian Policy.

The *Regina Leader* reviewed the day:

> *As soon as the Indian scouts galloped in announcing the
> approach of the vice-regal party, about sixty Indians moved
> out to meet them in the old style and the effect to the
> lookers-on from the Agency was most picturesque, espe-
> cially as the party drew near, with the advance guard of the
> NWMP riding solidly in front, the Indians alternately
> closing in and scattering around the cortege like a cloud.*[68]

Lady Stanley wasn't quite as enthralled. "When we were within a mile of the place, we were met by a lot of wild-looking creatures on wild horses. They all made the most hideous noises by way of welcome and joining our escort we entered the Cree Indian Reserve. After addresses from the English settlers and the schools for Indian children, the Chiefs were brought in. Fine looking with all painted and dressed in coloured clothes with rings around them and feathers in their hats. [Frederick] held a pow wow. Each chief made a speech. [Frederick] answered them and their noise of approval was so strange."[69]

Entering the reserve, the Governor General was welcomed by a triumphal arch that read, "Wah-chee-yea [we shake your hand]." A second arch read, "Kee-tah-tam-is-kat-tin-nan [we wish you all good luck]." A platform had been erected for the welcoming ceremony, decorated with flowers and flags. Yet another sign of welcome overhead: "Nan-ee-too, kit-tah kee-tan. Nab-way-e-mayo, kee chee kee too kee-mah, squam-e-nan [God save the Queen]. The Reverend Hugh McKay, principal of Round Lake School, stood by proudly as the schoolchildren sang 'God Save the Queen.'"[70]

Lieutenant Colonel Alan McDonald presented to Lord and Lady Stanley the four chiefs: Louis O'Soup, Kahkewista-haw, Ochapawace and Sakimay. Chief O'Soup of the Cowessess tribe addressed His Excellency in Cree, which was then translated into English by a government interpreter. Lord Stanley was greatly impressed. Chief O'Soup expressed that "the real wants of Indians are few; some cattle and a small grist mill."[71] The Governor General presented each of the four chiefs with very handsome pipes. The Regina newspaper continued:

> *Chief O'Soup then presented a trophy of his own hunting*
> *prowess in the shape of a most magnificent head and horns*
> *of an elk, and begged His Excellency's acceptance of the*
> *very handsome Indian chief's dress he was wearing, which*
> *His Excellency graciously intimated he would accept when*
> *the ceremony was concluded.*[72]

Following Chief O'Soup's speech, the children from Qu'Appelle Industrial School gave a short address to Lord and Lady Stanley. Mr. W. Tait, on behalf of the settlers from Cotham, then concluded with his address. Cotham was believed to be the most exclusively English settlement in Assiniboia and possibly the whole northwest. Lord Stanley replied, "While Cotham was justly proud in being an English settlement, Canada, with its free institutions, is a country adapted to be the home of persons of every nationality."[73] Stanley was mindful that these vast open areas would soon be populated by many different settlers who likely would not emanate from the Home Countries.

Luncheon was served at the home of Indian Agent McDonald. Afterwards, Lord and Lady Stanley were driven sixteen miles west across the prairie to Grenfell, where they were delighted to see the train depot decorated for the occasion. Hearty cheers rose from the large gathering. A local dignitary read a brief address to which Stanley replied, "The future lays in your own hands." The Governor General was pleased that the townspeople "were not putting all eggs in one basket and were experimenting with mixed farming." Always encouraging the settlement of the Prairies, the Governor General concluded, "Each individual is capable of making a first class immigration agent."[74]

Richard Hardisty, who was appointed Chief Factor of the Hudson's Bay Company in Edmonton in 1887, was named a senator from the District of Alberta by Sir John A. Macdonald that same year. Hardisty made the trip from Edmonton to Grenfell in order to greet the governor general's party. He was joined by Archibald McDonald, the Chief Factor from Fort Qu'Appelle. While crossing the track accompanying Lord Stanley and his party on the afternoon of 2 October, the carriage containing McDonald and Hardisty hit the steel rails and threw the gentlemen onto the tracks. "The vehicle was being driven by C. Dodd when it struck against the metal, causing the seat to turn over and throw the senator on the track." The Governor General's physician, Sir James Grant, rushed over to attend to the senator's injuries and stayed with him until a local doctor, Dr. Hutchinson, arrived. It was decided that the best course of action would be to remove Hardisty to the hospital in Winnipeg. The *Regina Leader* reported that Hardisty was "said to be suffering from concussion of the spine."[75]

Archibald McDonald sustained injuries from which he continued to suffer until his death in 1915. But Hardisty, the fifty-seven-year-old senator, never recovered and died on 15 October in Winnipeg at the General Hospital.

The Hardisty family was one of the most prominent in the region. In 1873, when Richard Hardisty was named chief factor in charge of Fort

Edmonton, he became the third generation to hold that position. Richard, the son of Richard senior and Margaret Sutherland, a Métis woman, ran in the first general election in the Northwest Territories, which took place on 30 June, 1888. The junior Hardisty based his platform on upholding the rights of the Métis, and although unsuccessful in getting elected, he was the first federal senator appointed from the District of Alberta and the first Métis senator in Canadian history. Senator Richard Hardisty's sister Belle (Isabella) was in a relationship with Donald Smith, later to be known as Lord Strathcona, when she gave birth to a daughter. Donald Smith later married Belle, and subsequently rose to become one of the most powerful businessmen in Canada.[76]

"We greatly regret the death because of the loss to his family, his country and his company," the *Regina Leader* lamented. "He was a man of great business power, sound judgement and his family are famous in the north for their hospitality."[77] Senator Hardisty's funeral took place in Winnipeg on Saturday, 19 October, 1889, and he was buried in St. John's Cathedral in that city.

* * *

Lord Stanley was met by Colonel Lake, an acquaintance from England, who drove the Governor General to his farm six miles outside Grenfell. Colonel Lake and his two sons had arrived in the area in 1883 and built a large home they called named Winmarleigh Grange. Their farm, one of the largest and most productive in the region, was devoted to raising cattle and growing grain. Winmarleigh was renowned far and wide for its hospitality, and Lord Stanley was the recipient of same. After supper, a carriage took Stanley back to town.

The train pulled out of Grenfell on Thursday morning, 3 October, and stopped thirty miles away at Indian Head, where a large gathering had assembled. The dust whipped up around the carriage wheels as the Stanleys were taken to the sixth annual exhibition of the Indian Head Agricultural Society. The highly successful Indian Head experimental farm, a 675-acre farm established in 1888, had been established just a mile outside of Indian Head. The exhibition took place in a large schoolhouse borrowed by the trustees for the event. Although the day began with cool temperatures, the air had warmed up substantially by the time the vice regal couple arrived.

Lord and Lady Stanley climbed the stairs to the upper storey, where, in the centre of the hall, they saw a long table covered with tubs of butter, turnips, cabbages, onions and mangold wurzels, a football-sized root fed to farm animals. On one side, the ladies' displayed their fancy work on a table the entire length of the hall, with sales benefiting the Anglican diocese. On the other side were grain and garden vegetables. Outside the hall, the finest horses, cattle, sheep and pigs were displayed. The Stanleys observed a horse being broken in — as the latter recalled, "Broncho broken in for us to see … we were not impressed with the wildness of the poor little horse, only with the terror shown by the men who handled him."[78] Lord Stanley expressed delight in the wonderful quantity and quality of the produce, which "equalled any I have seen in the Dominion."[79] He then thanked his host and once again boarded the train.

Leaving Indian Head at eleven o'clock, the *Victoria* chugged along the tracks and arrived in Regina, the capital of Assiniboia, just after noon. The burgeoning city boasted a population of two thousand, and was the site where the Executive Council of the Northwest Territories, embracing the districts of Assiniboia, Alberta, Saskatchewan and Athabasca, would meet.[80]

Elaborate preparations had been made for the arrival of Lord and Lady Stanley. A platform decorated in red, white and blue bunting was erected at the CPR station. Spanning the platform was an arch with Lord Stanley's family crest and motto "Sans Changer," with shields on either side. Banners hanging across nearby streets read, "Welcome to Regina," "The North-West Capital Greets You" and "Loyalty to the Crown."[81]

On the CPR station platform, the Governor General's party was welcomed by schoolchildren warbling "God Save the Queen," accompanied by the Regina Brass Band. Both Mayor J. W. Smith and Lieutenant Governor Joseph Royal addressed the esteemed guests. In his reply, Lord Stanley stated that there was "little doubt as to the future importance of these territories, and formed into provinces, they would achieve still more, and the time is not far distant when you will form the bulwark and the backbone of Canada."[82] Cheers emanating from the hundreds waiting at the train station indicated they were pleased with His Excellency's sentiment.

The brass band performed as the carriages departed the train station for the barracks of the North-West Mounted Police. "We were driven about in a most uncomfortable carriage with four horses and an escort,"[83] mentioned Lady Stanley in her journal. On arrival, they were given a Royal salute by the NWMP. Lord and Lady Stanley were guests at a luncheon hosted by NWMP Commissioner Lawrence W. Herchmer at the barracks. Afterwards, the Governor General inspected the mounted police — in Lady Stanley's estimation, "such magnificent men with such good horses all bred in the North-West and broken by the men."[84] A mounted parade was held outside the barracks square; a precursor to the Royal Canadian Mounted Police Musical Ride. Lady Stanley described it as a "most interesting event."[85] The parade was followed by an exhibition of skirmishing in the hill and gullies just south of the barracks.

Dinner was held at Government House. At eight-thirty that evening, a torchlight procession took place along South Railway and Broad streets, which were illuminated by wax candles. A ball, given by the police union, was held on the Governor General's first evening in Regina. "The ball was a very good one," wrote Lady Stanley. "The room was very nattily decorated. Every one was well dressed and the supper was excellent, everything being done and cooked by the ladies of the place. Considering that we were away in the far North-West, the whole thing was wonderful."[86]

Friday, 4 October began much more to the personal liking of Lord Frederick Stanley. At nine o'clock, the Governor General was taken by carriage to the first annual meeting of the Assiniboia Provincial Rifle Association. On hand to welcome him were Major Bedson of Stony Mountain Penitentiary and Nicholas Flood Davin, a member of Parliament who was also publisher of the *Regina Leader*. "Everything in readiness, His Excellency, rifle in hand, advanced to the firing point, knelt on one knee and taking careful aim, fired the first shot. Whizzing through the air, the bullet was heard to strike the target and the man in the pit at the other end marked a bull's eye."[87] Spectators cheered the accomplishment lustily. After the competition, the Governor General presented a silver and a bronze medal for the winners.

Mayor Smith hosted a reception for his vice regal guests at three o'clock in the afternoon. "Reception in the afternoon and was dreadful failure," reported Lady Stanley. "There are too few people at Regina to make a regular reception possible. We waited patiently for an hour and shook hands with about twenty people, much to the horror of the Lieutenant Governor's wife Mrs. Madam Royal, who told us they never 'give the hand'. The consequence is they are not liked. We held the reception in the room where Riel was tried."[88]

Afterwards, Lady Stanley was taken for a drive through the city (this time in a more comfortable carriage, drawn by four horses), joined by aide-de-camp Aubrey McMahon. Edward Stanley, his wife, Alice, and younger sister Isobel went out shooting, bringing back two ducks and some nice flowers. Lord Stanley and a party of twelve, including Mayor Smith, Commissioner Herchmer, Nicholas Davin and Mr. Justice Richardson, dined with Lieutenant Governor Royal at Government House.

A fancy ball took place that evening at the barracks. "I never was more bored," wrote Lady Stanley. "I was planted down in a chair under a balcony. I could not see the dancing."[89] Nevertheless, the Assiniboian capital was proud of hosting Lord and Lady Stanley. After their departure, the town's weekly newspaper summed things up: "His Excellency the Governor General's visit is over and he and his gracious lady have left an excellent impression of their unostentatious courtesy and simplicity of manner."[90]

A train took Lord and Lady Stanley and their guests to Long Lake, where they spent the next three days shooting. Lady Stanley reviewed the affair:

> *Left Regina in the night and found ourselves planted down in the wildest and most dreary place I ever saw. An uncompleted line of the railway. No station, only service tents but the shooting is good!!!*[91]

The group bagged several geese that day.

"We sat out and thoroughly enjoyed our rest," wrote Lady Stanley of Sunday, 6 October. "A glorious day."[92] The men got up before daybreak to shoot geese — a pursuit they were all successful in, as Constance confirmed in her journal. "They say the sky was quite thick with them."

In fact, Long Lake was well known for the vast numbers of nesting and migratory birds it harboured; so much so that it was feared that the Long Lake Railway would result in development that would harm the shoreline where the populations of these birds made their homes. To prevent the disruption of this wildlife habitat, in 1887 the Dominion government set aside parts of Long Lake and Last Mountain Lake as a bird sanctuary. The official word from Government House explicated:

> *Whereas the Minister of the Interior has reported that the*

*islands and shores of the north end of Long Lake, in the
North West Territories are favorite breeding grounds for almost all the different varieties of wildfowl in that country,
and that it is very desirable that steps be taken to retain
these grounds for such purposes, especially in view of the
probable extension of the Long Lake Railway, and the consequent settlement of the land in that neighbourhood.*

*His Excellency in Council … hereby ordered that the
following lands which are vacant and unsold be, and the
same are hereby reserved from sale and settlement, and set
apart as breeding grounds for wildfowl.*[93]

* * *

To say that Lord and Lady Stanley were surprised to be approached by the
son of the Imperial Chancellor of the Exchequer on Monday, 7 October
would be a resounding understatement. Next to the Prime Minister, the
Chancellor of the Exchequer is the highest post in the British government.
Yet, twenty-three-year-old George Joachim Goschen — who later married
Lady Margaret Gathorne-Hardy, whose father preceded Lord Stanley as
British Secretary of War — did not simply show up in Regina, but re-
mained with the governor general's party for the remainder of the
transcontinental train trip, right back to Ottawa that November. Lady
Stanley noted in her journal:

> *Young Mr. Goschen came on a freight train to pay his re-
> spects. He is very like both parents and very pleasant. I
> thought him rather a fool for not going out shooting with
> the others but found, poor fellow, that he was ill. Sir J.
> Grant prescribed for him.*[94]

Lady Stanley enjoyed bantering with the vice regal physician, and laughed
about one such incident in the pages of her tour diary:

> *… heard that Sir J. Grant was in the most awful fright be-
> cause on Saturday night, I said, 'only fancy if here in this
> lovely place the Indians were to attack our car, how helpless*

we would be!' We had a good deal of chaff about it but he took it seriously and went and implored Mr. White, for God's sake, to take us back to Regina and he told the others that if we ever left the place alive we might indeed be thankful![95]

The men returned from Long Lake after a highly successful shooting excursion on Tuesday, 8 October. It was duly noted that this was the wedding anniversary of Captain Charles Colville and his wife Ruby. Just prior to noon, the train pulled out of the station and spent the better part of the day speeding across the Prairies, past Moose Jaw and through the Cypress Hills. Constance described her dull day: "We only passed through Prairie and we saw a good large tract of the said land on fore. We also saw a coyote quite near to the line and two herds of antelopes at some distance off."[96] After continuing for just over two hundred miles, the train made a mid-morning stop on Wednesday. At Colley, the men thought they would try their hands at shooting some prairie chickens — medium-sized grouse that were plentiful on the Plains ever since the buffalo population had been so severely depleted, leaving the taller grasses as an ideal habitat for the birds. After lunch, the train continued, and at three-thirty arrived in Dunmore, just east of Medicine Hat. At Dunmore, the CPR advised that "remains of gigantic saurians and other extinct animals are abundant."[97] While Eddy and Alice went to shoot goats, Lord Stanley left for Medicine Hat, arriving at four o'clock with the mercury reaching a torrid ninety degrees.

The streets and buildings of Medicine Hat, which had a population of seven hundred, were "gay with flags, mottoes and bunting."[98] On a platform erected on the grass in the CPR garden, a Mr. Finley addressed the Governor General on this sweltering afternoon. Lord Stanley then examined gardens and an exhibit of grains and vegetables before visiting the new hospital, the first built in the Northwest Territories. The North-West Mounted Police band, furnished at the request of CPR Superintendent John Niblock, who had been heavily involved in the construction of the hospital, enlivened the reception with "their loyal airs."[99]

Lord Stanley left for Dunmore just past five o'clock, and was joined for supper by Elliott Galt, an Assistant Indian Commissioner and the son of Sir Alexander Galt, a Father of Confederation and Canada's High Commissioner to Great Britain. The younger Galt spoke excitedly about the vast coal reserves he was mining. By that year, the Galts, father and son, owned more than a million acres of prairie land.

The entourage left Dunmore for Lethbridge on Thursday, 10 October. Although a welcoming sign read, "Welcome Stanley of Preston: God Speed Our New Railroad," *Victoria* arrived in Lethbridge at quarter past three — some forty-five minutes late. A strong wind blew the decorations that had been used to welcome the vice regal party. Lord Stanley was presented with a civic address by C. A. Magrath, the president of the Lethbridge Board of Trade, who acknowledged that Lady Stanley was the first wife of a Governor General to venture west of Manitoba.

Afterwards, the carriages drove the party by the barracks and then to Galt's house — named, appropriately, Coaldale — which Lady Stanley pronounced "such a nice place." Coaldale was considered the finest residence south of Calgary at that time. The Galts had built a mining town around the coal deposits, originally calling it Coalbanks but changing the name in 1885 to Lethbridge to honour the company's president, William Lethbridge. Constance described the area: "at the foot of a hill into which we walked and found ourselves in a coal mine! Where the men can work standing upright and they know of sixty miles straight ahead of coal."[100] The Governor General and Lady Stanley spent the night at Coaldale.

On the morning of Friday, 11 October at eight o'clock, the vice regal travelled by carriages, accompanied by a North-West Mounted Police escort, to the Blood Reserve. "Such a picturesque drive over prairie," Lady Constance commented. "We had to ford two rivers, which was rather exciting as the currents were very strong and one felt very nervous that the carriage might go over."[101]

At the reserve on the Belly River, "Fred held the usual pow wow," yawned Lady Stanley in her journal. "The chiefs were not dressed in their war paint and clothes. They were wearing the coats provided by the Government. Dark blue coats and brass buttons are not so well worth seeing as paint and feathers."[102] Lord Stanley conversed with the head and minor chiefs. 'The interview followed the old well known lines and was very much the same that every Governor General or public official who has ever visited them has listened to before," sniffed the *MacLeod Gazette*.[103]

Lady Stanley was unsure of how to react to one particular display. "One chief, Calf Shirt by name, is a snake charmer [and] was beautiful all in yellow and skins hanging from his sleeves and head dress. He pushed through the crowd and came up to us and pushed into my hand his pipe of peace and his embroidered tobacco bag — really a very pretty one. I was very much taken aback but also much pleased."[104]

Calf Shirt, whose native name was Onistah-sokaksin, was born in 1844, near what was later known as Lethbridge. After the deaths of both his parents around 1870, the despondent Calf Shirt wandered off to spend time alone in the sand hills near present-day Medicine Hat. While there, he experienced visions in which a rattlesnake appeared in the form of man and offered to adopt him, claiming that all snakes were his brothers. Calf Shirt subsequently embraced the rattlesnake with reckless abandon and developed great skill in handling them. The native leader was so adept at handling the poisonous snakes that he would regularly mount demonstrations of his peculiar craft, charging spectators twenty-five cents apiece to watch his show. The *MacLeod Gazette* offered, "Calf Shirt claims to have subtle power over the snakes, and to see him take his present specimen up, she measuring about three-feet long, catch it by the neck and cram about eight inches of it, the deadliest reptile in America, head downwards down his throat, is calculated to make the marrow in any man's bones shiver."[105] Inside his log cabin, Calf Shirt kept a snakepit, and when he ventured outside, he usually carried a snake in his shirt.

During the late 1890s, when Calf Shirt was a performer at Regina's Territorial Exhibition, a doubtful spectator accused him of being a fraud, of using reptiles that had been defanged. Calf Shirt enticed his rattlesnake to bite one of the camp dogs. The doubter's claim was debunked when the dog keeled over minutes later, dead.[106]

Having aspired to become a chief for the better part of the decade, Calf Shirt and about forty followers established their own band, the Namopisi, or Crooked Back, in 1888 in an area near present-day Lethbridge. Ironically, the new chief established his band in the only part of what is now southern Alberta where rattlesnakes, which terrified his loyal followers, could be found. Calf Shirt, whom Indian agent William Pocklington called "probably the most reliable Indian on this Reserve" and who was identified as a "shrewd and intelligent man" by missionary John MacLean, was appointed a scout for the North-West Mounted Police just prior to Lord Stanley's visit.[107]

Sam Steele, the superintendent of the North-West Mounted Police, added, "When I arrived, the Indians had assembled in large numbers and when the Governor General and party arrived there, the chiefs were presented. After this part of the ceremony was over and the usual speeches made, the Indian warriors who had assembled gave a mounted war dance. This was really an illustration of what they would do in war, such as riding into the camp of an enemy and stampeding his horses. The braves were beautifully decorated, plumed and painted and all were well mounted and in high spirits."

Lady Stanley enthusiastically depicted the events:

> *The Indians formed up some hundreds of yards in front of us and the Governor General's party were on the veranda of the Agency. When his turn came, each centaur rode at full speed towards us, rolled up his blanket like a ball, both feet coiled up under him on the saddle and when he was close enough, suddenly unrolled himself and, standing erect on his horse, spread the blanket to the full extent of his arms like the wings of a bat, coming at us with wild yells, flapping it as he passed at a gallop round the flanks of my party. Others came waving the blanket in one hand and firing their rifles at us as they approached with their wild war-whoops. Many galloped in, firing as they advanced, or rode by yelling and shaking their rifles at us as if in defiance.*[108]

"The Indians danced a war dance on horseback,"[109] continued Lady Stanley. In *The Graphic*, Frederic Villiers described the war dance as a "barbaric fandango."[110] Following the powwow, the group lunched with Indian Agent Pocklington.

The group was driven to the largest ranch in the Dominion, the Cochrane Ranche. Constance complained that "the wind was too high to make the drive pleasant and the prairie dust was simply awful. Sir J. Grant and Mr. Villiers, who were in the last carriage, arrived with their faces black with it, which made Mr. Villiers very cross indeed!"[111]

As the Canadian Pacific Railway was being built, colonization was important to the union of British Columbia with eastern Canada. To prepare for settlement, treaties with the First Nations tribes were negotiated and the North-West Mounted Police inaugurated to maintain order on the land earmarked for settlement. The Canadian government established the

Dominion Lands Act in 1876, granting grazing leases in order to create large, elite ranches that would cover much of what later became Alberta and Saskatchewan. In 1881, the first of these leases was secured by an enterprising group of eastern capitalists headed by Senator Matthew Cochrane, who had effectively lobbied the Minister of the Interior for changes to the act that would allow cattle barons the opportunity to lease large tracts of land at nominal fees. For five hundred thousand dollars, Cochrane secured more than a hundred thousand acres of prime land, straddling the proposed route of the CPR, the lush Bow Valley and close to the burgeoning city of Calgary and two Indian reservations.

Bordering the prairie solitude and the magnificence of the Rockies, the Cochrane Ranche got off to a promising start, but suffered several challenges. The senator's son, Billy, took over management in 1885.[112]

By the time Stanley's party reached the Cochrane Ranche , the travellers had passed hundreds of horses in the lower valleys, herds of cattle on the terraces and sheep on the hilltops, creating a most interesting memory. The train arrived at six o'clock, with Lord Stanley, Isobel, Aubrey McMahon and George Goschen going out on horseback to witness the rounding up of six thousand cattle owned by the Cochrane Ranche. Constance proclaimed that "the cattle were wonderful. All in a circle and kept in order by a few cowboys."[113] William Cochrane had his cowboys give the vice regal party a display of ranch work, roping and branding of steers.

"Mr. Cochrane's house is quite a log hut," wrote Lady Stanley. "We had all to double up very tight and the gentlemen were in tents." But one thing that impressed the entire party was the first glimpse of the majestic Rocky Mountains. Constance exclaimed that the Rockies looked "too lovely!"[114] Lady Susan Agnes Macdonald, the Prime Minister's wife, had eloquently noted the magnificence of the Rockies on her trip west in 1886:

> *And lo, through an opening in the mist, made rosy with early sunlight, we see, far away up in the sky, its delicate pearly tip clear against the blue, a single snowpeak of the Rocky Mountains. Our coarse natures cannot at first appreciate the exquisite aerial grace of the solitary peak that seems on its way to heaven, but as we look, gauzy mist passes over, and it has vanished.*[115]

Travelling by carriage, the party set out from Cochrane for Fort MacLeod on Saturday morning. Lady Stanley's journal entry noted:

> *We all enjoyed ourselves except Captain Colville who, because His Excellency rode, thought it necessary to do ditto and [Frederick] never saw anyone so uncomfortable — his back showed how he was suffering in vain. F. told him to get into the carriage. He bore his misery till we returned for luncheon at Mr. Cochrane's house. About three we started again riding and driving, leaving Mr. Colville with regret.*

It wasn't just Captain Colville who left with a souvenir. "He [Billy Cochrane] gave us two coyote brushes as a remembrance of our visit."[116]

Lady Stanley's longest journal entry of 1889's transcontinental trip continued:

> *We saw great quantity of buffalo heads and bones. We picked up what was thought to be good in order to have the bones polished. The entry to Fort MacLeod was picturesque. There were lots of Indians about us. They had been paid their money the day before so they had come into the town to spend it at the Hudson Bay store. The men fired [hunted] and we were a large cavalcade. Colonel Herchmer said the horses were all pretty nearly done, for in the two days, we had done one hundred miles.*[117]

The vice regal party stayed at the house of Dr. John W. Allen, "a dreadful old man with a still more dreadful son," according to Lady Stanley. But Constance tempered her opinion: "they were very kind to us and did their best to make us comfortable and we found lots to laugh at. They were so vulgar."

During the day, a representative of the Mormons arrived to greet Lord and Lady Stanley, hoping to deliver an address which the *MacLeod Gazette* reprinted:

> *Owing to some hitch, they were not able to do so and waited upon Lord Stanley on Monday morning before he*

> left. 'We, the Latter-Day Saints resident in the North West
> Territories of Canada, do most cordially unite with our
> fellow settlers of Alberta in welcoming to the district the
> representative of that Sovereign Power which, as pictured
> to us by the last of the old Republicans, has dotted the sur-
> face of the globe with Her possessions and military posts,
> whose morning drum-beat, following the sun, and keeping
> company with the hours, circles the earth with continuous
> and unbroken strain of the martial airs to England.' Signed
> by request of the Latter-Day Saints in the Canadian North-
> West, Charles Ora Card, president.[118]

Card, who had been arrested for polygamy after marrying his fourth wife in Utah in 1885, escaped custody and fled to southwestern Alberta. There he started a fledgling Mormon community close to the Blood Indian Reserve, where he hoped his brethren might carry out missionary work.[119]

Lord Stanley replied to the president of the Latter-Day Saints, welcoming the church to Canada and saying that "the country is free to all creeds, and to as many of their people as desired to come."[120]

A reception took place that evening, but it too, as the newspaper attested, was a disappointment. "Reception in the evening a regular farce as there was no one to be received." Of course, an address was presented. Lord and Lady Stanley "remained in the hall less than half an hour and, consequently, only a very few were presented, the others arriving too late."[121]

On Sunday, 13 October, the party took the day to reflect and worship. "Went to a dear little church where we had such a bright nice Harvest House service," wrote Lady Stanley. "It did seem odd to look out of the window and to see a lot of Indian faces looking in! Fred and the men went to have luncheon with Colonel Herchmer at the Barracks. We were left to the tender services of the two Colonel Allens, but they were rather interesting as they told us how the Indians had stolen the younger Mr. Allen's child away from its Mother. They were the first people to come settle in Fort MacLeod. The Indians were quite wild there and they wanted something done and watched their opportunity and came and took the child out of its cot. They had rather difficulty in getting the poor little thing back again."[122]

While waiting for the return of Lord Stanley, Lady Stanley bought a few items from the Hudson's Bay store and was then taken to see "Indian curiosities." Lady Stanley was dismayed:

> *The man had got two scalps which were horrid. He had*
> *also got some of the ivory sticks used by the Indians in their*
> *sun dance. When they make the 'braves', they cut the mus-*
> *cles of the chest. They pass these sticks through and then*
> *hang up to a tree till the flesh tears away. They are then*
> *'braves' and may marry.*[123]

After supper, as the Stanleys readied themselves for a second church service, they received another surprise guest. "Mr. McPherson, brother of one of our friends at Quebec, came with us. We were so surprised to hear of him as none of the family had ever mentioned him. He was under a cloud for twelve years but is now forgiven and has got his commission this year upon which Sir David, his father, sent him a thousand dollars." Sir David Lewis McPherson was a railway czar and the business partner of Sir Casimir Gzowski. "The Evening Service as nice as the morning one was. Mr. Hutton was the name of the clergyman."[124]

Monday was remembered by Lord and Lady Stanley as the seventeenth birthday of their son George. Constance noted:

> *[Frederick], Mr. McMahon, Mr. Goschen, Mr. Allan left*
> *early in the morning to do three days ranching. We left in*
> *our carriage of four to drive to Mr. Galt's house again. Very*
> *uneventful hot drive. Saw a coyote which Captain Colville*
> *tried to shoot. Mr. Galt gave us an excellent luncheon and*
> *took us to the top of the coal mine to show us how the coal*
> *was delivered from the mine.*[125]

The ladies were driven to Banff and arrived at seven o'clock.

The village of Banff was best known for "a medicinal watering-place and pleasure resort." The CPR declared that "no part of the Rockies exhibits a greater variety of sublime and pleasing scenery, and nowhere are good points of view and features of special interest so accessible, since many good roads and bridlepaths have been made."[126] After sulphur springs were discovered in the area in 1883, the Canadian Pacific Railway immediately recognized the potential as a tourist destination and, in 1888, constructed the elegant Banff Springs Hotel. As beautiful as the village was, the family's thoughts were elsewhere. "Found poor Chump very ill," Lady Stanley lamented. "When we got to Banff we sent for a doctor who said he had the worst form of distemper. We took him away to nurse him but have little hope of his recovery."[127]

Aubrey McMahon went to stay at the Banff Springs Hotel with Mr. McPherson. Lady Stanley wryly assessed McPherson as "such a nice amusing ugly little man."[128]

In the meantime, Lord Stanley left Fort MacLeod on Monday to visit a number of area ranches. The New Oxley (Canada) ranch Fort MacLeod was the first stop, and he was welcomed by W. Stanley Pinhorne, the ranch's manager.

Thirty miles west of Fort MacLeod in High River, Stanley was the honoured guest of the North-West Cattle Company, whose managing director was the engaging Fred Stimson. Financed by Hugh Allan, one of Canada's wealthiest men and whose other business interests included shipping, trains and banking, the company, with its 150,000 acres and 500 horses, was one of the foremost ranching operations in Canada's New West. Stimson's Ranch, as it was most often called, was noted for its hospitality, and was a favoured spot for visitors from eastern Canada and England.

Stimson was an engaging storyteller and fluent in Blackfoot, so he was a favourite among the First Nations tribes of the area. Stanley stayed at the North-West Cattle Company's ranch for two nights. On the first evening, he was persuaded that he must be fatigued and should retire early, which he did so, willingly. Stimson and the remaining visitors then proceeded to "make merry and a right royal time was enjoyed." The next night, Lord Stanley insisted on joining in the merriment as well.[129]

On Wednesday, His Excellency visited the Quorn Ranch, which was better known as Barter's Ranch after its manager, J. J. Barter. The Quorn Ranch was just west of High River. There, as the *Calgary Herald* reported, "an evening of mirth, wit and humour was spent, unrestrained by the formalities of court etiquette."[130]

On Thursday, joined by several Calgary dignitaries, the Governor General travelled over the Dewdney Bridge and Mission Hill to MacLeod Trail, where he visited the North-West Mounted Police. One of those who travelled with Stanley was Arthur D. Braithwaite, the manager of the Bank of Montreal. Braithwaite, whose wife had given birth to a daughter just four months prior, accompanied Lord Stanley on the remainder of his overland trip. The Bank of Montreal had opened its first Calgary branch in a rented space in 1886 and built a permanent branch in 1889.

* * *

The Honourable Edward and Lady Alice rejoined the vice regal party on Tuesday, 15 October, boasting of a very good time but no luck in shooting goats. In the afternoon, the suite was taken by carriage for a tour of Banff, with the promise of a visit to the sulphur springs the next day.

There are any number of hot springs that occur naturally within the Rockies. Hot springs form when moisture seeps through the many cracks and crevices found in the mountain rock. The water eventually works its way down through to the earth's crust, where it is boiled by the intense heat occurring at the core of the globe. Pressure then forces the heated water back to the earth's surface, where it pools in areas within the mountain range. The water is greatly affected by the type of rock present, so some springs, like the one enjoyed by the Stanleys near Banff, have a sulphuric smell due to the amounts of hydrogen sulphide that are released naturally during the heating process. Although not always pleasant-smelling, the sulphur baths are very soothing and therapeutic. While constructing the CPR, builder William Cornelius Van Horne installed "the finest bathing establishment on the continent" at the Banff Springs Hotel, making it one of the most popular stops on the transcontinental route.

Confirming an earlier apprehension, Lady Stanley wrote on Wednesday, 16 October, "Poor Chump died this morning. We were all most dreadfully cut up for he was a dear dog. Fred feels it very much indeed." Perhaps in an effort to escape the sadness, the entire party enjoyed a sulphur bath later that day. Constance had hers at the Sanitarium. "Went to the Minnewanka Lake in the afternoon. Had tea there."[131] Lake Minnewanka, about five kilometres north of the town of Banff, was a very popular spot for visitors, specifically affluent Europeans who were drawn to the Rockies once the railway had been built.

Lord Stanley rejoined the rest of the vice regal suite on a sun-drenched Thursday, 17 October, and the entire party proceeded by train to Calgary. A private car carrying William Whyte, the general superintendent of the CPR's Western Division, and Colonel Villiers of Winnipeg were added to the Governor General's train. After leaving Banff, Victoria followed the Bow River through some of the most extraordinary sights imagined — forested valleys and a series of lakes amid the impressive mountain peaks.

The city of Calgary owes its very existence to the Canadian Pacific Railway, which linked the young (first settled in 1874) community with eastern Canada as well as the Pacific, enabling a number of industries — not the least of which was cattle ranching — to not only grow but flourish.

The vice regal procession arrived at the train depot, where they were greeted not only by hundreds of loyal citizens, but by an arch decorated with evergreens that bid the Governor General welcome.

The local North-West Mounted Police played "God Save the Queen" for the guests. Among the civic dignitaries there to greet Lord and Lady Stanley was Calgary Mayor Daniel W. Marsh. Marsh had been working for T. C. Power and Brother, a well-known mercantile company in the north-western United States, when he realized the opportunities in the Canadian west made possible by the railway. A year after opening a store in Maple Creek, Saskatchewan, on behalf of his employer in 1883, he did the same in Calgary. While managing the Calgary store, Marsh became a respected money-lender. He was elected mayor on 21 January, 1889. In 1893, the company sold its Calgary store to Marsh.

Mayor Marsh delivered a stirring address, which was followed by the obligatory reply by Lord Stanley:

> *During my extended trip through the north-west, I have everywhere met with expressions of deep-rooted loyalty to the Queen, but at none of the many places which I have had the pleasure of visiting has that feeling been more enthusiastically manifested than at Calgary. I have found that feeling so general that even the dust of your streets has risen up to meet me.*[132]

The crowd laughed at Stanley's remark. Those in attendance offered three cheers for Lord Stanley, followed by three for his wife.

The Governor General was introduced to Bishop William Cyprian Pinkham, Calgary's Anglican bishop. Known as Chief Holy Rest by the Blood Indians, Pinkham's diocese covered three thousand square miles at that time.

LORD FREDERICK ARTHUR STANLEY, THE EARL OF DERBY

"He is fair, with full beard which is just slightly streaked with grey, has a ruddy complexion, blue eyes, aquiline nose," reported Toronto's *The Globe* in October 1888. "He has a fine, broad forehead upon which the hair is becoming thin."

(photographer unknown / Library and Archives Canada; C-022832)

LADY CONSTANCE STANLEY

"Lady Stanley is a charming matron," wrote *The Progress* in October 1888. "She has the fresh, beautiful complexion of all her country women, dark blue eyes and a most charming smile." Although insisting on remaining in the shadow of her husband, Lady Stanley was a tireless worker for hospitals and children in the Ottawa area.

(photographer unknown / Library and Archives Canada; PA-025668)

RIDEAU HALL, OTTAWA, ONTARIO, CIRCA 1895

Oft-maligned in its earliest configuration as the vice regal residence in Ottawa, this was nonetheless the most accommodating principal residence of Lord and Lady Stanley and family while in Canada.

(Wm. Notman & Son / McCord Museum, Montreal; VIEW-2563)

STANLEY HOUSE, NEW RICHMOND, QUEBEC

Purchased soon after their arrival in Canada in 1888, Stanley House offered the family a respite from much official business and a haven for relaxing and fishing on the Cascapedia during summers in Canada. The home, seen as it exists today, has been lovingly restored and is owned by J. Edgar LeBlanc, who operates the historic home as Auberge La Maison Stanley.

(Photo courtesy of J. Edgar LeBlanc)

UNVEILING OF THE SHARPSHOOTERS MONUMENT

One of the first official duties presided over by the new governor general was the November 1, 1888 unveiling of The Sharpshooters Monument, created by British sculptor Percy Wood.

(Photographer unknown / Library and Archives Canada; PA-027139)

THE GOVERNOR GENERAL'S XI

Lord Stanley proudly stands back row centre (in top hat) amongst his cricket team, the Governor General's XI, along with assorted supporters. The team sported the uniform made famous by the Marylebone Cricket Club (MCC), which was founded in 1787.

(photographer unknown / Library and Archives Canada; C-019506)

COMPOSITE, MONTREAL CARNIVAL, QUEBEC, 1889

The Notman studio pioneered the use of composite photographs, like this elaborate representation of the Montreal Winter Carnival of 1889 at which Lord Stanley and his family first witnessed a hockey game. In the lower left, Stanley is being tossed in the air by a snowshoe club.

(Wm. Notman & Son / McCord Museum, Montreal; VIEW-1998.1)

His Excellency, Lord Stanley and snowshoes, Montreal Quebec, 1890

Most dignitaries visiting Montreal found themselves having their portrait taken at William Notman's studio, and Lord Stanley was no different. Likely taken during the course of the Montreal Winter Carnival of 1890.

(Wm. Notman & Son / McCord Museum, Montreal; II-91495)

SKATING ON THE RIDEAU HALL RINK
A group of skaters enjoy an outing on the Rideau Hall Rink.
(Photographer unknown; Library and Archives Canada; PA-033915)

A PARTY OF SNOWSHOERS AT RIDEAU HALL
The Stanley family prepares for a day of snowshoeing on the steps of Rideau Hall. Lord Stanley stands back row, second from left in light-coloured toque. Isobel is seated bottom left while Edward is beside his sister on the stairs.
(Topley / Library and Archives Canada; C-020478)

LORD STANLEY ON FRONT OF CPR TRAIN

While in British Columbia, nearing the conclusion of the transcontinental journey, the vice regal family road on the train's cowcatcher in order to better observe the extraordinary scenery. Seated left to right: Lord Stanley, Miss Lister, Isobel Stanley and aide-de-camp Aubrey McMahon. William Whyte, the CPR's Western Division General Superintendent, stands behind them.

(photographer unknown / Canadian Pacific Railways Archives; A.17333)

STATUE OF LORD STANLEY IN STANLEY PARK, VANCOUVER, BC

The Vancouver World reported on the vice regal events of October 29, 1889: "Lord Stanley threw his arms to the heavens as though embracing within them the whole of one thousand acres of primeval forest, and dedicated it 'to the use and enjoyment of people of all colours, creeds, and customs, for all time'. Then, as he slowly poured champagne on the virgin earth, Lord Stanley added, 'I name thee Stanley Park.'"

(Walt Neubrand / Hockey Hall of Fame)

LORD AND LADY STANLEY

Both born into aristocratic British families, Lord Frederick Stanley and Lady Constance Stanley (nee Villiers) were married 31 May, 1864. Lady Stanley gave birth to ten children, eight of whom lived to adulthood.

(photographer unknown / Hockey Hall of Fame Archives)

The Rideau Rebels

Following the Montreal Winter Carnival, Arthur Stanley put together a loosely-organized hockey team comprised largely of parliamentary assistants. This 1889 photo includes (standing, left to right) Captain Wingfield, Arthur Stanley, Senator Lawrence Power, Henry Ward, J. de St. Lemoine (seated, left to right) Edward Stanley, James Creighton, Aubrey McMahon, John Barron, H.B. Hawkes.

(photographer unknown / Hockey Hall of Fame Archives)

Ottawa Hockey Club (Ottawa, O.H.A. Champions, 1891-2-3)

The storied Ottawa Hockey Club attracted much attention in the nation's capital. It was at a banquet to the championship team that Governor General Stanley bequeathed a challenge trophy. Top row, left to right—W.C. Young, F.M.S. Jenkins, H.Y. Russel, R. Bradley. Bottom row, left to right—A. Morel, Dr. H.S. Kirby, C.T. Kirby, J. Kerr.

(photographer unknown / Hockey Hall of Fame Archives)

THE GOVERNOR GENERAL'S PRIZE

On March 19, 1892, *The Montreal Gazette* reported that Lord Kilcoursie, on behalf of Lord Stanley, had attended a banquet honouring the Ottawa Hockey Club, and announced the creation of a trophy for the best amateur hockey club in Canada. The trophy would be known as the Stanley Cup.

(The Montreal Gazette; *March 19, 1892*)

THE FIRST WINNERS OF THE STANLEY CUP

In 1893, the Montreal Hockey Club, part of the Montreal Amateur Athletic Association (MAAA), became the first recipients of Lord Stanley's challenge cup. Billy Barlow, one of the team's stars, is seated far right. Note the Stanley Cup front and centre, along with other championship trophies.

(*photographer unknown / Hockey Hall of Fame Archives*)

HORSES AND SLEIGH OF THE GOVERNOR GENERAL

Wrapped in bear fur, Lord and Lady Stanley employed this coachman, sleigh and team of horses to provide winter transportation while in Canada.

(Photographer unknown / Library and Archives Canada; PA-033962)

NEW YEAR'S SKATING PARTY

Rideau Hall was the site of many a winter party, with guests enjoying tobogganing, snowshoeing and skating along with the Stanley family. Note the 'Happy New Year' sign erected on the trees behind the party posing on the Rideau Hall Rink.

(photographer unknown / Library and Archives Canada; PA-013245)

1902 GUILD COIN

The 16th Earl of Derby and Countess Derby were depicted in profile on a coin minted in 1902 to commemorate the Preston Guild, celebrated every twenty years. The Earl had been selected as Guild Mayor, the highest honour that Preston could bestow upon an individual.

(Hockey Hall of Fame Archives)

BUST OF THE 16TH EARL OF DERBY

This extraordinary sculpted likeness of the 16th Earl resides at Liverpool Town Hall, commemorating Stanley's term as Lord Mayor of Liverpool.

(Pamela Raman / The Lord Mayor's Office, Liverpool Town Hall)

PORTRAIT OF FREDERICK ARTHUR STANLEY, 16TH EARL OF DERBY

This magnificent painting of the Earl was created by Sir Hubert Von Herkomer, and hangs in the Derby estate at Knowsley. Stanley most likely sat for the portrait later in his life.

(K-305; (c)The Right Hon. The Earl of Derby)

ORIGINAL STANLEY CUP

The incredible trophy that fuelled a nation's obsession, the Stanley Cup, seen here almost exactly as donated by Lord Frederick Stanley, was originally to be named the Dominion Hockey Challenge Cup. This original bowl is on permanent display at the Hockey Hall of Fame.

(Doug MacLellan / Hockey Hall of Fame)

STANLEY CUP AT ITS HOME IN THE HOCKEY HALL OF FAME

The proud 'descendent' of Lord Stanley's original Cup resides in the magnificent Great Hall of the Hockey Hall of Fame, and is viewed by over a quarter-million visitors each year.

(Hockey Hall of Fame)

HISTORIC PLAQUE MARKS PURCHASE LOCATION OF STANLEY CUP

The Stanley Cup, or as it was originally known, the Dominion Hockey Challenge Cup, was purchased in 1892 from G.R. Collis & Co. at 130 Regent Street in London, England. In April 2006, a plaque was affixed to the building, now housing Boodles jewellery. Officiating at the unveiling were The 19th Earl of Derby and Lord Mayor of Westminster Tim Joiner.

(Philip Pritchard / Hockey Hall of Fame)

STANLEY CUP ON-ICE PRESENTATION

In a ceremony beloved by hockey fans, gloved custodians of the Stanley Cup Philip Pritchard (left) and Craig Campbell (right), both of the Hockey Hall of Fame, carry Lord Stanley's prize to centre ice in Washington after the Red Wings captured the Stanley Cup on June 16, 1998.

(Dave Sandford / Hockey Hall of Fame)

Although Lord and Lady Stanley were quite pleased with their Calgary reception, the *Calgary Herald* bemoaned the poor attendance: "Nothing short of a visit from the Queen Herself would have induced some farmers, who are behind with work, to lose a day of such grand weather as that which prevailed during the Governor General's trip."[133]

* * *

Prior to Stanley's appointment, relations between the vice regal office and the First Nations of Canada had been strained. The Indian Advancement Act had been passed by the Dominion government in 1884 and was based unashamedly on the premise that First Nation citizens and culture were inferior to those of white settlers. The act gave increased powers to Indian agents, and among other things, attempted to control the manner in which chiefs were elected. In a letter to all Indian agents, Sir John A. Macdonald, in his role as Deputy Superintendent-General of Indian Affairs, wrote, "The object of the Department is to endeavour to promote their advancement in civilization and intelligence with a view to eventually attaining to an equality in those respects with the white portion of the population."

Ottawa's efforts were unsuccessful and the life of the aboriginals proceeded as usual. One Mohawk community, Tyendinaga, sent a petition to Lord Stanley dated 29 October, 1888, requesting that they be allowed to continue employing their own methods to choose leaders.

> *Brother! We do not want our Council Fire extinguished because it was the custom and manner of our forefathers. We lay before your Excellency of our main object to do away with the way of electing council committee, that we have entirely lost confidence in them and that there is division among themselves.*

Without a favourable reply from Stanley, the band reminded him of promises the British Crown had made to "remain in its own vessel and the Indian in his birch bark canoe" and that the British "will never make any compulsory laws for the Six Nations and the treaties between them shall remain unmolested forever." There was a not-so-subtle reminder to Lord Stanley that the Royal Proclamation of 1763 stated that Indian land would be secured to them free of molestation and was delivered with the solemn promise of peace and friendship:

> *We will remind you of the Covenant Chain of Peace and Friendship between the English people and the Six Nations. When our forefathers first made the Covenant Chain with the English, both parties engaged to keep the ends of it fast in their hands: that they would take care to keep it from breaking, or from getting any rust or filth upon it. We, the old people [are sorely grieved] of receiving such a document from the Privy Council stating that our wishes cannot be complied with. It fills us with great concern. Neither can we visualize any account for it, having always lived in the strictest friendship with the British Government, and our forefathers faithfully served and assisted them in all their wars back against the French and in the Revolutionary War. The treaties were sealed in the blood of our forefathers to benefit and to promote their children's children's welfare. It is necessary in order for the preservation of our liberties and rights, privileges and customs. The Canadian Government which does not recognize us fully looks upon the Six Nations as minors and treats them as such.*
>
> *Brother! We quote the words of Lord Dufferin, one of your predecessors, saying the people of Canada and the people of Britain will not cease to recognize these obligations. Never shall the word of Britain, once pledged, be broken. Brother! We now beg to assure you that our feelings of loyalty to the British Crown are as deep, as sincere, and as true at this day as they were in the days of our forefathers of old. We are your most obedient, and most humble and devoted friends.*

Edgar Dewdney, the newly-appointed Superintendent-General of Indian Affairs, to whom Stanley referred the matter, simply suggested to the Privy Council that correspondence be discontinued as Lord Stanley was unable to accede to their request.

A First Nations delegation from the Bay of Quinte approached the

Governor General in 1889 and pointedly asked, "What is your power and authority to rule our people?" This challenge, too, was ignored. A further petition to the Governor General pleaded even more furiously for equality:

> *Brother! We remember still that when our forefathers first met with you, when you came with your ship and our fore-fathers kindly received you and entertained you and entered into an alliance with you. Though our forefathers were then great and numerous, and your people were in-considerable and weak, and they knew that, they entered into a Covenant Chain with you and fastened your ship therewith, being apprehensive the bark would break away and your ship be lost. Brother! We are inconsiderable and weak, and you are now a great and numerous people, and you know that we are entered into a Covenant Chain of Brotherly Love, and therefore we also like to be entertained and recognize our request concerning our just rights from the Government. But Sir, we are sinking fast because our treaty right is neglected.*[134]

* * *

At nine-thirty on the morning of Friday, 18 October, a ceremony was held at the CPR station in Calgary to bid goodbye to Lord Stanley and his party as they proceeded to the First Nations reserve at Gleichen. Sir James Grant, the physician travelling with the vice regal suite, had visited western Canada seven years prior and noticed substantial progress. "The prosperity is general. Passing on through Brandon, Medicine Hat and Calgary, no better proofs could possibly be given of the rapid growth of the country than evidenced in these three centres."[135]

Cautious but undaunted, the entourage was driven eighty miles east of Calgary to the Blood Reserve at Gleichen on Friday, 18 October. Edgar Dewdney, the Deputy Superintendent-General of Indian Affairs, acted as host for the Governor General's visit.

As a divisional point for the CPR, Gleichen was an important stop for trains in the late 1800s. The community was named in 1883 by the CPR to honour Count Albert Edward Wilfred Gleichen, a financial supporter of the railway who had visited the area at that time. Gleichen is the home of the Siksika Reserve. Part of the Blackfoot Confederacy, which also included the Bloods and Peigans from southern Alberta and the Blackfoot in Montana, the Siksika were longtime buffalo hunters who successfully employed a natural rock formation two miles north of Gleichen as a buffalo jump. The tribe would drive herds of buffalo to the cliff, forcing them over the edge to their demise, then butcher the carcasses for meat, use the skins for clothing and the bones as needed for tools.

Sixty horses and wagons transported the vice regal party. The Governor General, his daughter Isobel and Miss Lister, along with some of the other men, rode part of the way on horseback. At eleven-thirty, and several miles outside of the reserve, an Indian scout signalled the pending arrival of their special visitors. Almost immediately, the sombre hills came alive with more than a hundred braves on horseback, whooping and firing their guns as though to capture an enemy. Chief Crowfoot greeted Lord Stanley on his arrival, joined by almost a thousand Blackfoot men, women and children and a large number of horses and dogs.

Lord Stanley sat across from Chief Crowfoot and his councillors and smoked the pipe of peace with them. Then, Stanley addressed the Native chiefs. "Chief Crowfoot, Old Sun and warriors, your Great Mother across the salt sea, although unable to come and see you herself, is always glad to hear of your welfare and prosperity and your loyalty to the throne." Crowfoot responded in Blackfoot, his address translated for Stanley through Alexander Begg, the CPR's immigration agent. Lord Frederick Stanley was given the name "Son of Love," as he had been sent from the Great Mother, Queen Victoria. Crowfoot referred to the failure of the local potato crop and the need for extra rations and medicine. Stanley instructed Agent Begg to place "three fast steers" at the disposal of the tribe as a personal gift.

The Blackfoot nation was routinely discouraged from performing ritual dances for the entertainment of visiting dignitaries. Dances of celebration or to curry the good will of the spirits was to be kept private. But Lady Stanley expressed interest in taking photographs of Native dancing, so the tribe obliged Her Excellency.[136] Dewdney was concerned that such an exhibition might give the Governor General the impression that he was observing savages, and that that impression would undo any accomplishments that had been made to that point in "civilizing" the Natives.

Lady Stanley reviewed her time with the Blackfoots:

> *Drove to the Blackfoot Indian's ranch, the best we have seen. They rode out to meet us shouting and yelling and firing guns from their horses. Old Crowfoot the Chief is a very fine old man. F. had the usual pow wow. They danced a war dance and showed us their sign language. The Blackfoot Indians seem to paint their faces, especially their eyes, with a bright red, making them look quite sore, and they also paint their horses' eyes and tails!*[137]

In a dispatch published later that year in *The Graphic*, Frederic Villiers wrote:

> *A captive of one of the chiefs of the Blackfeet is a little white girl about nine years old. She was brought into camp on a pony. Dressed in rich beadwork vestments, which ill became her fair hair and little white face. Full of intelligence, she sat to be sketched and photographed. I only hope that publicity will be the means of this child being handed over to people of her own colour, though she is treated with every care and great affection.*[138]

These sorts of dramatic accounts helped to sell publications a world away in the urban centres of the Empire.

A luncheon was held at the home of Alexander Begg, then the entourage returned to Calgary. After a hectic day, Lord and Lady Stanley were the guests of honour at a reception at the Calgary Opera House.

While Stanley went to inspect the police barracks with Lawrence Herchmer, the red-headed commissioner of the North-West Mounted Police, the ladies went shopping on Saturday, 19 October. "Met Mr. Goschen, who looked more dead than alive," stated Lady Stanley. "He confides his loves and sorrows to everyone. He told us he had been sent away from England on account of his heart! We thought it was disease but have found out that it is love!"[139]

The suite left Calgary at noon and arrived at Banff, where a civic address was delivered at the CPR station.

The Stanleys took advantage of a beautiful day to go for a walk in both the morning and afternoon of Sunday, 20 October. That evening, they attended a service at the Presbyterian Church Chapel. "Bishop Pinkham preached. Oh so dull," Constance sighed.[140]

Lady Stanley was asked to lay the cornerstone of the newly constructed St. George's-in-the-Pines Anglican Church in Banff National Park on Monday, 21 October. The limestone was quarried from a spot across the river from the Banff Springs Hotel. Constance recalled:

> *I had to lay the foundation stone of the new English Church. A nice little service. The church will stand in a most lovely position. I was given a little trowel in a very nice holder made out of the bark of the cotton and carved by a man at Minnewanka Lake.*[141]

According to Lady Stanley's journal, a ball given that evening in honour of the Governor General and his wife turned out to be rather interesting:

> *Great jealousy between the two sisters-in-law Mrs. Commissioner Herchmer [wife of Lawrence] and Mrs. Colonel Herchmer [wife of Lawrence's brother, William, an NWMP superintendent]. The former told me that her sister-in-law is very fat. Mrs. Allan had been to have a sulphur bath in the afternoon and that they were both so fat that they came to the top in vain. They tried to hold one another down. It was of no use.*[142]

The vice regal family spent the night at the Banff Springs Hotel. Lady Stanley described what happened that night: "Mr. Goschen ill in the night. Called Mr. McMahon, who went for Eddy and got a doctor, who said he had nothing the matter with him, he was only hysterical!"[143]

The entire vice regal suite commented on how wonderfully and professionally they had been treated by Sam Steele and the North-West Mounted Police. "Said goodbye to the Mounted Police with some regret for they have been so good to us." The *MacLeod Gazette* reported:

> *Superintendent Steele was highly complimented by the Governor upon the way in which the men in his district*

> *had turned out. It was the best guard of honour he had had*
> *since he came to the North-West. When they arrived at*
> *MacLeod, the escort worked as one man, and their splendid*
> *appearance was the subject of much favourable comment.*[144]

The trip through the Prairies had been both enlightening and entertaining for the Stanleys, who frequently commented on the particular leg of his journey throughout their term in Canada.

* * *

The Governor General's train pulled out of Banff at nine o'clock on the morning of 22 October, and within a few hours had crossed the border into the province of British Columbia. Lady Stanley's journal entry depicted the conditions: "Cloudy morning but became fine enough for us to see the beauty of the Rockies ... when we reached Field, the clouds lifted from off the top of Mount Stephen."[145] The massive mountain, rising to a height of 10,496 feet (3,199 metres), was named in 1886 after George Stephen, who in 1881 became the first president of the Canadian Pacific Railway.

Lord and Lady Stanley had the opportunity to observe firsthand the magnificence of Canada's western landscape. "It was very grand indeed and we saw all the beauties to perfection as we were on the cowcatcher."[146] The cowcatcher was made of iron and was fixed to the front of train engines in order to throw off animals that might wander onto the tracks. Lady Macdonald had enjoyed travelling through much of the Canadian west on the cowcatcher during her trip in July 1886.

What is now southeastern British Columbia had been left all but untouched by human footsteps until the 1860s. The rugged mountains made early transportation all but impossible and foiled attempts at agriculture. The winters were not only frigid but dangerous, with substantial amounts of snow falling on the area each year, much of which contributed to terrifying avalanches. But the beauty of the scenery held an unmistakable allure.

Although others, as early as 1865, had tried to discover a path through the Selkirk Mountains that would accommodate railway trains, it wasn't until 1881, when a surveyor named Major Albert Bowman Rogers and his adventurous crew struggled up from a valley (later to be named Illecillewaet Valley). Rogers earned five thousand dollars, and immortality, by discovering a narrow pass at the summit of the Selkirks that bears his name.

In order to complete the railway, the CPR was forced to build a massive trestle at Mountain Creek that stretched more than 330 metres in length and rose 50 metres above the mountain river. A few kilometres further along, a bridge rising 64 metres above Stoney Creek was constructed. Then, as the rails entered the Illecillewaet Valley, engineers were with a dangerously steep descent. Although it lengthened the track by five kilometres, an intricate series of loops in allowed trains to pass successfully through the Selkirks and, by 1886, successfully span the breadth of the Dominion.[147]

"We stood still on the ugliest bridge in the world which is very wonderful but rather awful," Lady Constance wrote, "and after the hills, what struck us most was the beautiful colour of the Columbia River. It is a lovely bright blue sort of green."[148] Lady Stanley took photographs from the door of the railway car.

The scenery along the railway route suggested great potential for tourism for the CPR. A grand hotel was built nearby in 1886, helping to entice travellers to what had been wilderness just a few years before. Although Glacier House was primarily intended to eliminate the need for trains to pull heavy dining cars through the steep mountain grades, the glacier very quickly became an immensely popular tourist attraction. It boasted an extraordinary view of the headwall of the Illecillewaet Glacier just five hundred feet away. Passengers were able to enjoy a view of the great glacier from the seats of their railway car. The hotel offered not only accommodation and meals, but also sightseeing, mountain climbing and another recently popularized pastime, bowling.

That same year, the federal government set aside 1,349 square kilometres of wilderness to establish Glacier National Park, which CPR president William Cornelius Van Horne described as "the climax of mountain scenery." Rogers Pass is located in the centre of the park.[149]

The vice regal party arrived in Glacier at 4:45 on a rainy Wednesday afternoon, 23 October and was received by local dignitaries. Although most who visited Glacier were impressed with what man had carved out of nature's enormity, not everyone was so pleased. "Very dull place shut in by the hills," wrote a nonplussed Lady Stanley. "The party all went up to the glacier. I remained at home. Ditto Isobel who had a very bad cold." Lady Stanley seemed rather more interested in the fact that "the time goes back an hour" as the wonders of nature.[150]

The party departed Glacier at dawn on Thursday, 24 October. Riding on the train's cowcatcher in order to view the landscape, Lady Stanley commented, "The clouds were so low we could see nothing of the hills." The train crossed the Columbia River and briefly stopped in Revelstoke and Sicamous on its way to Kamloops. "We took more photos of Shuswap Lake," continued Lady Stanley. "The railroad goes along the shore of this lake for twenty miles. And the mountains all around are very beautiful."[151]

The train arrived in Kamloops at six on Thursday evening, 24 October, and almost as soon as Lord and Lady Stanley had stepped from the vice regal train, they were addressed by John Mara and a committee of citizens. Mara, a politician and land speculator, had arrived in Kamloops in 1872, and over the next several years had become one of the richest and most powerful men in British Columbia. The Governor General, his family and staff remained in Kamloops overnight.

"Left Kamloops at 7:30," wrote Lady Stanley. "Very slow journey to North Bend. Part of this is line is dangerous and no train is allowed to go quickly over it. The line is laid too near to the steep hill going straight down into the river. The scenery all day was glorious."[152] The train arrived in North Bend at five o'clock that afternoon.

North Bend, located on the Fraser River, had been known as Boston Bar until 1885, when the CPR was completed through the town. The name was changed to North Bend, while the name Boston Bar was reassigned to a place on the other side of the Fraser. Although the railway built a hotel in North Bend, it was little more than a stopover until later in the century, when it became very busy for those venturing north to prospect for gold.

After a night in North Bend, the Stanleys and their staff left the next morning, destination Vancouver. "The country very beautiful," penned Constance. "Stopped at Hope for breakfast and at Hastings for luncheon." As the party neared Vancouver, Lady Stanley noted how similar the area was to her memories of home, "the country much more cultivated looking, like English parks and gardens."[153]

The engine pulling *Victoria*, with its tastefully decorated smokestack, smoke box and cowcatcher, pulled into Vancouver at one in the afternoon and was greeted with great enthusiasm by dignitaries and citizens who had braved the threatening clouds and occasional sprinkles to wait for the governor general at the Canadian Pacific depot. "Very good reception indeed," noted Lady Stanley.

A procession, led by Lord and Lady Stanley, their son Edward and Vancouver Mayor David Oppenheimer, was driven by carriage to the Hotel Vancouver. The lead vehicle was followed by coaches bearing the remainder of the Governor General's suite, as well as city officials, some of whom were forced to walk as there were not enough carriages for all. With an estimated three thousand citizens lining the street leading up to the hotel, the carriages passed under a railway bridge with one banner spelling out "Stanley" and another "God Save the Queen." "Two of the most lovely arches I ever saw," noted Lady Stanley.[154] Lord Frederick Stanley smiled when he observed others: a sizable arch that included a lifesize transparency of Queen Victoria, the Masonic emblem on the left and that of the Oddfellows on the right, and a large revolving globe with "Vancouver Welcomes Lord Stanley" inscribed beneath and another that read "Welcome to our Governor General: Happy people without a grievance."[155]

Once at the Hotel Vancouver, Mayor David Oppenheimer addressed the special guests. Lady Stanley wrote: "Great enthusiasm shown. Mr. Oppenheimer, the mayor, most civil and seems very unhappy about the weather, but of course, made the remark that he could control everything in this city but the clouds would not obey him!" She also confided, "Our remarks have been heard before. We were not in the least original!"[156]

Eight hundred Vancouver schoolchildren greeted the Governor General from stands erected at the hotel. "All the children were there with such a very good band," Lady Stanley entered in her journal.[157]

At five o'clock, the reception over, the vice regal party returned to their train. Lord and Lady Stanley, along with aide Aubrey McMahon, had made plans to stay with the Bishop of New Westminster. "We stayed with the Bishop of New Westminster and Mrs. Sillitoe," Constance recounted. "The poor man has the misfortune to be called 'Windeyer'. He used to be at Darmstadt and knew Princess Alice very well."[158]

Acton Windeyer Sillitoe was the first Bishop of New Westminster, a position he accepted at thirty-nine years of age on All Saints' Day in 1879. The Australian-born Sillitoe oversaw two prominent Anglican churches in New Westminster — Holy Trinity Cathedral and St. Mary the Virgin — and played a vital role in spreading Christianity throughout southern British Columbia during its earliest days as a province. Bishop Sillitoe was well-known to Lord Stanley. While chaplain to the British delegation at Darmstadt, Germany, Sillitoe tutored Princess Alice, daughter of Queen

Victoria, at the time of her marriage to Prince Ludwig of Hesse.[159]

Lady Stanley commented in her journal on their stay in New Westminster. "It was so curious to have China boys for servants. Nothing else can be got and they seem to do the work very well and to be very clean and quiet."[160]

The vice regal couple attended Holy Trinity Cathedral on Sunday, 27 October. Before spending a restful day in their train car, Lady Stanley commented, "Very nice service. The national anthem sung quite beautifully."[161]

The party left Vancouver by boat at 9:45 on Monday morning, sailing aboard the *Premier* up English Bay and Howe Sound. "It would have been charming had it not been damp and cold," began Lady Stanley. "The wooded hills right down to the water's edge are very beautiful. The Indians came out in their canoes all decorated with lamps arranged in arches over each boat. The effect was perfectly lovely."[162]

At eleven, Premier John Robson hosted the Governor General, Lady Stanley, their family and staff for an excursion up the Fraser River on the *Samson*. With a hundred and sixty guests on board, the steamer travelled up the North Arm, around Burrard Inlet and out to Howe Sound, then back to Vancouver by four.

A band played throughout the trip. During a stop at the Bon Accord cannery, Lord Stanley expressed deep interest in the processing of salmon.

After supper, the party followed a torchlight procession to the harbour for an exhibition. Fifty canoes paddled behind a tug named Senator. A second procession of sixty boats, all from the Vancouver Boating Club and similarly illuminated, followed the canoes. *HMS Champion* flashed its searchlight in every direction like a beacon. Afterwards, the harbour exploded in light from a massive fireworks display.

* * *

History will mark Tuesday, 29 October, 1889, as a special day for citizens of Vancouver. On that day, one of the most significant landmarks in the city was officially dedicated.

Stanley Park is located on a thousand-acre tongue of land that has been inhabited for at least eight thousand years. Newcomers who arrived at the peninsula in the late 1700s discovered that the area had served as a home to generations of aboriginal peoples.

The most populated region of what we know today as Stanley Park was located on the north shore of the peninsula. Referred to by European colonizers as *Whoi Whoi*, the name was written much like it sounded to those not familiar with the Squamish dialect, which spelled the name of the area as *Khwaykhway, xw'ay xway* or *Quoiquo*. The area, also known as Lumberman's Arch, played an important role in Squamish life through the decades, hosting massive potlatches where feasts for two thousand took place along with dancing and gift exchanges.

In August 1863, while visiting the first sawmill opened on the shores of the Burrard Inlet, British Columbia Attorney General H. P. P. Crease referred to a map created after a Royal Engineers' survey from earlier that year. Lance Corporal George Turner of the Royal Engineers had surveyed the area and written "Indian House" at a location near Prospect Point. He also added the notation, "Suple Jack," and at Whoi Whoi, he scratched in "Squamish Ranch."

Supple Jack, misspelled by Crease, was the son of a Squamish chief named Khahtsahlano, whose name has been borrowed for Kitsilano. Chief Khahtsahlano had constructed a house on a high bank — in Squamish, a chaythoos — west of Whoi Whoi near Prospect Point. The house, referred to as Chaythoos, later was home to his son Khaytulk, also known as Supple Jack.

Supple Jack was well known to those in the area. In July 1859, Lieutenant Governor Richard Moody, in a letter to his brother Tom, referred to Khaytulk:

> *We were visited by an Indian named Supple Jack, who used occasionally to come with messages from the (Royal Navy ship)* Plumper. *He was anxious to accompany us but as he belonged to another tribe (than the Indians paddling our canoes), and was noted for his partiality to whiskey, we managed to convince him, after hard feeding, that we could get on without him.*[163]

In 1876, a census of the area we know as Stanley Park revealed that fifty Squamish, led by Chief Supple Jack, were residing in the area known as Prospect Point. The British Columbia Reserve Commission wished to have what they referred to as "squatters" removed from the land, but, led by Supple Jack, the families at Chaythoos resisted, insisting that they had every right to remain on their land, which their families had inhabited for a generation.

Supple Jack was killed in an unfortunate accident in 1883. "My mother told me that he, my father, was sick one month and a half and he died," his son August Jack Khahtsahlano told Vancouver historian Major J. S. Mathews. "He was milking a cow and the cow gave him a kick and he bumped on the wall of the stall."[164]

Supple Jack's body was laid in a coffin covered with a red blanket and placed in a type of hut on cedar posts above ground measuring ten feet in length and six feet in width, and covered by hand-split cedar shingles.

The Canadian Pacific Railway, eager not only to complete its trans-Canadian train line but also to acquire vast tracts of land it could later sell to settlers, requested ownership of the southern half of the peninsula in January 1885; the Dominion government rejected the request. Denied this opportunity, the railway was convinced that if they couldn't own the beautiful (and valuable) land, then no one should. Arthur Wellington Ross, a member of Parliament aligned with the CPR's vision, proposed in March 1886 that the area "would be quite an attraction to tourists travelling over our national railway." The response from Sir Adolphe Caron, Minister of Militia in Ottawa, indicated that the government might have designs on the peninsula for a military reserve.[165]

* * *

William Van Horne, wielding his power as a vice president with the Canadian Pacific Railway, insisted that the name of the city be something other than the suggestions being discussed — Granville, Gastown or even Liverpool. "This is destined to become a great city, perhaps the greatest city in Canada," he proclaimed. "We must see to it that it has a name commensurate with its dignity and importance, and 'Vancouver' it shall be if I have the ultimate decision!" On 6 April, 1886, the city formally came into existence, using the name Vancouver — which incensed residents of Vancouver Island as well as those of Vancouver, Washington. How dare someone steal the name Captain George Vancouver himself had bestowed on them? Although the anger led to boycotts and letters to the editor, history shows that the protests had little if any effect.

Just over one month later, Vancouver's first city council petitioned the

Dominion government to lease to the citizens "the whole of that part of Coal Harbour peninsula known as the Government Reserve" to be conveyed to the City of Vancouver for a public park.

After numerous letters back and forth between the two governments, the Dominion government agreed. "The Minister reports that he sees no objection to this proposal provided the Corporation keep the Park in proper order, and the Dominion Government retain the right to resume the property when required at any time." The original intention, however, was to name the tract of land Strathcona Park to honour Donald Smith, 1st Baron Strathcona and a principal with the CPR. Smith modestly demurred, proposing instead that the Vancouver park be named to honour the new Governor General, Lord Stanley.

Plans for the park included the building of a road around the perimeter, using existing trails long followed by aboriginal settlers and logging operations, as the basis for the route. But as this thoroughfare was being built, construction crews stumbled upon a massive repository of discarded mollusk shells, or midden, that covered three acres and was eight feet deep. Although such heaps are not unusual in coastal zones, this one proved especially interesting because of its size and the discovery of human skulls and other bones in the vicinity. Because middens give archaeologists solid clues about the day-to-day lives of residents, researchers should have spent copious amounts of time poring over the discovery. Instead, the broken shells were used to help pave the road. In June 1891, the Vancouver Parks Board described the material used for three miles of road construction "being clam shells, which packed closely present a remarkable white appearance, adding greatly to the attractiveness of the park."[166]

As the road took its form, there was little regard for the inhabitants of what would become Stanley Park. Squamish families were often forced out of their homes, and they watched in horror and confusion as their houses were destroyed or expropriated with no regard for either heritage or compensation. They were also outraged at the use of the midden to pave the road. August Jack, in an interview some fifty years later, recalled:

> *When they make Stanley Park road, we was eating in our house. Someone make noise outside. They chop the corner of our house. We all get up go out see what was the matter. When they cut roadway, they go right through our house, my*

*father's, Supple Jack's. Grave was about one hundred and
forty feet west of our house. Our little house in front facing
water. Been there long, long time. Long before my time.*[167]

Just prior to eleven o'clock on 27 September, 1888, Vancouver Mayor David
Oppenheimer led a procession of vehicles from City Hall to a grassy spot
near where Supple Jack's grave had been located. There, in front of hundreds of observers, Mayor Oppenheimer officially opened Stanley Park,
stating that the new park would provide "a place of recreation in the
vicinity of a city where its inhabitants can spend some time amid the beauties of nature away from the busy haunts of men."[168]

On 1 August, 1889, a public meeting at Vancouver City Hall unanimously approved a resolution that gave the Lord Stanley Reception
Committee the green light "to carry out arrangements and provide the
funds necessary for the reception of His Excellency, the Governor General."
The Stanley Arch, better known as the Coal Harbour Bridge, was constructed of small sticks cut from trees found within the park. It replaced an
earlier crossing which was nothing more than the trunk of a massive, fallen
tree used when the tide was low. The Arch was erected at the foot of Georgia
Street so that the vice regal party could pass under it en route to the dedication ceremony at Chaythoos, Prospect Point. The Stanley Arch was replaced
by the Causeway at the entrance to Stanley Park and First Narrows Bridge,
leading to North Vancouver, West Vancouver and the mountains.

It was a day of drizzle on 29 October, 1889, when Lord Stanley, along
with wife Lady Constance Stanley, son Edward and daughter-in-law Alice
as well as several aides, attended a ceremony for the dedication of the massive park named in Stanley's honour.

The entourage left their hotel at Carrall and Powell streets at eleven in
the morning and their carriages wound through the downtown streets, led
by a local band. A plank bridge served as a park entrance for the entourage,
which followed the newly constructed road around Brockton Point to the
site of the stage.

This second ceremony took place at the same spot as the first, a grass-
covered area at the extreme north end of what is now known as Pipeline
Road, overlooking the narrows to the north shore. A temporary platform
was erected close to the burial spot of Squamish Chief Supple Jack, who
had, throughout his life, been outspoken about his opposition to that land

being turned into a park. A flagpole was erected so that the Union Jack could be displayed upon Lord Stanley's arrival.

The school children of Vancouver were brought to the dedication of Stanley Park. "When Lord Stanley came to the park to open it, the school children of Vancouver all went out to the end of the old Pipe Line Road, now closed up, where there was a little grassy spot. Lord Stanley spoke and the children sang," recalled Sarah Harris, the daughter of Henry Avison, Stanley Park's first ranger. "I was only about five years old. I went to the 'West End School' on Burrard Street."[169]

"I recall when Lord Stanley dedicated the park. I stood right beside him when he cut the ribbon. That was in October 1889," reminisced Mrs. W. E. Newcombe in a 1958 interview. "Down at what is now the Causeway, there was an old wooden bridge and there was a white ribbon stretched across the bridge. Then, after Lord Stanley had cut the ribbon, all the people went into the park. I remember him making a speech. He was tall and good-looking, but I don't remember what he said. I was seven at the time."[170]

The *Vancouver World* commented on what followed the speeches delivered by local dignitaries that day:

> *Lord Stanley threw his arms to the heavens as though embracing within them the whole of one thousand acres of primeval forest, and dedicated it 'to the use and enjoyment of people of all colours, creeds, and customs, for all time'. Then, as he slowly poured champagne on the virgin earth, Lord Stanley added, 'I name thee Stanley Park'. Those in attendance burst into enthusiastic applause. The Governor General then descended from the platform and laid the stones for a commemorative cairn. 'A cairn will perpetuate your visit to this park,' began Mayor Oppenheimer in his address. 'Herewith, Your Excellency will find a sketch of what the cairn will represent when fully completed. The decoration will be of flowers, trailing plants, specimens of British Columbia's minerals and tablet on which will be recorded this memorable event. The samples of some of the stones to compose the structure now before you, galena ore and red hematite, are intended to represent the mineral wealth of Your province'.*[171]

Rockets were fired into the air, and after bursting, bits of paper shaped like flags, lions, elephants and pigs floated slowly down to the ground, with the school children excitedly running to collect as many as possible.[172] *The World* added, "Owing to the inclemency of the weather, the ceremony was much curtailed."[173]

"The land was granted last year to the City by the Dominion Government for a park," wrote Lady Stanley.

> *It is all in the rough still and our only fear is that man will spoil nature. The trees are grand, some of fifty feet in diameter. The Douglas Pine and the hemlock are such beautiful trees and grow to a great size and height. We had seen in some of Mr. O'Brien's pictures — trees with their branches covered with a thick hanging moss. We thought we must have imagined some of it but we saw in Stanley Park how true he had been to nature for this moss beautifully hangs down from the branches and it does not seem to destroy the trees.[174]*

An illuminated scroll was presented to the Viceroy:

> *We, the citizens of Vancouver, desire to express the gratification which we feel at the arrival in our midst of the Representative of Her Most Precious Majesty The Queen, and we beg to tender You and Lady Stanley hearty welcome.*
>
> *The first occasion on which a Viceroy of Canada has visited this, the youngest city in the Dominion, we hail the arrival in Vancouver of Your Excellency as the official recognition of the completion of that great national work, the Canadian Pacific Railway, an undertaking to which Vancouver owes its existence, and of which it is the Western Terminus.*
>
> *From that circumstance and from the favourable geographical situation which our city occupies, we believe Your Excellency will realize the important part which Vancouver is destined to take in the future commercial development of the Dominion.*

It was with the highest feelings of satisfaction that we learned that Your Excellency's Government, in conjunction with the Imperial Government, had decided to subsidize a line of mail steamships between our city and the ports of the Orient, whereby the trade of the Dominion will be enlarged, her commercial relations with the teeming population of China and Japan be extended, a new field be opened for Canadian manufacturers, and the sources of employment for our artisans be widened.

During Your Excellency's sojourn in our midst, we trust you will be pleased to visit our city and to observe the progress which we as a people have made in building it up. But little more than three years have elapsed since Vancouver was totally destroyed by fire and the public and private buildings which you see today have all been constructed since then, and are but an earnest of what under the prosperity brought about by the wise measures and prudent legislation of Your Excellency's Government we hope to accomplish in the future.

We also hope that Your Excellency will be pleased to visit that noble tract of forest, which granted by Your Government for the benefit of our people, you were pleased to consent should be called by your illustrious name, and to view the proportions of this noble gift to the people of this city for their use and enjoyment for all time to come.[175]

The illuminated scroll, nearly five feet long, was presented to Lord Stanley by the citizens of Vancouver on 29 October, 1889 and hung at Knowsley House for fifty years. In 1949, the scroll was returned to the City of Vancouver by the 17th Earl of Derby, Edward Stanley, who had acted as an aide de camp to his father during the transcontinental trip.

On 19 October, ten days before Lord Stanley's dedication, a document had promised an appropriate monument to the Governor General to commemorate the naming of the park. Through the years, this promise had been forgotten, and it wasn't until Vancouver archivist J. S. Matthews discovered the letter in 1950 that the city realized it had never fulfilled its obligation. Matthews mounted a fund drive to correct the omission and although it took a decade, on 19 May, 1960, an eight-foot bronze statue of Lord Stanley, created by British sculptor Sydney March, was unveiled in Stanley Park by Governor General Georges Vanier. Located across from the heritage clubhouse of the Vancouver Rowing Club, the statue of Lord Stanley stands near a monument to Queen Victoria as well as a statue honouring poet Robert Burns. The dedication articulated by Stanley in 1889 was inscribed onto the granite base of the Governor General's trophy: "To the use and enjoyment of people of all colours, creeds, and customs, for all time." For a representative of the quintessential Imperial man, Stanley harboured some progressive ideals.

A decade later, the City of Vancouver paid the federal government one dollar for a renewable ninety-nine year lease on Stanley Park, which has since been renewed. The Vancouver Park Board celebrated the park's centennial in 1988, holding a modest ceremony on the spot where Lord Stanley would have dedicated the park. A commemorative bronze plaque marks the spot. Located just above the seawall before Park Drive switches to Prospect Point, the plaque summarizes both openings of Stanley Park and pays homage to the Squamish legacy: "This area was known to the native Indian people as 'Chaythoos' or high bank."

Following the ceremony, a number of picnics were held, and Vancouver's citizens were invited to attend. "Fred went after luncheon to the Indian Village. It was too wet for us to go," Lady Stanley reported. The plan to stage an illumination of the city in honour of the vice regal visit was thwarted by rain.[176] Later that evening, the Mayor and Mrs. Oppenheimer hosted the largest ball ever held in the city at the Opera House. The fire department orchestra provided the entertainment.

The entourage toured the city by carriage on Wednesday, 30 October. At three-thirty, a reception was held at City Hall. "We were at the City Hall at the appropriate time and waited for fifteen minutes," remarked Lady Stanley. "No one came so we went away. Only sorry for the poor Mayor. Quantities of people arrived after we had gone."[177]

A fancy ball, open to citizens, took place that evening. Lady Stanley enjoyed herself, especially watching the participants. "There were three new dances — 'The Jersey', 'The Ripples' and 'The Rockaway', all variations on a valse but very funny and rather pretty."[178]

The Governor General's visit to Vancouver had proven to be one of the highlights of the tour, and was enjoyed immensely by the entire suite.

"Vancouver is a city which has grown up with most promising rapidity, and now attracts the attention of capitalists far and near," wrote Sir James Grant. "Nature seems to have designed it for a city of great importance. Supported as it is by the lumber, fishing and mining industries and the rapidly increasing commercial interests, it is not at all surprising that this city should already have established a wide-ranging prestige."[179]

1 'Canada', *Encyclopædia Britannica* (Encyclopædia Britannica Premium Service: 2006).

2 *Toronto Star* (8 January, 2006).

3 A. B. Hart & H. Ferleger (*ed*), *Theodore Roosevelt Web Book* (Westport: Greenwood Publishing Group: online).

4 *Toronto Star* (8 January, 2006).

5 *British Colonist* (Vancouver: 20 July, 1871), p.2.

6 J. A. Macdonald, as quoted in, P. Berton, *The Impossible Railway* (New York: Knopf, 1972), p.V.

7 D. Hodge, *The Kids Book of Canada's Railway and How the CPR Was Built* (Toronto: Kids Can Press, 2000).

8 D. McDonald, *Lord Strathcona: a biography of Donald Alexander Smith* (Toronto: Dundurn Press, 1996).

9 Cowan, *Canada's Governors General*, p.53.

10 'Kodak Camera advertisement', *Outing* (February 1888).

11 Gemmill (ed), *The Canadian Parliamentary Companion*.

12 *MacLeod Gazette* (October 10, 1889), *edition cover page*.

13 *Ottawa Daily Citizen* (17 September, 1889), p.2.

14 *Canada (Ontario Boundary) Act*, 52–53 Victoria, c.28 (1889).

15 *Lady Stanley's Journal*, from the National Archives of Canada,(17 September, 1889).

16 CPR, *Transcontinental Route* (Canadian Pacific Railway, Eastern Division: 1889), p.14.

17 *Lady Stanley's Journal* (18 September, 1889).

18 CPR, *Transcontinental Route*, p.15.

19 *Lady Stanley's Journal* (18 September, 1889).

20 CPR, *Transcontinental Route*, p.16.

21 *Lady Stanley's Journal* (19 September, 1889).

22 Ibid.

23 *Lady Stanley's Journal* (20 September, 1889).

24 Ibid.

25 Ibid.

26 *Daily Mercury* (Quebec: 20 September, 1889), *edition cover page*.

27 *Lady Stanley's Journal* (20 September, 1889).

28 *Lady Stanley's Journal* (21 September, 1889).

29 Ibid.

30 *Lady Stanley's Journal* (23 September, 1889).

31 *Ottawa Daily Citizen* (24 September, 1889), *edition cover page*.

32 *The Graphic* (London: September, 1889).

33 *Winnipeg Free Press* (24 September, 1889), *edition cover page*.

34 Ibid.

35 Ibid.

36 Ibid

37 *MacLeod Gazette* (3 October, 1889), p.4.

38 *Lady Stanley's Journal* (23 September, 1889).

39 *Winnipeg Free Press* (5 September, 1889).

40 In 1891, Bedson moved to Ottawa to be an *aide-de-camp* for the Governor General

41 *Lady Stanley's Journal* (24 September, 1889).

42 *Winnipeg Free Press* (25 September, 1889).

43 *Lady Stanley's Journal* (24 September, 1889).

44 *Lady Stanley's Journal* (25 September, 1889).

45 'Alexandre-Antonin Taché', *New Advent* (Catholic Encyclopedia, On-Line & CD-ROM: c2000).

46 The 'Red River Jig' was a popular dance at the time, created by the Métis and based on the movements of a prairie chicken during mating season.

47 *Lady Stanley's Journal* (25 September, 1889).

48 *Lady Stanley's Journal* (26 September, 1889).

49 Ibid.

50 Ibid.

51 *Lady Stanley's Journal* (27 September, 1889).

52 *Manitoba Liberal* (October 1889).

53 *Lady Stanley's Journal* (28 September, 1889).

54 *Lady Stanley's Journal* (29 September, 1889).

55 Ibid.

56 Ibid.

57 CPR, *Transcontinental Route*, Western Division, p.19.

58 'Saskatchewan Homestead Index', *Canadian History News: Canada's Past in Perspective* (*www.northernblue.ca*).

59 From, *Canadian Confederation: Alberta and Saskatchewan* (Ottawa: National Library and Archives of Canada, *www.collectionscanada.ca*).

60 D. Owram, *Promise of Eden: The Canadian Expansionist Movement and the Idea of the West — 1856–1900* (Toronto: University of Toronto Press, 1980).

61 *The Dominion Illustrated Monthly* (9 November, 1889), p.295.

62 *The Dominion Illustrated Monthly* (9 November, 1889), p.295.

63 *Lady Stanley's Journal* (1 October, 1889).

64 *Regina Leader* (8 October, 1889), *edition cover page*.

65 A thicket of small trees.

66 CPR, *Transcontinental Route*, Western Division, p.19.

67 Ibid.

68 *Regina Leader* (8 October, 1889), p.4.

69 *Lady Stanley's Journal* (2 October, 1889).

70 *Regina Leader* (15 October, 1889), *edition cover page*.

71 Ibid., p.4.

72 Ibid., *edition cover page*.

73 Ibid., p.4.

74 Ibid.

75 Ibid.

76 A. Redford, 'Donald Alexander Smith', *Dictionary of Canadian Biography On-Line* (Ottawa: National Library and Archives of Canada).

77 *Regina Leader* (22 October, 1889), p.4.

78 *Lady Stanley's Journal* (3 October, 1889).

79 *Regina Leader* (15 October, 1889), p.4.

80 CPR, *Transcontinental Route*, Western Division, p.20.

81 *Qu'Appelle Vedette* (10 October, 1889), p.3.

82 *Regina Leader* (15 October, 1889), p.4.

83 *Lady Stanley's Journal* (4 October, 1889).

84 Ibid.

85 Ibid.

86 Ibid.

87 *Regina Leader* (8 October, 1889), p.4.

88 *Lady Stanley's Journal* (4 October, 1889).

89 Ibid.

90 *Regina Leader* (8 October, 1889), p.4.

91 *Lady Stanley's Journal* (5 October, 1889).

92 *Lady Stanley's Journal* (6 October, 1889).

93 Official Document, Government House (Ottawa: 8, June, 1887).

94 *Lady Stanley's Journal* (7 October, 1889).

95 Ibid.

96 *Lady Stanley's Journal* (8 October, 1889).

97 CPR, *Transcontinental Route*, Western Division, p.21.

98 *Regina Leader* (15 October, 1889), p.1.

99 Ibid.

100 *Lady Stanley's Journal* (10 October, 1889).

101 *Lady Stanley's Journal* (11 October, 1889).

102 Ibid.

103 *MacLeod Gazette* (24 October, 1889), p.4.

104 *Lady Stanley's Journal* (11 October, 1889).

105 *MacLeod Gazette* (2 November, 1894).

106 H. Dempsey, *The Amazing Death of Calf Shirt, and other Blackfoot Stories: Three Hundred Years of Blackfoot History* (Saskatoon: Fifth House, 1994).

107 H. A. Dempsey, 'The Snake Man', *Alberta History*, 29, 4, (Calgary: 1981), pp.1–5; *Macleod Gazette* (2 November, 1894); *Manitoba Free Press* (15 Aug. 1889); *Toronto Daily Mail* (28 Jan. 1886).

108 Cowan, *Canada's Governors General*, pp.50–1.

109 *Lady Stanley's Journal* (11 October, 1889).

110 F. Villiers, 'To the New West With the Governor General of Canada over the Canadian Pacific Railway', *The Graphic* (14 December, 1889).

111 *Lady Stanley's Journal* (11 October, 1889).

112 R. J. Heintzmann, 'The Cochrane Ranche Site', *Archaeological Survey of Alberta Occasional Paper, 16* (Cochrane: Alberta Culture Historic Resources Division 1980).

113 *Lady Stanley's Journal* (12 October, 1889).

114 Ibid.

115 CPR, *Transcontinental Route*, Western Division, p.23; S. A. Macdonald, 'By Car and Cowcatcher', *Murray's Magazine* (c1889).

116 *Lady Stanley's Journal* (12 October, 1889).

117 Ibid.

118 *MacLeod Gazette* (24 October, 1889), p.4.

119 D. Godfrey & B. Y. Card (*ed*), *The Diaries of Charles Ora Card: The Canadian Years, 1886–1903* (Salt Lake City: University of Utah Press, 1993), p.668; *Canadian Historical Review, 76, 2*, (Toronto: University of Toronto Press, June 1995).

120 *MacLeod Gazette* (24 October, 1889), p.4.

121 Ibid.

122 *Lady Stanley's Journal* (13 October, 1889).

123 Ibid.

124 Ibid.

125 *Lady Stanley's Journal* (14 October, 1889).

126 CPR, *Transcontinental Route*, Western Division, p.24.

127 *Lady Stanley's Journal* (14 October, 1889).

128 Ibid.

129 *Calgary Herald* (16 October, 1889), p.4.

130 Ibid.

131 *Lady Stanley's Journal* (16 October, 1889).

132 *Calgary Herald* (18 October, 1889), *edition cover page*.

133 Ibid.

134 *The Best of Akwesasne Notes: How Democracy Came to St. Regis & The Thunderwater Movement* (Akwesasne: Akwesasne Notes Newspaper, 1974). <booklet>

135 Sir James Grant, as quoted in, *Ottawa Daily Citizen* (20 November, 1889), p.8.

136 J. H. Thompson, 'Forging the Prairie West', *The Illustrated History of Canada* (Toronto: Oxford University Press, Don Mills, 1998).

137 *Lady Stanley's Journal* (18 October, 1889).

138 F. Villiers 'To the New West With the Governor General of Canada over the Canadian Pacific Railway', *The Graphic* (December 14, 1889).

139 *Lady Stanley's Journal* (19 October, 1889).

140 *Lady Stanley's Journal* (20 October, 1889).

141 *Lady Stanley's Journal* (21 October, 1889).

142 Ibid.

143 Ibid.

144 *MacLeod Gazette* (24 October, 1889), p.4.

145 *Lady Stanley's Journal* (22 October, 1889).

146 Ibid.

147 A. O. Wheeler, *The Selkirk Range* (Ottawa: Government Printing Office, 1905).

148 *Lady Stanley's Journal* (22 October, 1889).

149 In 1916, the railway was rerouted through the Connaught Tunnel under Rogers Pass. Shortly afterwards, the glacier receded. As a result, hotel visitation declined substantially and in 1930, the once-grand Glacier Hotel was demolished.

150 *Lady Stanley's Journal* (23 October, 1889).

151 *Lady Stanley's Journal* (24 October, 1889).

152 *Lady Stanley's Journal* (25 October, 1889).

153 *Lady Stanley's Journal* (26 October, 1889).

154 Ibid.

155 *Ottawa Daily Citizen* (Ottawa: 30 October, 1889), p.5.

156 *Lady Stanley's Journal* (26 October, 1889).

157 Ibid.

158 Ibid.

159 Rev. H. H. Gowen, *Pioneer Church Work in British Columbia: Being a Memoir of the Episcopate of Acton Windeyer Sillitoe, First Bishop of New Westminster* (London: Mowbray, 1899).

160 *Lady Stanley's Journal* (26 October, 1889).

161 *Lady Stanley's Journal* (27 October, 1889).

162 *Lady Stanley's Journal* (28 October, 1889).

163 A. B. McLeod & P. McGeachie, *Land of Promise: Robert Burnaby's Letters from Colonial British Columbia, 1858–1868* (Burnaby: City of Burnaby, 2002), p.102.

164 J. Barman, *Stanley Park's Secret* (Madeira Park, British Columbia: Harbour Publishing, 2005), p.42.

165 Ibid., p.89.

166 Ibid., p.21.

167 Ibid., p.92.

168 *Vancouver News Advertiser* (27 September, 1887).

169 *Interview with Sarah Harris* from the City of Vancouver Archives (11 February, 1958) at her daughter's North Vancouver home.

170 *Interview with W. E. Newcombe* from the City of Vancouver Archives (16 April, 1958).

171 The cairn has since been lost or destroyed.

172 Paper ephemera and descriptive note in City of Vancouver Archives.

173 *Vancouver World* (29 October, 1889), City of Vancouver Archives.

174 *Lady Stanley's Journal* (29 October, 1889).

175 Commemorative scroll presented to Lord Stanley on October 29, 1889 now housed at the City of Vancouver Archives.

176 *Lady Stanley's Journal* (29 October, 1889).

177 Ibid.

178 *Lady Stanley's Journal* (30 October, 1889).

179 *Ottawa Daily Citizen* (20 November, 1889), p.6.

CHAPTER ELEVEN

Narrow Escape from a Watery Grave

In 1842, James Douglas was hired by John McLoughlin, Chief Factor of the Hudson's Bay Company at Fort Vancouver, to search for a prime location on which to build a new British settlement. Douglas targeted an area on the southern coast of Vancouver Island, an agriculturally rich area inhabited by the local Songhees, who called it Camosack. Citing the advantages of the area's extensive grasslands, by the next spring, Douglas had begun construction on Fort Victoria, named after the reigning British monarch.

In 1913, renowned naturalist Berthold Seeman described the area. "In walking from Ogden Point to Fort Victoria, a distance of little more than a mile, we thought we had never seen a more beautiful country. It is a natural park; noble oaks and ferns are seen in the greatest luxuriance; thickets of the hazel and the willow, shrubberies of the poplar and the alder, are dotted about. One could hardly believe that this was not the work of art."[1]

HMS Herald arrived at Fort Victoria in June 1846. For seven shillings a year, the Crown granted control of Vancouver Island to the Hudson's Bay Company under a January 1849 charter. In return for proprietary rights, the Hudson's Bay Company was to promote colonization. That same year, Fort Victoria replaced Fort Vancouver as the company's headquarters on the Pacific Coast; it also joined a network of Royal Navy bases that included Aden, Bombay, Cyprus, Gibraltar, Hong Kong, Malta, St. Helena, Sydney and Trincomalee (Ceylon).

Victoria, located at the extreme southeast tip of Vancouver Island, was aided in its development by its status as the first available port north of San Francisco; and with Esquimalt but three miles away, any size of vessel could be accommodated. By water, Victoria is 72 miles from Nanaimo, the same distance from Vancouver, 73 from New Westminster, 100 from Seattle, 128 from Tacoma, and 750 from San Francisco. The Canadian Pacific steamship *Islander* left for Vancouver every morning except Monday, connecting with the CPR, while other steamers ran back and forth at different times.

The sealing trade of British Columbia was almost entirely controlled from Victoria, and most of the vessels employed in the business were built there and wintered there. The seal trade was one of B.C.'s most important, and for many years it yielded large returns. Victoria was probably more affected by the Behring Sea dispute than any other port in Canada.

* * *

After five enjoyable days spent in Vancouver, Lord Frederick and Lady Constance left early on Thursday, 31 October for their next stop: the capital of Canada's newest province. *HMS Champion* took the vice regal suite across the strait to Vancouver Island. "To our disgust, we had to leave the landing stage at 7:30 in the morning," harrumphed Lady Stanley. "It was wet and we did not go on board *HMS Champion* quite in a happy frame of mind. However, Captain Sinclair was so kind to us and gave us such a good breakfast."[2] While the *Champion* cruised with Lord and Lady Stanley aboard, it encountered a steamer named the *Premier*. As was protocol, the *Champion* dipped her flag in salute but the *Premier* did not return the compliment, "causing great displeasure at the steamer's lack of courtesy."[3]

The Stanleys had looked forward to enjoying the magnificent view of the landscape from *Champion*'s deck, but they were disappointed to discover that a thick fog had enveloped the countryside, obscuring the view completely until just before noon, when a beautiful day presented itself. In spite of the fog, the ship was only marginally tardy, docking at the Hudson Bay Company's outer wharf just past the expected two o'clock arrival. The *Sir James Douglas*, a local steamer, came alongside to receive the party and escort them to the inner wharf. The *Victoria Daily Colonist* explained: "The clock had just struck three when the steamer bearing the Governor General and his party rounded the bend and steamed quickly up the harbour, with all colours gaily flying."[4]

The vice regal party arrived at two-thirty and was greeted by a sizable welcoming committee that included Lieutenant Governor Hugh Nelson; Mayor John Grant; members of municipal council; George Anthony Walkem, Chief Justice of the Supreme Court of British Columbia; members of the Senate, the House of Commons, and the Legislative Assembly; the admiral; bishops; the clergy; mayors from other British Columbia cities; Victoria's captains of industry; and the military band.

Lord Stanley's carriage, pulled by six horses, was included in a large parade that swept the Governor General from the landing, up Wharf Street to Yates and then to the corner of Government, where they arrived at a welcoming arch. With Union Jacks flapping proudly in the breeze, the Governor General read the arches: "God Blass Our Wide Dominion," "138 Degrees West and Still in Britain" and "In the Name of the Sovereign, Greetings."[5]

While the procession drove along Fort Street, several young ladies poised on a nearby balcony waited until the Stanleys' carriage passed and threw three lovely bouquets of chrysanthemums towards it. Each of the bouquets missed the carriage and tumbled instead to the street. Lady Stanley requested that the carriage be stopped and an aide-de-camp summoned a policeman, who picked up the best of the bouquets and handed it to Lady Stanley.[6]

Before a large throng that included a large number of school children, Mayor Grant welcomed Lord and Lady Stanley:

> *We, the Mayor and municipal council, on behalf of the citizens of Victoria, British Columbia, desire to extend to Your Excellency and Lady Stanley, a most cordial and hearty welcome to this city … It is a source of gratification to us that Your Excellency and Lady Stanley have been enabled to traverse this vast Dominion of Canada, from east to the west, through changing scenes, on bands of steel laid by Canadian energy and enterprise, believing, as we do, that the Canadian Pacific Railway is the most important factor in cementing as one the various provinces of the Dominion of Canada, and in binding together the British commercial interests of the Occident and Orient, while giving increased facilities for the defense of our common flag.[7]*

Stanley replied, "I am now, as you are aware, approaching the completion of a journey lasting more than two months, in the course of which I have traversed, from east to west, this great Dominion of ours. It is our desire that the union of the provinces should be so perpetuated that the Dominion, gaining strength from unity, shall be enabled to press forward to the great future which is in store for it."[8]

The Lieutenant Governor then smugly suggested that the Governor General's place of residence in Ottawa not be a fixture and that he consider residing for part of his term in Victoria. Lord Stanley replied:

> *In all parts of the Dominion, I have met with kindness so spontaneous and overpowering that each place I have visited I would like to make my home. I lost my heart to Quebec, I am thoroughly content to remain in Ottawa once I reached there, I was charmed by Ontario, pronounced Manitoba a splendid place for a man to make his home, and find British Columbia unequalled among them all. This westward journey has been a pleasant one. I have found the provinces rich in all that makes a country great, only waiting for the hand of man, capital and skill to develop that with which Providence has so richly enjoyed it.*

The eloquent remarks of the Governor General were greeted with extended and enthusiastic applause, concluding in three rousing cheers.[9]

The speeches were received enthusiastically when Alderman Harris's young daughter presented Lady Stanley with a bouquet of flowers. In honour of the visit of the Governor General, the Mayor issued a proclamation appointing the remainder of the day a civic holiday. All businesses were closed for the afternoon to honour the visit of Lord Stanley.[10] The procession then re-grouped and marched to Government House, the thirty-six-acre residence of the Lieutenant Governor, once known as Cary Castle and located on Rockland Avenue. It was here that the vice regal party would reside during their six-day visit.

At seven-thirty that same evening, Stanley was the guest of honour at a civic banquet held in the Assembly Rooms of Government House. For five dollars, the public was able to attend.

Lady Stanley commented on her first day in the British Columbia capital. "[Frederick] and the men dined at a city banquet where of course the usual number of speeches had to be made. Alice and Eddy and I dined alone and our hostess bored us off to bed at 10! We talked without ceasing the whole time."[11]

On Friday morning, 1 November, Admiral Sir Algernon Heneage made a formal call on His Excellency at Government House. Later that afternoon, Lieutenant Colonel E. G. Prior escorted Lord and Lady Stanley and their children, Edward and Alice, through Chinatown, which was lavishly and tastefully decorated in honour of the Governor General's presence.

Many Chinese immigrants had been lured to Canada and the Pacific Northwest states to help in the construction of the railway. Upon completion of the CPR in 1885, many of these labourers settled in Victoria. They found a measure of comfort in assembling in communities that came to be known as Chinatowns, where they were able to maintain their language and cultural traditions. Victoria's Chinatown is recognized as the oldest in Canada and, with thirty-five hundred permanent Chinese residents, was the largest of its kind in Canada.

The Governor General's party was fascinated, thrilled with the sights and smells of Chinatown — fragrant incense blended superbly with the aroma of foods not common to the vice regal household. The party spent much of the afternoon examining goods carried by some of the Chinatown merchants, inspecting the Chinese method of bookkeeping and visiting the local joss houses[12] where the community worshipped.[13] On a dreary, wet morning, Constance wrote in her journal:

> It cleared in the afternoon and we went with Alice and Eddy and Colonel Prior to visit China Town. We went to see the temple where the great joss is kept. There was some beautiful work. Altogether it was curious. We then went to a sort of business room and were introduced to some of the head men and we made them write things for us. Alice and I and about a half-dozen Chinese sat around a table writing with the odd brush pens they use. It was very amusing. Fred and Eddy walked home and Colonel P. took us to some Chinese shops where we poked about for a long time and bought some trash and were each presented with an embroidered handkerchief.[14]

At four that afternoon, Lord Stanley and selected guests made the three-mile trip west to Esquimalt, the headquarters of Her Majesty's fleet in the north Pacific Ocean. "We went on a drive with Admiral Heneage on board the Swiftsure. He gave us such a good dinner and his cabins were quite lovely," stated Lady Stanley.[15] In the evening, they drove back through Chinatown to see the area illuminated by an elaborate exhibition of fireworks, which drew wonder and admiration from the Governor General's party.

That evening, the *Daily Colonist* claimed, "the most brilliant social event of the season was the fleet ball given in honour of His Excellency and Lady Stanley at the Naval Yard." The newspaper further elaborated, "Without any exception, it was the most complete and the most admirably arranged affair of the kind ever given in the province."[16]

The ballroom was, according to the *Colonist*, "a blaze of light; a wreath of fragrance and dream of beauty." The once-barren sail loft had been converted into a palace of light and extravagance with hundreds of cut and potted plants and flowers that lent a sweet fragrance to the room. As Lord and Lady Stanley and their entourage arrived by carriage, they were escorted through a grand entrance adorned by tropical plants and aromatic blossoms. The newspaper review went on: "At the end of this airy promenade was placed a small cannon, polished to the highest degree of brightness. The grim sign of war rose through a pyramid of flowers and its threatening muzzle was wreathed with a garland of sweet lilies."

Opposite the stairway was an exquisite fairy grotto, constructed of exotic plants and moss-covered fieldstone. The *Colonist* delightfully described the setting: "Peeping out from beneath the drooping ferns and fragrant blossoms, nestling among the glowing lilies and apparently shining in their very hearts were scores of fairy lamps and tiny incandescent lights, while in the centre stood two large fountains; the crowning triumphs of the enchanting scene."

The ballroom itself was as elaborate as the proscenium leading to it. The room was adorned in flowers similar to the hallways leading to it. A dais, surrounded by tropical plants and flowers, was placed in front of overstuffed chairs for the comfort of Lord and Lady Stanley, while the Royal Coat of Arms and the flag of England served as background. To the rear of the ballroom, a retiring room was prepared for the vice regal party.

Chinese parasols hung from the ceiling as though dancing in the wind above the long table that ran down the centre of the room, stretching from one end to the other. The finest crystal, gleaming silver cutlery and Irish linen adorned each place setting.

At eight o'clock, all celebrants took their assigned places in the ballroom; then, at ten-thirty, the first in a series of toasts was proffered — "To the Queen!" shouted the assembled multitude in chorus. The toast to Benjamin Harrison, the newly elected president of the United States, was followed by prolonged applause, acknowledging the hoped-for improvement in commercial and social relations between the neighbouring countries.[17]

Senator William John Macdonald, a prominent local merchant who had been appointed to the Senate by Sir John A. Macdonald in 1871, chronicled the governor general's transcontinental trip; this was followed by toasts to the Army, the Navy and to the volunteers.

Lieutenant Governor Hugh Nelson then spoke:

> *Lady Nelson and I are particularly honoured in having His Excellency and Lady Stanley as our guests at Government House … In all the Dominion, in every part of the British Empire, in the British Isles themselves, I am sure there are no more loyal subjects of Her Majesty to be found than in the Province of British Columbia.*

Victoria's mayor, John Grant, then proffered the final toast, a short speech that expressed appreciation for the visit by the Governor General. "It is not often that the occasion is presented of honouring so illustrious a gentleman as the city's distinguished guest," he began as the assembled smiled and nodded in agreement.

> *[Stanley] has had a brilliant career and been entrusted with many most important missions, which he has conducted with high honour to himself and satisfaction to his Sovereign. He has filled the important position of Lord of the Admiralty, Secretary of State for War, Secretary of State for the Colonies and now, as Governor General of Canada, he is here tonight to enjoy and brighten with his genial presence, the present occasion.*

Mayor Grant referred to the difficulties of transcontinental travel prior to the construction of the railway, which he believed "has enabled His Excellency and Lady Stanley to traverse the Dominion quickly, enjoyably and with comfort and pleasure.

"After what he had seen in the province, it is our wish that His Excellency would be able to take back a thorough knowledge of British Columbia and its resources, which could enable him in advising the government in effecting many measures for the development of the most western province in the Canadian confederation, which would place it in its proper position of second to none."

After the toast, Lord Stanley rose and addressed the crowd. "I find it difficult, if not impossible, to put into words the deep sense of gratitude which I feel at the cordial manner in which my health has been drunk as the representative of her majesty," began His Excellency. "I am forced to pronounce the Canadian Pacific Railroad as unrivalled in the world as a marvel of engineering triumph." The trip had given the Governor General a new appreciation of the country. "Nothing struck one coming from the Old Country to this more than the vastness of the land."[18] In appreciation, the assembled gave the Governor "three cheers and a tiger."[19]

The cream of the province's aristocracy and wealth who made up the three hundred and fifty invitees enjoyed a sumptuous dinner, served at midnight. In preparation for after-dinner relaxation, rooms had been set aside for smoking and for playing whist, a card game particularly popular in England during the nineteenth century.

Lady Stanley clearly enjoyed the evening, as evidenced by her final entry of 1 November. "We went to the ball given to us by the fleet. The decorations of the room too pretty and done as only sailors know how. The whole thing was a great success. We did not get home until three."[20]

Lady Stanley, her daughter Isobel and daughter-in-law Alice were taken to the stunning and newly redesigned Beacon Hill Park, located on the Strait of Juan de Fuca, where they took photographs. Beacon Hill Park had long been owned by the Hudson's Bay Company, but was granted in trust to the City of Victoria in 1882.

On 9 January, 1888, while campaigning for mayor, John Grant stated, "This city should be made more attractive and a sum of money should be expended in beautifying Beacon Hill." When he won the election, tenders were let out to design a beautifully improved park.

Victoria's *Daily Colonist* wrote:

> *Every day sees some new improvement at Beacon Hill Park.*
> *Every day, something fresh is added to increase the attrac-*
> *tions of Victoria's most popular afternoon resort. There*
> *have been more improvements made during the last six*
> *months zoo was populated by six deer, two black bear cubs,*
> *a wolf, a 'hair seal', sheep, a rock pheasant, a bald eagle and*
> *two swans.*[21]

The large park was fashioned after England's magnificent gardens of that time, with immaculately manicured flowerbeds and graceful trees as well significant amounts of grassland, a swamp and the magnificent Douglas fir trees. Meanwhile, Lord Stanley and the men of the vice regal suite travelled to the temporary quarters of "C" Battery, where they were hosted by Lieutenant Colonel E. G. Prior, Commander of the Artillery Garrison.

The Victoria Jockey Club, which was instituted in 1861, hosted a spate of horse races attended by Lord and Lady Stanley and their guests at the Driving Park on both Saturday, 2 November and Monday the fourth. A special grandstand was erected for the vice regal party, which arrived just prior to the events that began at noon both days. Victoria boasted a magnificent day on the Saturday. "The air was so clear that Mount Baker seemed not twenty miles away," reported the *Colonist*. Under sunshine and blue skies, the largest crowd ever to witness racing events on Vancouver Island watched the afternoon's heats.[22]

The Governor General's party observed the better part of the day's program, which included trotting, pacing, hurdles and a *gymkhana* — a timed obstacle race on horseback. First up was the half-mile, and while the spectators cheered on their favourites, a brass band performed musical selections.

"The best event of the day, the race for Indian horses and riders, was thoroughly enjoyed by all," wrote the *Colonist*.[23] Lord Stanley, who inherited his father's love of horses, couldn't have enjoyed an afternoon more thoroughly. On the other hand, Lady Stanley wrote, "Races in the afternoon very stupid with the exception of the Indian race that was rather funny." She was spellbound, though, by the sight of Mount Baker, a volcano in northern Washington that had last erupted in 1880. Most of the summit of Mount Baker is covered by glaciers. "Perfection. It is 80 miles and about 11,000 feet high."[24]

Lieutenant Governor Nelson hosted a dinner for the vice regal party and twenty-two guests on Saturday evening at Government House.

As was de rigueur each Sunday, Lord and Lady Stanley attended church at Victoria's Christ Church Cathedral, the seat of the Diocese of British Columbia, which included all of Vancouver Island as well as the islands on the Gulf of Georgia. "Very dull service and server," commented Lady Stanley. "View from the church quite beautiful. Went with F. & Isobel in the afternoon to see Mr. Dunsmuir's house. Bored to death in the evening by the chatter of our hostess."[25]

James Dunsmuir had followed in the footsteps of his father and become an exceptionally wealthy coal baron, whose interests also included ownership in the Esquimalt and Nanaimo Railway. Dunsmuir's wife, Laura, enjoyed her husband's prominence because it allowed her to steadily climb British Columbia's social ladder.[26] In the evening, Lord and Lady Stanley attended a second church service, this time at St. John's Church, commonly known as "the Iron Church."[27]

Monday, 4 November, 1889, was a glorious day, according to the journal kept by Lady Constance Stanley. "F. paid formal visit to the Admiral [Heaneage] and inspected the ships, dockyard and dry docks. Had luncheon with the Admiral on board the *Swiftsure*. He was very funny. The five ships manning the yards and saluting. Such a lovely sight. We tried to get some photographs of it."[28] Including Lady Stanley, Isobel and Miss Lister, Admiral Heneage entertained eleven ladies at lunch aboard *HMS Swiftsure*.

In the Treasury Building at one o'clock that afternoon, the Governor General received a deputation from the local Sealers' Association regarding the highly volatile Behring Sea controversy. The Association pleaded for the Governor General's support, detailing facts and disputing fictions. Stanley appeared genuinely interested in and deeply concerned by the grave concerns expressed by the Association, vowing that the Dominion government had great interest in the sealing matter and, with information gleaned in part from the Sealers' Association, hoped to resolve the dilemma. Little did he know that the matter would still not be entirely resolved by the time he returned to England.

Government House was the location for yet another ball honouring the Governor General: this one included five hundred of the B.C. capital's most important residents. "Society has been in a delightful whirl of excitement for the past week," exclaimed the *Colonist* on its front page of 5

November, 1889.[29] "Mrs. Nelson's balls are always looked upon, rightfully, as assuredly enjoyable and successful."[30]

Dressed in the most elegant of attire, guests enjoyed refreshments while the string band from *HMS Swiftsure* provided music for dancing, filling the air and making the lofty rooms "ring with merriment." Lord and Lady Stanley led a procession of one hundred couples in the first of twenty-two dances, starting promptly at nine o'clock. The first dance was led by Lord Stanley and Mrs. Nelson, the Lieutenant Governor's wife, as well as Mayor Grant and Lady Constance Stanley; Lieutenant Governor Nelson and Lady Alice Stanley; and Lady Stanley's private secretary, Miss Lister, accompanied by Captain Hulton of *HMS Amphion*. "From that time until midnight, the well-polished floor was in constant use," reported the *Colonist*. In fact, the dancing did not finish until after three the next morning. "At 11 o'clock, the vice regal party left the ballroom but it was not until daylight began to break that the last of the dancers departed and the grand ball was over."[31]

For those less inclined to dance, there were a number of areas to which one might steal away, as the *Colonist* eloquently reported: "The tastefully decorated and illuminated conservatory was pronounced the most charming of retreats by those who had tender confidences to exchange."[32]

Lady Stanley, of course, commented on the evening:

> *Ball at Government House went off very well and was very cheery considering there was no supper, only light refreshments. We had taken the precaution of trying some food which we, Alice, Eddy and Freddy and self enjoyed extremely when we came up to bed.*[33]

In fact, a feast was served from midnight until three in the morning, with salmon, halibut, crab, lobster, *pâté de fois*, turkey, eggs in aspic, lamb, and wonderful desserts. The *Colonist* proclaimed that "the glory of the supper table was an immense crown of Derby beef, wonderful in construction, which was placed in front of the seat occupied by His Excellency.... Nothing was left undone to increase the happiness of those attending."[34] Regrettably, not everyone attending shared the same levels of happiness. Lady Stanley admitted in her diary, "Citizens ball very good but I felt so low that I would have cried and for no reason only deeply depressed."[35]

The Esquimalt and Nanaimo Railway, managed by James Dunsmuir, put a special train at Lord Stanley's disposal. At nine o'clock on the morning of 5 November, Dunsmuir, the Governor General, Captain Colville, Aubrey McMahon, Premier John Robson, Lieutenant Colonel Prior, journalist Frederic Villiers and Douglas Sladen — a London-born travel writer, poet and author of note — boarded the train for the seventy-two-mile trip up the eastern coast of Vancouver Island to Nanaimo.

The group left Victoria in the specially outfitted car *Maude*, along with two passenger coaches, and stopped at Duncan, about midway between the B.C. capital and Nanaimo. Five hundred people, mostly school children, met the train. The station was beautifully decorated with flowers, mosses and evergreens. A civic address was read by Henry Croft, Dunsmuir's brother-in-law and the Member of Provincial Parliament from nearby Cowichan. Lord Stanley made an eloquent reply to the civic dignitaries. W. H. Lomas, the Indian agent for the Hul'qumi'num-speaking residents on the eastern and southern sides of Vancouver Island, acted as translator for several local chiefs who also presented addresses. In the absence of Lady Stanley, the children presented the Governor General with a bouquet. As the train pulled out of the station following the brief stop, the crowd gave a hearty three cheers.

The party arrived in Nanaimo by train promptly at noon on 5 November. Mayor Mark Bate, the town's aldermen, and many civic-minded citizens met the Governor General at the station. Mayor Bate introduced Lord Stanley to several public-school scholars who had been specially selected for the occasion. After the civic address from Bate and an appropriate reply, those gathered at the train depot gave the Governor General three cheers and a tiger. The Nanaimo brass band then struck up "God Save the Queen."

A procession, led by the brass band and a fife-and-drum band, was followed by uniformed firemen, who marched from the firehouse to the Nanaimo railway station alongside their steam-powered fire engine. The engine was beautifully decorated and pulled by four horses. A carriage carrying Lord Stanley, Mayor Bate, Premier Robson and Lieutenant Colonel Prior followed. The procession followed a route whose destination was the office of the New Vancouver Coal Company. The Governor General donned a waterproof suit and, joined by two executives from the company, descended down the No. 1 esplanade shaft.

Luncheon was served at Windsor House, and then the Governor General and his guests boarded their private car *Maude* and returned to Victoria. "The run down was pleasant and the train reached Victoria at 6 p.m., His Excellency being delighted with his trip and the pretty scenery along the railroad," said the *Colonist*.[36]

Yet another civic ball — the third at which the Stanleys were guests of honour — took place that evening in Victoria, in the Assembly Rooms on Fort Street, providing a fitting conclusion to an adventurous but most enjoyable cross-Canada trip. Admission for the public was a hefty ten dollars.

According to the *Colonist*, the rooms were beautifully decorated:

> *At the upper end of the ball room, a screen of evergreens and flags illuminated by fairy lamps separated the ball room from the supper room. In front of this partition of foliage, a fountain, surrounded by lovely potted plants in luxuriant bloom, their branches holding fairy lamps which threw a softened light upon the scene, sent its feathery spray into the air.... The Governor General himself expressed surprise and pleasure at the beauty of the room.*[37]

The sixth of November, 1889, began with the Governor General visiting the children attending Victoria's public schools. With boys in one line and the girls in another, fourteen hundred students were marshalled to the grounds of Central School, where they sang "God Save the Queen" for His Excellency. Lord Stanley turned to the children and asked if they would sing the anthem for him once again. As the *Colonist* observed, "The national anthem was given with an enthusiasm never surpassed, the music of the sweet, young voices being heard many blocks away."[38] The Governor General then thanked the children by giving them a holiday on Friday, 8 November. Governor Robson led the schoolchildren and dignitaries in three cheers and a tiger, first for Lord Stanley, then again for Lady Stanley. Several children selected in advance presented Lady Stanley with a basketful of beautiful flowers.

Carriages took the vice regal party to the harbour, where Lord and Lady Stanley bade grateful goodbyes to Mayor Grant and the other dignitaries who had made their stay so memorable. It had been a most enjoyable stop for the Governor General and his suite. "Lord and Lady expressed the hope that before a very distant day, they may again visit this city, where they may be sure they will always receive a cordial welcome."[39] Sir James Grant later wrote:

> *Victoria, the gem of the Pacific, has an established reputa-*
> *tion for solidity and commercial prosperity generally, being*
> *the great naval depot of the west. Those who have settled*
> *there enjoy a degree of wealth and influence that speaks*
> *well for its present prosperity.*[40]

HMS *Amphion* had been detailed and was standing ready to take its special passengers back to the mainland, where a visit to New Westminster would complete the journey and set the stage for the governor general's return to Ottawa.

* * *

"*Prepare to abandon ship!*" shouted Captain Edward Grey Hulton, commander of HMS *Amphion*. There was no mistaking the horrific explosion of sound as metal ground against rock.

Amphion was considered the finest warship of the Pacific squadron, and she had been brilliantly readied to carry the vice regal party from Victoria back to New Westminster on Wednesday, 6 November, 1889. Named for a son of the Greek god Zeus, *Amphion* was the fourth and last of a series of steam cruisers known as the *Leander* class. She was 315 feet long, fitted with ten six-inch guns and four torpedo tubes and carried a crew of 278 officers and men. The *Amphion* was one of the first ships to use the drydock at Esquimalt, which had only just been completed in 1887 after scandal delayed the project by eleven years.[41]

With Hulton, who knew the area's waters well, at the helm, *Amphion* left Victoria Harbour at ten in the morning at a speed of seventeen and a half knots. The *Colonist* submitted that "the dismal fog, which had covered the water and the straits for two days, rendering navigation dangerous as well as difficult, still hung over the water,"[42] making sightseeing all but impossible. Nevertheless, the vice regal suite were enjoying the trip.

"On that morning, we were particularly desirous of returning to the mainland," reported Captain Colville in an interview, "and though there were belts of fog hanging about, it was thought safe enough to venture across. We wanted to keep an appointment in New Westminster, where a grand reception was in preparation, and the vessel, after clearing the harbour, ran at a good rate of speed."

The vessel slipped through the dangerous narrow channel known as Plumper's Pass, but a mile and a half later, as the vessel entered Haro Channel at a reduced speed of fifteen knots, Captain Hulton failed to notice a submerged reef. At seven minutes to noon, the ship glanced off the rocks, but the collision left a considerable split in the side. Water rushed into the compartments of the ship. Passengers were in a state of great confusion, but fears were quickly allayed by the coolness of the capable crew, who quickly restored the confidence of the passengers.[43]

Colville described the chaos:

> We were below, enjoying ourselves as usual, when we were startled by a great crashing sound, followed immediately by the noise of a rush of water into the compartments.... For a moment, there was confusion, but then the excellent discipline of the ship made itself felt, and Captain Hulton and his officers, having given the crew the necessary instructions as to starting the pumps and preparing the boats for embarkation, if necessary, soon convinced all on board that the safe course was to quietly await developments.

As the *Ottawa Daily Citizen* attested, "He was inspecting the ship with one of the officers and either at the time of the accident or a moment before, was at the very spot where the rock crashed through the side."[44]

Lady Stanley's eyewitness account of the accident is recorded in her journal:

> We were all in high spirits and every thing went well for about three-quarters of an hour. And then such a fog came on that we went below and were very comfortable in the Wardroom because we felt the vibration of the screw less there than in the Captain's cabin. We were asked to move because of the officer's luncheon and were collecting our books, etc. when suddenly, there came a crash and then a

loud cracking sort of noise and the ship seemed to quiver, every thing in the cabin came down on our heads. F. and the gentlemen were going around the ship ahead and only just left the place where the blow came. They were all knocked down. We all went on deck and I am happy to say none of the women made fools of themselves. All were perfectly quiet. The faces of all the men told us that something most serious had happened. And we could see for ourselves that we were on a rock. I'm glad we were so close to the land that we seemed as if we could touch it. It happens that the current took us fifty yards further west and we should have been clear. We were not thirty yards from the shore. Some say that we had slowed, others that we had not. The ship keeled over most dreadfully. They thought that four of the water tight compartments were full. We could not go down to see what damage had been done.[45]

When the ship glanced off the sawtooth-sharp rocks, Lady Constance Stanley, Lady Alice Stanley, Mrs. Colville and Miss Lister were seated in the *Amphion*'s dining room. At the moment the crash was felt, Lady Stanley loudly exclaimed, "Oh my!" Afterwards, Lady Stanley proposed that the area where the crash occurred should be renamed "Oh My."

As soon as the gnarl of metal against rock was heard, all hands were ordered to the steam pumps, but the surging water couldn't be controlled and four compartments filled up quickly. The *Amphion* began listing fairly significantly to the starboard. While some of the crew manned the pumps, others dealt with the passengers who, although confused, were calmed and reassured that no lives would be lost. In the meantime, the captain and crew realized that the most appropriate course of action was to turn the *Amphion* around, in spite of it being in "dangerous and precarious condition," and sail straight to the dock at Esquimalt.[46] While the compartments of the *Amphion* were pumped, the ship sat at the spot of the crash for three-quarters of an hour. During that time, Miss Lister took several photos of the ship with her new camera.

* * *

The welcoming committee in New Westminster was waiting anxiously, the city decorated in bunting and banners, the band seated and ready to strike up "God Save the Queen." Word had not yet reached them that the Governor General's ship was not going to arrive that day but was instead limping into Esquimalt. The *Colonist* reported that New Westminster never had been "in a greater state of excitement than today, and now, the whole city mourns, for the vice regal party has not arrived as per programme." The newspaper further stated, "There is great disappointment in consequence of the postponement and the elaborate preparations and programme prepared will now necessarily have to be curtailed."[47]

At eight that evening, the welcoming committee in New Westminster received word of the accident, along with the Governor General's apologies for not being able to attend the reception planned for him. The fog lifted briefly as the badly damaged *Amphion* slowly made its way into the mouth of Esquimalt Harbour, and late that night, with much credit given to the dogged efforts of the ship's crew, the *Amphion* was able to anchor safely in Constance Cove, opposite the naval yard, where it was forced to wait until the tide was high enough to enter the dock.

"The ship was safely docked and what might have been a frightful calamity, attended with great loss of life, ended in a most dangerous accident," confirmed the *Ottawa Citizen*.[48] The nerves of the passengers were "naturally unstrung at the thoughts of the terrible ordeal through which they have passed and their feelings are of great thankfulness that it was no worse." They were carefully taken ashore. The shaken Governor General and his party were housed at the Driard Hotel in Esquimalt. Meanwhile, divers from *HMS Swiftsure* and *Amphion* were sent down to evaluate the damage but were forced to return to the surface as they were unable to use submarine lights.

Colville gave his account:

> *The rock was struck about mid-day and until eight that evening, the* Amphion *groped her way slowly through the fog, the water all the time gradually gaining on the pumps. They were anxious hours, you may be sure, for Captain Hulton and his men. As the compartments on the starboard side filled with water, the ship listed in that direction, so that when she came into Esquimalt, one stepped with*

ease from the deck into a rowboat. However, we got safely in and the ship being docked, we discovered that the sharp end of a rock had badly ripped the side of the vessel, an immense gap being left. We were in a very serious predica-ment indeed during the weary voyage home, for there were not boats enough for all hands had the vessel sunk, and some of us were apt to meet a watery grave. But the best of order prevailed, the ladies of the party setting a grand ex-ample and happily, the vessel was kept afloat until the dock was reached.

Notes from Lady Stanley's journal complete the saga:

The Captain decided to return to Victoria. He had the boats provisioned and all was ready to lower them at a moment's notice. Mr. McMahon was told by the first Lieutenant which boat F. and I were to use. We struck St. Juan [sic — Kellett's Bluff] at noon and we did not get into Victoria till 8:30 and we only did so then by the merciful chance of the moon rising and lifting the fog for about five minutes. The Captain then saw where we were. He saw a stump which was a mark on the torpedo ground. All this time we were 'making our penance' but the ships in harbour only thought we had put back owing to the fog. At last the flagship understood that we were in distress and sent off her boats and very thankful we were to leave the poor beautiful Amphion. *So much was she keeling over that we stepped off her entering port into the jig alongside! The damage done is found to be cut seventy feet long with two or three holes. Ten out of twelve water com-partments full of water. Five feet of water in the stoke hole. Two bad leaks in the deck. The water gained twenty inches an hour before we landed.*[49]

"We got rooms at the hotel and were very glad to go to bed after the terrible experience of the day," Colville said. "We all felt so much for the poor Captain and we shall be most anxious to know what will be his fate. Some fear that it will go hard with him."

* * *

At daybreak, using ropes attached to the masts, the ship, which had careened more than twenty-two degrees to starboard, was able to be righted to its proper position. Once reviewed, it was discovered that the damage was more serious than originally believed. Even though protection mats and sails had been thrown over the side of the ship to protect it seconds after hitting the rock, an examination revealed that the starboard side had been scraped and dented by the rock fifty feet down the ship's length. It was determined that the rock had penetrated both the outer and inner linings of the hull's double casing; an immense puncture measuring four feet long and six inches wide, some forty feet from the bow, as well as several smaller holes from the sharp rocks, were noted. The keel was badly bent in intervals of twenty-five feet, while the bilge keel, one of the two fins running lengthwise and attached along the ship's bilge, had been doubled almost in half. Many of the rivets had been pulled right out of the ship. All four blades of the starboard propeller had been bent out of shape and one was half gone. The iron frame of the ship was bent. Five of the *Amphion*'s compartments had filled with water. The dockyard fire engine and a pump from the Victoria Fire Department helped keep the water under control.

Interested readers back in Ottawa, who had been following the vice regal tour, were dumbfounded to read the headline in the *Daily Citizen* on Friday, 8 November: "Struck a Reef, Miraculous Escape of GG & Family Yesterday. Disaster to *HMS Amphion*."[50] The next day, another story began was flagged, "Narrow Escape from a Watery Grave."[51]

For Lord Stanley, his family and staff, there was more to be thankful for on that Thanksgiving Day, Thursday, 7 November, than the blessings of an abundant harvest. Although the fog had finally burned off the west coast, the governor general's party decided to remain at the Driard Hotel all day and return to the mainland the next morning to fulfill the postponed engagements. Meanwhile, the work of pumping out the water taken in by the ship continued, and by Friday the disabled ship stood dry and the canvas removed.

"The Admiral has again placed the *Champion* at our disposal and we should have started this morning but there was a fog and we were all thankful not again to run any risk," wrote Constance.

We spent the day walking and driving. It was so hot at 12 o'clock as to be almost disagreeable for walking. The Admiral came to pay us a visit. Of course, he was very reserved as to the accident but his face was not exactly hard when he spoke about it. Captain Sinclair dined with us. We hope that all will go well with Captain Hulton. All our party went on board the Amphion but could not see anything as the water had not yet been got out of.[52]

The bravery of Captain Hulton, who piloted the damaged *Amphion* through the fog to Esquimalt, was noted in the *Colonist*. "Captain Hulton, his officers and crew acted with the most consummate courage and coolness and are much praised. Under the trying circumstances, they navigated the ship into Esquimalt harbour as if nothing had happened."[53]

The cost of repairing *HMS Amphion* came to $180,000, a staggering amount of money in 1889 dollars and took many months to complete. The damaged ship was patched by Albion Iron Works in Victoria, then returned to England for more extensive repairs.

* * *

Shaken but undaunted, at 9 o'clock on the morning of 8 November, the vice regal party sailed for the mainland aboard the *Champion*. "Most lovely day and we made a very quick and good passage," detailed Lady Stanley. "At one time, we came into a fog but it only lasted a short time. It was most interesting to see the island and the rock on which we struck. And it certainly filled one with wonder that the ship did not instantly go down. People were kind when we landed at Vancouver."[54]

* * *

Before being posted to search for explorer Sir John Franklin's lost expedition, which had disappeared while searching for the Northwest Passage between the Atlantic and Pacific oceans, Captain Henry Kellett had been commissioned by the Royal Navy in 1846 to survey the Strait of Juan de Fuca. The strait separates Vancouver Island from the mainland — the state of Washington due east and the British Columbia mainland to the northeast. Kellett had discovered a maze of islands scattered through the strait, as well as a number of dangerous reefs submerged just below the water's surface. He noted at that time that several of the most dangerous reefs had already been marked by beacons before his arrival in the area.

In 1865, the Royal Navy relocated its Pacific Fleet headquarters from Valparaiso, Chile, to Esquimalt on Vancouver Island. The officers and crew introduced many of the social and sporting activities familiar from their British homes to the area, including cricket matches, band concerts and formal balls.

The San Juan Islands, located within the Strait of Juan de Fuca, were the traditional territory of the Salish, who had inhabited the area for thousands of years. Henry Island, located about twenty miles east-northeast of Victoria, is separated on its west side from the northern tip of San Juan Island by Mosquito Pass. On the southern end of Henry Island is a steep, rocky bluff. The waters around Kellett Bluff have strong currents and are teeming with marine life, inhabits the nooks and crannies that define the area. Cloud sponges, anemones, starfish and orange coral dot the rocky bluff, while rockfish and orcas thrive in the chilly waters.

There had been much debate over who controlled the islands located in the Strait of Juan De Fuca. Long-lingering tensions between Great Britain and the United States were resolved in 1872 when Kaiser Wilhelm I of Germany acted as arbitrator and ruled that the boundary line between Canada and the United States would run through the Haro Strait between Vancouver Island and the San Juan Islands, placing the islands of the Strait of Juan de Fuca under American jurisdiction.

U.S. President Ulysses S. Grant dealt with the situation in his State of the Union address of 2 December, 1872:

> *By the thirty-fourth article of the Treaty of Washington, the respective claims of the United States and of Great Britain defining the boundary line between their respective territories, were submitted to the arbitration and award of His Majesty the Emperor of Germany, to decide which of those claims is most in accordance with the true interpretation of the treaty of 1846. After a patient investigation of the case and of the statements of each party, His Majesty the Emperor, on the 21st day of October last, signed his award*

*in writing, decreeing that the claim of the Government of
the United States, that the boundary line between the territories of Her Britannic Majesty and the United States
should be drawn through the Haro Channel, is most in ac-
cordance with the true interpretation of the treaty
concluded on the 15th of June, 1846, between the
Governments of Her Britannic Majesty and of the United
States. The line so defined shall be deemed to be the international boundary, as defined and established by Treaty
provisions and the proceedings there under as aforesaid,
from the forty-ninth parallel of north latitude along the
middle of the channel which separates Vancouver's Island
from the mainland and the middle of Haro Channel and of
Fuca's Straits to the Pacific Ocean.*[55]

* * *

HMS Amphion served the Royal Navy after it was repaired in England, and
curiously, was involved in another collision involving a reef. In the early
weeks of 1902, the *Amphion* was badly damaged when she struck rocks
while travelling along the west coast of South America between Panama
City and Callao, Peru. Repaired again, the *Amphion* remained in service to
the Royal Navy until 1906 when it was sold for scrap.[56] All that remains of
this once-proud vessel is the rusted and crumpled keel, now found in the
northwest corner of Beacon Hill Park in Victoria, beside the entrance sign
at the corner of Douglas and Southgate streets. A plaque, which was placed
on 6 December, 1974, reads:

*Crumpled Keel Has a History. On November 6, 1889, Lord
Stanley, Governor General of Canada, embarked for
Vancouver following a visit to Victoria. HMS Amphion
carried the vice-regal party and, while travelling in fog,
struck a sunken reef at Kellett Bluff, Henry Island. The ship
was extremely damaged but returned safely to Esquimalt.
The bilge keel or rolling chock was crumpled like a con-
certina, as exhibited here.*[57]

* * *

The telegraph dispatch from Lord Stanley to Sir John A. Macdonald dated 7 November, 1889, read: "Serious accident to ship in which we sailed has thrown my arrangements three or four days later than proposed."[58]

Stanley's party arrived in New Westminster at ten o'clock on a rain-soaked Saturday, 9 November, 1889. Mayor William B. Townsend greeted Their Excellencies on behalf of the town, and was joined by other civic dignitaries, including Bishop Sillitoe.

Addresses were presented by the city councils of New Westminster, Surrey, Maple Ridge and Delta. His Excellency replied to all four parties at once, "making a very handsome speech, complimentary of the city and district."[59]

Boarding the steamer Samson, the party travelled up the Fraser River, visiting the salmon hatchery. Lord and Lady Stanley took a surprising interest in the scientific lecture on the incubation of salmon ova. Lady Constance asked several questions about procuring eggs and was told that ten million eggs were nurtured at the hatchery. The group returned to the ship and stopped briefly at the Bon Accord cannery and the Royal City Planing Mills. "Went in a steamer to see the salmon hatching establishment and then on to some lumber mills where we saw big forest trees being handled and cut up as if they were twigs," mentioned Lady Stanley.[60]

After luncheon, the vice regal suite continued first to inspect the penitentiary and then at Queen's Park. Lady Stanley was to plant the first tree in the park but was indisposed, so the Governor General performed the honour in her place. After the ceremony was over, the spade used to turn the sod was presented to Lady Stanley as a souvenir of the occasion. Constance briefly noted in her journal, "Was given a lovely silver spade."

That evening at six, a reception was held at the opera house. Lord and Lady Stanley stayed for two hours. The *Colonist* described the night: "The city was gaily illuminated this evening, and when the train bearing the vice regal party left for the east at eight o'clock, Their Excellencies were accorded a right hearty send-off by the people of the Royal City."[61]

* * *

With the transcontinental trip concluded, the train pulling *Victoria* took the governor general's party home, speeding east from British Columbia to Ottawa. Frederic Villiers, the correspondent for *The Graphic*, stayed in British Columbia to spend more time travelling across Canada. George Goschen, the son of the Imperial Chancellor of the Exchequer, travelled back across the Dominion with the Stanleys. The ceremonial visits and addresses were over, so on the way back, there were no stops other than to sleep at night — the train travelled only by daylight so that none of the scenery would be missed. "There was no end of fun amongst the party and a not important element in this arose out of the amateur photography practiced by nigh all of the party, there being no less than five complete photographic outfits on hand," wrote *The Citizen*.[62] The passengers were treated to spectacular meals throughout the entire journey. Many local delicacies were brought on board and prepared fresh for the vice regal suite: Fraser River salmon, trout, antelope steaks, prairie hens and the finest cuts of beef supplemented the standard fare of roast lamb with mint sauce, stewed lamb, leg of mutton and caper sauce, roast beef, roast turkey and cranberry sauce, and haddock in cream sauce.

Sunday, 10 November was recognized by the party as Captain Colville's birthday. The day was spent at the British Columbia town of St. Mary's Mission, today known simply as Mission. "Great Roman Catholic Mission," stated Lady Stanley. "The sisters do a great deal of good with the Indians."[63]

After spending the night, the train pulled out of Mission early on Monday, 11 November and arrived at Kamloops. Lady Stanley noted, "We got snow today. Mr. McMahon got bad news of his father."[64]

The party left Kamloops at 6:45 on the morning of Tuesday, 12 November. "Changed time at Donald. One hour forward," began Lady Stanley, ever impressed with the time zones. "Took photos of Revelstoke and Glacier. We saw the wonderful loop in the railway at the latter place better than we had done in our outward journey. It takes three turns round the side of the hill. Looking down you see the line in the shape of an S."[65]

Victoria departed from Glacier early on Wednesday. "Soon after we were up, we saw our last view of the Rockies and I for one felt very sorry," Lady Stanley recounted.[66] The train arrived in Medicine Hat, where the temperature had dropped substantially, although it was not snowing. A telegraphed message was received from Ottawa informing Lord and Lady Stanley that their youngest child, Bill, had the chicken pox.

Thursday took the suite from Medicine Hat to Broadview. It turned out to be the last day of the trip on which the Governor General's party saw First Nations people and their teepees on the plain along the tracks. Friday the 15th began in Broadview and ended in Rat Portage, with a brief stop in Winnipeg. "The Schultzes came to see us and were most cordial," remarked Lady Stanley in her journal.[67]

Saturday was a day of rocks, trees and travel. The party left Rat Portage at five-thirty in the morning and arrived at Schreiber at seven-thirty that night. Lady Stanley noted, "A broken spring to the engine on the way!"[68]

Sunday was spent entirely at Schreiber, which lies on the most northerly point of Lake Superior. Lady Stanley described the village as "rather a pretty place with a beautiful view of Lake Superior," punctuating the entry with "it was a glorious day."[69]

The final day of the Governor General's exhaustive transcontinental trip was Monday, 18 November. Leaving Schreiber at five in the morning, the vice regal train raced all but nonstop towards Ottawa, pausing only for fuel, oil and water in Cartier. The train pulled into the nation's capital at eleven that morning, greeted by pouring rain. "We left our dear car with many regrets," sighed Lady Stanley in the final entry of her travel journal. "It had been a happy house for nine weeks and our most enjoyable trip to the North-West was over."[70]

"Ottawa received back the Governor General and party after their interesting and unparalleled tour across the continent," stated the *Daily Citizen.*[71] Ottawa Mayor Jacob Erratt and Aldermen Heney, Gordon and McLean were part of a small delegation to welcome Their Excellencies back to the capital. The vice regal party were escorted to carriages that took them back home to Rideau Hall after a tour of sixty-three days that had been enjoyed thoroughly from start to finish.

* * *

Lord Dufferin, Canada's fourth Governor General, was the first vice regal to make the trip across the Dominion of Canada. Beginning 31 July, 1876, Lord and Lady Dufferin set off by train from Ottawa on a month-long journey to Canada's west coast. One of the main reasons for the trip was to help him understand the controversy developing between the British Columbia government and that of the Dominion of Canada in regards to the building of the transcontinental railway. Like Stanley, Dufferin also met with a number of aboriginal Canadians.

Stanley's extensive trip served a number of purposes. Besides allowing him to view the country over which he served as Governor General, it enabled him to appreciate the vastness of the country, experience the wide range of weather conditions enjoyed by Canada and, possibly most importantly, meet many of the citizens of the Dominion.

"It is understood that His Excellency's impressions of 'new Canada in the west' are highly favourable," wrote *The Citizen*. "His reception along the route was loyally enthusiastic."[72] Physician Sir James Grant added:

> At every point, it was enthusiastic in its character and made it plain that there was no lukewarmness in the loyalty felt towards the Queen's representative. The people as a whole were deeply interested in His Excellency's visit and appreciated the deep interest he exhibited in all that pertains to the welfare of the New West.[73]

But the trip served so many other functions. It also permitted Stanley to observe the effectiveness of the North-West Mounted Police, an organization in which he took great pride. *The Citizen* elaborated:

> The Governor's party seemingly cannot say too much by way of praise of the magnificent appearance, drill and discipline of the force, the pride every member of it appears to take in the organization and the tone of satisfaction with the service heard on all sides and all ranks.[74]

The cross-Canada excursion also gave the Governor General a firsthand look at the efficiency of the Canadian Pacific Railway. Lady Stanley commented, "We are filled with wonder and admiration for the minds that conceived the idea of this wonderful railroad and the energy and courage of those who carried it out."[75] Grant further noted, "Had it not been pushed through to completion, no one would have come into this district. It is quite impossible at present to estimate the vast importance of the Pacific Railway to the entire population of the Dominion."[76]

Lord Stanley continued to encourage further settlement of the Dominion, especially the vast prairies. And his official visits helped cement relations with the residents of the country, most notably with Canada's First Nations people. *The Citizen* surmised:

> *The Indians on the several reserves were delighted when told that their visitor was no less a personage than the representative of their great white mother, the Queen. They vie with the white residents in their expressions of loyalty, and if they have not reached that stage of civilization productive of the 'address of welcome', their sentiments were none the less plainly made known.*[77]

* * *

Lord Stanley scribbled a note to Sir John A. Macdonald on 19 November, 1889. "I write one line tonight myself to you on arrival here, after a very successful trip and I hope also one which may be of use. I shall now be here at your command at any time."[78]

* * *

After their exhaustive transcontinental trip, Edward and Alice left for a brief visit to England the week of 13 November. For his part, the Governor General settled in at Rideau Hall for the winter with no out-of-town engagements scheduled until the new year. Political affairs, on the other hand, would keep him more than occupied.

---

[1] E. O. S. Scholefield, *British Columbia from the earliest times to the present, I & II*, (Vancouver: S. J. Clarke Publishing Company, 1914), p.483.

[2] *Lady Stanley's Journal* (31 October, 1889).

[3] *Victoria Daily Colonist* (1 November, 1889), *edition cover page*.

[4] Ibid.

[5] Ibid.

[6] *Victoria Daily Colonist* (2 November, 1889), p.4.

[7] *Victoria Daily Colonist* (1 November, 1889), *edition cover page*.

[8] Ibid.

[9] Ibid.

[10] *Victoria Daily Colonist* (31 October, 1889), *edition cover page*.

[11] *Lady Stanley's Journal* (31 October, 1889).

12 The word "joss" is a bastardized version of the Portuguese word "Dios," meaning God. The Chinatown joss houses were shrines to patron saints.

13 David Chuenyan Lai, *Chinatowns: Towns Within Cities in Canada* (Vancouver: University of British Columbia Press, 1988)

14 *Lady Stanley's Journal* (1 November, 1889), National Archives of Canada.

15 Ibid.

16 *Victoria Daily Colonist* (2 November, 1889), *edition cover page.*

17 Ibid.

18 Ibid.

19 When "three cheers and a tiger" was called for, the first portion was constituted of three "hurrahs!" The "tiger" portion began as a growl from the crowd, slowly rising in volume and pitch until it became a loud roar at the conclusion.

20 *Lady Stanley's Journal* (1 November, 1889).

21 *Victoria Daily Colonist* (21 July, 1889), p.2.

22 *Victoria Daily Colonist* (3 November, 1889) p.4.

23 Ibid.

24 *Lady Stanley's Journal* (2 November, 1889).

25 *Lady Stanley's Journal* (3 November, 1889).

26 In 1900, James Dunsmuir became Premier of British Columbia, and in 1906, the province's Lieutenant Governor.

27 The original church was constructed of corrugated iron and sent from England by ship, along with two workmen to re-erect it in Victoria.

28 *Lady Stanley's Journal* (4 November, 1889).

29 Ibid.

30 Ibid.

31 Ibid.

32 Ibid.

33 *Lady Stanley's Journal* (4 November, 1889).

34 *Victoria Daily Colonist* (5 November, 1889), *edition cover page.*

35 *Lady Stanley's Journal* (4 November, 1889).

36 *Victoria Daily Colonist* (6 November, 1889), *edition cover page.*

37 Ibid.

38 *Victoria Daily Colonist* (7 November, 1889), *edition cover page.*

39 Ibid.

40 *Ottawa Daily Citizen* (20 November, 1889).

41 Premier George Walkem, who had ordered $30,000 worth of cement from England to complete the project, was forced to resign when the cement was lost in a mysterious warehouse fire. The project, initiated in 1876, incurred massive cost overruns and forced the resignation not only of Walkem but of several contractors. The Dominion government interceded to get the project completed.

42 *Victoria Daily Colonist* (7 November, 1889), *edition cover page.*

43 Ibid.

44 *Ottawa Daily Citizen* (8 November, 1889), *edition cover page.*

45 *Lady Stanley's Journal* (6 November, 1889).

46 *Ottawa Daily Citizen* (8 November, 1889), *edition cover page.*

47 *Victoria Daily Colonist* (7 November, 1889), *edition cover page.*

48 *Ottawa Daily Citizen* (8 November, 1889), *edition cover page.*

49 *Lady Stanley's Journal* (6 November, 1889).

50 *Ottawa Daily Citizen* (8 November, 1889), *edition cover page.*

51 *Ottawa Daily Citizen* (9 November, 1889), p.4.

52 *Lady Stanley's Journal* (7 November, 1889).

53 *Victoria Daily Colonist* (7 November, 1889), *edition cover page.*

54 *Lady Stanley's Journal* (8 November, 1889).

55 State of the Union address delivered by U.S. President Ulysses S. Grant on 2 December, 1872.

56 *Toronto Daily Star* (15 January, 1902), p.2.

57 A plaque at the entrance to Beacon Hill Park in Victoria commemorates the sinking of *HMS Amphion* with Lord Stanley aboard.

58 F. A. Stanley, *Telegraph to J. A. Macdonald*, from *Sir John A. Macdonald Papers*, (7 November, 1889).

59 *Victoria Daily Colonist* (10 November, 1889), p.4.

60 *Lady Stanley's Journal* (9 November, 1889).

61 *Victoria Daily Colonist* (10 November, 1889), p.4.

62 *Ottawa Daily Citizen* (November 20, 1889), p.2.

63 *Lady Stanley's Journal* (10 November, 1889).

64 *Lady Stanley's Journal* (11 November, 1889).

65 *Lady Stanley's Journal* (12 November, 1889).

66 *Lady Stanley's Journal* (13 November, 1889).

67 *Lady Stanley's Journal* (15 November, 1889).

68 *Lady Stanley's Journal* (16 November, 1889).

69 *Lady Stanley's Journal* (17 November, 1889).

70 *Lady Stanley's Journal* (18 November, 1889).

71 *Ottawa Daily Citizen* (November 20, 1889), p.2.

72 Ibid.

73 Ibid.

74 *Ottawa Daily Citizen* (20 November, 1889), p.2.

75 Ibid.

76 Ibid.

77 Ibid.

78 F. A. Stanley, *Letter to J. A. Macdonald, from Lord Stanley Papers*, (19 November, 1889).

Chapter Twelve

1890

In a ceremony rife with pomp and circumstance, Lord Frederick Stanley was conferred with an Honorary Doctor of Laws degree (LL.D.) from Queen's University in Kingston on the afternoon of 18 December, 1889. Chancellor Sandford Fleming presided over the event held in Convocation Hall. Sir John A. Macdonald spoke to those assembled:

> *Principal [George Munro] Grant presented the name of Lord Stanley of Preston, Governor General of Canada, as a fit and proper person to be enrolled on the list of Doctor of Laws of the university. The intimation was received with cheers. His Excellency replied in a pleasing way.*[1]

Joining the Governor General in receiving his honourary degree that day were the Reverend Dr. Ebenezer Jenkins, W. Kingsford and Dr. E. C. Roose.[2]

* * *

A month later, on 16 January, the Governor General opened the new session of Parliament.

> *In calling you together again for the consideration of Public Affairs, I may fairly congratulate you on as continuance of the progress and prosperity of the country.*
> *During the recess, I visited Manitoba and the North-West Territories and British Columbia, and everywhere I*

found myself received with the loyalty and goodwill which I have learned to be characteristic of Canada. A comparison of my own observations with those of my predecessors shows clearly the great progress which has marked this part of the Dominion, in the settlement of the country and in the development of its great agricultural capabilities, of mineral wealth and of its other natural resources.

In consequence of the repeated seizures by cruisers of the United States Navy of Canadian vessels, while employed in the capture of seals in that part of the Northern Pacific Ocean known as the Behring Sea, my Government has strongly represented to Her Majesty's Ministers the necessity of protecting our shipping, while engaged in their lawful calling, as well as of guarding against the assumption by any nation exclusive proprietary rights in those waters. I feel confident that those representations have had due weight, and I hope to be enabled during the present session to assure you that all differences on this question are in the course of satisfactory adjustment.

Having observed the close attention which has recently been given by the Imperial Authorities and on the continent of Europe to the improvement in the methods of catching, curing and packing fish, I deemed it expedient to cause a Commission to be sent to Scotland and Holland to examine and report upon this subject during the fishing season. The report of the delegates will be laid before you; it will, I am sure, give our fishermen most valuable information and instruction as to the best means of improving and developing this important industry.

My Ministers have carefully considered the difficulties which surround the administration of the rights of the Dominion in its foreshores, harbours, lakes and rivers, and a measure will be submitted to you for removing uncertainty as to the respective rights of the Dominion and of the provinces and for preventing confusion in the titles thereto.

Certain amendments to the Acts relating to the North-West Territories, calculated to facilitate the administration of affairs in that region, as also a Bill further to promote the efficiency of the North-West Mounted Police, will be submitted for your consideration.

Measures will be laid before you relating to Bills of Exchange and Promissory Notes, to improve the laws respecting patents of invention and discovery, to amend the Adulteration Act, and the laws respecting the Inland Revenue, to amend also the Act respecting the Geological and historical Nature Survey of Canada and to provide for the better organization of the National Printing Establishment.

* * *

In February 1888, the University of Ottawa noted that:

The rink [located on the front lawn of what is known today as Tabaret Hall] of this year is superior to that of any former year in our remembrance. We should like to see a good hockey match on the rink before long. No winter pastime reaches hockey in excitement, and none requires such skill and dexterity that it may be played with success. By all means, let hockey be inaugurated!

Far from oblivious to the hockey teams organized at McGill University in Montreal, Queen's in Kingston and Osgoode Hall in Toronto, and responding to the excitement generated in the capital by the Rideau Rebels and the Ottawa Hockey Club, the University of Ottawa formed its own hockey team, which began play in 1890.

In February of that year, the university challenged the Ottawa Hockey Club's second squad to a contest. A grandstand was erected in anticipation of a large crowd. The uncovered rink was surrounded by the flags of many nations, but in spite of the appearance of many dignitaries, including the Governor General, Lord Stanley of Preston, the unseasonably mild Ottawa weather rendered the ice unusable. The game was salvaged when it moved over to the Rideau Hall Rink, where the ice had been better maintained. The Ottawa Hockey Club defeated the "unpractised, slower, yet plucky" squad from the university by a 4-0 score. The next year, a city league was formed as part of the new Ontario Hockey Association, and it included the Ottawa Hockey Club (who went on to win the league championship), the Rideau Rebels, Dey's Rink, the Capitals and the University of Ottawa.[3]

Lord and Lady Stanley were joined by Sir John A. and Lady Macdonald at an impromptu dance at Ottawa's Riverview. Members of the Rideau Rebels were also in attendance,[4] as evidenced by a photograph taken that evening, which captured members of the Rebels conversing with members of the capital's social elite.

* * *

In April 1859, Sir Casimir Gzowski, acting on behalf of the Toronto Turf Club, petitioned Queen Victoria to sponsor a thoroughbred horse race; in July, Her Majesty replied that she was "graciously pleased" to grant a Plate of fifty guineas for the race, "to be run for in Toronto or such other place as Her Majesty might appoint." With that, the mile-and-a-quarter Queen's Plate, the oldest continuously-run thoroughbred race in North America, was born. Today, the Plate is the first jewel in Canadian racing's Triple Crown.

The first Queen's Plate was held at the Carleton Racetrack in Toronto on 27 June, 1860; Don Juan, ridden by jockey Charles Littlefield for owners James and John White of Milton, Ontario, was the winner.

In time, the race moved to Toronto's Woodbine Park, located on Queen Street East between Woodbine and Coxwell avenues. According to *The Dominion Illustrated Monthly*:

> *The Park itself is delightfully situated, and a more lovely spot is hard to find. From the grandstand directly south, a magnificent stretch of Lake Ontario's blue waters greets the eye, and refreshing breezes wafted from it serve to mitigate the intensity of the sun's rays. On a clear day, from the roof of the new members' stand, it is possible to see the spray from the Falls of Niagara.[5]*

Lord Stanley indulged his love of horse-racing and agreed to present the fifty guinea prize to 1890's Queen's Plate winner. Much to the chagrin of William Hendrie, president of the Ontario Jockey Club, by race day a steady downpour had turned the track into a muddy mess. The race was postponed until the next day; as a result, horsemen and spectators alike turned up at the track on 22 May, only to find the doors locked. The next day, a cold, damp afternoon, twelve thousand spectators jammed Woodbine Park, but only seven of the thirteen horses entered ran the race.

Before the race began, Aide-de-Camp broke away and threw its rider, Charles Butler, knocking him unconscious. Although a replacement rider was found, Aide-de-Camp never challenged and finished fifth.

In the early running, it was La Blanche out front, pursued by Kitestring and Flip Flap. In the backstretch, Kitestring took the lead but surrendered it briefly to Flip Flap. Rose Maybud, one of the early favourites, broke well but collapsed, landing on jockey Harvey "Dup" Douglas, who suffered a broken leg. The mare, Rose Maybud, suffered a broken hip and had to be destroyed. Coming into the stretch, Kitestring took over the lead and never relinquished it. Flip Flap backed off the pace to finish third behind La Blanche.

Dup Douglas, the injured jockey, recalled that two steeplechase races were run before a carriage ambulance reached him. He looked on in anguish as Kitestring crossed the finish line first. A collection was taken around the paddock, and about one hundred thirty dollars was collected for Douglas.

Thomas Hodgens, who had been the mayor of London, Ontario, and later helped establish the Imperial Oil Company, was the owner of Kitestring, a three-year-old black filly ridden by Fred Coleman that day.

> *A happier man than Mr. Hodgens was probably not to be found on the course when he accepted the hearty congratulations from the chief executive of the Dominion, Lord Stanley of Preston. The Governor General presented Hodgens with the symbolic fifty guineas that accompanies a Queen's Plate winner.*[6]

The Queen's Plate had been so enjoyable that successive Governors General always considered the Ontario Jockey Club's spring meetings, which coincided with the annual Plate, a fitting time to make their annual visits to Toronto.

Rider and Driver, a New York-based magazine, also endorsed Toronto and the Queen's Plate as a destination worthy of the attention of fans of the "sport of kings":

Toronto is the recognized headquarters of Canadian racing. The May meeting at Toronto has achieved a great reputation — the attendance is enormous. Balls and parties go on all the week. For an outing and jollification, we cordially recommend the trip.[7]

* * *

A Grand Ball, hosted by Lord and Lady Stanley, was held at The Citadel in Quebec City on 18 September, 1890. Eight hundred guests craned their necks to see His Royal Highness, Prince George of Wales, who entered the ballroom as the band began playing "God Save the Queen."

The twenty-five-year-old George, second son of the heir to the British throne and grandson of Queen Victoria, wore the uniform of the Royal Navy, where he held the rank of captain. In 1890, he would have had no expectation of becoming king; but after his brother's death in 1892, followed by his father's passing in 1910, he became King George V, reigning until 1936.

Over the course of the ball, the brilliant searchlights of *HMS Pylades* and *HMS Bellerophon* were thrown upon the party, whose guests included the Prince, Lord and Lady Stanley, Lieutenant Governor Angers and Sir Ambrose Shea, the Governor of the Bahamas. "The universal verdict upon the entertainment was that a more charming ball had never been given in Quebec," stated *The Citizen*.[8]

* * *

By the winter of 1889, Sir John A. Macdonald had sketched out what, in his opinion, were the key points in the Behring Sea dispute that directly affected Canadians. First, Macdonald wanted to attack the American premise that seals themselves were in danger of extermination, and that if the Americans really felt this was true, a proposal should emanate from their side of the fence. Next, Macdonald wanted to know what Britain expected from the Dominion, should Canada open negotiations with the U.S. in order to expedite the matter. Finally, if the British government wished for the Canadians to engage with the Americans, Macdonald listed the major terms that he wanted to secure from the negotiations:

a) That the mare clausum [closed sea] claim shall first be abandoned and any American legislation apparently supporting that conclusion repealed or amended.

b) That Canada shall be directly represented on British Commissions as in cases of Washington Treaty 1841...

c) Conclusions arrived at to be subject to approval by Canada.

d) Negotiations as to compensation and seizures to be conducted by Great Britain, United States and Canada without Russia.[9]

Considering the influence Russia had on previous negotiations (and the minuscule role Canada had played), this was a tall order. Too tall, in fact; Macdonald described Salisbury's report to Stanley grimly: "The Behring Sea cable is disheartening."[10]

Sir John Tupper arrived in Washington in late February 1890, his presence irritating U.S. Secretary of State James Blaine, who understood that "the British Government and the United States administration would agree upon a close season [a ban on pelagic hunting of seals] in the interests of this great and important industry and then submit the agreement to Canada for approval."[11] Tupper, however, did not allow Blaine to sidestep Canada's legal right to be involved in negotiations that directly affected it.

The Canadian government was deeply suspicious — some historians might argue, with good reason — that their official mail to Washington was being tampered with and delayed. In the delicate and important negotiations of March 1890, the Canadians took no chances; Stanley's eldest son and aide-de-camp Edward George Stanley was recruited to hand-deliver communications to the Canadian liaisons in Washington.[12] Sir Julian Pauncefote, the British minister at Washington, later told Stanley that everyone in the American capitol thought Edward was "the most charming of youths and he took Washington Society by storm."[13]

Pauncefote prepared a draft convention on behalf of the Anglo–Canadian delegation, to be presented to the Americans after it was reviewed in Ottawa in March 1890. The previous convention — the North Atlantic Fisheries Treaty — had been flatly rejected in the American Senate in 1888. The main provision of the new draft called for a mixed commission of experts which would study the conditions of fur-seal life and submit a plan for the regulation of the fishery within two years. During this study period, the capture of seals was to be suspended.[14] (The "study" portion of this convention was vital to Macdonald's aim to test the necessity of a close season.)

The revised edition of the new treaty that Tupper presented to Pauncefote in April 1890 called for the study to include an examination of fur-seal life on the Pribilof Islands, which were owned by the United States. This addendum went straight to the heart of the matter concerning fur-seal life and tested the Americans' expressed desire for the reduction of the indiscriminate slaughter of seals on land and on the high seas.

The details for the close season itself were also taking shape: the area to be observed by was determined and all but settled. There was, however, some question as to the duration of the season and the treaty itself. The Canadians wished for the treaty to last ten years, after which the parties had the right to terminate it upon giving one year's notice. Stanley felt that these two points were reasonable and worth a little bother: "Two things we can still fight for: the duration of the close season and the duration of the Treaty. As to the first, can we not delay any definite proposal until we got more expert advice on our side?"[15]

Stanley saw the benefit of making a concession to the U.S. by way of a temporary close season until more data was available to the Canadian contingent. In turn, Stanley suggested that if the definite details of a close season could be left open for two years or less, until "an expert commission chosen by both sides has verified some of the questions as to the habits of the seal about which at present little seems to be really ascertained." The American contention, of course, was that sealing in the close season would have serious ecological ramifications — Stanley wanted to press the United States on this claim: "Our best way of meeting the American contention was to throw on them the burden of verifying their assumptions."[16] This reasoning reinforced the strategy that would leave the onus on the Americans to allow science, and not commerce, to establish the need for a close season.

The terms the Canadians sought made Pauncefote extremely uncomfortable, a fact Tupper secretly confirmed to Macdonald:

> *I cannot refrain from urging that in future negotiations*
> *with the United States, no British Minister at Washington*

should act for us. It is apparent that there is always present on his part a desire to make his future residence in Washington as pleasant as possible, and he is to some extent therefore unable to take and keep a firm and independent position.[17]

Pauncefote was still very much unwilling to take even the smallest steps without British approval, as Tupper telegraphed Macdonald: "Pauncefote declines to present our draft until he hears from England."[18] Macdonald later related his feelings to Lord Stanley that, in regards to the matter of sealing during the close season, Sir Julian had "caved in and yielded" to the Americans.[19] As frustrating to the Canadians as this was, it was beginning to grate on the nerves of the Governor General, too.

Lord Stanley, for his part, was now beginning to take Canadian interests to heart and was not so easily roped into undermining the "colonial" prerogative, even through correspondence with British politicians, including Salisbury. In a letter to the Foreign Secretary, Stanley demonstrated an acute understanding of Canadian needs in the dispute:

As to the Behring Sea, we shall follow your lead though we shall grumble. I feel strongly that reasonable compensations to our sealers would be worth your while. They are ruined by an act of the Imperial Government … and I do not think that we can quite accept the position laid down in your telegram of the 28th of May that it is a matter which only interests Canada and is quite immaterial to Great Britain.[20]

While he was not necessarily about to take Salisbury to task, neither would Stanley censor his, or the Dominion's, displeasure with the Home Government. And, judging from the volumes of correspondence during his term in Canada, never did the Governor General never choose to refer to Canadians as inferior colonials — even though his British colleagues might have conducted their discourse in that old familiar British manner.

Stanley had received a deputation from the local Sealers' Association when he visited Victoria on 4 November, 1889, during his transcontinental trip. The Association had recently been formed to help preserve the sealing industry. Spokesman Richard Hill began the address:

> *It has been published in England as well as in America that for every one seal taken by our sealers and placed on the market, ten seals are destroyed. We believe that this statement, persistently made and seldom or never contradicted, has created, especially in England, a prejudice against our sealers. We have abundant evidence that the actual number of seals killed by our sealers, but not actually captured, does not exceed six in every one hundred. We are charged also with the wholesale destruction of female seals while carrying and nursing their young, thus destroying immense numbers of young seals as well. To answer this charge, it is only necessary to say that the females breed upon the islands in Behring's Sea about midsummer, that they remain with their young for about two months, seldom going more than a few miles from the islands for food and consequently, do not come within reach of our sealing vessels. The great majority of seals taken in Behring's Sea by our sealers are what are known as 'bachelors' and 'barren cows'.*[21]

Stanley appeared genuinely concerned in hearing Hill's account of this most delicate of issues. The report continued:

> *It has been stated that the matters in dispute will probably be settled by a compromise in the nature of a close season from May to December in each year for seal hunting in Behring's Sea. As the only period of the year when seal hunting can be carried on in Behring's Sea falls between May and December, a close season means practically the complete closing of the Sea to our sealers and a monopoly of the fur seal trade by the Alaska Commercial Company or other lessee on the same rights and privileges now enjoyed by that company from the Government of the United States.*[22]

Lord Stanley responded:

> *I thank you for having given me the opportunity to procure*
> *your views today. The matter on which we have met is one*
> *of the most difficult and delicate questions I could have to*
> *speak upon. It concerns not only your interests but the inter-*
> *ests of the Dominion and the Imperial government, and the*
> *interest of nations. I am glad to have had the opportunity of*
> *assuring you that the government has no desire to pass this*
> *great question by, and also of showing you the importance*
> *of my receiving from you definite information based on*
> *your knowledge of the facts, which I can transmit at once to*
> *the home government through the proper channels.*[23]

Stanley also shared his concern with the Russians' influence over the negotiations: "Russia will do anything she can against us, to say nothing of the
generally friendly feeling which she has maintained at all times towards the
United States."

The finished proposal was received by Blaine and the Americans on 29
April, 1890. A pregnant silence followed and lasted nearly a month before, on
22 May, the United States Cabinet rejected the proposal. In the wake of the
rejection, the mood was sombre, and as Creighton suggested, "relations with
the United States had been nearly as bad as they could have been."[24] Now,
more than ever, there was the possibility of a confrontation in the Behring
Sea. A small squadron of the Royal Navy was stationed at Esquimalt, British
Columbia, and with this move, the possibility of war — or, at the very least,
the end of diplomatic relations — was strengthened greatly.

* * *

Stanley's father had also faced the possibility of a Canadian-American war
when he was the Colonial Secretary in the 1840s. Edward Geoffrey Stanley
called for a dramatic improvement in the undermanned and sadly trained
Canadian militia. Some fifty years on, Edward's son was calling for the
same overhaul of the Dominion's militia.

From a British perspective, there was as little incentive for Britain to
wage war against America in 1890 as there had been in 1840. Writing in

The Dominion Illustrated Monthly, J. C. Hopkins offered:

> ... *if we consider the matter for a moment from a British point of view, that to go to war with the United States for any of the causes which have so far arisen; to expend millions of money and the lives of thousands of men, as well as to lose countless millions of dollars more by stoppage of trade, would be an enormous responsibility to assume. And for what? For the sake of a colony where the leaders of one great party are advocating closer union with the States and discrimination against British trade, while at the same time attempting to create dissatisfaction against the Mother Country for not acting with sufficient vigour in defence of our interests.*[25]

Yet logic would not necessarily dictate the outcome.

* * *

Further adding to the overall stress of the moment was the shift in American commercial policy represented by the McKinley Bill, which promised a comprehensive tariff that would drastically affect the export of Canadian grains (including barley, which was superior to the American variety), eggs and other farm products. If the Behring Sea was already a proverbial powder keg, the McKinley Bill had all the makings of one.

Wilfrid Laurier, among others, predicted that the McKinley tariff, which created a heavy burden for Canadian farmers to shoulder, spelled economic disaster for the Dominion.[26] Sir John A. Macdonald believed that the aim of the proposed tariff was to "starve" Canada into annexation with the United States.27 This belief was valid. American politicians had — some secretly, others, more transparently — hoped that the Canadian national "experiment" had run its course. American politician Erastus Wiman declared that "a prolonged dose of McKinleyism will bring Canada into commercial union."28

As early as 1888, *The Dominion Illustrated Monthly* plainly showed its disgust for Americans who sought to bring about annexation and for those Canadian publications that attempted to facilitate the idea:

A glance over the whole field of public opinion, during the past three months, reveals a strengthened and a loftier national feeling than existed before. It is more general, too, stretching from the east to the west. Partisan papers may seek to explain that sentiment away, but they cannot do it … some of the papers, whose object it would not be hard to fathom, complain bitterly that the writers and speakers should be called traitors who would hand over their country to another, on the transparent plea of a material improvement which cannot be shown, and which does not justify the risk of political change, Yet, traitor is the word. It conveys precisely what is meant. Canada is well as it stands. Its institutions are no longer experimental, but entering fast upon results of practical thrift. We are a nation now, and need no officious bolstering.[29]

Many Americans were not so sure. American "rebels" had played a peripheral role in the rebellions of 1837–38. And every time there was an undue strain on the legitimacy of Canada as a separate entity, be it Papineau's movement in the late 1840s, Nova Scotia's initial opposition to Confederation or Louis Riel and the North-West Rebellion, certain American opportunists were always close at hand to help fractious elements in the Dominion champion the cause of annexation to the United States. During the Riel Rebellion, the United States refused passage to Canadian troops on American railroads. Some time later, American Senator Sherman did not mince words, predicting that the Dominion would be annexed to the Republic in less than ten years.[30]

The majority of Canadians were not, however, in favour of the idea of annexation; most upheld the belief that Confederation was a success, a conviction echoed in *The Dominion Illustrated Monthly*. "The experiment of Confederation is not yet a quarter of a century old. Those who can recall what these provinces were before 1867 will hardly despair of its success so soon, when they look upon the results already achieved."[31]

Numerous American newspapers endorsed a policy of hostility towards Canadian interests as long as it remained a British possession.[32] Canadian periodicals shot back. *The Dominion Illustrated Monthly*, while praising the republic on its wonderful progress, warned in no uncertain terms that Canadians "inherit too much patriotic felling and national pride to wish to exchange a British birthright for a foreign-alliance."[33]

Gains enjoyed by the Democratic Party in the House of Representatives at the end of 1890 gave Macdonald and others reason to believe that the American people were rallying against the McKinley tariff and that, after the administrations of Harrison and Cleveland, the pendulum might swing in Canada's favour. However, the Republicans remained very much in power until March 1891. And until that time, Blaine and company were committed to weakening the Dominion's power.

* * *

On 29 September, 1890, Lord Stanley and his party embarked on another railway trip, this time to the Atlantic provinces of New Brunswick, Nova Scotia and Prince Edward Island. They would return to Quebec on 26 October. With this journey, Stanley could genuinely claim to have completed toured Canada *a mari usque ad mare* — from sea to sea. Like his 1889 journey to the west, the Governor General would take the opportunity to involve himself in civic duties, meet the citizens of the area and, of course, be addressed in each city, town and hamlet visited.

When New Brunswick and Nova Scotia joined Confederation in 1867, Prime Minister Macdonald's government had promised a railway linking them to Quebec and Ontario. That year, construction of the Intercolonial Railway began under the watchful eye of Sandford Fleming, engineer-in-chief. Nine years later, in July 1876, the railway was open for business, connecting Rivière-du-Loup, Quebec, with Truro, Nova Scotia. Before the completion of the Intercolonial Railway, the only available route between the Atlantic provinces and the rest of Canada was by taking a ship to Portland, Maine, and then following a trail inland from there.

Once again, Lord and Lady Stanley would travel in their private car, *Victoria*; members of the party included Edward Stanley, who acted as an aide-de-camp, and his wife, Lady Alice, along with another aide, the Honourable William Walsh; Isobel and Arthur Stanley; Mr. Streatfeild; and Miss Marjorie Middleton, the daughter of General Sir Fred Middleton, who was in command of the forces in Canada at that time.

Stanley's train left from Quebec City on Monday, 29 September and travelled easterly around the Gaspé Peninsula, pulling into Campbellton,

New Brunswick, later that afternoon. Lord Stanley was fairly well acquainted with the area, as he would have passed Campbellton on trips to his summer home, Stanley House. The Stanleys stayed the night at the luxurious Inch Arran Hotel in Dalhousie, enjoying the extended veranda and watching with amusement as guests played croquet and quoits.

Edward Stanley notified the towns of Newcastle and Chatham that the Governor General would be arriving the afternoon of 30 September. Although the notice was short and precluded elaborate plans, the two communities decided to receive the vice regal party collaboratively.

A large throng of admirers greeted Lord Stanley as he and his party arrived at Newcastle's Muirhead Wharf at noon. After they were greeted by a nineteen-gun salute fired by the Newcastle Field Battery, the local band began playing "God Save the Queen." Then the group was driven down Water Street, treated to the sights of homes, businesses and streets decorated with flags and banners of welcome.

At the Masonic Hall in Newcastle, a civic address was delivered by A. D. Shirreff, who operated a brewery in town and owned Middle Island and its fishery, about a mile from Chatham. Included in his response, Stanley expressed a desire to see the Miramichi Railway and its bridges, an idea which was greeted enthusiastically by those assembled.

Many of those in attendance accompanied the Governor General to the public wharf. Local businessman Jabez Bunting Snowball served as host to Stanley throughout the afternoon. Snowball was at the centre of both the economic and social life of Chatham, as most of the region's economy was based on his various enterprises. His Chatham sawmill, one of the largest in Canada, cut 170,000 feet of timber a day. Snowball also owned three smaller mills, a grist mill, a cannery that shipped lobster to England, and the Miramichi Steam Navigation Company, which operated six steamers that transported raw materials to his mills and carried away his cut timber for export. In 1886, Snowball financed the Chatham Branch Railway, which connected his mill in Chatham to the Intercolonial Railway more than six miles away. At the time of Stanley's visit in 1890, J. B. Snowball & Co. employed a thousand men.

The vice regal party climbed aboard Snowball's yacht, the *St. Nicholas*, and anchored at his mill in Chatham. "Visitors got an exciting and realistic idea of how lumber is made and shipped on the Miramichi," according to one newspaper account.[34] After the tour, the group departed, and at four o'clock they stepped through the imported-wrought-iron gates of Snowball's prestigious Wellington Villa, where they were served luncheon. Lord Stanley and his party were taken by carriage to the Chatham railway station at five that afternoon, and they departed for Moncton.

There was much excitement in the region about the Saint John Exhibition taking place at that time. In fact, Mayor Sumner and several aldermen were visiting Saint John when the Governor General arrived in Moncton at eight in the morning on the first day of October, 1890. In the mayor's stead, Stanley and his party were officially greeted by David Pottinger, the general manager of the railway. A reception was held at eleven o'clock that morning in the Opera House, and the Moncton Cornet Band performed several selections as the local public school children gathered to meet Lord and Lady Stanley.

The Governor General visited various sites around Moncton that day, and on Thursday the second he, too, attended the exhibition taking place in Saint John.

Edward, who routinely proceeded ahead of the vice regal train to ensure that details were in place for the Governor General's arrival, boarded the train at Petitcodiac and rode along as far as Sussex with his family and the remainder of the suite.

As the vice regal train approached Saint John at 11:55, a salute was fired from nearby Fort Howe. Not many years prior, Saint John had boasted a population larger than Toronto, but a devastating fire in 1877 put a quick halt to the town's burgeoning prospects.

The Governor General was greeted by three cheers and the welcoming handshakes of a number of prominent Saint John citizens, including Mayor W. Albert Lockhart; the Lieutenant Governor of New Brunswick, Sir Leonard Tilley, along with Lady Tilley and their son, Lieutenant Herbert Tilley; J. B. Snowball; Judge John R. Armstrong; the Commanding Officer of the Regiment, Lieutenant Colonel Armstrong; the Honourable L. J. Tweedie; the Honourable Samuel James Mitchell; and Mrs. A. G. Blair, wife of the Premier of New Brunswick. It was a beautiful day as the artillery band played an appropriate air in King Square.

Sir Leonard Tilley, seventy-two years of age at the time of the Governor General's visit, had held the office of finance minister of the Dominion of Canada until 1885, when his health faltered and he accepted the less labour-intensive position of Lieutenant Governor of New Brunswick.

Mayor Lockhart and Lieutenant Governor Tilley joined Lord Stanley for a short drive to the outskirts of Saint John. The city had a festive air, with many businesses and residences decorated with bunting and flags. Upon the group's return, they were joined by Lady Stanley for a luncheon in the vice regal train car. At 3:20, Stanley was driven through streets lined by throngs of onlookers to the Saint John Exhibition.

George Moffatt was giving an organ recital, performing an 1870 hymn entitled "Rescue the Perishing," when he saw a flurry of activity at the main entrance and surmised that the Governor General was arriving. He immediately began playing "God Save the Queen."

Exhibition president Charles A. Everett welcomed Lord Stanley, who responded, "I thank you very much indeed." Lady Stanley was unable to join her husband at the exhibition because of an injury to her knee.

The exhibition was packed with industrial and agricultural innovations as well as curiosities, and Stanley seemed amused and intrigued by the array of displays. *The Progress*, a Saint John newspaper, mused that there was quite a competition for Lord Stanley's attention between exhibition president Charles A. Everett and Alderman Connor. The paper termed them "rival cicerones," or tour guides. Visitors to the exhibition were uncertain which of the men was the Governor General: several pointed at Lord Stanley's son Edward, while others, ironically, thought it was Alderman Connor.

As the group strolled through the exhibition, each few steps brought them to a new, interesting exhibit. There was a fruit display, a nail exhibit and a discourse on rope making. British Columbia had presented an exhibit and there was a butter section. Passing by Patterson's haddies, the lightly smoked and delicately flavoured haddock, Lord Stanley tipped his hat and said, "Nice fish, these." Mayor Lockhart plucked a sample of peat moss to demonstrate its quality for Lord Stanley. The Governor General showed interest in the gun sights and Crawford's electric oven and praised the bricks manufactured by the Lee Brothers.

There was mild embarrassment when Lord Stanley stopped at the Trinidad Court. "Mr. Everett, in an absent-minded sort of way, removed a card which, apparently by accident, lay over the face of a framed photograph. This unveiling disclosed a perfectly nude native of Trinidad, whereupon Mr. Everett's face assumed a look of chart indignation."[35]

A large number of people were already milling about Ganong's candy pagoda by the time the Governor General strolled by. New Brunswick's

Ganong brothers, Gilbert and James, opened a candy factory in St. Stephen in 1873. While preparing for a fishing trip, James's son Arthur and candy maker George Ensor mixed chocolate with nuts and wrapped pieces individually to snack on while they waited for the fish to bite. This idea prompted the idea of producing chocolate bars, which were first manufactured by the Ganong candy factory.

Lord Stanley was escorted to the art gallery, watched a taxidermy demonstration and stopped at an exhibit of speed skates from the J. A. Whelpley Company of Greenwich, Kings County. Whelpley produced several brands of skate, including the Volant hockey skate and the Long Reacher speed skate, both renowned throughout the province. Both kinds of skates were strapped onto the boot of the skater with a pair of leather straps. People in the region were particularly interested in skating, stoked by the success of local boy Hugh McCormick, holder of world speed skating records in 1886 and 1887. In 1890, McCormick defeated Norwegian Axel Paulsen in two out of three races to win the World Professional Speed Skating championship in Minneapolis, Minnesota. "There probably has never been a more popular Saint John athlete than he," stated the *Evening Star* in 1926 about Hugh McCormick. "[McCormick's] ascent to the pinnacle of Champion Skater of the World in 1890 made no difference in his amiable relations with the great number, rich and otherwise, who were glad to be among his friends."[36]

The Governor General chuckled as he addressed C. W. Taylor of the Gananoque Carriage Company. "I have been trying for the last twelve months to break one of your carriages and have not yet succeeded." A carriage the company sold to the Earl of Dufferin, who was Governor General between 1872 and 1878, served each of the subsequent Governors General — the Duke of Argyll, the Marquess of Lansdowne and Lord Stanley.

Stanley concluded his visit with a firm handshake and a salute to the organizers. "I can sincerely say that it is with utmost satisfaction on all I have seen around me what are marks of the great progress that is being made in all useful industries, but also in the arts and sciences in this province."

On Friday, the party was driven by carriage to Saint John's court house, where an address was presented by B. Lester Peters, the Common Clerk and Police Magistrate, whom *The Globe* had described in 1884 as "of fine figure, dignified in appearance" and "one of Saint John's most eligible bachelors."[37]

At 1 p.m., the tug *Dirigo* carried Lord Stanley to Partridge Island at the entrance to the Saint John harbour. Stanley visited the lighthouse and its keeper, an entertaining soul named James Wilson, who demonstrated the steam-powered fog whistle and explained his "fog factory" and the "mysteries of the beacon," but then took the opportunity to dwell in eloquent detail on the various improvements he wanted the government to make.

As the *Dirigo* continued, it was saluted by ships in the harbour. Lord Stanley showed great interest in the history of French settlements on the Saint John River. He was shown the location of two ancient forts, Fort Nashwaak and Fort Jemseg, as well as the first French farm and the old settlements of Sheffield and Maugerville. The wind turned cold and strong, so the party decided against sailing further to Kennebacis.

Approaching Fort Howe, the Governor General was greeted by a cannon blast. "The sail had been a delightful one and while the guests were charmed with what they saw, the citizens who accompanied them are equally delighted with the unassuming manner and cordial friendliness of the distinguished guests." That evening, a grand levee was held with Lord and Lady Stanley as the guests of honour.

The party left Saint John by train and arrived in Fredericton just past noon on Saturday, 4 October, met by the Royal School of Infantry. The Stanleys were recipients of the traditional civic address, which was followed by a response from the Governor General. The crowd then delivered a hearty three cheers and a tiger. The vice regal couple, joined by Lord and Lady Tilley, were driven up Queen Street in barouches to visit the Normal School.

The couple ate luncheon in their train car *Victoria*, then departed for Victoria Public Hospital on the south bank of the Saint John River, just east of Government House, followed by a visit to King's College.

In the evening, Lord Stanley received an address at the Legislative Building, and then was guest of honour at a public reception. With thousands looking on, the firemen put on an outstanding pyrotechnic display, which was followed by a torchlight procession through the main streets of Fredericton. The cathedral bells chimed as residents celebrated in the streets. Lord and Lady Stanley spent the night at the Governor's House, also known as Old Government House, the official residence of New Brunswick's Lieutenant Governor.

A driving rain soaked the region on Sunday as the Stanleys prepared to attend church service at Christ Church Cathedral in Fredericton. To this day, the cathedral, a sensational example of Gothic architecture built in

1853, holds the letter patent from Queen Victoria that constituted Fredericton as a Cathedral City. The first two pews of the middle aisle were reserved for the vice regal party, which also included Sir Leonard and Lady Tilley and Lieutenant Colonel Armstrong. Following the service, the ladies took carriages back to the train while Lord Stanley and the men walked. In the afternoon, the Stanleys attended a second service, this time at Metropolitan Cathedral, then returned and dined in their train car.

At nine o'clock on the morning of Monday, 6 October, the vice regal suite took barouches for the short trip to Marysville and its prospering cotton mill. Run by "Boss" Gibson, the mill was at the hub of what had become a very industrious town, named after Gibson's wife, Mary. Lord Stanley seemed to be as impressed by the mill's electric lights as he was by the efficiency of the cotton mill.

At eleven that morning, Lord and Lady Stanley, along with forty guests, boarded the steamer *David Weston* for the trip back to Saint John. Steamers played an integral role in the life of New Brunswick residents, transporting goods and people between communities. The *David Weston*, named after its first captain, was built by the Union Line Steamship Company and began making regular runs between Fredericton and Indiantown, which is now part of Saint John, in 1866. The ship, which could carry more than two hundred passengers, boasted luxurious accommodations, including a dining lounge that seated ninety at any one time, a circular staircase, marble-topped tables and plush chairs.

The Governor General and his party arrived in Indiantown just past five in the afternoon. Robert Visart, Count de Bury, an Austrian who had relocated to Saint John and owned a sizable mansion there, spent much of the journey chatting with Lord Stanley. After docking, carriages took Lord and Lady Stanley to Saint John, where they spent the night.

Tuesday, 7 October began in Saint John. Joined by Mayor Lockhart, Lord Stanley visited the Centennial School on Brussels Street, where the seven hundred students assembled to greet the Governor General. While touring the school, Stanley gripped a piece of chalk and wrote on the blackboard in large, block letters: "HOLIDAY." The students, as one might imagine, applauded wildly.

At half past three, the Governor General was escorted to the university in time for opening exercises. There, he witnessed a lecture being presented on Physics in Modern Life. He then visited the Normal School, a teacher's college. Afterwards, the Governor General visited the Harris Car Works, a company that manufactured railway cars.

Stanley left later that day for Amherst, Nova Scotia, accompanied by Lieutenant Governor and Lady Tilley and Amherst-based Senator Robert Dickey, who was part of the Legislative Council of Nova Scotia and who had been one of the Fathers of Confederation. Upon arriving in the town, which had been incorporated in 1889, the vice regal suite was driven down Victoria Street to the town's court house. While the Amherst Cornet Band played, Mayor Dunlap greeted the Governor General and Lady Stanley.

Stanley responded to the address by noting the decorative arch he had observed on his drive into town. "On the handsome arch under which I passed, I see that the emblems of your town are two figures which represent the motto 'hand in hand'. I hope that this country will always pass hand in hand with the old country."

The Cornet Band played "God Save the Queen," and the five hundred schoolchildren attending the ceremony joined in. As was the case at other schools, these students were also given a holiday by the Governor General.

The entourage was then driven to Fort Lawrence, a British fort built on the former site of Beaubassin, a French settlement burned to the ground in an attempt to keep it from falling under control of the British.

The specific purpose of the visit to Amherst was to inspect the Chignecto Marine Transport Railway, which was nearing completion but had experienced mammoth challenges over the course of its construction. The Isthmus of Chignecto links Nova Scotia and New Brunswick and separates the Bay of Fundy from the Gulf of St. Lawrence. In the late seventeenth century, the Governor of New France (Quebec) realized that if a canal could be sliced through the isthmus, it would create a much quicker shipping route between Port Royal, the French capital of Acadia, and Quebec City. It took almost two hundred years, but Henry Ketchum, a New Brunswick engineer, devised a plan that would allow vessels to be transported across the isthmus by way of a railway, thus substantially reducing the sailing distance between ports on the St. Lawrence and those on the Bay of Fundy. The proposal called for the construction of a seventeen-mile railway that would extend from Fort Lawrence, located on the Bay of Fundy, to Tidnish Dock on the Northumberland Strait. At docks at either terminus, vessels would be lifted by hydraulic presses onto special railway cars, then hauled across the isthmus using the power of two locomotives, to be lowered back into the water at the other end.

After years of negotiation, the Dominion government agreed in 1888 to subsidize the railway, provided that Ketchum finish the project by 1892. His company, the Chignecto Marine Transport Railway Company, hired four thousand men to begin work on the project, creating a small town near Amherst. But the company faced massive obstacles right from the start. For one, the flow of the Tidnish River had to be altered. Heavy rains later flooded the project, delaying work for several months. The swamp-like nature of the land forced one sizable section to be excavated and filled with rock six feet deep in order to create a solid foundation for the tracks.

Lord Stanley was shown a hole in the ground where the great Chignecto Marine Transport Railway was being built. He inspected the work and commented that it appeared to be moving along with some efficiency. Little did the Governor General know that by the next year, 1891, most of the project would be completed, but both Ketchum's company and the contractor would run out of money. Work was suspended, and when the deadline passed, Parliament cancelled both its subsidy and the charter of the Chignecto Marine Transport Railway Company.

* * *

Lady Stanley's reception took place beginning at eight o'clock in the evening at the residence of the recently deceased Adam Hudspeth, a local lawyer who had been the member of Parliament for Victoria South, an Ontario riding that consisted of the town of Lindsay as well as the townships of Emily, Mariposa, Ops and Verulam.

The cynical *Progress* newspaper yawned and wrote, "The public has been bored so much by accounts of the vice regal party that I omit all references to them this week. I am sure that hundreds of retailers will thank me."[38]

* * *

Lord Stanley arrived in Annapolis Royal at seven o'clock on Wednesday, 8 October. Rather than staying overnight on the vice regal train *Victoria*, Lord and Lady Stanley spent the night at the Hillsdale House, an inn built in 1849 that found itself home to most luminaries who arrived in the area.

At eleven o'clock the next morning, Warden Roop addressed the

Governor General. The vice regal party then boarded the steamer *Evangeline* and sailed to Digby in the afternoon. After a short visit, the ship returned to Annapolis Royal at six. Two hours later, the Hillsdale Cornet Band led a torchlight march through the town. The performance of "God Save the Queen" later that evening served as a signal that the Governor General's official duties within the town had come to a conclusion.

* * *

As a city, Halifax assumed a decidedly British feel, in large part due to the presence of the navy and military. A steady parade of British vessels in and out of the Halifax harbour, instilled a strong, patriotic fervour in most Haligonians, and ties to the Empire were resoundingly strong. British customs took precedence, especially in regard to social activities. Halifax very likely was the spot where the first hockey-like games were played — influenced, no doubt, by games of shinty and bandy imported from the United Kingdom.

Two thousand residents gathered at Halifax's North Street station to await the arrival of the Governor General's party on Friday, 10 October.

The cracking of railroad torpedoes placed on the rails between Richmond and North streets signalled to all that the vice regal party had arrived. The Governor General was greeted by Alderman J. N. Lyons, the acting mayor in the absence of Mayor David McPherson. Malachy (Mally) Daly, who had only been sworn in as Nova Scotia's Lieutenant Governor in July of that year, was also on hand to greet Stanley, as was Sir John Ross, the general officer commanding the forces in Canada and the man who had acted as Administrator of the Government of Canada during the month that separated the departure from Canada of Sir Henry Petty-Fitzmaurice, the Marquess of Lansdowne, and the arrival of Lord Stanley of Preston.

The vice regal party walked past a guard of honour of one hundred fifty men from the 66th Battalion, the Princess Louise Fusiliers, and stepped into waiting carriages which transported them, along with a guard of honour from the Duke of Wellington's West Riding Regiment, through Barrington, Granville and Hollis streets, ending the trip at Bellevue House on Spring Garden Road as guests of Sir John Ross.

At Bellevue House with Ross, the vice regal party was greeted by a performance by the St. Patrick's Band of "God Save the Queen." Inside, Lord

Stanley sat in the mayor's chair with Lady Stanley to his left while a civic address was delivered in the council chamber at eleven o'clock. Afterwards, carriages picked up Stanley and his party and drove them back to the vice regal train while a band performed "Farewell to Thee" — an appropriate air written in 1884 by Edgar Selden Gaines.

That evening, a red light situated on the centre of the flagstaff indicated to those assembled that the vice regal train was in town.

* * *

Far removed from the endless political invitations and business greetings was the manner in which the Governor General and his party spent the afternoon of Saturday, 11 October.

Woolnough's Pleasure Ground, located on McNab's Island, was a popular location for outings. Concerts and dancing were regular features in the pavilion on the grounds, although many visitors preferred a game of croquet, quoits or other athletic pursuits before the final ship left the island for the Halifax mainland each evening at eleven.

Four days later, on a bitterly cold Wednesday, a gymkhana was staged at the Riding Grounds in Halifax. Among those in attendance were Lord and Lady Stanley and Prince George, who was serving with the Royal Navy on *HMS Canada*. Sir John Ross was also on hand. Lord Stanley wore an ulster, a long overcoat made of a heavy, rugged fabric, to protect himself from the chill. Lady Stanley wore furs and heavy wraps.

Gymkhana competitions enjoyed great popularity in the mid-nineteenth century. The games, all involving riding, had been devised by British troops serving in India. The word gymkhana is an Anglicized version of the Hindi word *gendkhana*, which means "ball-playing area."[39] The contests, at that time quite lighthearted and spirited, combined British and Indian feats of skill and were usually mounted on Sunday afternoons by cavalrymen to hone their horsemanship. Non-participants regularly gathered, finding the games most entertaining.

Attendance on this date was less than expected, as fewer than two hundred spectators braved the chill. A polo match was first on the agenda. Teams were chosen alphabetically — players whose surname began with the letters A through L wore red sashes, while blue was worn by those whose names began with M to Z. Prince George participated, playing on the red team with Captain Bruce, Colonel Clarke and Captain Jenkins. The blue team was made up of Major Mansell, Major McDonnell, Lieutenant McGowan and Captain Stewart. Given the piercing cold and the softening of the field from the recent rains, the field's condition was much less than optimal, but the contest, which ended in a 4–4 draw, was entertaining nonetheless. "There was some brilliant playing, which was much enjoyed by the visitors," according to one newspaper. Much attention was devoted to Prince George, who, even though he was given the best polo pony in the garrison, proved to be a fine polo player on his own merits. "Prince George was not only much observed from his rank, but his fine playing attracted great attention."

Next up was a tug of war, followed by other competitions that were not nearly as well known. The cheroot and umbrella race, for example, saw contestants light a cigar, saddle a pony, put up an umbrella, then mount the pony and ride around a post fifty yards away, circle back, dismount and then drink a cup of hot coffee. The cigar had to stay lit and the umbrella up through the entire race. The Lloyd Lindsay Competition, named after a military captain of the era who had introduced an experimental shooting competition in 1873, saw teams of three ride over hurdles fifty yards apart, dismount, break ten bottles with stones at ten yards, mount, and ride back over the hurdles. The Postillion Race asked competitors to ride one pony and lead another over a quarter-mile track, pick up weights just over a hundred and sixty pounds, then finish over a flight of hurdles. As politically incorrect as it would be today, the gymkhana also featured a contest called Spearing the Afghan. Britain had just battled Afghanistan and annexed what is today Pakistan's northwest frontier province, which had been Afghan territory prior to 1891. In the game, a stuffed figure was laid on the ground just beyond a hurdle. Contestants speared the figure as they leapt over the hurdle on their horse. The stuffed figure had a heart marked on its breast, and the winner was the contestant who not only finished the race in the fastest time, but who "speared the Afghan" closest to this target.

* * *

Sunday, as always, was a day of rest for the Governor General and his travelling party. The 12th of October began with a service at St. Paul's, the oldest Protestant place of worship in Canada. Designed to resemble St.

Peter's in London, England, Halifax's St. Paul's was built in 1750 of timber imported from Boston and bricks made locally.

On Monday, Lord and Lady Stanley visited *HMS Bellerophon*, a British battleship launched in 1865, with General Ross and Vice Admiral George Watson, the Commander-in-Chief of North America and the West Indies for the Royal Navy. The Governor General was given a seventeen-gun salute on his arrival, after which he observed, with great interest, the performance of manoeuvres.

The group then visited a succession of government buildings, including the Provincial Building, the Customs House and the Post Office.

Sir John Ross accompanied the Governor General to the forts at York Redoubt and McNab's Island. York Redoubt sits on a bluff overlooking Halifax Harbour, and was originally built in 1793, at the outbreak of war between England and France, to secure Halifax from attack by sea. During the nineteenth century, signal flags were used between York Redoubt and Citadel Hill in order to keep both informed of activities on the Atlantic.

McNab's Island divides the entrance to the Halifax Harbour into two channels, and the fort located there offered an outstanding vantage point from which to observe activity on the waters surrounding the Nova Scotia capital.

At nine o'clock that evening, the Stanleys were the guests of honour at a Grand Ball hosted by officers of the Duke of Wellington's Regiment. The regiment's 2nd Battalion had been deployed to Bermuda in 1886, then moved to Halifax in 1888, before being sent to the West Indies in 1891, and ultimately to South Africa two years later.

The regiment's quarters had been:

> … *metamorphosed completely and from the matter of fact every day quarters, the skillful hands of the decorators had laid a most pleasing ballroom and all the etceteras necessary for the grand display of 'fair women and brave men' who assembled after 'the gun had gone'.*[40]

Beyond the garlands that decorated the hall, suspended from the ceiling were lifebuoys from *Bellerophon*. Both Prince George and Lieutenant Victor Stanley, stationed with the Royal Navy in Halifax at the time, were on the reception committee and assisted in decorating the hall.

Placed at the centre of a table in the supper room was a trophy won by the Duke of Wellington's Regiment in a rifle contest held in Bermuda. Nearby was a refreshment table that offered coffee, tea, ice cream, ices and champagne cups. Dancing took place in the mess room from ten-fifteen until four the following morning. Afterwards, guests called the event the "best ball since the visit of the Prince of Wales thirty years ago."[41]

On Tuesday morning at 9:15, Lord Stanley visited the professors and students of Dalhousie College. The undergraduates lined the hall and stairway from the main entrance to the examination room, where the Governor General received an address, fashioning a reply afterwards. After the addresses, Stanley was serenaded with an exuberant version of "For He's a Jolly Good Fellow," followed by the traditional three cheers and a tiger. The Governor General presented gold and silver medals achieved during the annual academic competition, then was shown through the library, laboratories and classrooms. As the Governor General appeared in yet another hallway, the students made the corridors resound to a series of college songs, concluding appropriately with "God Save the Queen."

Next on the itinerary was the Convent of the Sacred Heart, established in the 1850s to teach academic subjects as well as the "ornamental branches" (art, music, sewing) to young Roman Catholic girls. The school, located on Spring Garden Road, offered room and board for students from outside the city and was highly regarded for its "respectable character" and outstanding scholastic standards.

Archbishop Cornelius O'Brien escorted Lord Frederick and Lady Constance to various sites within the city, including St. Joseph's Roman Catholic Orphanage, which was rebuilt in 1884, and St. Patrick's Home, a reformatory and industrial school opened by O'Brien in 1885.

Then, the Stanleys visited the Halifax Ladies' College, today known as Armbrae Academy. The college was established in 1887, and was affiliated from its outset with the Halifax Conservatory of Music. Reverend Robert Laing founded the Conservatory, with C. H. Porter appointed as the school's first director. At the time of the vice regal visit in 1890, two hundred and forty students were attending the Conservatory. That same year, Dalhousie University had granted the Halifax Conservatory of Music the right to confer Bachelor of Music degrees to its graduates. A special concert was presented for the vice regal couple by the students.

Mindful of Lady Constance Stanley's deep interest in health and, subsequently, hospitals, a visit to Victoria General Hospital was built into the Halifax itinerary. Established in 1867, Victoria General quickly garnered a poor reputation, accused of offering poor medical care. The province assumed control of the facility in 1887 and attempted to transform Victoria's image by opening a nursing school, the first of its kind in Nova Scotia, at the hospital in 1890. The measure succeeded, and the hospital ultimately established a sterling reputation for the quality of its medical care and training. In 1892, Stanley's successor as Governor General, Lord Aberdeen, presented diplomas to the six young ladies and two men who comprised the first graduating class of the Victoria General Hospital School of Nursing.

The party then was taken for a tour of the Dartmouth Ropeworks. By the late 1800s, many in Nova Scotia believed that the region was on the verge of becoming Canada's industrial heartland. The newly completed Intercolonial Railway provided access to the burgeoning markets of central and western Canada, and there was generally great optimism in the Atlantic provinces. For a brief period in the late nineteenth century, Nova Scotia was quite prepared to turn its back on the sea and, for a short time, prospered in doing so. William J. Stairs was a major figure in the region's industrialization, with interests in ship-owning, steelmaking, banking, sugar refining and, in 1868, the Dartmouth Ropeworks.

When shipbuilding reached its peak around 1875, there were 2,787 registered vessels in Nova Scotia alone, and all of them needed rope. Stairs believed that Confederation offered exciting new opportunities for the sale of his product — not only to the traditional maritime markets in the shipping industry and the expanding fisheries, but to the farms of Ontario and the Prairies. Stairs remained committed to an industrial future for Nova Scotia long after many of his colleagues had abandoned hope. The Stairs family decided to build an enormous complex of six buildings in what had been swampy land between Wyse and what became Victoria streets in Dartmouth to manufacture rope of all types, including massive hawsers used to tie up or anchor ships.42

* * *

In a CBC radio interview conducted in 1968, Halifax native George M. Robinson recalled a random meeting with the Governor General:

While [Lord Stanley] was here on an official visit, he sent word to the stable that he'd like to get a carriage to drive him. I went up after him. He said, 'I want to see Frederick Fraser.' He was the head of the Blind School and it was the first blind school in Canada. [Stanley] had never met him. He was very much interested in the blind. He said, 'Do you know him?' I said, 'Oh yes, I know him very well.' So I drove him down to the Blind School and went to the door and got Frederick Fraser and I introduced him to the Governor General. I left him and he said, 'Take Lady Stanley. She wants to visit a friend of hers down in the south end.' So I drove her down.

Charles Frederick Fraser, blind himself since the age of seven, had trained at the Perkins School for the Blind near Boston, Massachusetts, the alma mater of both Helen Keller and her instructor, Anne Sullivan. Fraser was appointed principal of the much-heralded Halifax School for the Blind, and under his guidance and spirit, the school and its reputation grew exponentially. In 1915, to honour his seminal work, King George V bestowed a knighthood upon Fraser. He remained superintendent of the Halifax School for the Blind for more than half a century. In 1874, the school added students from New Brunswick and Prince Edward Island, and in 1887 it admitted the first students from Newfoundland. Although no provincial measures were taken to educate blind children in the school's earliest years, in 1882, through the efforts of Frederick Fraser, the Nova Scotia Legislature passed an act that gave free education to any child in Nova Scotia who, through reason of blindness or insufficient sight, was unable to attend public school. This law was duplicated by New Brunswick in 1892.

Robinson continued:

[Stanley] had this big coachman on the carriage with me. Big fellow. Weighed about two hundred pounds. We both had beaver hats on. I left her [Lady Stanley] at the house and she said, 'Come back in an hour.' Well, I thought it would almost take an hour to drive home and back so I just thought I'd loaf around here somewhere for an hour before I picked her up. So I thought [that since] the coachman had

*never been here before, I'd take him down by Pine Hill and
show him our natural park. So I drove down the serpentine
drive down by the shore.*

> *We took our time walking up to the carriage but there
was no carriage there. The carriage ran away with all Lady
Stanley's stuff in it. So I started running. I got up to the top
of the hill which is up by the tower. It's a mighty hard run,
going up there with a big beaver hat and coat on, so I fired
them down in the bush and I kept running in my shirt-
sleeves. I got over on the other side where the road went up
to Barrington Street. The carriage had passed and gone up-
town. I met a boy with a couple of my cushions and I said,
'Them's my cushions! Leave them down here.' I met the
man coming back that stopped the carriage on Barrington
Street and went back. It took me about twenty minutes to
find the coachman. He got lost in the woods. I got some
grass and wiped the sweat off the horses and drove back.
Lady Stanley came out and pulled out her watch and said,
'My, you're just in time.' I often wondered if she [ever]
knew what happened in the meantime!'*[43]

After visiting the various Halifax schools through the course of the day,
both Lord and Lady Stanley commented on how pleased they were with the
substantial progress being made in education in the province of Nova
Scotia. The couple dined at Government House that evening as guests of
Lieutenant Governor Ross.

Wednesday, 15 October, saw the Governor General and his party
leave the Nova Scotia capital after better than four busy days. The next
destination was Mulgrave, a small town on the Strait of Canso just west of
Cape Breton.

* * *

Local merchants Hector MacDougall and Edward A MacNeil, envisioning
the potential for tourism to Cape Breton Island, built the Grand Narrows
Hotel in 1887. MacDougall had been one of the principals behind the
Intercolonial Railway, which was being expanded to serve central Cape

Breton. Sir John A. Macdonald had a decided affinity for Cape Breton, and often visited the island, "sometimes just to escape the bickering of Ottawa." He was a frequent guest at the Grand Narrows Hotel,[44] which was an important stop for railway travellers.[45]

Key to the completion of the stretch of railway from New Glasgow to Sydney (expediting the export of coal from the island's mines) was the construction of a bridge across the Barra Strait. The Prime Minister is reputed to have been gazing at the scenery from the front stoop of the hotel when he decided, "That is where the new bridge will go," pointing northward. A seven-span iron bridge was completed at that spot in 1890. The opening of the island to rail travel was immensely beneficial to the coal mining and steel industries, allowing the Cape Breton economy to prosper accordingly.

The Prime Minister sent Lord Stanley a letter dated 13 September, requesting that he take part in the official opening of the Grand Narrows Bridge as part of his Atlantic visit.[46] At midnight on Wednesday, 16 October, Stanley's five-car train left Mulgrave and was ferried across the Strait of Canso on the *S.S. Mulgrave*, the newest addition to the Intercolonial Railway's fleet of vessels. The train cars were then reassembled at Point Tupper, where they were hitched to the Intercolonial Railway's locomotive number 166. At Iona, on the morning of Friday the seventeenth, Lord Stanley officially declared the railway to Sydney open to traffic. He personally sat at the controls of the first train to drive across the Grand Narrows Bridge, reaching Sydney at seven-ten that evening and instigating celebrations that lasted though the night.[47]

After spending Saturday in Sydney, the largest town on beautiful Cape Breton Island, the vice regal party returned to Mulgrave, where they spent Sunday, before departing for New Glasgow on Monday. A seventeen-gun salute greeted Lord Stanley on his arrival in New Glasgow at seven-thirty that evening. The New Glasgow Cornet Band, perched on the balcony of the Vendome Hotel, performed for the special guests.

Three hundred young girls, all dressed identically in white, sang the "Dominion Hymn" ("God Bless Our Wide Dominion"). The song, now long-forgotten, was appropriate not only for its patriotic subject matter, but for the circumstances under which it was composed. The lyrics were written by Stanley's predecessor as governor general, the Marquis of Lorne, while the melody was provided by Sir Arthur Sullivan — the musical half of the renowned team of Gilbert and Sullivan — who was the Marquis's guest on an 1880 visit to Canada.

> *God bless our wide Dominion, our fathers' chosen land*
> *And bind in lasting union, each ocean's distant strand.*
> *From where Atlantic terrors our hardy seamen train*
> *To where the salt sea mirrors the vast Pacific chain*
> *O Bless our wide Dominion, true freedom's fairest scene*
> *Defend our people's union, God save our Empire's Queen.*[48]

The Reverend George Munro Grant, known as the "New Glasgow poet," composed a special verse of greeting for the Governor General:

> *His Excellency will be here!*
> *His visit fills our hearts with cheer!*
> *Representing our Gracious Queen*
> *The greatest lady ever seen.*
> *Welcome, thrice welcome, our liege lord*
> *We bow to thee with one accord:*
> *May heaven's blessings thee attend*
> *And follow thee, time without end.*

A fireworks display followed the musical performances.

* * *

The vice regal suite spent the night in New Glasgow, visiting Humphrey's Nova Scotia Glass Factory and the Fraser Brothers Iron Foundry in nearby Trenton the next day. Stellarton, due south of New Glasgow, was their next destination. Stanley commented on the immense Allan coal shafts situated next to a row of miners' cottages. A tour of Standard Brick and Tile was also undertaken.

Early on the afternoon of Tuesday, 21 October, the Governor General left for Pictou, arriving in the beautiful town perched near the Northumberland Strait at two o'clock. Mayor Allan Ferguson, who also owned the Pictou Foundry, greeted Lord and Lady Stanley and drove by carriage with them to Prince Street Hall, where he read an address to the

Governor General on behalf of his town. The party then drove to the academy, where schoolchildren greeted the Governor General with song.

The Pictou Railway, which connected the town with Stellarton, had opened in 1887, and the next year a ship began making regular runs between Pictou and Prince Edward Island. The "short line" between Pictou and Oxford Junction had opened just prior to Stanley's arrival. As the town of Pictou flourished, it looked as though the area was going to be an important centre for Nova Scotia. Sadly, a fire destroyed much of the town's core just over a month after Lord Stanley's visit.

* * *

At noon on Thursday, 23 October, *HMS Canada*, a British-built corvette and the first ship to enter the Halifax dock the day it opened on 20 September, 1889, dropped anchor at the wharf in Charlottetown, Prince Edward Island, greeted by a nineteen-gun salute. The Governor General was taken by carriage to visit the Lieutenant Governor, Jebediah Slason Carvell, a former mayor of Charlottetown. At three o'clock, the Governor General was addressed in the Legislative Council Chamber. In his reply, Stanley stated, "The object is to weld more closely all the interests of the Dominion," a theme he reinforced at every opportunity. At seven in the evening, he was escorted by local firemen to a dinner party at Government House, which was followed by a Grand Ball.

The next day, the Governor General visited city schools, was guest of honour at a banquet and enjoyed an "at home" at Government House.

Lord Stanley enjoyed Thursday and Friday on Prince Edward Island, and on Saturday, 25 October, the *Canada* returned the party to Pictou. The vice regal train took its passengers to Truro, where they spent the night.

On Sunday, 26 October, after attending church in Truro, the train returned to The Citadel in Quebec City. Lord Frederick Stanley had now travelled the full breadth of the Dominion of Canada. The journeys had given him an excellent overview of the potential, as well as the challenges, that faced the country over which he presided.

---

[1] *British Whig* (Kingston: 19 December, 1889).
[2] *The Dominion Illustrated Monthly* (4 January, 1890).

3 See, 'The Owl', *www.geegeehockey.com.*

4 *The Dominion Illustrated Monthly* (15 March, 1890)

5 *The Dominion Illustrated Monthly* (18 February, 1893), p.282.

6 L. Cauz, *The Plate: A Royal Tradition* (Toronto: Deneay, 1984) p.77; K. Shea, *Interview with Louis Cauz*, Archivist Woodbine Entertainment, (January, 2006).

7 *The Rider and Driver* (New York: 4 February, 1892).

8 *Ottawa Daily Citizen* (22 September, 1890).

9 J. A. Macdonald, *Private Brief, Lord Stanley of Preston Papers*, from the Public Archives of Canada in London, (Ottawa: 6 December, 1889).

10 J. A. Macdonald, *Letter to F. A. Stanley, Lord Stanley of Preston Papers*, from the Public Archives of Canada in London (Ottawa: 13 February, 1889).

11 Blaine, as quoted by Tupper to Macdonald, *Macdonald Papers* (National Archives of Canada: February, 1890).

12 Creighton, *John A. Macdonald*, p.541.

13 J. Pauncefote, *Letter to F. A. Stanley, Lord Stanley of Preston Papers*, from the Public Archives of Canada in London (Washington: 15 March, 1890).

14 Creighton, *John A. Macdonald*, p.541.

15 F. A. Stanley, *Letter to J. A. Macdonald, Lord Stanley of Preston Papers*, from the Public Archives of Canada in London (Ottawa: 7 March, 1890).

16 F. A. Stanley, *Letter to J. A. Macdonald, Lord Stanley of Preston Papers*, from the Public Archives of Canada in London (Ottawa: 7 March, 1890).

17 Tupper to Macdonald, *Macdonald Papers* (National Archives of Canada: 27 April, 1890).

18 C. S. Tupper, *Telegram to J. A. Macdonald*, as reproduced in J. A. Macdonald, *Letter to J. A. Macdonald, Lord Stanley of Preston Papers*, from the Public Archives of Canada in London (Ottawa: 12 April, 1890).

19 J. A. Macdonald, *Letter to F. A. Stanley, Lord Stanley of Preston Papers*, from the Public Archives of Canada in London (Ottawa: 1 May, 1890).

20 F. A. Stanley, *Letter to Lord Salisbury, Lord Stanley of Preston Papers*, from the Public Archives of Canada in London (Ottawa: 4 June, 1891).

21 *Victoria Daily Colonist* (Victoria: 2 November, 1889), p.2.

22 Ibid.

23 Ibid.

24 Creighton, *John A. Macdonald*, p.544.

25 J. C. Hopkins, 'The Britannic Empire', *The Dominion Illustrated Monthly* (3 May, 1890), p.287.

26 Creighton, *John A. Macdonald*, p.546.

27 Macdonald from, *Empire*, 11 (12 November, 1890); Creighton, *John A. Macdonald*, pp.546–7.

28 E. Wiman, as quoted in J. C. Hopkins, 'Canada and American Aggression', *The Dominion Illustrated Monthly* (Montreal: December 1892), p.701.

29 *The Dominion Illustrated Monthly* (20 October, 1888), p.242.

30 J. C. Hopkins, 'Canada and American Aggression', p.701.

31 *The Dominion Illustrated Monthly* (10 August, 1889), p.83.

32 Creighton, *John A. Macdonald*, p.548.

33 *The Dominion Illustrated Monthly* (21 February, 1891), p.170.

34 *Gathorne-Hardy Papers* (National Archives of Canada).

35 'Daily Exhibition', *Progress* (Saint John, NB: 3 October, 1890).

36 *Saint John Evening Star* (c.1926).

37 *The Globe* (Toronto: 1884).

38 'Daily Exhibition', *Progress.*

39 *The Hindu* (India: 17 May, 2003).

[40] *Gathorne-Hardy Papers* (National Archives of Canada).

[41] Ibid.

[42] J. D. Frost, 'Dartmouth Ropeworks: 1869-1958', J. Candow (*ed*), *Industry and Society in Nova Scotia: An Illustrated History* (Black Point, NS: Fernwood Books, 2001).

[43] B. McNeil, 'Interview with George M. Robinson', *Voice of the Pioneer* (Toronto, Canadian Broadcasting Corporation, 22 December, 1968). <*radio broadcast*>

[44] J. Underwood, 'Every Bridge Tells a Story', *Canadian Rail* (March–April, 2004), pp.43–5.

[45] Alexander Graham Bell, who owned a summer home inland at Baddeck called 'Beinn Bhreagh' (beautiful mountain), frequently stayed at the Grand Narrows Hotel and took the steamboat *Blue Hill* to Baddeck.

[46] J. A. Macdonald, (Ottawa: 13 September, 1890).

[47] Underwood, 'Every Bridge Tells a Story', pp.43–5.

[48] 'Dominion Hymn (God Bless Our Wide Dominion)', music by Sir Arthur Sullivan, lyrics by the Marquess of Lorne, (c.1880).

CHAPTER THIRTEEN

1891

St. Bartholomew's Anglican Church, located across the street from Rideau Hall, had served as the place of worship for the vice regal family since Confederation. To this day, a pew is reserved for the Governor General and family, even though it is no longer a given that he or she will be Anglican. The church also served a social function, and one evening in mid-January of 1891 a "screamingly funny farce" entitled *Ici On Parle Français* was mounted in the auditorium. The role of Major Regulas Rattan was played by Eric Streatfeild, a nephew of Lord Stanley's military secretary, Captain Charles Colville. Algernon and Billy Stanley, children of the Governor General and his wife, also performed in the play.

On 7 February, Lord and Lady Stanley attended *Tableaux and Theatricals* at the Grand Opera House in aid of the organ fund of Grace Church. Built in 1874, the thousand-seat Grand Opera House was located on Albert Street at O'Connor and was one of several such auditoriums that sprang up in Ontario during the late 1800s, including Toronto's St. Lawrence Hall (1850), the Grand Theatre in Kingston (1879) and the Orillia Opera House (1895). Opera houses also opened in Montreal in 1875, Winnipeg in 1883 and Vancouver in 1891.

Over the course of the evening, attendees enjoyed tableaux entitled "The Child's Dream," "Jeptha's Daughter," (written by Lord Byron) and "Our Wife." Handel's "Angels Ever Bright and Fair" was performed brilliantly by the Governor General's Footguards Band, and the evening concluded with "God Save the Queen."[1]

* * *

When the season arrived, hockey was never far from the minds of the Stanley family. In a letter written to Prince George by Lady Alice, daughter-in-law of the Governor General and Lady Constance, in February 1891, she described a game at Rideau Hall:

> … *after three days shooting, the men joined us at hockey and we had some splendid fun. You would have laughed to see some of them. Colonel Brabazon was as brave as a lion. He had skated three times before only; but quite un-daunted, he threw himself into the fray and had fall after fall. Always too falling on the same place in a sitting posi-tion. Colonel Vivian was also a skater of the same calibre but he must have something wrong with his balance as whenever he tried a step forward, he tottered, waved his stick round his head and fell heavily. Eddy got one terrible whack from someone just on his knee, so Sir Oscar Clayton comforted him by saying that something most important had burst and that Eddy would have to lay up for at least six weeks. However, next day, found him playing hockey and the knee has been well ever since.*[2]

In 1890, the recently formed Hamilton Yacht Club petitioned Queen Victoria for the privilege of adding the Royal designation to its name. On 14 February, 1891, it was Lord Stanley's duty to inform the club that he had consented, on behalf of Her Majesty, to the request. The newly minted Royal Hamilton Yacht Club's vessels (above a certain weight) were also granted the authority to fly the Blue Ensign of Her Majesty's Fleet. "The prestige associated with 'Royal' clubs has lost some of its lustre," general manager John Todorovic recently observed, "but nevertheless, there are but a few clubs in the country that enjoy the patronage of the Royals."[3]

* * *

Previous governors general had begun a delightful tradition of holding skating and toboganing parties at Rideau Hall, and Lord and Lady Stanley were pleased to maintain the practice.

On 28 February, Lord and Lady Stanley hosted one of their always-enjoyable "at homes," a fancy dress carnival, at Rideau Hall. The walls of Rideau Hall were draped in bunting made up of flags from different nations. At eight-thirty, Lord Stanley, Edward and wife Alice, Mrs. Colville (the wife of Stanley's military secretary) and Miss Lister entered the area at the south end of the rink. Once seated on the raised dais, they were welcomed by three cheers and a tiger.

Seven clowns, playing against a selected team, put on an entertaining exhibition of hockey that saw them easily defeat their opponents. It was assumed that the seven clowns included at least two of the hockey-playing Stanley boys. Later, a grand march ensued, in which thirty costumed skaters participated. Isobel, the daughter of the Governor General, was dressed as Cinderella, Alice as a Chocolate Girl[4] and Miss Lister as a witch.

Seven hundred and fifty people enjoyed a variety of events, including skating and tobogganing. "To the left were seen on the miniature lake the happy skaters circling in graceful curves and waltzes to the Governor General's Guards band," reported *The Dominion Illustrated Monthly*. Huge bonfires crackled to warm the attendees, while the grounds were illuminated by thousands of Chinese lanterns. "The slides were admirably worked by red light signalling, and though there were one or two spills, such only added to the zest and enjoyment, as no injury was sustained."

Supper was served in the curling rink at nine o'clock that evening, and at eleven-thirty the playing of the national anthem signalled the conclusion of the day's festivities.[5] "Their Excellencies Lord and Lady Stanley and the members of the vice regal household," according to *The Citizen*, "were unremitting in their gracious attentions to their guests, who one and all will certainly entertain the most pleasant recollections of the joyous evening spent at Rideau Hall."[6]

Among those who performed at the Rideau Hall rink was George Meagher, who "went through several beautiful figures and glided through with an ease and grace that bespoke a long acquaintance with ice," according to the *Daily Citizen*.[7]

The *Brooklyn Eagle*, commenting on George Meagher, remarked:

> *He learned to skate when a child. As he became more expert he added more tricks and originated others until he gained the undisputed title of champion of the world in his profession. His repertoire of steps, tricks and figures is now*

a long one. Among other things, he can do twenty-three dif-
ferent grapevines, fourteen spins and seventy-four figure
eights, and over one hundred anvils on foot without stop-
ping. He does all these things with a grace and suppleness
which leave the novice little idea of the real intricacy and
difficulty of the figures and the risks he takes in his jumps.8

But as fine a figure skater as George Meagher was, he was equally adept in a hockey game: "Mr. Meagher is an expert with the hockey stick, as those who have seen him practicing against half a dozen players at once at the new rink will testify." Meagher helped introduce hockey to New York in 1896, and he can also be credited with introducing hockey to Europe.

Like many Canadians of his era, Meagher was passionately interested in hockey. Apparently, it ran in the family: Meagher's older sister Mary married William Farrell, a Montreal politician. Their son, Arthur, was a member of two Stanley Cup champions with the Montreal Shamrocks, in 1899 and 1900. Art Farrell is also recognized as having written Canada's earliest book on hockey — *Hockey: Canada's Royal Winter Game*, published in 1899. He is enshrined as an Honoured Member of the Hockey Hall of Fame.

While visiting Paris in 1894 to demonstrate his figure-skating prowess, Meagher was astonished to find that the French were not familiar with hockey. He had packed hockey sticks for his trip, and during the seven months he spent in the French capital, he formed *le Hockey Club du Paris*, the city's first official hockey team. He later organized another, *le Club des Patineurs de Paris*. Although it has not been confirmed, Meagher may very well have created a loosely knit league that played as often as four times a week. After Paris, Meagher went on to London, where he is also reported to have formed a hockey league, then on to Glasgow, where he staged hockey games. In Germany, Meagher introduced hockey to Nuremberg, followed by a trip to St. Petersburg, Russia. "Hockey is going to take here as it has in other cities," he stated. "It is exciting and scientific and an excellent exhibition game, so why shouldn't it be popular?"

In 1895, Meagher published a book entitled *Lessons in Skating*. Stanley, who had by then returned to England and assumed the mantle of 16th Earl of Derby, was asked to write the foreword.

I understand from Mr. Meagher, the author of the present work, that he wishes me to write a few words of introduction. I am very willing to comply with his request, although I cannot myself claim to rank as a figure skater, still less as an authority on the subject. But as I was at Ottawa as Governor General of Canada, and in the exercise of my duties, presented him with the medal which he then won at an open competition as the World's Champion for figure and fancy skating, Mr. Meagher is entitled to the tribute which I readily give. My first, or almost my first, acquaintance with Mr. Meagher was upon the occasion when he won the medal aforesaid, but he was even more well known as a good and graceful skater, and held that rank at Montreal amongst those who were certainly qualified to be critics. He was, if I recall rightly, at that time skating on the public rinks and afterwards at Government House, Ottawa, and was always most kind, not only in giving a display of his own powers, but also in instructing those who were novices in the art of which he is a master. Since the year 1891, Mr. Meagher has received many trophies from various skating clubs in America, and also, I believe, from similar clubs in Europe.

Mr. Meagher's book will, no doubt, be favourably judged upon its own merits. I can only, in conclusion, wish both to the work and to the author, all the success they deserve.[9]

* * *

On 6 April, 1891, a celebration was held by the Governor General's Foot Guards, attended by, among other guests, their patron and guest of honour, His Excellency the Governor General. The band began with a number entitled "A Morning Call." The Citanos Mandolin and Guitar Club, based in the Ottawa area, performed "Gypsy." Following a march-past and a military salute, a group of vocalists performed a comedic song called "Hush! The Bogie" that had been performed in an 1889 British burlesque musical, *Ruy Blas*, or the *Blasé Roue*. One reviewer reported that Victorian audiences loved the show, which starred Fred Leslie, laughing "with an hysterical 'Ho, ho ho!' or even a rapturous, long-drawn 'Ha ha!'"[10] Lord Stanley threw his head back and clapped his hands with delight when he heard the chorus.

The Foot Guards performed a cavalry sword exercise, followed by a fencing demonstration and a series of ordinance drills. Then the band completed the program with a song called "There's Nothing Like a Freshning Breeze." To complete the evening, the band saluted the Governor General with the traditional closing anthem, "God Save the Queen."

* * *

On Thursday, 30 April, 1891, Lord Stanley opened Parliament for another session:

> *I am glad to welcome you to the duties of the first Session of a new Parliament, which I hope will be memorable for wise deliberations and for measures adapted to the progress and development of the Dominion. The season in which you are assembled has opened auspiciously for the industries of our people. Let us hope that their labours may be crowned with fruitful returns from land and sea, and that the great resources of Canada may continue to reward the toil and enterprise of its inhabitants.*
>
> *My advisers, availing themselves of opportunities which were presented in the closing months of last year, caused the Administration of the United States to be reminded of the willingness of the Government of Canada to join making efforts for the extension and development of the trade between the Republic and the Dominion, as well as for the friendly adjustment of those matters of an international character, which remain unsettled. I am pleased to say that these representations have resulted in an assurance that, in October next, the Government of the United States will be prepared to enter on a Conference to consider the best means of arriving at a practical solution to these important questions.*
>
> *Under these circumstances, and in the hope that the proposed Conference may result in arrangements beneficial*

to both countries, you will be called upon to consider the expediency of extending, for the present season, the principal provisions of the protocol annexed to the Washington Treaty, 1888, known as the Modus Vivendi.[11]

A disposition having been manifested in the United Kingdom to impose on sea-going ships engaged in the cattle trade, increased safeguards for life, and greater restrictions against improper treatment, a careful enquiry has been made as to the incidents of that trade in so far as this country is concerned. The evidence elicited on this enquiry will be laid before you. While I am glad to learn that our shipping is free from reproach in that regard, your attention will be invited to a measure which will remove all reasonable apprehensions of abuses arising in the future in connection with so important a branch of our commerce.

The early coming into force of the Imperial Statute relating to the Vice Admiralty Courts of the Empire has made it necessary to revise the laws in force in Canada respecting our courts of maritime jurisdiction, And a measure will therefore be laid before you designed to reorganize those tribunals.[12]

* * *

Lord Stanley returned to Toronto for the running of the Queen's Plate. In a most peculiar situation, the winning horse, owned by the Seagram family of distilling fame, had not been named. The duty fell to Stanley, who put one hand on his chin, thought for a few moments, and proclaimed, "Victorious! The horse's name shall, of course, be 'Victorious.'" The 1891 victory was the first of eight successive wins by a Seagram horse.

* * *

From the moment she landed on the shores of Canada, Lady Constance Stanley was actively involved in aiding benevolent societies within Ottawa. Perhaps it was the fact that she appreciated the substantive blessings given her, but Her Excellency was a strong proponent of involvement in causes that assisted those less fortunate.

Just prior to the holidays, which the Stanleys spent in Ottawa at Rideau Hall, Lady Stanley took the opportunity to demonstrate her generosity towards those less fortunate in the Ottawa area. Having already become a key contributor to what would become the Children's Aid Society and the Ottawa Humane Society, on 28 November she presented an "ambulance wagon" to the City of Ottawa. Lady Stanley was so quiet and unassuming in public that she insisted her husband speak on her behalf. Lord Stanley remarked that "she wished him to express her very great satisfaction in having been able to take a part, however humble, in this good work."[13]

* * *

As the Behring Sea question continued to lack a concrete resolution, Canadians were, by 1891, beginning to entertain doubts about their future as a Dominion. Editorialist J. C. Hopkins, who supported the idea of remaining fiscally free of the United States while developing closer ties with Britain, spoke to the crossroads that many Canadians felt they had reached:

> *Finger-posts are pointing in three different directions, and guides are to be found who are willing — nay, anxious — to lead her in one or the other of the directions pointed out — Annexation, Independence or Imperial Federation. A change is certainly imperative. No nation of the growing importance of this Dominion can long remain in leading-strings and retain either its own self-respect or that of others.*[14]

If a tangible uncertainty about Canada's future had permeated some of the more moderate publications, the more radical papers continued to challenge the legitimacy of the nation and, in no small way, entertained the American government's line of reasoning. This sympathy did not help Canada's case in the question of fishing rights.

One way in which the American administration tried to undermine the official Canadian position in the Behring Sea was to begin negotiating a separate treaty for Newfoundland that promised the latter a more open line of trade. The hope was to divide British North America and turn it against itself. In a letter to Salisbury, Stanley rightfully accused Blaine, the U.S.

Secretary of State, of trying to create turmoil for Britain through these talks.

> *Blaine is playing a game with us, in which your Newfoundland negotiations have accidentally helped him. He will take the line that unrestricted reciprocity and discrimination against the U.S. are the only conditions on which any negotiations can proceed — and if even we come here to a tariff framed against English interest and dictated in terms at Washington, we shall not be very far from the frame of mind which would lead Canada to annexation to the U.S.*[15]

By 1891, Stanley recognized that there was a reasonable likelihood that the Dominion might be lost as a result of the clever politicking of Blaine and company. At the very least, Newfoundland might be persuaded to join the republic, as this was a time when Newfoundland joining Confederation was not a foregone conclusion.

Another modestly effective tactic on the part of the Americans was to implore Ottawa to negotiate informally, dangling a lucrative, if vague, Reciprocity Treaty as the prize. Macdonald did not have much of a stomach for this approach, as it allowed Washington to change its tune as it wished. Stanley shared Macdonald's wariness, refusing to underestimate the lengths to which the U.S. Secretary of State would go to undermine Canadian aims. He said as much in a communiqué with Macdonald in which he offered this advice: "The more I think of the situation the more I should be disposed to advise that we should go right ahead — Blaine or no Blaine."[16]

Popular opinion in Canada reflected that of the Governor General, as *The Dominion Illustrated Monthly* explained:

> *What concerns us chiefly is the foreign policy of [President Grover Cleveland's] successor, especially as it affects the vexed question of the Fisheries. If Mr. Harrison's own voice were alone to be heard on the subject, we might await the course of events with a measure of confidence … [Harrison's] Secretary of State, Mr. J. G. Blaine, has at times presented an attitude towards Great Britain which the most favourable interpretation could not pronounce*

friendly. On him, as the President's chief minister, a great
deal will depend.[17]

Perhaps the most underhanded tactic employed by the Americans, however, involved the informal interviews that Blaine and his representatives
were conducting with Edward Farrer, one of the chief editors of the
Toronto daily *The Globe* which — not surprisingly, as it had been founded
by leading Grit George Brown — was the Dominion's chief Opposition
newspaper. Still, Macdonald was up for a fight. Macdonald and Sir John
Tupper were the principal speakers at a high-profile Conservative rally at
the Academy of Music in Toronto. The two publicly attacked Farrer and
brought into question both his integrity and his loyalty to Canada.
Remarkably, the Conservative party was able to secure a pamphlet that
Farrer had produced, aimed at a small group of Americans who had asked
for his advice on trade policy with Canada, in which he recommended
levying duties on Canadian vessels, suspending bonding privileges in the
United States, and the cessation of ties with the Canadian Pacific Railway
at Sault Ste. Marie. In another inspired speech in Halifax, Macdonald did
not mince words and pointed the finger squarely at the Liberal party, which
he felt had given "aid and comfort" to the Americans and their commercial
warfare campaign against Canada.[18]

While the character assassination of Farrer was comprehensively effective, Macdonald still faced the rather large hurdle of reopening
communications with the U.S. Despite the humiliation Blaine had caused
him, the Prime Minister cunningly pushed on for negotiations to resolve
trade issues between the two nations. These talks, however, failed to resolve
the varied and complex issues between the countries, and by 1891 James
Blaine was public enemy number one in Canada.

In his systematic poor treatment of Canadian interests, Blaine might
only, at least in his mind, have been politicking for the sake of some of his
constituents. He had promised Irish-Americans that he would "tweak the
Lion's tail," referring to the British Lion — and Canada as an extension of
it.19 Still, in Canada, and to a lesser extent Britain, Washington's aggressive
foreign policy had taken a heavy toll and war was now, more than ever, a
real possibility.

If, in previous months, *The Dominion Illustrated Monthly* had bandied
about the possibility of war with America as a remote scenario, the period-

ical had a decidedly different tone when the matter remained unresolved in January of 1891:

> *We venture to think that on calm reflection, the Congress of the United States will decline to commit themselves to a course of action which will not only stultify themselves in the eyes of the world, but which will have the far more serious effect of bringing on a war for which their nation is totally unprepared.*[20]

Canadians wanted the Americans to arbitrate on the matter of the Behring Sea — a policy suggested by Lord Salisbury. Many felt that the whole question might be resolved quickly — and more importantly, war might be avoided. Yet the Americans, perhaps because they felt their case was not terribly compelling, opted instead for a cat-and-mouse game; all the while, tension in the Pacific grew with every passing month.

Although Macdonald was ill with a severe bronchial cold, his political savvy had secured another election victory in 1891 and the Conservatives remained in government. The vice regal household was pleased, not only because of the fine relationship between Sir John A. Macdonald and Lord Stanley, but also because the result pleased the Queen. The Dominion appeared sound again.

Macdonald, however, was not sound; indeed, his illness worsened. In one meeting with the Governor General, Macdonald was simply unable to articulate his words. Stanley was aware of this new disability and politely excused himself back to Rideau Hall, promising to return later on. When he returned, Macdonald was still crippled with this inexplicable affliction and, in a state of panic, he implored Sir John Thompson to attend the rescheduled meeting to be his voice in front of Stanley. As Macdonald explained to his secretary, Joseph Pope, "He must come at once because he must speak to the Governor for me, as I cannot talk. There is something the matter with my speech."[21] The eventual meeting was unproductive, and when Stanley left Macdonald and Thompson, he noticed that one side of the Prime Minister's face was drawn and slightly twisted.[22] Macdonald was experiencing the onset of a paralysis that would claim his life within less than a month.

Less than a week before Macdonald's death, Stanley informed the Queen by cable that the Prime Minister was dying. Not only did Stanley ignore quiet calls for a plan of succession, but he assured all concerned that nothing was to be done until after the state funeral. Perhaps Creighton best echoed Stanley's rationale for honouring the Prime Minister to the fullest when he observed that Macdonald "was ruling Canada from his death bed — he would rule Canada until he had been buried in its earth."[23] This show of respect caused Stanley some grief as pressure began to be applied for a plan of action; Sir John Thompson, asked why there was a delay in the constitutional process.

At the same time as he assured others that there was no need for concern, Stanley privately expressed his grave misgivings about the Dominion's future to Salisbury: "Of late years, Sir Macdonald has not had many colleagues who could advise with him on matters of high importance." While Stanley praised Langevin Thompson, he felt that "the others are of no use outside their own Departments."[24] Ultimately, Stanley and Canada were poised to lose not only their Old Chieftain, but perhaps the one man in the Government who had an understanding of the breadth of the key issues facing the nation — naming an adequate successor would be no mean feat.

On 29 May, 1891, Sir John A. Macdonald suffered a massive stroke from which he never recovered. On 2 June, his personal physician cautioned that the Prime Minister was unlikely to survive the night. At five the following morning, the Prime Minister lost all consciousness, although he was still alive. "Sir John passed the night composedly and comfortably, without any drawback. As I write this bulletin, he is sleeping," stated his personal physician, Dr. P. W. Powell.[25] Queen Victoria sent daily telegrams to Lord Stanley inquiring about the condition of the Prime Minister: "Am very anxious about Sir John Macdonald. Make personal enquiries in my name," Victoria wrote from her home in Balmoral on 4 June.[26] Two days later, on 6 June, 1891, Sir John A. Macdonald lost his battle.

"Sir John is Dead," blared the headline of *The Globe* on Monday, 8 June. At 10:25, the Prime Minister's private secretary, Joseph Pope, stood outside the gate at Earnscliffe and told the gathered correspondents, "Gentlemen, Sir John Macdonald is dead." He added, still in a husky voice, "He died at 10:15 without pain and peace."[27]

The seventy-six-year-old Prime Minister, the Dominion of Canada's first, had suffered a series of smaller strokes before being felled by the massive stroke that robbed him of his speech on 29 May. Stress and alcohol are considered to have played a role, but the warning signals, including a gallstone attack in 1870, had been virtually ignored.

Stanley was terribly fond of Macdonald and deeply affected by his passing. One month prior, Stanley encouraged his friend to relinquish some of his duties:

> *My dear Sir John, I can only plead two reasons in apology for this letter: first, the frank confidence which I am glad to think that existed between us ever since I came to this country, three years ago — and, second, that you have enabled me to feel that our official and other relations have ripened into something more than ordinary friendship. I want to ask you to remember of what inestimable value your life and health are to the country, and how essential they are to your party, and how dear to your friends and family and not to refuse, in this condition, to consider whether some arrangement cannot be made by which your present crushing work could be lightened.*[28]

Stanley had witnessed Sir John A. suffering a mild stroke just prior to their meeting on 12 May. "It appears that from the day three weeks ago when the Premier was struck speechless while in the presence of the Governor General, he was conscious that his end was near, although he fought against it and insisted that there was no danger and that he must work, evidently trying to convince himself that his fears were unfounded."[29]

Yet, Stanley knew well that it was in his friend's character to continue on until he was physically incapable of doing so, and that is exactly what Prime Minister Macdonald did.

Macdonald slipped away with his family gathered around his bedside. *The Globe* bid an eloquent farewell:

> *The bright young spirit who had arduously and valiantly won a wide fame and remained in later years in the front of battle, had at length reached the brink of eternity. At last without a struggle his heart stopped beating, the breath of life left the body, and Azrael*[30] *departed with the soul of Sir John Macdonald.*[31]

A messenger was sent at once from Earnscliffe, the Prime Minister's residence, to Rideau Hall in order to convey the sad news to Lord Frederick Stanley. The Governor General sent Captain Charles Colville, his secretary, to Earnscliffe to express deep sympathy on behalf of himself and Lady Stanley. He then cabled Queen Victoria and British Prime Minister Lord Salisbury with the news.

The Governor General was one of a select few friends and associates who spent a brief moment with the deceased Prime Minister, who lay in his deathbed dressed in the uniform of an Imperial Privy Councillor, before Macdonald's body was moved for the impending funeral.

As bells tolled throughout Ottawa for the deceased Prime Minister, grieving citizens arrived by the thousands to pay their respects while Sir John A. Macdonald's body lay in state in the Parliament Buildings. The funeral was held 9 June, 1891. As the train departed Ottawa for Kingston, hundreds of Canadians lined the tracks to say one final goodbye. Sir John A. Macdonald, Canada's first Prime Minister, was buried in Kingston's Cataraqui Cemetery.[32]

On the recommendation of Lord Stanley, Sir John A. Macdonald's widow, Agnes, was given the title Baroness Macdonald of Earnscliffe, a title she apparently appreciated receiving but despised.

* * *

Although there had been much speculation as to who would succeed the Prime Minister, Macdonald had apparently never indicated his preference, which triggered a crisis in Cabinet. Although Lord Stanley was certain that Sir John A. had named his successor in his will or in papers written at his bedside a week prior to his death, no evidence of any such decision could be found. The Conservative government remained in turmoil for two weeks as Stanley refused to act until after Sir John A.'s funeral. Finally, however, the responsibility of choosing Canada's new prime minister fell squarely on the shoulders of the governor general, as the *Montreal Gazette* reported:

> *Whenever the Governor General deems it proper to exercise his prerogative of entrusting some person with the formation of a ministry, and action cannot long be delayed, work will be proceeded with on the lines already made known in*

*measures throughout the Dominion, and no apprehension
may be feared that a crisis in public affairs will occur or
that the continuance of the Conservative party in office will
be jeopardized.*[33]

Stanley considered two candidates: Sir John Thompson and John Abbott.
Thompson, at forty-seven years of age, was clearly Stanley's choice, but he
was Roman Catholic, having converted for his marriage, and there was
great fear that his religion would offend Ontario Protestants and reduce the
ruling Conservatives' chances in the next election. When Stanley sent for
him and asked him to form a government, Thompson politely but firmly
declined the opportunity and advised the Governor General to select
Abbott instead. In Thompson's estimation, Abbott would be better suited
to lead the party into the next election. Abbott ultimately accepted the position, albeit with great reluctance. "The position which I tonight have the
honour to occupy, which is far beyond any merits I have, has come to me
very much probably in the nature of comprise," Abbott told the Senate
shortly after taking office. "I am here very much probably in the nature of
compromise. I am here very much because I am not particularly obnoxious
to anybody."[34]

Unbeknownst to many, Thompson had another reason to decline the
role of prime minister. His third daughter, whom he affectionately called
"Frankie," was only ten years old but suffered from a disease to her hip
joints that necessitated a battery of treatments and operations. Frankie was
close to death in October 1891, and Thompson, the Minister of Justice, was
consumed with her condition at the time of Macdonald's death. Thompson
was, however, the last minister to visit the Prime Minister before his stroke
of 29 May.

Stanley had relied heavily on the advice of Sir John Thompson when
he invited Abbott to lead the government. Remarkably, Thompson, the
former Minister of Justice who had been mentored by Macdonald, would
succeed Abbott in the Dominion's most important post.

Stanley's choice of Abbott garnered him some measure of criticism.
The Dominion Illustrated Monthly defended the Governor General:

> *It is a curious phase of the Canadian politics of to-day that
> the most hostile criticism on the Governor General's action*

in having entrusted the position of First Minister to the Honourable Mr. Abbott is not on the ground of the personal unfitness of that gentleman for the position, but largely because he has been connected in a legal capacity for many years with one of our two great railways. The attack is the more unjust from the fact of it being well known that Mr. Abbott promptly resigned all connection with the road immediately on his acceptance of the Premiership, and went to the rather extreme point of disposing of all his stock in the Company.[35]

In a letter to Pauncefote in Washington, Stanley confessed to a lack of knowledge of the nation's new prime minister:

The fact is that it is only within the last few days, and since the prorogation of Parliament, that I have been able to have any real conversation with Sir John Macdonald's successor, Mr. Abbott. Although he had been for a long time a trusted member of the Cabinet, he had no portfolio, and he lived at Montreal and I had therefore less knowledge of his personal views than I had of those of his colleagues. He accepted the Premiership at a moment of danger and difficulty and he had so much to do that I contented myself with receiving the assurance that the general policy of his Predecessor towards the United States Government would not be materially altered and I let him carry on the work of the session without interference.[36]

Macdonald's "general policy" regarding the United States had not secured arbitration of the Behring Sea debate, nor had it engendered, though not for lack of trying, any good faith with American diplomats when it came to Canadian interests.

John Abbott remained prime minister for just seventeen months, when ill health forced him to resign on 24 November, 1892. "I hate politics, and what are considered their appropriate methods," he had written on 4 June, 1891, just prior to being named prime minister. "I hate notoriety, public meetings, public speeches, caucuses and everything that I know of that is apparently the necessary incident of politics, except doing public work to the best of my ability."[37] Abbott died on 30 October, 1893, in Montreal.

Upon Abbott's resignation, the position was finally accepted by Sir John Thompson, whom most believed should have had the job in the first place. His first speech as prime minister, given in Toronto in January 1893, concerned the possibility of Canada being annexed by the United States. Two months later, he was one of the judges on a tribunal to settle the dispute between Canada and the U.S. over the seal harvest in the Behring Sea. Thompson helped decide in Canada's favour that there was no justification for U.S. claims that the Behring Sea should be closed to all except American seal hunters.

Thompson solidified the Conservative party and substantially grew its popularity. He was recognized as a master of government business and a key strategist. But tragedy befell Thompson just two years into his term as prime minister. While visiting Queen Victoria at Windsor Castle, where he was being made a member of the Privy Council, Thompson suffered a massive heart attack and died 12 December, 1894. He was just forty-nine years of age. Stanley, by now back in England, sent a letter of condolence to Lady Thompson from his estate at Knowsley in Lancashire.

Although both succeeded Sir John A., neither Abbott nor Thompson shared the same intimacy that he had enjoyed with the Queen's representative.

* * *

Following the frantic pace of the summer of 1891 to that point, Lord Stanley and his family spent August at Stanley House, their summer home near New Richmond, Quebec.

Also on the Governor General's agenda later that summer was to hire another aide-de-camp. He selected Frederic Rudolph Lambart, who was born at Ayot St. Lawrence, Hertfordshire, England, on 16 October, 1865. Lambart, better known as Lord Kilcoursie, later became the 10th Earl of Cavan. After attending Eton College and the Royal Military College, Sandhurst, Kilcoursie joined the army and, in 1885, was commissioned as a second lieutenant in the Grenadier Guards.

Stanley's offer to Kilcoursie was not the first that he had received. Sir William des Voeux, appointed Governor of Hong Kong in 1887, had also offered Lord Kilcoursie a position as aide-de-camp. But, just before he could leave for his new posting, Kilcoursie's battalion was ordered to report to Bermuda, and the commander-in-chief, Lord Wolseley, insisted that he remain with the unit. It may have been a blessing in disguise: the man who took Kilcoursie's place as des Voeux's ADC contracted a fever within a month of arriving and died.

While in Bermuda, Kilcoursie received Stanley's telegram asking him to come to Ottawa as an aide-de-camp; he requested, and was granted, sanction to accept the position. Sir Baldwin Walker, captain of *HMS Emerald*, was in Bermuda at the time and offered Kilcoursie passage to Halifax if he could be ready by the next morning at ten o'clock. "I had no outfit but hot weather khaki," Kilcoursie wrote, "but I accepted at once." Captain Walker lent him some warm clothes for the trip.

Arriving in Halifax, Kilcoursie took the Intercolonial Railway to Ottawa to meet the vice regal family and staff. "Willie Walsh was the other ADC. Extremely capable but extremely reluctant to get up in the morning," he laughed. "Consequently, all the day's orders and all the early jobs fell to my lot."[38]

Kilcoursie's memoirs offer the reader an insider's insight into the personality of the Governor General.

> *Imagine my distress when, on descending the stairs, His Excellency looked me up and down and said, 'Your overalls are creased the wrong way.' Lord Stanley had been a Grenadier in the (1860s) and had always been taught to crease his trousers sideways and not fore and aft as in the modern way. How could I guess this? And what was to be done? Luckily, Willie Walsh and Colville, the military secretary, both more modern Grenadiers, appeared with the fore and aft rig, and so we were allowed to proceed to the ceremony as we were.*[39]
>
> *His Excellency was punctiliously neat and tidy in all his business. Whenever I took a document to his room, it was punctured, numbered and tied with blue ribbon, then put away. Alas, if asked for a week later, it could never be found, but such is life.*[40]

Kilcoursie chuckled when he wrote about one of his early efforts at placing guests in the correct spots at vice regal dinners. "'Dear sir,' the letter began — 'I cannot understand why I was made to sit further away from His Excellency than Mrs. XXX, seeing that I am the rankest lady.'"[41]

On another occasion, a local newspaper ran a contest, offering a prize to the person who could create the greatest number of words out of the letters of "Northumberland":

> *I had plenty of spare time that winter and took a dictionary and sent in an enormous list. I received a copy of Tennyson's work as the prize and a form which I was asked to copy saying that the competition was a bona fide concern and that I had received the prize. That I did, foolishly on Government House paper. This letter received a prominent place in a later edition of the newspaper. I never knew exactly what happened, but I know that I was summoned by His Excellency to explain. He showed me the stupidity of my action and the wrongful use of Government House paper and I never forgot the lesson.*[42]

Lord Kilcoursie remained in the employ of the Governor General until 1893, when he returned to his regiment in England. A lifetime of military service saw Kilcoursie, who succeeded his father as the Earl of Cavan, serve in the Boer War, then rise through the ranks until he retired from the army to his estate near Wheathampstead, in Hertfordshire, in 1913.

But with the outbreak of the First World War, the 10th Earl of Cavan was summoned to return to active duty, and he rose to become one of the British Army's most important commanders. In 1918, Cavan assumed command of the British forces in Italy. Following the war, he travelled to the United States as military adviser at the Washington Conference in 1921. The Earl was Chief of the Imperial General Staff from 1922 until his retirement in 1926. Lord Kilcoursie, the Earl of Cavan, died in London on 28 August, 1946.

* * *

Returning to The Citadel in September 1891, many on the Governor General's staff indulged their love of cricket, fashioning a team to compete against the "B" Battery Regiment, using the historic Plains of Abraham as their pitch. His Excellency's Household, as the team called itself, consisted of Arthur, Ferdy and George Stanley; their twenty-seven-year-old cousin Edward Bootle-Wilbraham, the 2nd Earl of Lathom[43]; military secretary Charles Colville; and aides-de-camp William Walsh and Lord Kilcoursie. On the afternoon of Monday, 7 September, they defeated the regiment 133 to 77. *The Citizen* exclaimed, "Lord Lathom showed that he had lost none of his old cunning both behind the wickets, with the gloves and in front of the wickets with the bat."[44]

The next day, His Excellency's Household was challenged to a cricket match by the Cavalry School Corps, known today as the Royal Canadian Dragoons. The final score was 171–87. "The Honourable William Stanley was undefeated in both innings and played in a style that gave promise of future excellence," reported *The Citizen*.[45] The game featured Arthur, Ferdy and George as well as their youngest brother and Lord Kilcoursie.

Kilcoursie's memoirs recall times like this:

> *Cricket on the Plains of Abraham and dinners on board the flag ship I shall not forget, especially the latter. I was in attendance on Their Excellencies when dining with the Admiral one very hot night. A glass of what I thought was plain water was by my plate and I drank freely. It was a mineral water and an air lock formed in my throat. I got purple in the face and collapsed. Luckily, the sailor man next to me did the right thing and gave me a good punch at the back of the neck which, I suppose, burst the bubble, and in a few minutes, all was well.*[46]

* * *

Lord Stanley returned to Toronto on a number of occasions, but he only visited the Toronto Industrial Exhibition once more after his 1888 appearance. On 17 and 18 September, 1891, the Governor General attended the final days of the thirteenth annual fair. On both days, he was again escorted through the fairgrounds once again by Exhibition president J. J. Withrow. "His Excellency was one of the most observant of the visitors who attended the exhibition yesterday,"[47] reported *The Globe*. Thursday, 17 September was American Visitors' Day. On Friday, the Governor General observed the Edison phonograph again, stopping at the exhibit in the Main Building as he wandered over to inspect the quality of pianos at the display of R. S. Williams & Sons.[48]

The vice regal party made an enjoyable foray into Ontario's Cottage Country and Kawarthas region on 25 September, 1891, visiting Lindsay, Lakefield, Bobcaygeon, Deer Lake and Stoney Lake. Isobel made good use of her camera, taking pictures of the sensational scenery, chipmunks and deer.

* * *

In late 1891, Lord Stanley became embroiled in an issue regarding the Canadian flag. On 7 November, 1891, the North American Commander-In-Chief, Vice Admiral George Willes Watson wrote to the Governor General:

> *I have read with much interest the correspondence relating to the Canadian flag. It will certainly be a great pity if the Home Government insists on its abolition. As a matter of feeling and sentiment, I know for certain it will cause very great dissatisfaction in the colony, and I can see no good result from the enforcement of the order, but on the contrary I think a change enforced might give rise to trouble and will certainly cause general ill-feeling. They are proud of their flag, and their pride in my opinion should be encouraged not dampened.[49]*

Roughly a year before, on 13 November, 1890, Sir Charles Tupper, the Canadian Minister of Marine and Fisheries, had also advised Stanley: "Since about 1869, our ships have been encouraged by the Government of Canada to use the red ensign with the Canadian coat of arms in the fly. These ships are in every quarter of the globe."

Stanley, on the recommendation of Tupper, requested that the Canadian red ensign be permitted for use both at sea and on land. In correspondence with the Colonial Secretary on 12 December, 1891, Stanley wrote:

> *It has been one of the objects of the Dominion, as of Imperial policy, to emphasize the fact that, by Confederation, Canada*

> *became not a mere assemblage of Provinces, but one united*
> *Dominion, and though no actual order has ever been issued,*
> *the Dominion government has encouraged, by precept and*
> *example, the use on all public buildings throughout the*
> *provinces, of the red ensign with the Canadian badge in the*
> *fly. Of course it may be replied that no restriction exists with*
> *respect to flags which may be hoisted on shore, but I submit*
> *that the flag is one which has come to be considered as the*
> *recognized flag of the Dominion, both ashore and afloat, and*
> *on sentimental grounds, I think there is much to be said for*
> *its retention, as it expresses at once the unity of the several*
> *Provinces of the identity of their flag with the colours hoisted*
> *by the ships of the mother country.*

Lord Stanley's implied request for use on land went beyond the jurisdiction of the British Admiralty, but it relented and authorized "the red ensign of Her Majesty's fleet with the Canadian coat of arms in the fly, to be used on board vessels registered in the Dominion."[50] On land, the national flag remained the Union Jack.

* * *

Lord and Lady Stanley hosted a combined musical and theatrical evening at Ottawa's Grand Opera House on 15 December, 1891. The Prague-born Grunfeld brothers performed before a full house. Heinrich, a cellist, and Alfred, a pianist, were court musicians of the emperors of Germany and Austria and performed pieces by Beethoven, Boccherini, Schumann and Wagner. The brothers undertook successful concert tours in North America, Austria, Germany and Russia through the final decades of the nineteenth century. Of Heinrich, one newspaper stated, "Everywhere, his beautiful tone and his tasteful rendering were appreciated.' The program that evening also included 'Cut Off with a Shilling' and 'Dearest Mama,' two short plays that included members of the vice regal family and staff."

---

[1] National Archives of Canada

[2] Lady Alice Stanley, *Letter to Prince George* (February 1891); Churchill, *Lord Derby*, p.30.

[3] K. Shea, *Interview with John Todorovic*, Royal Hamilton Yacht Club, (November, 2005).

[4] A chocolate girl was charged with serving hot cocoa to guests.

[5] *The Dominion Illustrated Monthly* (14 March, 1891).

[6] *Ottawa Daily Citizen* (2 March, 1891), p.4.

[7] *Ottawa Daily Citizen* (2 March, 1891), p.4.

[8] *Brooklyn Eagle* (13 December, 1896).

[9] G. Meagher, *Lessons in Skating* (Toronto: George N. Morang & Company, Ltd., 1900).

[10] Gaiety Theatre, *Souvenir Brochure* (London: December 1889). <*programme*>

[11] *Modus vivendi* — Latin, meaning two parties who are not in agreement but have agreed to live with their differences.

[12] Library of Parliament, *www.parl.gc.ca*.

[13] *Ottawa Daily Citizen* (29 November, 1890), p.4.

[14] J. C. Hopkins, 'The Britannic Empire', *The Dominion Illustrated Monthly* (29 March, 1890),p.109.

[15] F. A. Stanley, *Letter to Lord Salisbury, Lord Stanley of Preston Papers*, from the Public Archives of Canada in London (Ottawa, 12 February, 1891).

[16] Stanley to Macdonald, Macdonald Papers (National Archives of Canada, 30 January, 1891).

[17] *The Dominion Illustrated Monthly* (16 March), p.183.

[18] Creighton, *John A. Macdonald*, p.555.

[19] *The Dominion Illustrated Monthly* (10 January, 1891), p.47.

[20] *The Dominion Illustrated Monthly* (10 January, 1891), p.26.

[21] J. Pope, *Memoirs of the Right Honourable Sir John Alexander Macdonald, G.C.B., First Prime Minister of the Dominion of Canada*, 2 (London: 1894), p.259.

[22] Stanley to Knutsford, *G 13, 85* (Ottawa: 4 June, 1891); Creighton, *John A. Macdonald*, p.562.

[23] Creighton, *John A. Macdonald*, p.574.

[24] F. A. Stanley, *Letter to Lord Salisbury, Lord Stanley of Preston Papers*, from the Public Archives of Canada in London (Ottawa, 4 June, 1891).

[25] *The Globe* (Toronto: 3 June, 1891), edition cover page.

[26] Queen Victoria, *Telegraph to Lord Stanley*, National Archives of Canada, (June, 1891).

[27] *The Globe* (Toronto: 8 June, 1891), *edition cover page.*

[28] F. A. Stanley, *Letter to J. A. Macdonald, Lord Stanley of Preston Papers*, from the Public Archives of Canada in London (Ottawa, 6 May, 1891).

[29] Ibid.

[30] Azrael was the Angel of Death.

[31] *The Globe* (Toronto: 8 June, 1891), edition cover page .

[32] *The Dominion Illustrated Monthly* (20 June, 1891), p.596.

[33] *Montreal Gazette* (15 June, 1891).

[34] J. Abbott, *Speech before the Senate* (17 June 1891).

[35] *The Dominion Illustrated Monthly* (27 June, 1891), p.602.

[36] F. A. Stanley, *Letter to J. Pauncefote, Lord Stanley of Preston Papers*, from the Public Archives of Canada in London (Ottawa: 11 October, 1891).

[37] J. Abbot, *Letter*, National Archives of Canada, (4 June, 1891).

[38] Kilcoursie, *Recollections Hazy But Happy*.

[39] Ibid.

[40] Ibid.

[41] Ibid.

[42] Ibid.

[43] Edward Bootle-Wilbraham, the 2nd Earl of Lathom, was the first cousin of Frederick Stanley, and the second cousin to his children.

[44] *Ottawa Daily Citizen* (8 September, 1891).

[45] *Ottawa Daily Citizen* (9 September, 1891).

[46] Kilcoursie, *Recollections Hazy But Happy*.

[47] *The Globe* (Toronto: 18 September, 1891), p.2.

[48] *Toronto Daily Mail* (19 September, 1891), p.3.

[49] G. W. Watson, *Letter to Lord Stanley*, National Archives of Canada, (7 November, 1891).

[50] J. S. Ewart, 'The Canadian Flag', *The Canadian Magazine, 30, 1,* (1907), pp.332–5.

CHAPTER FOURTEEN

1892

The new year began on a sad note, as Prince Albert Victor Christian Edward, the Duke of Clarence and grandson of Her Majesty, Queen Victoria, died of typhoid on 14 January, 1892. Eddy, as he was known, was the son of the Queen's eldest son, Edward, who was the Prince of Wales and became King Edward VII on his mother's death in 1901.

In an address to Parliament, Stanley stated:

> *The lamented and untimely death of His Royal Highness, the Duke of Clarence and Avondale, has aroused a feeling of profound sorrow. The sympathy with Her Majesty and their Royal Highnesses, the Prince and Princess of Wales, in their bereavement, which has prevailed in the Dominion on this melancholy occasion, has found expression in respectful messages of condolence from my Ministers, from the Provincial Governments and from many other representative bodies.*[1]

Eddy had been engaged to Princess May of Teck, who, following Eddy's death, married his brother George, who later reigned as King George V. On 19 January, 1892, Lord and Lady Stanley received a telegram conveying the thanks of Queen Victoria and the Royal Family on the messages of condolence extended by the citizens of Canada.

* * *

On January 15, 1892, Lord and Lady Stanley hosted a presentation of *The Messiah* at the Grand Opera House in Ottawa. The cast included soprano Anna Birch from New York City, tenor Douglas Bird from Toronto, contralto J. Aumond of Ottawa and basso Barrington Foote of London, England. Also on the stage that evening was Edouard Remenyi, a friend of Franz Liszt and the man credited with introducing Johannes Brahms to the world after discovering the eighteen-year-old playing piano in a saloon on the Hamburg, Germany, waterfront.

* * *

On 25 February, 1892, Lord Frederick Stanley addressed the opening of Parliament:

> *It affords me much gratification to meet you at the commencement of the Parliamentary Session, and to be able to congratulate you upon the general prosperity of the Dominion and upon the abundant harvest with which Providence has blesses all parts of the country.*
>
> *The negotiations with respect to seal fishing in Behring Sea have been continued with a view to the adjustment by arbitration, of the difficulties which have arisen between Her Majesty's Government and that of the United States on that subject. Commissioners have been appointed by both Governments to investigate the circumstances of seal life in Behring Sea; to report thereon; and to suggest the measures, if any, which they may deem necessary for its proper protection and preservation. The Commissioners are proceeding with their deliberations in Washington, and the results will shortly be communicated to Her Majesty's Government. I trust that their investigations and the determination of the Arbitrators who are to be appointed, may lead to a just and equitable settlement of this long-pending difficulty.*
>
> *The meeting which had been arranged with the United States' Government for a day in October last, for an informal discussion on the extension of trade between the two countries and on other international matters requiring*

adjustment, was postponed at their request. But, in compliance with a more recent intimation from that Government, three of my Ministers proceeded to Washington and conferred with representatives of the Administration of the United States on those subjects. An amicable understanding was arrived at respecting the steps to be taken for the establishment of the boundary of Alaska, and for the reciprocity of services in cases of wreck and salvage. Arrangements were also reached for the appointment of an International Commission to report on the regulations which may be adopted by the United States and Canada for the prevention of destructive methods of fishing and the pollution of streams, and for establishing uniformity of close seasons, and other means for the preservation and increase of fish. A valuable and friendly interchange of views respecting other important matters also took place.

An important measure respecting the Criminal Law, which was laid before you last session, has been revised and improved as a result of the expression of views elicited by its presentation to Parliament, and will be submitted to you. Your attention will also be directed to measures for the redistribution of seats consequent upon the census returns; the establishment of the boundaries of the Territories and the amalgamation of the Departments of Marine and Fisheries. Bills will also be presented to you for the amendment of the Civil Service Act, the Acts relating to real property in the Territories and of those respecting the fisheries.[2]

* * *

On 5 March, the Governor General invited members of the Canadian Press Association to Rideau Hall for an afternoon of skating and tobogganing. Afterwards, the vice regal couple and the press corps attended a fancy ball at the Russell Hotel; the other guests included five hundred of the crème de la crème of Ottawa society. *Le Canada* reported that the Governor General's impressive speech was "*un tres beau discourse, plein d'esprit.*"[3]

There was no thoroughbred racing in Ottawa during Stanley's tenure as governor general, so he was forced to indulge in his passion, inherited from his father, while visiting other cities. For the third year in a row, Stanley attended the Queen's Plate at Toronto's Woodbine Riding and Driving Club, later known as Greenwood Racetrack. On 25 May, Stanley presented the fifty-guinea prize to O'Donohue, a horse owned by Joseph Seagram, who was the winning owner for the second straight year.

* * *

Although historians have frequently suggested that Frederick Stanley was an unimaginative speaker, at times he displayed a wicked sense of humour. In July 1892, a messenger sent by Peter White, the Speaker of the House of Commons, mistakenly arrived at Rideau Hall, requesting a deck of cards for the use of guests visiting his office. The messenger, who had been intended to call on the Rideau Club across Wellington Street from the Parliament Buildings, arrived at the Governor General's residence in time to catch Lord Stanley in the midst of dinner. But Stanley obliged in good humour, excusing himself from the table and securing two decks of cards, which he asked the messenger to deliver to White with his compliments. "Needless to say, the blunder has caused considerable hilarity in town," said *The Citizen*.[4]

* * *

On 21 July, the Governor General closed the seventh Parliament of the Dominion of Canada. From Rideau Hall, His Excellency was accompanied by a mounted escort from the Princess Louise Dragoon Guards. The Governor General's Foot Guards met Stanley in front of the Parliament Buildings. In summary, *Qu'Appelle Vidette* offered, "the session, which closes today, is one of the most uneventful, as far as practical legislation is concerned, that has taken place since Confederation."[5]

Officers of the military battery held a festive "at home" at their camp in Lévis, Quebec, in honour of the Governor General on 30 July. While there, Lord Stanley presented badges and a five-hundred-dollar prize to members of Canada's bisley team, a rifle competition.

Invitations sent to Quebec's high society late in August 1892 promised the recipients an unforgettable experience: "To have the honour of meeting HRH Prince George of Wales" was engraved across the gilt-edged invitation. Word throughout Quebec City was that balls given by Lord and Lady Stanley in Quebec were always "very brilliant affairs," so great excitement greeted the news that the Prince of Wales was to be a very special guest at the Vice Regal Ball being held on 18 September at The Citadel. Eight hundred guests attended the event, which lasted from ten in the evening to two o'clock the next morning. The *Evening Journal* reported, "Prince George sustained his well-established reputation for gallantry by making himself the most agreeable partner in the Ball Room to as many as possible of the handsome young ladies in attendance."[6] His Royal Highness included on his dance card Lady Stanley and Madame Angers, the wife of Auguste-Réal Angers, the Lieutenant Governor of Quebec.

Lord Stanley took advantage of any opportunity to shoot game, and late in September 1892, while visiting Port Dover, Ontario, his hosts took the Governor General out for a successful afternoon of duck hunting.[7] Lord Kilcoursie remembered the day well:

> *After a great duck shoot on some lakes nearby and the gathering of some eighty or ninety in sacks, we heard that curious sound like a distant pack of hounds increasing to a chorus like ten packs of hounds as thousands and thousands of geese came in to feed. We had no more cartridges, so simply lay very still and watched the descent from heaven, the placing of the outposts and the instant warning given by the sentry who was patrolling just fifty yards downwind of our hide. Every head and neck went up like arms raised at physical drill but the leader, after two minutes of absolute silence, said 'Honk-ka-honk,' which, being interpreted, can only have meant, 'The sentry's a fool. Go on feeding,' for down went all the necks and the evening meal began. We lay very still for some time when I thought we should be getting home. The buckboard was to come for us some time in the evening.*[8]

On 10 October, Lord and Lady Stanley sponsored a series of tableaux on marriage at the Grand Opera House in Ottawa. *The Daily Citizen* surmised:

> ... *if all the marriage dramas in real life ran their course as smoothly and beautifully as did the 'Marriage Dramas' on the stage of the Grand Opera House last evening, the Divorce Committee of the Senate would find time hang so heavily on its hands that it would have to go out of business altogether.*[9]

Lady Stanley's train was late arriving in Ottawa, so the vice regal couple was not present on opening night, but they did attend the performance on its second evening.

* * *

Of the many pastimes enjoyed by Lord Stanley, few were loved as much by His Excellency as fishing and shooting. On the first day of November, the Governor General took a party that included his son Edward and Lord Kilcoursie out for a ride in their shooting phaeton, on the hunt for coyotes and prairie wolf. Lord Kilcoursie, quick with a quip and skilled at penning doggerel, left a memory of the day:

THE WOLF HUNT

I'll tell you a tale of a glorious ride
On a boundless ocean of grass
A tale of the prairie, wild and wide
Where sight into haze can pass.

A day when the lungs with might expand
And the breezes a vigour give.
So keen, that for very joy we stand
And thank our God we live!

Look! Down in the coolie beneath the hill
What's that sitting up to listen?
Ye gods, t'is a wolf! Oh, it's hard to be still
When your eyes with excitement glisten.

We are galloping still and are galloping fast
We are gaining — no — yes, we are gaining.
But the wolf is as game as a fox to the last
Though the hounds' every muscle are straining.

They have got him — whohoopp! But t'is only one part
For he fights with a grim desperation.
And to see him snarl still with the knife in his heart
Seems to baffle the laws of creation.

I could pity the varmint his terrible fate
Were he only a common marauder
But a slayer of colts! Ah, the sin is too great
So his death is of justice the order.

We skinned him and cut off his cruel grey head
Which is mounted to help me remember
Though foxes were absent, we killed him instead
On Monday, the first of November.[10]

* * *

On the first day of December in 1892, while on a visit to Toronto, Stanley visited Upper Canada College, where an address was delivered in Latin by head boy B. K. Sandwell. Astonished students heard the Governor General respond in Latin. *The Globe* reported, "Lord Stanley's impromptu reply in Latin to the head boy's address of welcome was in truth a remarkable performance which few, if any, even among college professors, could have equalled. [Stanley] spoke slowly and deliberately, but with scarcely a falter or any hesitancy for a word, and in grammatical construction and pronunciation, the effect was marvelously accurate and scholarly."[11]

It had been twenty-eight years since Lord Stanley had spoken a word of Latin in public, and insofar as he had not heard of the Latin address which was to be tendered to him until he reached the college, "he hoped they would pardon his somewhat faulty grammatical construction and original pronunciation; he was afraid his remarks had been couched in the *Latin caninum*, or dog-Latin style."

In fact, although Lord Stanley had not had the need to use his Latin for a number of years, "as a student at college and university, he spoke and wrote Latin as fluently as English, a statement easy of credence after his speech of yesterday afternoon."[12]

At a dinner that same evening, Stanley spoke at the Medical College of the University of Toronto. "When he admitted that he, too, was 'a state-aided institution,' there was an unrestrained outburst of laughter," reported *The Globe*.[13]

∗ ∗ ∗

Stanley suspected that the Americans were trying to sidestep many of the provisions in the proposed resolution of late 1891. In a letter to Salisbury, Stanley confessed:

> *United States politicians will take advantage in a way which at home we should consider beneath contempt, and if Ministers here have insisted on arbitration and damages being parts of one agreement, it is because they and the general body of their constituents are firmly convinced that the U. S. will wriggle out of the payment of damage (should the case be given against them) after they have once secured the arbitration and the sealing regulations, which are the considerations offered on our side.*[14]

James Blaine, the American Secretary of State, had been ill during the tedious and dreadfully long negotiations on the Behring Sea matter. By 1892, American newspapers were reporting that he was no longer capable of conducting business at a high level. As the American politician Henry Watterson reported in the *Buffalo Courier*:

> *I saw Mr. Blaine last week and had a long talk with him. I*

have no hesitation in saying that he could never serve out his term if elected, even if he lived to be inaugurated. He is slowly dying at the top, as anybody can see who is admitted to his confidence. He is incapable of mental work. He cannot carry on a conversation without lamentable signs of mental decay. He flits from topic to topic. His lapse of memory is almost painful. He needs constant prompting as to names, dates, and occurrences: and there are times when his struggles to collect himself are almost pitiable.[15]

Watterson's estimation of the Secretary may have been slightly oversold to safeguard against ruminations that Blaine would run for the presidency. Nevertheless, it is perhaps no coincidence that Canadian representatives were making more headway in the arbitration of the Behring Sea question, now that the obstacle of Blaine was being slowly removed from the equation.

Lord Salisbury was able to finally secure a settlement through arbitration by informing American representatives that if they chose not to arbitrate, the *modus vivendi* that allowed the United States to fish off of Canadian shores would not be renewed and, perhaps more importantly, Canadian sealing rights would be protected by the Royal Navy. This tough talk from Westminster was, in the opinion of many Canadians, long overdue, but was nevertheless effective.

Despite his advancing illness and weakening mental powers, it was Blaine who finally agreed to arbitration on the condition that his points would be laid before the arbitrators. The main questions that were to be considered by the arbitrators were:

i) *What were the ostensible boundaries in the Behring Sea that Russia understood to be within its jurisdiction prior to the sale of Alaska to the U.S.?*

ii) *Were Russia's claims of jurisdiction in regards to the sealing industry observed by Great Britain?*

iii) *Was the Behring Sea included in the definition of 'Pacific Ocean' as it was referred to in the 1825 treaty between Russia and Great Britain, and did Russia claim or exercise any rights in this area against Great Britain following the signing of the treaty?*

iv) *Did the United States assume jurisdiction of the seal*
fisheries in the Behring Sea east of the water boundary
following the sale of Alaska?

v) *Do the United States have any right of property and*
protection in those fur seals that frequent the islands of
the Behring Sea when those seals are found outside of
the three-mile limit?

These questions, along with the agreed component of a joint commission to investigate the nature of seal life and the preservation thereof, were part of a treaty that was approved by the United States Senate on 29 March, 1892, and ratified by the President just over a month later.

The arbitration began in February 1893 and lasted well into the summer. The U.S. and Great Britain agreed that each country was allowed to appoint two arbitrators and that the kings of Italy, Norway and Sweden, along with the French president, were to appoint one arbitrator each. A Justice of the Supreme Court, J. M. Harlan, and Senator J. T. Morgan, were the two arbitrators appointed by the U.S. Britain's representatives were Lord Hannen and Prime Minister Sir John Thompson of Canada. The Baron de Courcel, the Marquis Visconti Venosta and Gregers Gram were the neutral arbitrators appointed by the other parties.

Arbitrators did not uphold the American claim that pelagic sealing was "illegitimate." The matter was finally and rightfully settled in Canada and Great Britain's favour on 15 August, 1893. Damages amounted to approximately half a million dollars, or $13,000,000 in Canadian currency today.

Stanley had only five months left in Canada when the hearings had begun; by the time they were completed, he had returned to Britain as the 16th Earl of Derby. Still, Stanley's stewardship, as confidante to Pauncefote, Salisbury, Abbott, Thompson, and his good friend Macdonald, had exacted a victory. Stanley was thrilled with the decision, even though, like his famous Cup, he had not been in Canada long enough to witness its effect on the Dominion.

---

1 Library of Parliament, Parliament of Canada website, *www.parl.gc.ca*.
2 Ibid.
3 *Le Canada* (Ottawa: 5 March, 1892), p.3.
4 *Ottawa Daily Citizen* (2 July, 1892), p.6.

[5] *Qu'Appelle Vidette* (21 July, 1892), *edition cover page.*

[6] *Evening Journal* (Ottawa: 19 September, 1892).

[7] *Le Canada* (Ottawa: 30 September, 1892), p2.

[8] Kilcoursie, *Recollections Hazy But Happy.*

[9] *Ottawa Daily Citizen* (11 October, 1892), p.8.

[10] Kilcoursie, *Recollections Hazy But Happy.*

[11] *The Globe* (Toronto: 2 December, 1892), p.6.

[12] Ibid.

[13] Ibid.

[14] F. A. Stanley, *Letter to Lord Salisbury, Lord Stanley of Preston Papers,* from the Public Archives of Canada in London (Ottawa, 11 October, 1891).

[15] H. Watterson, as quoted in *The Buffalo Courier,* reprinted in, *The New York Sun* (1 June, 1892).

CHAPTER FIFTEEN

Birth of the Stanley Cup

A banquet, both raucous and ribald, was held at the Russell House Hotel on 18 March, 1892, to honour another triumphant season for the victorious Ottawa Hockey Club, one of several sporting clubs affiliated with the Ottawa Amateur Athletic Association. As Ottawa's *Daily Journal* reported:

> … *a record as honourable in the making as it was splendid in success…. Nine championship matches won; a single match lost, by the narrowest possible shave. Fifty-three goals taken in championship contests against the best teams in Canada; only nineteen goals the other way. This was the record of a genuine amateur team playing for pure love of sport and treating all comers as they wished to be treated themselves.*[1]

More than seventy-five of the team's most enthusiastic supporters were in attendance at the five-storey Russell House, located at the corner of Sparks and Elgin streets and considered the finest hotel in the city. The dinner was the first held under the auspices of the Ottawa Amateur Athletic Association. The Governor General's Foot Guards provided musical entertainment. Just before ten o'clock that evening, with the dishes cleared and business ready to begin, a number of ladies arrived and were seated in a wing of the dining room, where ices were served.

The president of the Ottawa Amateur Athletic Club, J. W. McRae, hosted the dinner, flanked by team members H. Y. Russell and F. M. Jenkins. The vice-presidents' chairs were occupied by past president Phillip Dansken Ross, publisher of the *Ottawa Journal*, and vice-president Georges-Edouard Desbarats, publisher of the weekly *Canadian Illustrated News*.

McRae proposed a toast to Queen Victoria, then Ross raised a glass to Governor General Lord Stanley, and "referred to the great interest manifested in hockey by His Excellency."[2]

Lord Kilcoursie, an aide de camp to Lord Stanley, attended the banquet on his behalf. He thanked those in attendance for their kind words, then read a letter from His Excellency:

> *I have for some time past been thinking that it would be a good thing if there were a challenge cup which should be held from year to year by the champion hockey team in the Dominion. There does not appear to be any such outward and visible sign of a championship at present, and considering the general interest which the matches now elicit, and in the importance of having the game played fairly and under rules generally recognized, I am willing to give a cup, which shall be held from year to year by the winning team.*
>
> *I am not quite certain that the present regulations governing the arrangement of matches give entire satisfaction, and it would be worth considering whether they could not be arranged so that each team would play once at home and once at the place where their opponents hail from.*[3]

Continuing, Kilcoursie stated that Captain Charles Colville, who had earlier acted as military secretary to the Governor General and who was now living in England, had been commissioned by Lord Stanley to order an appropriate cup. It would be held in Ottawa by trustees until the end of the following hockey season, at which time it would be presented to the champions.

The reading of the letter was greeted by wildly enthusiastic applause. The president of the O.A.A.C. then proposed a toast to the health of the Ottawa hockey team. Friends of the team members stood on their chairs to salute the team.

The first to respond to the toast was the captain, H. Y. Russell, "who did great honour to his team in a speech that was full of humour, and which was heartily appreciated by all present."[4] Russell's teammates then spoke in turn. F. M. Jenkins recalled the times when he, H. Kirby and J. Kerr had battled the "Winged Wheelers" of the Montreal Amateur Athletic Association team. Kirby and Kerr then took their respective turns. W. C. Young earned hearty applause by referring "to the good fellowship that existed among the clubs of the O.A.A.C. and their members."[5] Bradley, unable to attend because of illness, was remembered by his teammates. A. Morel and Chauncy Kirby concluded the speeches, the latter delivering his oration while standing on the table.

Mr. Moss, travelling into Ottawa from the Osgoode Hall club in Toronto, stood and raised his glass. "Our sister clubs," he smiled, joined by Mr. McCarthy of the Ottawa College team, Mr. Walsh of the Montreal A.A.A. and Mr. Laurie, the secretary of the Ontario Hockey Association. The president then read a telegram received from the Quebec team: "Quebec regrets that she cannot send a delegate and do honour to the finest hockey team in Canada."

Captain Russell toasted the ladies, followed by a toast to the press. Then, a Mr. O'Grady offered one final toast to honour the Ottawa Amateur Athletic Club. President McRae stood, bowed, and saluted those present.

Final speeches were made by Clarence Martin and a Mr. Palmer of the Rideau Rebels.

Lord Kilcoursie, who was not only an aide to the Governor General but was also a member of the Rideau Rebels, with whom he played alongside Stanley's sons, composed a song for the occasion, "winding up with a rousing chorus which was rendered in stentorian style by all the members."[6]

THE HOCKEY MEN

There is a game called hockey
There is no finer game
For though some call it 'knockey'
Yet we love it all the same.

This played in His Dominion
Well played both near and far.

There's only one opinion
How 'tis played in Ottawa.

Then give three cheers for Russell
The captain of the boys.
However tough the tussle
His position he enjoys

And then for all the others
Let's shout as loud we may
An O, a T, a T, an A
A W and A!

Now list' to me one minute
I'll tell you where they play
And why it is that eagerly
We welcome them today.

They vanquished in their revel
Quebec and Montreal
The gallant club, the Rebels
And the Queen's and Osgoode Hall.

Well, first there's Chauncy Kirby
He's worth his weight in gold
For though he is not very big
He's very, very bold.

Supported by his brother
They make a wondrous pair
For either one or t'other
Is invariably there.

And on the left there's Bradley
And on the right there's Kerr.
And when the centres pass it
There, on either side, they are.

Lord Stanley

And that's what's won the battles
Their fine unselfish play
Cool heads that nothing rattles
In the thickest of the fray.

At coverpoint — important place,
There's Young, a bulwark strong.
No dodging tricks or flying pace
Will baffle him for long.

At point we have the captain
And if he gets the puck
Will very near the goal he'll shoot
And get it too, with luck.

There's yet another member
Impregnable Morel.
He's had his share of work to do
And done it very well

And there is also Jenkins
Who played in matches twain
So well that in Toronto
They don't wish for him again.

And now, my friends, forgive me
The moral of my song
I'll soon explain in twenty words
Nor keep you very long.

We've here eight bright examples
Of fine unselfish play
And that's the secret of success
And why they're here today.

Just one word to the audience

And every player too
(Forgive me, though, a novice,
In dictating this to you).

Don't question a decision
However wrong it be.
And little boys, for manners' sake
Don't hoot the referee![7]

The assembled hooted and clapped with every player reference, and the entire hall erupted at the conclusion of Kilcoursie's doggerel.

After further songs were presented, the gathering sang "Auld Lang Syne," then dispersed into the night, having little comprehension of the history that had been made at the banquet that evening.

* * *

Hockey was in its infancy in the late 1800s, tottering on unsteady legs as it found its place in society; although it couldn't be known at the time, the sport was at the hub of a remarkable transformation in sporting tastes. Outing, the monthly New York-based periodical of sport and recreation akin to the *Sports Illustrated* of its day, announced on its masthead that it would offer brief outlines of:

> *... reputable sports of the period: On the ball fields, it will embrace cricket, base-ball, lacrosse, foot-ball and lawn tennis. On the bays and rivers, yachting, rowing and canoeing. In the woods and streams, hunting, shooting and fishing. On the lawns, archery, lawn tennis and croquet. Together with ice boating, skating, tobogganing, snowshoeing, coasting and winter sports generally, as also the in-door games of billiards, chess, whist, draughts, etc.*[8]

No specific mention of hockey was made, although results of games played by the Amateur Hockey Association of Canada, as well as New York-area contests, were published.

James George Creighton, born in Halifax, Nova Scotia, in 1850, is credited with the introduction to a widespread audience of a game that came to be known as hockey. Having observed the sport in his hometown, Creighton moved to Montreal and organized what historians cite as the first game of hockey that may be recognized as such. It took place on 3 March, 1875, at the Victoria Rink.

> *At the rink last night a very large audience gathered to wit-*
> *ness a novel contest on the ice. The game of hockey is not*
> *much known here, and in consequence the game of last*
> *evening was looked forward to with great interest. The*
> *match was an interesting and well-contested affair, the*
> *efforts of the players exciting much merriment as they*
> *wheeled and dodged each other, and notwithstanding the*
> *brilliant play of Captain Torrance's team, Captain*
> *Creighton's men carried the day, winning two games [as*
> *goals were then called] to the single of the Torrance nine*
> *[each team utilized nine players]. The game was concluded*
> *about half-past nine, and the spectators then adjourned*
> *well satisfied with the evening's entertainment.*[9]

While attending McGill in Montreal, Creighton and his colleagues played regularly. By 1877, he had formed a team known as the Metropolitans. That year, he and some other McGill students drafted a set of seven rules, borrowing heavily from British field hockey.

During the decade that began in 1875, organized hockey was played almost exclusively in Montreal, where Creighton's Metropolitans competed against teams from McGill University and the Victoria Skating Rink. The significance of the tournaments played at the Montreal Winter Carnival cannot be understated. In 1882, Creighton moved to Ottawa, where he held the position of Law Clerk of the Senate but also helped introduce the game to Canada's capital as a member of Arthur Stanley's Rideau Rebels.

* * *

The Montreal Amateur Athletic Association was created on 20 June, 1881, bringing together the Montreal Lacrosse Club, the Montreal Bicycle Club and the Montreal Snowshoe Club. "They surrendered their individual autonomy in order that a larger umbrella organization might look after the affairs of the three organizations more effectively and with the idea that the pooled resources would allow the activities of all three to flourish." The constitution of the M.A.A.A. stated that objectives were to be "the encouragement of athletic sports, the promotion of physical and mental culture and the providing of rational amusements for its members."

At a board meeting in late November 1884, Tom Paton, an M.A.A.A. board member and one of its founding members, approached the Association about forming a hockey club. Paton, an early hockey enthusiast and netminder, recognized hockey's increasing popularity as a winter recreational activity. The idea was immediately embraced and approved. Within four days, the "Montreal Hockey Club" was a reality. The name was recorded as such in the minutes of the M.A.A.A.'s next meeting.

The new Montreal Hockey Club practised at the Crystal Rink, and in early 1885 it entered the extremely popular hockey tournament at the Montreal Winter Carnival. Astonishingly, the Montreal Hockey Club won the series and was awarded the Birks Cup, which they brought back and displayed in the M.A.A.A.'s clubhouse. The success of the hockey club was a source of great pride for the Association.

In the early days, the M.A.A.A.'s board of directors covered the team's expenses. Eventually, however, the team tapped a source of revenue by charging admission to its games; these monies, shared with the rink management, enabled the team to largely pay its own way, requiring only occasional loans that were repaid from gate receipts during the course of the season.

* * *

On 8 December, 1886, representatives from the teams most often associated with the Montreal Winter Carnival hockey tournament met at the Victoria Skating Rink to discuss the formation of an association "to improve, foster and perpetuate the game of hockey in Canada, to protect it from professionalism and to promote the cultivation of kindly feeling among the members of the hockey club."[10]

Jack Arnton of the Victorias acted as chairman, while his teammate J. Monk took the role of recording secretary. The Victorias were also represented at the meeting by J. Muir; the others included C. H. MacNutt,

Holden and Wylde from McGill; Laing and McCaffrey from Montreal's Crystal Rink; E. Sheppard and Billy Barlow from the Montreal Hockey Club; and T. D. Greene and Hamilton from the Ottawa Hockey Club. "Mr. Monk said that he had, as requested, written to Quebec and Ottawa, asking them to send a representative to this meeting," reported Montreal's *Gazette*. "Ottawa had complied with his request but he had not received any word from Quebec."[11]

The association was named the Amateur Hockey Association of Canada, also occasionally as the Dominion Hockey Association. Charter members were the Crystals, the Victorias, McGill, the Montreal Hockey Club and the Ottawa Hockey Club. A constitution was adopted and an executive elected for the upcoming season. T. D. Greene from the Ottawa Hockey Club was elected president; Jack Arnton of the Victoria Rink was chosen first vice-president and R. Laing of the Crystals, second vice-president; E. Stevenson of the Victorias secretary-treasurer. A council was formed consisting of James Stewart of the Crystals, J. G. Monk of the Victorias, H. A. Budden from McGill, the Montreal Hockey Club's E. Sheppard and Ottawa's Percy Myles. Rules were approved, including the use of seven players per side. Teams in the AHAC played by the McGill Rules, which were published in the Montreal *Gazette* on 23 December, 1886.

The AHAC employed a challenge system whereby a championship team would face a new challenger each week for the title. "The club holding the championship trophy will accept all challengers in the order of their reception and shall be obliged to play all such championship matches with an intermission of not more than seven days between each match." Teams wishing to challenge the championship team were to mail a letter to the secretary of the team being challenged. If a championship team was defeated, it was required to deliver the trophy to the victorious team within seven days — there was, in fact, no championship trophy at first, but the Victoria Rink contributed fifty dollars, and although the Crystal Rink refused to participate in the purchase of a trophy, the AHAC's board of directors did buy one, at a price of seventy-five dollars, to be awarded to the champion.

The AHAC's season was to begin no earlier than the first of January and conclude no later than 15 March. These dates conformed to nature's will, as each of the teams played on natural ice. The first game played by the Amateur Hockey Association of Canada was a 3–1 win for the Crystals over McGill at the Crystal Rink on 7 January, 1887. The first title change occurred one week later when the Victorias defeated the Crystals by a 4–0 score. The Victorias held the title until 11 March, 1887, when the final challenge game was held. The Crystals won 3–2 in what was their third successive challenge to win the initial title of the Amateur Hockey Association of Canada. The Victorias played six games that season, the Crystals played five, and McGill, the Montreal Hockey Club, and the Ottawa Hockey Club each played once. Jack Arnton and J. Craven of the Victorias led all scorers with four goals apiece. Jack's brother T. Arnton recorded two shutouts in the Victorias' six games. Because of the long run enjoyed by the Victorias, it was decided to switch to a series system in 1888.

Ottawa chose not to participate in the AHAC schedule during 1888 due to the expense of travel, leaving the league with the four Montreal-based teams. At the end of the schedule, the Victorias and the Montreal Hockey Club were tied for first place. A tie-breaking game was scheduled, but two of the Victorias players were injured and unable to participate, paving the way for the M.A.A.A.'s team to capture the championship with a 2–1 victory over the defending champion Victorias. The Montreal Hockey Club, often tagged the Winged Wheelers because of the emblems on their red flannel sweaters, won five games and lost but one over the course of the schedule, scoring twenty-three goals and allowing just six. Goalkeeper Tom Paton of the champion Montreal Hockey Club recorded two shutouts.[12] The AHAC reverted back to a challenge system in 1889.

Whenever possible, Lord Stanley and members of his family tried to make plans to watch the Ottawa Hockey Club play at the Rideau Hall Rink. The Viceroy was on hand to watch as Ottawa defeated the visiting Victorias during February 1891. "The Ottawa hockey team, much to their own surprise as a couple of their first seven were ill, succeeded in carrying off the honours of the hockey match with the Victorias of Montreal on Saturday evening. The soft ice spoiled a little what would otherwise have probably been a wonderfully rapid game, but the contest was nevertheless fast and exceedingly close throughout." The 1–0 final, on an Ottawa goal by Kirby, came in a contest that provided "good, clean hockey free from roughness or temper."[13] After the game, the Governor General hosted a reception for the visiting team.

Later that year, Lord Stanley, along with a sizable crowd of hockey fans, witnessed a contest between the Ottawa Hockey Club and the Quebec Hockey Club. "For nearly three hours, the Rideau rink rang with the cheers of a thousand spectators of probably the finest [hockey] match ever played in Canada." It took overtime to decide the victor, with Ottawa outlasting the blue-and-white-sweatered Quebec squad.

By 1892, the AHAC was being recognized as the pre-eminent hockey league in Canada. At their annual meeting, held in Montreal on 15 December, the AHAC elected its officers for the 1893 season: F. M. Jenkins of Ottawa as president, J. Crathern of the Victorias as first vice-president and A. Laurie of Quebec second vice-president, while J. A. Findlay of Montreal was chosen as secretary-treasurer. In addition, a council of A. Ritchie of the Crystals, G. Carpenter of the Shamrocks, M. Costigan of McGill, A. Palmer of the Ottawa Rebels and J. Farwell of Sherbrooke was selected.

Five teams — the Crystals, the Victorias, the Montreal Hockey Club, the Ottawa Hockey Club and the Quebec Hockey Club — competed in an eight-game schedule to be played between 7 January and 17 March. The Montreal Hockey Club finished the season in first place, winning seven and losing one, scoring thirty-eight goals and relinquishing eighteen, earning the laurels as the champions of 1893. Their single loss was at the hands of Ottawa in the season's opening contest. Second-place Ottawa won six against two losses, and scored forty-nine times while allowing twenty-two goals. The Crystals, Quebec and the Victorias finished in that order.[14]

* * *

Although arguments rage over the location of hockey's true birthplace, there is no question that Ottawa played a substantial role in nurturing the fledgling sport in its earliest days, helping propel it into a national obsession. Geography, climate and wealth nourished the pastime into what soon became Canada's national sport.

As the initial waves of explorers, traders and settlers arrived in Canada, many followed the current of the St. Lawrence from the Atlantic Ocean to the Ottawa River, helping the Ottawa Valley, on both the Ontario and Quebec sides, get a head start on settlement. But it wasn't until the latter quarter of the nineteenth century that organized sport truly became an integral part of Ottawa's social life.

Lord Dufferin, Canada's Governor General between 1872 and 1878, contributed $1,624.95 of his own money for the construction of a skating rink at Rideau Hall, an amount later reimbursed by the government. Skating parties at the Rideau Rink immediately became prime social events in the Ottawa area.

In the 1870s and '80s, hockey was largely confined to universities, garrisons and athletic associations. Ontario's first official hockey team, the Ottawa Hockey Club, was no different. Formed in 1884, the Ottawa Hockey Club was part of a larger organization, the Ottawa Amateur Athletic Association, which mirrored the arrangement that saw the Montreal Hockey Club operate under the auspices of its parent organization, the Montreal Amateur Athletic Association.

* * *

After attending a hockey game during the Montreal Winter Carnival in February 1889, the Stanley family enthusiastically embraced the new sport. In early March of that year, Isobel played for a Government House team that defeated a Rideau ladies team in what is regarded as the first women's hockey game. The contest was played on the rink at Rideau Hall.

Edward Stanley's enthusiasm for the sport was quickly shared with his brothers Arthur and Victor. Arthur, like his siblings, was a natural athlete who had excelled in many sports, especially cricket, while living in England. But he possessed a leadership quality that rose above that of his siblings. In late February 1889, Arthur organized a game of hockey on the Rideau Rink, forming a five-man squad that included Edward and Victor as well as Captain Josceline Bagot and Lieutenant Aubrey McMahon, both aides-de-camp to the Governor General. The team faced a Parliamentary quintet that included John A. Barron, the Liberal MP for North Victoria (the area around Lindsay, Ontario) and Henry A. Ward, the Liberal member for the East Durham riding (Port Hope, Ontario).

What began as casual fun evolved into a regular series of games between like-minded enthusiasts culled from a pool of senators, members of Parliament and Parliamentary assistants. As time permitted, regular participants included the three Stanley brothers, Lord Stanley's aides-de-camp Bagot, McMahon and Captain Wingfield, MPs John Barron and Henry Ward, Sandford Fleming Jr. and Philip D. Ross, publisher of the *Ottawa Evening Journal,* who acted as a surrogate coach while also starring with the Ottawa Hockey Club in the AHAC. The squad came to be known as the

Rideau Rebels, and they sported crimson flannel sweaters, white trousers and white caps when they faced their competition. "I remember so well its initiation," recalled Edward Stanley, the 17th Earl of Derby, just prior to his death in 1948, in a letter to Vancouver city archivist Major J. S. Matthews:

> *It was in connection with a small group of hockey enthusiasts of whom four or five, if not more, were members of the staff of my father, Lord Stanley, the Governor General. We formed a team of ourselves, our name 'The Rebels'. I'm glad to think that from that very small beginning there has developed the present contest for the Stanley Cup, which you tell me is now the greatest ice hockey contest in North America, and that means in the world.*[15]

In March 1889, just over a month after Lord Stanley viewed his first hockey game, he invited the St. James Club of Montreal to visit Ottawa for a game against the Rideau Rebels on the rink at Rideau Hall. The Stanley boys did not play in this match, but several prominent names in hockey's early history did. Joining Captain Bagot on the Rebels were James G. Creighton and Philip D. Ross. Playing for St. James that day was Montagu Allan, who, nineteen years later, donated the Allan Cup for the senior amateur hockey championship of Canada. Both Allan and Ross have been inducted into the Hockey Hall of Fame as builders.

Enthusiastic as he was about hockey, Arthur Stanley was frustrated by the poorly organized games and envisioned a situation not dissimilar to the one he would have been familiar with back home in England in cricket and other sports, where organized teams formed a league, developed rules, set schedules and decided a championship. It was to take a little time, but Arthur's vision would soon be realized.

* * *

Arthur Stanley, with assistance from John A. Barron, instigated a series of contests for the Rebels during their second season, hoping "to stimulate interest in the game." Barron, a frequent member of the Rebels while he resided in Ottawa, was a Toronto-born lawyer with a practice in Lindsay. He was elected to the House of Commons in 1887. In December 1889, after

Lindsay built its first covered rink, Barron was elected the inaugural president of the Lindsay Skating Club. He joined the first Lindsay Hockey Club as a player and was an exuberant participant. "We expected to see a vacancy in the electoral district of North Victoria and the MP thereafter may yet be responsible for manslaughter," Lindsay's Canadian Post wrote in a January 1890 editorial.[16]

The touring Ottawa team included Arthur Stanley, Philip D. Ross and Henry Ward. James Creighton and Senator Lawrence Power had intended to participate, but both excused themselves at the last moment due to Parliamentary duties.

The *Canadian Post* described the relatively new game for the benefit of neophytes:

> *It appears to be a mixture of football, shinny and lacrosse. It has all the excitement of football, with about the same number of upsets; all the rush and move of shinny, with about the same number of broken shins; all the science of lacrosse with about the same number of players laid out each game.*[17]

The Rebels' first match, held 7 February, 1890, involved a visit to Lindsay at that town's new rink. "Mr. Barron's combined Parliamentary and Government House hockey team's promised visit to Lindsay aroused our Lindsay players to unheard-of exertions at practice. Mr. Hudspeth, M. P., accompanied the visitors, whom he entertained at luncheon after a one-hour practice at the Lindsay rink."[18]

The Rebels wore their familiar red flannel shirts while the Lindsay team wore white flannel shirts tucked into knickerbockers pants, black stockings and black and white caps. Barron played goal for the Rebels. "It quickly became apparent that the Lindsay team were better skaters, but the visitors were more experienced and their teamwork made the game very even," reported the *Canadian Post*.[19] At halftime, the score was tied 2–2. In the second half, Aubrey McMahon scored once and P. D. Ross scored his second goal of the game for the Rebels. One of Lindsay's goals was disputed but allowed by the Rebels. "The puck struck the end of the rink, bounced through the flags [which served as goal posts] from behind, struck the goal-keeper's foot and rebounded through the goal to give a game [goal] for

Lindsay."[20] The game ended with Ottawa victorious over Lindsay by a 4–3 score. Following the contest, the visitors were treated to dinner by the Lindsay Hockey Club.

The next morning, the victorious Rebels left Lindsay by train for Toronto. "An endeavour will be made for the Lindsay to travel to Ottawa for a return match."[21]

Hockey had generated little in the way of interest in Toronto prior to the arrival of the Rideau Rebels hockey club that February. "If Montreal hockey clubs can attract thousands of spectators to see their games, there is no reason whatever why Toronto should not support the game equally as well," wrote *The Mail*, a daily newspaper in Toronto. "It is a lively winter game and is the only one that can take the place of lacrosse, baseball, etc. for the enjoyment of spectators."

On the afternoon of Saturday, 8 February, 1890, the Rebels beat a team from the Toronto Granite Club by a 5–4 score, with P. D. Ross once again scoring a pair of goals for the victors. That same evening, the Rebels faced Toronto's St. George's team at the Victoria Rink and lost 4–1. Ross scored the Rebels' only goal. Both games were littered with fights and high sticks, to the point that hockey received its first appreciable coverage in Toronto, albeit through editorials denouncing the violence of the game.

Nonetheless, over celebratory drinks, Arthur Stanley was able to elicit support from representatives of both opposing sides, convincing both the Granites and St. George's of the need for a hockey association and planting the seeds for the growth of the sport throughout Ontario.

Later that month, the Rebels hosted Lindsay at the Rideau Rink, edging the visitors 2–1 in the morning, after which the teams were entertained at a luncheon held in Rideau Hall. That evening, a rematch was held with Lord Stanley in attendance. Arthur Stanley and P. D. Ross played for the Rebels, who won for the second time by a 2–1 score. Following the contest, the teams retired to the exclusive Rideau Club, then returned to Rideau Hall for dancing, skating and tobogganing.

In March 1890, the Rebels went barnstorming to Kingston, where they faced the Queen's University team at the city's new covered rink. The more experienced Queen's club, attired in striped tricolour flannel sweaters, spanked the Rebels 8–1. James K. Smellie, who would later be named a registrar of the Supreme Court of Canada, scored four of the goals on the Rebels' netminder, Wingfield. After the game, the Rideau Rebels, including

Ross and Barron, visited the studio of James W. Powell for team photographs.

On that same trip, the Rebels, minus the Stanleys, faced the Royal Military College of Kingston and were thumped 7–2. The *Kingston Daily News* explained that the sons of the Governor General were "prevented from attending by circumstances under which they had no control."[22]

The excitement of these hockey challenge contests prompted serious discussions between Arthur Stanley and the various players he encountered along the way. These games provided the basis for an organized league. "Out of that series of games was evolved the Ontario Hockey Association," reported the *Toronto Daily Star*. The newspaper continued:

> *The game has taken a tremendous hold upon the interest of the Canadian people and it is not strange, for it typifies wonderfully the sturdy pluck, the courage, the stamina, the resolution, the dash and go that is lifting this country up and up to the heights of splendid achievement.*[23]

* * *

Before heading to Toronto from Ottawa on 26 November, 1890, Arthur Stanley convinced his father to be patron of what he hoped would be known as the Hockey Association of Ontario, an organization that would aid in the promotion of the game. Stanley urged two of his teammates, John Barron of Lindsay and Henry Ward from Port Hope, to join him in Toronto for the meeting.

Arthur's train connected at Kingston with the Grand Trunk's express train between Montreal and Toronto. Barron took the Lindsay train, one of twenty-one that made the daily commute to Toronto, and met Ward in Port Hope, where the two rendezvoused with Stanley's train. The three arrived in Toronto on an evening when the weather was raw, complete with blowing snow that set the three back on their heels as they crossed Front Street from the station to the Queen's Hotel.

Stanley, Barron and Ward discussed their plans for the next day's meeting. Meanwhile, back in Ottawa, other members of the Rebels convened with representatives of the Dey's Rink Pirates and Ottawa College with plans of forming a civic league in Ottawa.

On 27 November, Stanley, Barron and Ward were joined by thirteen other men to discuss the formation of a hockey association. At this point, a few teams were playing what *The Globe* identified as "the winter game of hockey, which may be roughly described as 'shinny' on skates and reduced to rules."[24]

Joining John Barron from Lindsay were Fred Knowlson, the town clerk, and A. F. D. MacGachen. Representing Durham was Bowmanville lawyer D. Burke Simpson. James Smellie, one of the prominent players for Queen's University, attended, as did W. A. H. Kerr from Royal Military College. William Hendrie Jr. arrived from Hamilton. Toronto's delegates were F. W. Jackson of the St. George's team, W. Robinson of Toronto's Athletic Lacrosse Club, C. R. Hamilton from the Victoria Rink, H. Green and J. S. Garvin, players with the Granites, J. Thompson from Osgoode Hall and Army Captain Thomas Dixon Byron Evans from "C" Company at Toronto's Royal Infantry School (a.k.a. the "New Fort").

The sixteen convened in an upstairs parlour at the Queen's Hotel, where the Ontario Hockey Association's meetings would be held every year through 1898.

Barron was chosen to chair the proceedings. The *Toronto Mail* reported:

> *Mr. Barron said the meeting had been called to organize a hockey association for Ontario, and he said this was very necessary, as he had found on his playing visit to Toronto with the vice regal and Parliamentary Hockey Club Rebels the previous winter that the Toronto clubs played too roughly, probably because they had no knowledge of the rules. The other representatives, all being evidently of the opinion that stringent rules should be formed against charging or any other form of rough play.*[25]

The league was born "on the motion of Mr. [Arthur] Stanley, seconded by Mr. [Henry] Ward, that the Hockey Association of Ontario should be organized."[26] The motion was approved unanimously, with all members in agreement that officers and other pertinent matters should then be discussed.

A letter was read from P. D. Ross, who regretted his inability to attend but promised that at least three first-rate hockey clubs from Ottawa would compete in the championships of the new association. One of the three

Ottawa teams would be the Ottawa Hockey Club, which had been a member of the Amateur Hockey Association of Canada since 1886. Having been an inaugural member of both fledgling leagues, the Ottawa Hockey Club continued to play in both until the 1895-96 season, when it dropped out of the OHA to concentrate exclusively on the AHAC.

Officers were elected. "It is not clear whether other persons joined the meeting or their ascent to election was obtained in advance, or was simply not obtained."[27] A. Morgan Cosby, manager of the London and Ontario Investment Company of Toronto and a player with the Victorias, was named the association's first president. Barron and Ward were named vice-presidents. C. K. Temple of St. George's became the first treasurer; C. R. Hamilton of the Victorias, its first secretary. A committee consisting of Ross, Smellie, Evans, Garvin, Hendrie, MacGachen, Kerr and Temple was put in charge of compiling a set of rules for the teams and by-laws for the association. Ten rules were drafted before the first season got underway.

Lieutenant-Colonel Cosby agreed to donate a trophy for the winner of the first series between the founding teams. The official rules stated:

> *The cup shall be called the Cosby Challenge Cup. It shall be open for competition only to clubs in the Ontario Hockey Association, and shall be played for under the regulations, rules of competition and rules of the game of that Association. The Secretary of the Association shall be, to all intents and purposes, the legal holder of the Cup, in trust, for the Association.28*

The OHA Challenge Cup, also known in its first three seasons as the Cosby Challenge Cup, is older than the Stanley Cup by two years, and was a "loving cup"[29] manufactured of silver with a gold wash on the interior and measuring fourteen-and-a-half inches from top to base.

The original association comprised thirteen teams, who were then divided into three groups — six from Toronto made up one grouping, the four Kingston clubs another, and the three Ottawa teams were joined by the team from Lindsay for the third group. An entrance fee of two dollars per team was set, with annual dues of another three dollars per club.

The new association was greeted with great enthusiasm. *The Canadian Illustrated News* opined:

The formation of the Ontario Hockey Association is good news for all lovers of the dashing winter sport. For years past, Montreal was practically the only place where really good hockey could be seen. But the western [Ontario] men have gone about it this time in the proper way and there is no reason why they should not be successful.[30]

* * *

The first season of the Ontario Hockey Association got underway with Ottawa playing host to Lindsay. Both the Rebels and the Ottawa Hockey Club played contests against the Lindsay squad, who lost both games by a goal. The Rebels then ventured to Kingston for a game in February 1891. Philip Ross, a key component on the team, described the trip in the *Ottawa Journal*. "The trip, both going and coming, was made extremely comfortable by the kindness of the Governor General, who loaned the team his private [railway] car."[31] The Stanley boys were not in the line-up for this contest; the Kingston team, made up of players from both the Royal Military College and Queen's University, played very well. "With the exception of the point [captain Guy Curtis], the home team played a thoroughly gentlemanly game and the match, although vigorous, was good-humoured and enjoyable throughout," reported Ottawa's *Journal*.[32] Ross scored one goal while Lord Kilcoursie also connected for a goal in a 3–2 loss for the Rebels.

The Toronto teams faced a serious challenge during this initial OHA season — they couldn't secure a rink. Most proprietors made a significant amount of income from pleasure skating and were unwilling to surrender their ice time to a sport that was considered more a nuisance than an asset. The Toronto final between St. George's and the Granites was scuttled when the Granites' rink was unavailable and the teams were unable to agree on a substitute. The Granites declined any further play, so St. George's was crowned Toronto's champion.

Meanwhile, in Kingston, Queen's blanked the Royal Military College and edged the Kingston club 4–3 to finish the season undefeated, and thus qualified to meet the Ottawa champion. But Ottawa hadn't yet declared a champion. The Ottawa Hockey Club,[33] led by P. D. Ross, was slated to play Lindsay for the championship, but Lindsay sent a telegraph cancelling the game and then folded its team. Ottawa then faced the Dey's Rink Pirates.

Lord and Lady Stanley and their family attended the contest at the Rideau Hall rink. With a goal contributed by Ross, the game ended in victory for Ottawa, the score either 3–0 or 4–0.[34] As a result, the Ottawa Hockey Club moved ahead to play Ottawa College for the division final. But the Ottawa Hockey Club was also part of the Amateur Hockey Association of Canada, and was scheduled to play the Montreal Amateur Athletic Association for what was being billed as the Canadian championship. Ottawa, with P. D. Ross absent from the lineup, lost to M.A.A.A. A few days later, with Ross back in the lineup, the Ottawa Hockey Club edged Ottawa College, 3–2.

On 28 February, 1891, the Ottawa club boarded the train for Kingston to challenge Queen's, where they thumped the university 4–0. While staying at the British American Hotel, the visitors discovered that the hotel was also hosting Prime Minister Sir John A. Macdonald, who had cut short his election campaigning to recover after becoming confused and weak during a speech in Napanee.

The general election, slated for 5 March, had forced the Rideau Rebels to withdraw from the playoffs as many of their players, including Barron and Ward, were involved in campaigning for re-election.

The championship contest took place 7 March, 1891, at Ottawa's Rideau Hall Rink. Amidst a thousand spectators sat Lord and Lady Stanley, there to witness Toronto's St. George's challenge against the Ottawa Hockey Club, both of whom were unbeaten in league play. "At 8:15, Mr. A. Z. Palmer, the referee, whistled the teams to their places for the opening face-off," reported *The Globe*. The Ottawa squad won handily, recording a 5–0 shutout. *The Globe* stated that the loss by St. George's was due to "inferiority to the Ottawas principally in skating and lifting of the puck."[35]

The Governor General hosted a party to celebrate the Ottawa Hockey Club's victory and to thank the St. George's club for their good sportsmanship. Ottawa were crowned the OHA champions on 7 March, 1891: A. Morel in goal, J. Kerr at point, W. C. Young at coverpoint, P. D. Ross, H. Kirby, C. Kirby and J. Smith at forward. Captained by Ross, the team was presented with the the Cosby Cup. Today, the ornate silver goblet is on permanent display at Queen's University in Kingston, Ontario, home of the OHA champions of 1895, 1896, 1897 and 1899.[36]

At the OHA's annual meeting on 3 December, 1898, John Ross Robertson, an MP for East Toronto, came forward with a magnificent solid silver challenge trophy to replace the Cosby Cup:

The cup, which is of tazza form, is made of purest Canadian silver. It is lined with Canadian gold and richly decorated with bas-relief of lions, masks and fells, which stand out from the piece in high relief. A striking feature of this cup are three leopard handles, beautifully modelled and chased. When Mr. Robertson made the presentation, the delegates were filled with delight and his speech emphasizing his faith in amateur sport was enthusiastically received by the gathering.[37]

Two weeks after the Ottawa Hockey Club won the Cosby Cup in 1891, St. George's — bruised but unbowed — invited the Ottawa team back to Toronto for an exhibition contest at the Arena Gardens, later to be known as the Mutual Street Arena. Ottawa won 4–0. That same evening, Ottawa beat Osgoode Hall, 6–2.

* * *

When the OHA executive for 1891–92 was named, Colonel Cosby earned a second term as president, while H. D. Warren from Toronto's Granite Club joined John Barron as league vice-presidents. Warren would assume the league's presidency the next season. The Ottawa Hockey Club took championship honours again in 1892, defeating the team from Osgoode Hall by a 10-4 score. "I never missed a championship match and in '91 and '92, Ottawa had a great team," stated Lord Kilcoursie. "The Kirbys, Kavanagh, Russell were all star players."[38]

The game had attained great popularity in Montreal, Ottawa and Kingston, but had not been taken up by the young men of the west until the organization of the [Ontario Hockey] Association. Hockey gradually became the winter sport of every city, town and hamlet of the province, and as the players in each locality increased, a team was formed and after a period, they sought admission to the OHA and today, the Association embraces in its membership clubs from every section of Ontario.[39]

In the meantime, the Amateur Hockey Association of Canada elected its officers for the 1893 season. F. M. Jenkins of Ottawa was elected President, J. Crathern of the Victorias first vice-president and A. Laurie of Quebec second vice-president. J. A. Findlay of Montreal was chosen as secretary-treasurer, while the council comprised A. Ritchie of the Crystals, G. Carpenter of the Montreal Shamrocks, M. Costigan of McGill, A. Palmer of the Ottawa Rebels and J. Farwell of Sherbrooke.[40]

During the annual meeting, held in mid-December of 1892, the Ottawa Hockey Club suggested a championship series to determine the best team in Canada, rather than the usual challenge contests employed previously. The idea was adopted, and a series involving the Montreal Hockey Club, the Crystals and Victorias, and teams from Quebec City and Ottawa would compete in an eight-game home-and-home schedule. At the end of the series, the team with the most wins would be declared the champion of the Dominion of Canada. The season began 7 January and concluded 17 March. Curiously, there was no mention of a championship trophy of any sort, let alone the trophy promised by Lord Stanley at the Ottawa team's banquet earlier that year.

What is considered to be the pivotal game of the season took place on 18 February, 1893, when the Montreal Hockey Club hosted Ottawa, with both teams having lost but one game to that point. A special train was commissioned to transport Ottawa fans to Montreal for the contest. Montreal won handily, 7–1. Although Ottawa still had one game remaining on its schedule, fans dismissed it. "The glory of hockey seems departed but the town can fall back on shooting and curling,"[41] suggested the *Ottawa Daily Journal.*

The Montreal A.A.A. finished its schedule with seven wins against one loss, including a victory by default when the Crystals refused to continue their 2–2 tie to determine a winner. They scored thirty-eight goals during the schedule, and allowed just eighteen. The Ottawa club, often called the Generals, won six and lost two. They scored forty-nine goals, allowing twenty-two. The Crystals finished third (three wins and five losses, scoring twenty-five goals and allowing thirty-four) and Quebec fourth (two wins, five losses and a tie, with twenty-three goals for and forty-six against). The Victorias brought up the rear, winning just one game, losing six and tying a contest with Quebec. They scored twenty and allowed thirty-five goals.

The Montreal Amateur Athletic Association won the AHAC title and, as a result, were considered "world champions."

* * *

Reviewing the winter of 1892–93, H. J. Woodside said that it was marked:

> ... *by a wave of hockey that rolled over the North-West like a flood. No town or village with any pretensions but had its hockey club. In Winnipeg, the game basked in the popular and Vice Regal favour, and spread and flourished until the city poured out its teams as did Thebes its armies from a hundred gates.*[42]

With hockey evolving into a popular and highly competitive sport, the Stanley siblings showed great enthusiasm for the sport, a passion that rapidly permeated through social and political intimates of the vice regal family. "Algy was the best and his sister Isobel the neatest, but we were all just good enough to play for a club called the Rebels, and in our red shirts, to challenge amateur teams in many of the surrounding towns," recalled Lord Kilcoursie in his memoirs.[43] Stanley's sons had been surprised to learn that hockey was of relatively recent vintage and had grown quite proficient at the new game. Even Billy, the youngest Stanley, was becoming quite good at the game. With his shock of blond hair and blue eyes, the youngster was known to be an enthusiastic lover of drama, but in 1892 the *Ottawa Journal* reported that Billy, not yet fourteen years of age, "is a hockey player of no mean prowess."[44] Edward, Arthur and Algernon, along with Rebel colleagues Lord Kilcoursie and Philip D. Ross, persuaded Lord Stanley to donate a trophy for hockey.

But the idea, though both pertinent and important, was not necessarily original. As early as December 1890, *The Dominion Illustrated Monthly*, produced in Montreal, was calling for a symbol of hockey supremacy:

> *Why not have the champions of both associations (the Amateur Hockey Association of Canada and the Ontario Hockey Association) play off at the end of the season for the championship of the Dominion? If the secretaries of both*

associations would communicate with each other, there is hardly a likelihood of any difficulty being thrown in the way, and if a public interest, something similar to that taken in lacrosse, could be aroused, it would give a great impetus, especially in the West, than any the game has yet had.[45]

The idea was suggested again a year later:

Why not arrange a match for the championship of Canada, between the champions of Ontario and the champions of Quebec, after the manner of the football players? It seems to me it would need but a very small amount of negotiation, and if the newly elected council of the Hockey association would just consider the matter and make the first proposal, there would be scarcely and difficulty in coming to some satisfactory arrangement.[46]

The sport, as raw and underdeveloped as the land itself, was now being played in Montreal, Ottawa and Quebec City as well as Kingston, Toronto and a handful of smaller centres, and was beginning to find favour in western Canada, specifically in the Winnipeg area. There were now dozens of teams and a few leagues, but no indication on how a national champion was to be determined each year. Still, Lord Stanley "had contributed the last piece of the puzzle — the prize that went to the champion. The rest remained to be invented."[47]

Captain Charles Colville, who had served as Lord Stanley's secretary during the early years of his term as Governor General, was entrusted to purchase such a trophy. Colville, born into aristocracy as the first-born of Lord Charles John Colville, had, like Stanley, been a member of the Grenadier Guards. Prior to joining the Governor General in Canada, Captain Colville participated in the Zulu campaign in South Africa in 1879 and was aide-de-camp to the Commander-in-Chief of Bombay. He was appointed to the position of secretary to the Governor General in August 1888 at a salary of three thousand dollars per year. The thirty-eight-year-old Colville, along with his wife, the former Ruby Streatfeild, had been a member of the vice regal suite that travelled across Canada with Lord and Lady Stanley in 1889, but by 1892, Captain Colville had returned to

England, where he embarked on a search for the proper trophy for Lord Stanley to present to the hockey champion of Canada.

Colville's search began and ended in the shop of George Richmond Collis & Company.[48] Originally based in Birmingham, Collis's shop had relocated to 130 Regent Street in London's West End, just off Piccadilly Circus between Mayfair to the west and Soho to the east. From the time the street was built — and named to honour the Prince Regent, later to become King George IV — Regent Street has been a hub of commercial activity in London.

Captain Colville selected a silver bowl lined with a gold-gilt interior. At ten guineas, the price tag was roughly equivalent to fifty Canadian dollars; in today's dollars, however, the price would be between $5,500 and $8,900, making it a much more significant purchase than many realize.[49]

According to a document prepared on 30 July, 1992, by Robert C. Parks of Toronto-based Parks Johnson Fine Arts Services, Lord Stanley's Cup was described as:

> ... *a late Victorian electroplated silver punch bowl with a plain moulded rim above a repousse swirl-fluted and shaped band, above a plain inscription band crested and inscribed 'From Stanley of Preston' and 'Dominion Hockey Challenge Cup,' supported on a swirl-fluted pedestal base, the whole supported on an ebony column. Made in Sheffield, England and retailed by G.H. [sic] Collis, Regent Street, London, circa 1890.*[50]

Standing eighteen and a half centimetres (or about seven and a quarter inches) tall and twenty-nine centimetres (about eleven and a half inches) in diameter, under the engraved legend "From Stanley of Preston" is the Stanley family crest, consisting of "the eagle and child." There is a tale of great intrigue behind this crest.

Sir Thomas Latham, who died in 1385, had hoped to father a male heir with his wife, Joanna. When no child was conceived, likely due to Joanna's age, Latham had "a love intrigue" with a woman who bore him the son he so desired. Sir Thomas was delighted, but he needed to bring the child into the family without upsetting his wife. After a great deal of thought, Latham decided to leave the baby in a spot in a nearby park where an eagle was known to have her nest. Then, he would happen upon the baby as if by accident and adopt it.

The devious plan went as intended and Joanna was delighted, agreeing to raise the child as her own. The baby boy was named "Oskatell" after his true birth-mother, Mary Oskatell. In creating a family crest, Sir Thomas Latham adopted an eagle turning its head back as if searching for something lost.

As Sir Thomas aged, he realized it was important to put his house in order. He declared as his rightful heirs the children of his daughter Isabel, who had married Sir John Stanley, and Oskatell as his only son. Sir Oskatell Latham was denounced and supplanted, and the Stanley family reworked the crest to show their conquest over him. "The Eagle and Child" was created, this time, with the eagle looking down on the child as if it were prey. [51]

* * *

Realizing that his term as governor general was coming to an end, Lord Stanley invited two respected Ottawa businessmen to administer the new hockey trophy. These trustees were given "absolute authority in all situations or disputes over the winner of the cup."[52] The two men were Philip Dansken Ross and John Sweetland.

John Sweetland was born 15 August, 1835, in Kingston, Ontario. In 1858, at the age of twenty-three, he graduated with his medical degree from Queen's University, and he practised medicine in Pakenham, a small community west of Ottawa, until 1866, when he moved to the nation's capital.

For many years, Dr. Sweetland was an Ottawa coroner and a surgeon at both the Ottawa General Hospital and the Carleton County Jail. He was also the surgeon of the Unity Protestant Benefit Society, the Foresters and the Oddfellows. In 1877, he was named president of the Ottawa Medico-Chirurgical Society, and was later Ontario's secretary of the Canada Medical Association. For two years, the doctor was president of the Ottawa Poor Relief Society and a founding director of Ottawa Ladies' College. He was also a commissioner of the Ottawa Water Works during its construction. In 1880, he was made a sheriff in the County of Carleton, which gave him the title of Sheriff of the Supreme Court of Canada.

For seven years, Sheriff Sweetland was president of the St. George's Society of Ottawa, an organization that helped provide money, food and medical assistance to those in need who were of British origin.

One of the founding directors of the Beechwood Cemetery Company on its opening in 1873, Sweetland became its long-time president. Located close to Ottawa's Parliament Hill, Beechwood consists of one hundred sixty acres of former farmland that has become the final resting spot for politicians, builders and an astonishing number of hockey players. Among those buried in Beechwood Cemetery are Clint Benedict, Bill Beveridge, Buck Boucher, Punch Broadbent, Harold and Jack Darragh, Eddie Gerard, David and Billy Gilmour, Bowse Hutton, Rene Joliat, Harvey Pulford, Hamby Shore, Bruce Stuart and Harry Westwick.

The Governor General's choice of Sheriff John Sweetland was above reproach: "He is a man of very noble impulses and untiring in his efforts to aid in promoting the best interests of his fellow beings."[53]

Sweetland died on 5 May, 1907, in Ottawa. It is no surprise that he, too, is buried in Beechwood Cemetery. In fact, when his partner, Philip Ross, died in 1949, he too was buried in Beechwood.

* * *

Born in Montreal on New Year's Day, 1858, Philip Dansken Ross had earned his engineering degree from McGill by the age of twenty. An elite athlete, in 1855, his first year at the Montreal university, Ross made the school's rugby team, and captained the squad the next two years, including a victory over Harvard in 1878 in Canada's first international contest. Ross was the singles sculling champion of Quebec and he twice stroked four-oared crews to Canadian championships. He starred in lacrosse, was an expert gymnast, a fine fencer and a proficient boxer. While a university student, Ross organized and played for McGill's hockey team.

After working for a few months in 1878 as an engineer with the Montreal Harbour Commission, Philip began a career in newspapers, joining the *Montreal Star* as a reporter in 1879, earning five dollars per week. Within six months, he was promoted to city editor. After brief periods of employment with the *Toronto Mail* and the *Toronto Daily News*, Ross returned to Montreal in 1885 as managing editor of the *Star*.

In 1886, he moved to Ottawa to cover Parliament for the *Star*. That same year, using four thousand dollars he borrowed from his mother, P. D. bought a half interest in the *Ottawa Journal*. The paper teetered on the brink of bankruptcy until Charles Magee, president of the Bank of Ottawa and a colleague on the board of directors of the Central Fair, endorsed a note that allowed Ross to purchase the *Journal* outright in 1891. P. D. turned the daily around, and remained its president until his death in 1949.

Ross involved himself heavily in Ottawa's social and sporting circles. In 1886, he founded and was named first president of the Ottawa Amateur Athletic Association. In September of that year, a clubhouse was built at Elgin and Maria streets. Sir John A. Macdonald formally opened the clubhouse on 20 November, 1886.

Ross held the office of secretary for the St. Andrew's Society between 1888 and 1890, and was its second vice-president in 1890-91. The Society is an association that preserves Scottish culture while raising money for benevolent causes.

Most importantly to hockey's history, Philip Ross became a frequent teammate of the Stanley boys with the Rideau Rebels. An excellent forward with the Rebels, Ross also starred with the Ottawa Hockey Club between 1892 and 1895, leading the team to the Ontario championship in three of five seasons. Ross also later became president of the club. Although hockey was little more than a game played primarily in Ottawa, Montreal and Halifax when Ross was first finding his hockey legs, he helped infuse a great enthusiasm for the game in the Stanley boys. Together with Arthur Stanley, in 1892, Ross helped create the Ontario Hockey Association, becoming the fledgling league's first vice-president.

After the Governor General was persuaded to offer a trophy for Canada's hockey champion, he appointed Ross as one of the Stanley Cup's first two trustees, an honour which he held until late in his life.

Ross's selection as trustee was an intriguing choice. It didn't seem to concern anyone that P. D. Ross faced a conflict of interest by acting as a trustee at the same time he was president of the Ottawa Hockey Club, one of the teams that would compete for the new trophy. But Ross was an exemplary choice. He proved his integrity by never once allowing favouritism to shade his decisions. "An admirable citizen, a credit to his profession and a capable master of detail," stated an obituary. "He is a self-made man, having started at the bottom of the ladder and by his splendid qualities, become the head of the most quoted paper in Canada."[54]

Ross was so reliable and fair, in fact, that in 1901 he was appointed a trustee of lacrosse's championship trophy, the Minto Lacrosse Challenge Cup, also donated by a Governor General (this time, Canada's eighth vice regal, the Earl of Minto, who served between 1898 and 1904). However, Ross turned down the opportunity to also act as trustee of football's Grey Cup, donated in 1909 by the 4th Earl Grey, who between 1904 and 1911, served as Canada's ninth governor general. Ross was also active in local politics, first serving as an alderman in the City of Ottawa in 1902.[55]

When his colleague, Sheriff Sweetland, died in 1907, P. D. Ross appointed William A. Foran as his fellow trustee. Ross himself remained a trustee of the Stanley Cup until 24 February, 1946, when, at the age of eighty-eight, he felt that his age was such that he should appoint a successor. He chose J. Cooper Smeaton to succeed him. Philip Dansken Ross died in Ottawa on 5 July, 1949. In 1976, he was posthumously inducted into the Hockey Hall of Fame in the Builder Category.

* * *

The Dominion Hockey Challenge Cup arrived at Rideau Hall for the first time at the beginning of May 1893. The trophy, which has long enjoyed iconic status and worldwide recognition, made no such impression upon its donor. When a British sportswriter asked Lord Stanley to describe the Cup, he shrugged and replied, "It looks like any other trophy, I suppose."[56]

Although Lord Stanley had ordained in 1892 that hockey championship trophy would be donated, the regulations governing how the trophy would be awarded were not outlined until early in 1893. Stanley, who arranged to have the trophy kept at the residence of trustee John Sweetland, conferred with his trustees, in whom he vested "absolute authority in all situations or disputes over the winner of the cup," and devised these conditions for its presentation:

1. *The winner to give bond for the return of the Cup in good order when required by the trustees for the purpose of being handed over to any other team who may in turn win.*

2. *Each winning team to have at their own charge engraved on a silver ring fitted on the Cup for the purpose, the name of the team and the year won.*

3. *The Cup shall remain a challenge cup and will not become the property of any team, even if won more than once.*

4. *In case of any doubt as to the title of any club to claim the position of champions, the Cup shall be held or awarded by the trustees as they might think right, their decision being absolute.*

5. *Should either trustee resign or otherwise drop out, the remaining trustee shall nominate a substitute.*[57]

Complicating matters was the fact that Stanley hadn't specified that the Cup be awarded to the champion of any particular league; meanwhile, there were now two organizations, the Amateur Hockey Association of Canada and the Ontario Hockey Association, vying for the status of the Dominion's pre-eminent hockey league.

Philip Ross and Lord Kilcoursie, teammates on the Rideau Rebels, met in late April 1893 at the Rideau Club in Ottawa to discuss conditions for the new trophy. Then, as Stanley requested, Ross and Sweetland, the trustees, drafted their suggested guidelines to govern the competition for the new trophy. It is noteworthy that, although the Cup bore the legend "Dominion Hockey Challenge Cup," the trustees ordained that it would henceforth officially commemorate the name of its donor:

1. *The cup to be called the Stanley Hockey Championship Cup.*

2. *The Cup to be held by the M.A.A.A. team [Montreal Hockey Club] until the championship of the association to which the team belongs, namely the Amateur Hockey Association of Canada, be decided next year, when the Cup shall go to the winning team.*

3. *In order, however, that the Ontario Hockey Association shall have an equal interest in the Cup, the AHAC and the OHA are requested to each arrange its season so that there shall be an opportunity for a final match between the champion teams of the two organizations.*

4. *The trustees respectfully suggest to the associations that this could be done by each association arranging to close*

its separate championship contest not later than the first Saturday in March.

5. *If the above suggestion were adopted, the championship of the AHAC would accordingly be settled next year on 3 March, and also possession of the Stanley Cup so far as the association is concerned. Then the winner might be open to challenge from the champion club of the Ontario association.*

6. *Then and thereafter, a challenge from the champion club of one association to a champion club of the other holding the Cup might be sent under the following conditions:*

   a) *The fact that the club winning the Ontario championship may also belong to and have been defeated in the AHAC series, shall not debar it from challenging for the Stanley Cup; and vice versa, the fact that the Ontario champions may also have won it in the AHAC series shall not debar the second best team in the OHA series from challenging the champions for a final match. (The object of this is to continue the interest in the game up to the very close of the season.)*[58]

   b) *Should any representative provincial hockey association outside of Quebec and Ontario desire to compete for the Cup, the trustees shall endeavour to arrange means whereby its champion team may secure an opportunity to play for it.*

   c) *In case a senior league is ever formed representing the best hockey irrespective of local associations, the trustees may give its winning club the right to challenge for the Cup, and if successful, to hold it thereafter subject to new championship regulations.*[59]

The trustees would later add the following "Hockey Cup Rules":

1. *So far as any league or association in which the Cup is held is concerned, the Cup goes with the championship*

of that league each year without the necessity of any special or extra contest.

2. *Challenges are recognized by the trustees only from champion clubs of senior hockey leagues.*

3. *When a challenge is accepted, the trustees desire the competing clubs to arrange by mutual agreement, all terms of the contest themselves, such as choice of date or dates for matches, choice of rink, division of the gate money, selection of officials, etc., etc. The trustees do not wish to interfere in any way, shape or form if it can be avoided.*

4. *Where competing clubs fail to agree, the trustees have observed and will continue to observe as far as practicable, the following principles:*

   a) *Cup to be awarded by the result of one match, or of the most goals in two matches, as the trustees may consider fair.*

   b) *Contest to take place on ice in the home city, the date or dates and choice of rink to be made or approved by the trustees.*

   c) *The net gate money obtained from the arrangements with the rink to be divided equally between the competing teams.*

   d) *If the clubs fail to agree on a referee, the trustees shall appoint him, the two clubs to share any expense equally.*

   e) *If the clubs fail to agree on other officials, the trustees shall either appoint them, the expense, if any, to be shared equally by the competing clubs.*

   f) *No second challenge recognized in one season from the same hockey association.*

   g) *Except where the club which holds the Cup is willing to agree to an earlier contest, the trustees do not undertake to require a contest in any league season on a date earlier than 28 February in any year, so as to allow the league in which the Cup is held to complete its season before being called on to defend the Cup.*

5.   *The trustees do not consider eligible to play in a contest for the Stanley Cup at the close of the ordinary hockey season players who during that season were not regular members of the teams concerned. In the case of challenges accepted for matches to be played at or prior to the opening of the regular hockey season, the trustees will consider requests for the authorization of bona fide changes rendered necessary in the teams since the preceding season.*[60]

* * *

It was no secret which team Lord Stanley hoped would win the first Stanley Cup championship. "It had been the fond hope of its donor that the first holder of the sterling silver bowl would be his favourite Ottawa club," wrote Henry Roxborough in his 1971 work *The Stanley Cup Story*. "However, this wish was not fulfilled."[61]

The Ottawa Hockey Club, as expected, had been crowned champion of the Ontario Hockey Association in 1893. But in the Amateur Hockey Association of Canada, in which Ottawa also played, what is acknowledged as the championship game took place on 18 February, and resulted in a 7–1 win by the Montreal squad over Ottawa. "His Excellency directed that for the year 1893, the Cup should be presented to the Montreal Amateur Athletic Association," reported Montreal's *Gazette*.[62] The M.A.A.A. had "defeated all comers during the late season (1892–93), including the champions of the Ontario Association."

One of the terms under which the Stanley Cup was to be awarded to champions was that the victor was to assume responsibility for engraving its name and the year of its victory on the trophy. In parentheses, the terms included, "In the first instance, the M.A.A.A. will find the Cup already engraved for them," and so it was: "Montreal AAA 1893."

Lord Kilcoursie sent a telegram to the M.A.A.A., asking when the club's annual meeting would take place so that the Stanley Cup could be presented. Advised that it would be on the fifteenth of May, P. D. Ross informed M.A.A.A. secretary W.S. Weldon that Sheriff Sweetland would be arriving in Montreal on that date with the Cup. On the instruction of M.A.A.A. president James A. Taylor, Weldon informed Montreal Hockey

Club president James Stewart, also a member of the team, that he was to be present to receive the Cup. "It was going to be a grand occasion, and to emphasize the board's pride in the team's accomplishment, engraved gold rings would be presented to the players." Those who were to receive these rings included forward Billy Barlow, cover point Allan Cameron (by day, a salesman for Liebling's liquid extract and tonic invigorator), Archie Hodgson, substitute Alex Irvine (a bookkeeper), substitute forward Alex Kingan (also a bookkeeper), substitute George Lowe (a bank clerk), goalkeeper Tom Paton (a manufacturer's agent who was very active in the M.A.A.A. and is credited with introducing to the club the game of quoits[63]), Haviland Routh (the league's leading scorer with twelve goals in seven games) and point James Stewart.[64]

The press was invited to witness the special occasion. But executives with the Montreal Hockey Club declined to accept the trophy until "the proper representatives of said club had an opportunity of learning the conditions upon which said trophy was to be held."[65] Upon reading this missive, M.A.A.A. president Taylor grew furious and decided that the ceremony would commence as originally planned, and that *he* would accept the trophy on behalf of the hockey team.[66]

The M.A.A.A. board met an hour before the appointed time of the presentation, and agreed to accept Lord Stanley's Cup. Without a doubt, there were board members squirming in their seats — none more than Tom Paton, who not only served on the M.A.A.A. board but was an integral component of the hockey team. Almost immediately after the board meeting ended, the annual meeting began. "Mr. W. L. Maltby [a premier snowshoer with the Montreal Snowshoe Club and an executive of the Montreal Amateur Athletic Association] led a handsome-looking elderly gentleman to the platform, accompanied by a mahogany box. The gentleman proved to be Sheriff Sweetland of Ottawa, and the box contained the Governor General's hockey trophy.'"[67]

The first order of business that evening was to introduce Sweetland as the governor general's representative. *The Gazette* commented:

> *Mr. Sweetland said it gave him the greatest pleasure to meet*
> *the members of the M.A.A.A. for the first time. He quite un-*
> *derstood the courtesy of the president in suspending the*
> *regular order of business and he did not want to trespass on*

> their time. He would simply remark that His Excellency took
> great interest in hockey and had frequently made known his
> intention of giving a trophy. The only conditions attached to
> the Cup would be submitted officially at the annual meeting
> of the hockey association, and it was expected that the con-
> ditions would be agreeable to all clubs concerned. The last
> season, however, the Governor General thought that
> Montreal was justly entitled to the championship trophy.

Sweetland then presented the Stanley Cup, for the first time, to M.A.A.A. president Taylor, "owing to the unavoidable absence of Mr. Stewart, the president of the Montreal Hockey Club."[68] Taylor proudly accepted the trophy and made a short but dignified speech, which was followed by other congratulatory comments. Curiously, "the audience wanted to know if there was anything the matter with Mr. Sweetland, and finding out to their own satisfaction that there was not, the regular business of the meeting was proceeded with."[69] The members of the championship squad were then presented with their rings — the names of those who were actually present was not noted. Next, a Heintzman piano was presented to Tom Paton for services rendered to the M.A.A.A. *The Gazette* later reported that "none of the officials of the Montreal Hockey Club were present." Paton, incidentally, was elected president of the M.A.A.A. later that evening.

The problems between the Montreal Hockey Club and the M.A.A.A. were temporarily buried, until November 1893, when the Stanley Cup discussion resurfaced — led by new president Paton, who noted that his predecessor had contemplated returning the Stanley Cup to the trustees on behalf of the Montreal Hockey Club. The ensuing discussion insisted that "such action would tend to lower the name of this association in the eyes of the general public."

A committee was formed to meet with a group of hockey club representatives, including playing president James Stewart, to discuss the contentious issues. The committee returned, having discovered that the noses of the hockey club were out of joint at not having been consulted directly by the Stanley Cup trustees in matters regarding their championship. The M.A.A.A. asked the Montreal Hockey Club to poll all of its members (there were approximately thirty, which included players from both the championship senior team as well as an intermediate team) for their views;

the hockey club declined, arousing suspicion that the spokesmen who were taking a hard line did not necessarily speak for the entire group.

Meanwhile, proceeding as though the relationship was normal, the Montreal Hockey Club requested, as it did each year, a loan for initial expenses for the season ahead, to be repaid to the A.A.A. from gate receipts. What ordinarily was granted without thought was deferred, and ultimately the request for one hundred and seventy-five dollars was summarily denied. Curiously, at the conclusion of the 1893 season, the hockey team handed the M.A.A.A. board a cheque for $62.72 'in recognition of past financial assistance received by the Montreal Hockey Club.'[70]

The M.A.A.A. also decided to hold the Stanley Cup in trust until the trustees had decided how to handle the situation. The hockey club responded by contacting Dr. Sweetland directly, letting him know that they had not received the trophy and wondering how they could arrange to receive the Cup.

P. D. Ross, whose brother James was a board member of the M.A.A.A. and would surely have divulged the ongoing activities with the Cup, attended a meeting of the AHAC on 24 February, 1894. While there, he met with the Montreal Hockey Club's president, James Stewart, and that evening attended a hockey game with his brother. It appears that these meetings resolved the controversy, as three days later, separate letters were sent to the M.A.A.A. and the Montreal Hockey Club, signed by trustees Sweetland and Ross, confirming arrangements to present the Stanley Cup to the Montreal Hockey Club at the time when the 1894 championship was decided. The letter to Stewart referred to an "accidental misunderstanding" and let him know that the M.A.A.A. would comply with the transfer. To the M.A.A.A., Sweetland and Ross wrote that the directors of the association "are hereby requested and authorized to deliver the Stanley hockey challenge cup, which they have kindly had in their care, to the order of Mr. J. A. Stewart, president of the Montreal Hockey Club."

Between 5 and 15 March, 1894, the Stanley Cup was finally delivered to the Montreal Hockey Club for its 1893 win. On Holy Thursday, 22 March, the first actual Stanley Cup championship game took place in Montreal between the Montreal Hockey Club and the Ottawa Hockey Club. Lord Frederick Stanley, now the Earl of Derby, was not in attendance to watch as his trophy was competed for; he had returned to England the previous year.

Five thousand fans lined the edges of the Victoria Rink. "Never before in the history of the game was such a crowd present or such enthusiasm evident," reported the *Montreal Gazette*. "Tin horns, strong lungs and a general rabble predominated."[71] It was an exciting game enjoyed by all on hand. The Ottawa club broke the shutout early with a goal from Chauncy Kirby. Through the first half, Ottawa dominated on the strength of inspired play by Harvey Pulford, but were unable to add to their lead. "The Montreal defence seemed impregnable while the forwards rushed that puck around in a way that made the Ottawa men nervous."[72] Ottawa's Weldy Young was carried from the ice after fainting from exhaustion. Montreal then scored three unanswered goals and won the contest by a 3–1 margin. The moment the game concluded, fans crowded onto the natural ice surface and carried hero Billy Barlow, who had scored twice for the victors, off the ice on their shoulders.

For the Montreal Hockey Club, it was their second consecutive Stanley Cup championship. On 22 April, Secretary H. Shaw was instructed to send Lord Stanley's Cup out for engraving, and when the trophy was returned, it read, simply, "Montreal, 1894." Although the Montreal Hockey Club had been pleased to avail itself of the benefits that went along with being part of the Montreal Amateur Athletic Association, it had balked at being considered one and the same with the M.A.A.A., whose motto, ironically, is *"Jungor ut Implear"* — "I am joined in order that I may compete."[73]

---

[1] *Ottawa Daily Journal* (19 March, 1892).

[2] *Ottawa Daily Citizen* (19 March, 1892), *edition cover page*.

[3] 'Stars of the Ice-The Dinner to the Ottawa Hockey Team. Lord Stanley Gives a Challenge Cup Open to the Dominion, to be Competed for Next Year-A Successful Reunion', *The Ottawa Journal* (19 March, 1892), *edition cover page*.

[4] *Ottawa Daily Journal* (19 March, 1892), *edition cover page*.

[5] Ibid.

[6] Ibid.

[7] Kilcoursie, *Recollections Hazy But Happy*.

[8] *Outing* (New York: November 1886).

[9] *Montreal Gazette* (4 March, 1892).

[10] J. Whalen, 'Kings of the Ice', *The Beaver* (February/March 1994), p.31.

[11] *Montreal Gazette* (9 December, 1886).

[12] Paton was instrumental in introducing hockey to Toronto. In early 1888, he discovered that Toronto was not familiar with the game of hockey. He telegraphed back home to Montreal, asking that sticks and a puck be sent to him in Toronto. They arrived by train the next day and a group of men scrimmaged on the ice at the Granite Curling Club, located on Church Street. On February 16, 1888, the first recorded

hockey game in Toronto took place — a 4–1 win by the Granite Curling Club over the Caledonians Curling Club.

[13] *Ottawa Daily Journal* (1891); *Gathorne-Hardy Papers*, National Archives of Canada.

[14] A. Podnieks, *Lord Stanley's Cup*, (Toronto: Fenn Publishing, 2004), p.19.

[15] E. Stanley, *Letter to Major J.S. Matthews, City of Vancouver Archives*, (Vancouver: c.1948).

[16] *Canadian Post* (Lindsay: January 1890).

[17] Ibid.

[18] Ibid.

[19] Ibid.

[20] Ibid.

[21] *Canadian Post* (14 February, 1890).

[22] *Kingston Daily News* (February 1890).

[23] *Daily Star* (Toronto: 19 November 19, 1910), p.24.

[24] *The Globe* (Toronto); *Gathorne-Hardy Papers*, National Archives Of Canada.

[25] *Daily Mail* (Toronto: 29 November, 1890).

[26] *The Globe* (Toronto: 28 Nov, 1890).

[27] Young, *100 Years of Dropping the Puck*, p.15.

[28] Ontario Hockey Association, *Constitution, Rules of Competition and Laws of the Game, Groupings of Clubs and Schedule of Matches* (1914–15), p.8.

[29] An ornamental vessel made of silver and having two or more handles, given as an award at sporting events.

[30] 'Lacrosse on Skates', *Canadian Illustrated News* (August 1878).

[31] *Ottawa Daily Journal* (February 1891).

[32] Ibid.

[33] The team was referred to as either the Generals or the Capitals in various newspaper reports, but officially, the team name was simply the Ottawa Hockey Club.

[34] The fourth goal was scored as one of the Pirates broke his stick-which, according to the new rules, meant the play must immediately halt so that the sides could be evened up by having Ottawa lose a player to match the one the Pirates lost. In their reports, one Ottawa newspaper allowed the goal; the other did not.

[35] *The Globe* (Toronto: 8 March, 1891).

[36] K. Shea, *Interview with Henk Pardoel*, Sport Information Co-ordinator, Queen's Athletics, Queen's University, (Kingston: 9 January, 2006).

[37] Ontario Hockey Association, *Constitution*, p.8.

[38] Kilcoursie, *Recollections Hazy But Happy*.

[39] Ontario Hockey Association, *Constitution*, p.8.

[40] *Ottawa Daily Journal* (15 December, 1892).

[41] *Ottawa Daily Journal* (22 February, 1893).

[42] *Canadian Magazine*, "Hockey in the Canadian North-West," H.J.Woodside, January 1896

[43] Kilcoursie, *Recollections Hazy But Happy*.

[44] *Ottawa Daily Journal* (28 March, 1892).

[45] *The Dominion Illustrated Monthly* (Montreal: 20 December, 1890), p.405.

[46] *The Dominion Illustrated Monthly* (Montreal: 5 December, 1891), p.552.

[47] D. Jenish, *The Stanley Cup* (Toronto: McClelland & Stewart, 1992).

[48] *Toronto Daily Star* (17 March, 1909).

[49] E. Zweig, 'The Value of the Stanley Cup', *Society for International Hockey Research (SIHR) Journal* (Toronto: Fall 2005), p.68.

[50] Document housed at the Hockey Hall of Fame.

[51] F. Espinasse, *Lancashire Worthies* (London: Simpkin, Marshall, & Co. Stationers Hall Court, 1874).

52 One of the conditions of the Stanley Cup as outlined by Lord Stanley.

53 *1880 Canadian Biographical Dictionary and Portrait Gallery of Eminent and Self-Made Men* (Toronto: American Biographical Publications, 1880).

54 *Sault Ste. Marie Star* (6 July, 1949).

55 C. G. Roberts & A. L. Tunnel (*eds*), *Canadian Who's Who, 1936–37* (London: Times Publishing Co., 1936).

56 M. Abramson & B. Abramson, 'Lord Stanley's Priceless $48.67 Cup', *TWA Ambassador* (March 1973), p.8.

57 *Montreal Gazette* (1 May, 1893).

58 This condition was clearly aimed directly at the Ottawa Hockey Club, which was competing in both the AHAC and the OHA.

59 P. D. Ross, *Diary*, National Archives of Canada, (1 & 2 May, 1893).

60 Hockey Cup Rules, Hockey Hall of Fame Archives

61 H. Roxborough, *The Stanley Cup Story* (Toronto: McGraw Hill Ryerson Limited, 1971).

62 *Montreal Gazette* (23 February, 1894).

63 Quoits is a game similar to horseshoes.

64 Montreal Hockey Club members' day jobs from, Podineks, *Lord Stanley's Cup*, p.19.

65 *Board Minutes* from the Montreal Amateur Athletic Association.

66 Kitchen, 'They Refused the Cup', pp.20–4.

67 *Montreal Gazette* (16 May, 1893), p.8.

68 *Board Minutes* from the Montreal Amateur Athletic Association.

69 *Montreal Gazette* (16 May, 1893), p.8.

70 *Board Minutes* from the Montreal Amateur Athletic Association.

71 *Montreal Gazette* (23 March, 1894).

72 Ibid.

73 Kitchen, 'They Refused the Cup', pp.20–4.

Chapter Sixteen

1893

On 24 January, 1893, the Governor General's new military secretary, Major St. Aubyn, announced that two days later His Excellency, Lord Stanley, would open a Parliamentary session for the last time.

Precisely at three o'clock, Lord Stanley was introduced and began his address:

> *Honourable gentlemen of the Senate, gentlemen of the House of Commons. In meeting you at the commencement of another session of Parliament, it affords me pleasure to congratulate you on the continued progress which the history of the past year unfolds with regard to Canada.*
>
> *The increase in trade, as illustrated by the exports and imports during the period for which the official returns have been prepared, has been most gratifying, and that increase has continued down to the present time, with promise that the volume of trade during the current year will exceed that of any year in the history of the Dominion.*
>
> *The revenues of the country have likewise provided for all the services for which Parliament has made appropriation, and the operation of the Government railways has been less burdensome, as regards the difference between income and expenditure, than has been the case for a long term of years previously.*
>
> *In Manitoba and the North-West Territories, the increase in immigration has been decidedly encouraging, both*

as regards the number of persons who have come from other countries and as regards the number of homestead entries made by settlers of all nationalities.

Measures have been taken to carry into effect the agreements arrived at with the United States on the subjects of the boundary of Alaska, the boundary line in Passamaquoddy Bay, and the prevention of destructive methods of fishing and the preservation and increase of fish life. With regard to reciprocity in wrecking and towing, a correspondence has taken place which indicates that privileges are demanded for United States' vessels in Canadian canals, which were not anticipated, but it is not impossible that a satisfactory conclusion of the discussion may yet be reached.

During the recess, a friendly conference took place between delegates from my Government and from the Government of Newfoundland on the questions which were pending between the two countries. It is hoped and expected that the interchange of views which then took [place will be productive of beneficial results and lead to an amicable adjustment of those questions.

The Statutes of 1887 relative to a Department of Trade and Commerce and to the office of the Solicitor General having been brought into force, the appointments were made which were contemplated by these Acts.

It is to be regretted that the Government of the United States was unable to accept the suggestions made by my Government on the subject of canal tolls, and that the President should have thought it necessary to impose exceptional tolls on Canadians using the Sault Ste. Marie canal, which has so long been free to the people of both countries. My Government, while ready to consider in a friendly spirit any proposals which may be made by the Government of the United States, has caused efforts to be made to hasten the completion of the Canadian canal works, which will soon afford to the commerce of the Dominion, a highway within our own country.

> *Measures will be laid before you for the improvement*
> *of the Franchise Act, for the amendment of the laws relating*
> *to the Civil Service and the superannuation of civil ser-*
> *vants, for regulating the admission of evidence in cases and*
> *matters under the control of the Parliament of Canada, for*
> *extending the system of voting by ballot to the North-West*
> *Territories and for simplifying the laws relating to lands and*
> *land transfer in the Territories.*[1]

* * *

Lord Stanley and his guest, Major General Lionel Herbert, attended a hockey game at the Rideau Hall Rink on 24 February, 1893. Herbert had been an aide-de-camp to Queen Victoria's son Arthur, the Duke of Connaught (who would later serve as Governor General of Canada from 1911 to 1916), and at the time of his visit to Canada was Commander-in-Chief of the Bombay Army. He looked on with Stanley as the Rebels lost 10-4 to the Victoria Rink of Montreal.[2]

The Dominion Illustrated Monthly described the thrill of a contest during that era:

> *How much is known of hockey will probably never be ap-*
> *preciated by those who have simply seen it played in the*
> *championship form. Then there is a small rink and only*
> *seven to the side. But when the game is played on a big*
> *sheet of ice and there are fifteen men on each end, you see*
> *hockey in its original shape. This is just what happened on*
> *Christmas morning, when thirty good men and strong*
> *chased the 'puck' over what seemed to be to them a ten-acre*
> *lot. And it was a great deal more appetizing for the active*
> *participants on the steels than for the passive ones on the*
> *M.A.A.A. stand, who smothered themselves in furs and*
> *shivered, while making a big effort to look comfortable. The*
> *players all know how to skate — more or less — and most*
> *of them fell down just at the moment they didn't want to,*
> *but it was a rattling game for all that. It was a good old-*
> *time game, where skating and endurance told, and where*

*there was enough space to make the former particularly
visible. The score ... well, out of good nature, the score may
be forgotten or put down as a close one.*[3]

* * *

In early March, the Governor General returned to Montreal. He had last
visited on 30 October, 1890, at which time he was honoured to lay the cornerstone of McGill University. The purpose of this trip, two and a half years
later, was to officially open the new Macdonald Applied Science Building.

On the morning of Sunday, 5 March, Lord Stanley, accompanied by
daughter Isobel and one of his sons, attended service at Christ Church
Cathedral. That afternoon, the three Stanleys also worshipped at St. James
the Apostle.

The peal of the cathedral bell was tolling ten o'clock on Monday, 6
March, as Lord Stanley arrived at McGill University in the private sleigh of
Sir Donald A. Smith, later to be known as Lord Strathcona, who was chancellor of McGill at that time. The two were joined by the Governor General's
aides-de-camp, Kilcoursie and Walsh. As the sleigh pulled up in front of the
prestigious university, it was greeted with three cheers and a tiger from the
student body, followed by a chorus of "For He's a Jolly Good Fellow."

The new Macdonald Applied Science Building had been financed
through the monetary largesse of Sir William Macdonald, a tobacco mag-
nate and philanthropist who would later serve as chancellor of the
university and who, over the course of his life, would donate thirteen million dollars to the McGill. Because the building was intended for the
carrying out of physics experiments, no iron or steel were used in its construction — so as to keep magnetic interference to a minimum. Electricity,
light and heat were studied in the new laboratories.

Lord Kilcoursie recalled the visit in his memoirs:

*I remember my one visit to McGill. There was to be a
demonstration in the Faculty of Applied Science. There was
a huge compressing machine erected on the stage. I was in
the front row, the Governor General and staff were present.
A round, steel bar, four foot long was to be compressed.
Anything more alarming to the uninitiated than to be*

within a few feet of this gradual but resistless compression is difficult to imagine, but for the benefit of those as ignorant as myself, I may say that all that happens is an outward splintering of the steel and nothing flies off.[4]

Following the demonstration, the party was led outdoors. As Lord Stanley stepped forward, wearing a scarlet robe, the students sang "God Save the Queen." Then, in the presence of Donald Smith and Montreal Mayor Desjardins, Stanley laid the cornerstone of the building. He chuckled as he said, "I hope that stone was so laid that the masons have not occasion to come back at the dead of night and do the work again!" Sir William Macdonald then presented the keys to the building to Lord Stanley. Today, that same building houses the Schulich Library of Science and Engineering at McGill.

* * *

The Honourable Arthur Stanley left Canada for England to continue his military service in October 1892. Late the following February, Lord and Lady Stanley received startling news: "Lady Stanley was summoned from home by a cablegram announcing the serious illness of her distinguished son in London."

When the twenty-three-year-old Arthur first came down a sore throat, he thought little of it. But when he later developed a fever, abdominal pain and aching joints, he was diagnosed with rheumatic fever. The cables arrived at Rideau Hall in rapid succession: "Health of child, Arthur, took a turn for the worse," followed that afternoon by the more urgent, "Mr. Arthur Stanley much worse. Head symptoms very serious. Most critical. Can only hope for best." At nightfall, there was no change: "The same. Pulse quicker but quite unconscious."

Rheumatic fever damaged the heart, and was a leading killer of children. The fact that Arthur was so athletic and fit led many to believe his strength might save him. But at this stage, the prognosis did not look good. Throughout the capital, prayers were being offered up on behalf of the Stanleys.

A skating and tobogganing party at Government House, scheduled for Saturday, 4 March, went ahead as planned, although "many did not go … out of deference to the feelings of Their Excellencies, thinking that [because of] their anxiety for their sons in England, they would not care to see strangers."[5]

Isobel and one of her brothers received those who did attend. Lady Stanley had travelled to New York, where she was to board a ship that would carry her to her son's bedside in England. Lord Stanley chose to remain at Rideau Hall, but he initially chose not to attend the party.

Despite the atmosphere surrounding the event, six hundred guests did turn up for the outdoor "at home" at Rideau Hall. Coloured lanterns hung along the toboggan slide "looked like a coronet of great stars upon the Hall." Toboggans were provided for slides, while many took advantage of skating on the large rink near Rideau Hall. A smaller rink also existed, nestled amidst the pines.

That afternoon, the Rideau Rebels played host to a hockey game, described by the *Daily Journal* as such:

> *The fair sex turned out in large numbers to see the match between their friends, the invincible Rebels, and the Winnipegs. Many of the ladies in attendance wore a red ribbon pinned to their coat in support of the Rebels, who wore crimson sweaters. The women are as enthusiastic about hockey as the men, and I heard one fair damsel remark that she 'would rather go without her dinner than miss a game of hockey.'*[6]

While a massive bonfire crackled in the background, the Governor General's Foot Guards band played appropriate music. Lord Stanley relented and made an appearance, and he received hundreds of greetings from well-wishers, assuring each that Arthur's health was improving. "His Excellency is so kind, having a pleasant word and greeting for each."[7] Supper was later served in the curling rink.

While in New York, Lady Stanley received reassuring news that Arthur's condition had improved and he was on the road to recovery, so her trip to England was abandoned and Her Excellency returned to Ottawa. Arthur survived, but the strain on his heart caused by the rheumatic fever forced him to retire from hockey. He lived to the age of seventy-seven. Unmarried, Arthur died 4 November, 1947.

* * *

On 18 March, 1893, the Governor General watched portions of two games at the Rideau Hall Rink. In the first, the Ottawa Hockey Club walloped Quebec 14–0, followed by a 3–2 victory for the Rebels over the Aberdeens.

A most unusual, but highly entertaining, contest was played on the Rideau Hall Rink on the twenty-third. At 7:45 that evening, a team made up solely of players with surnames beginning with the letter K took on all others. Players from both the Ottawa Hockey Club and the Rideau Rebels took part in the "friendly." Lord Kilcoursie, two Kavanaughs, two Kirbys, a Kerr and a Kenny faced Bradley, Chittich, Grant, Russell, Spittall and Young. Kilcoursie recalled Arthur Stanley's participation, but it is improbable, as he had been suffering from rheumatic fever in England mere weeks before.

> *I reached the pinnacle of my hockey ambitions when a team was made up of the three Kirbys, Kavanagh and myself [Kilcoursie] plus two others and we played 'K's' against the rest and won 2-1. Little Kirby at centre forward yelled to me on the left wing, 'Pass'. Instead of passing direct to him, I banged the puck against the side wall [boards] to my left and it bounded out exactly right just ahead of the intercepting winger, who expected the direct pass, and went straight to little Kirby who shot the winning goal a minute from time. I was hot with joy and pride!*[8]

Between periods of the contest, the Governor General's Foot Guards performed. After the game, the rink was opened to public skating.

* * *

Early in April of 1893, Lord Stanley received a cable announcing the death of Captain Sir Aubrey McMahon. McMahon had come to Canada in 1888 as an aide-de-camp to Lord Stanley. He stayed with the Governor General for two years, then returned to England, where he became an adjutant of the 3rd Battalion, Grenadier Guards. McMahon was a favourite of the Stanley family, who greatly regretted losing his services. He was well liked among those with whom he dealt in his capacity as Stanley's aide, but even more popular with his teammates on the Rideau Rebels. The *Daily Journal* reported, "Among other things, the now generally popular winter game hockey owes a good deal to him, for until he and Mr. Barron, MP, took a team up west from Ottawa, the game was hardly known outside this city."[9]

While he was reeling from one serious blow, Lord Stanley received a second. On 22 April, Stanley received a telegram informing him of the sudden death of his brother Edward Henry Stanley, the 15th Earl of Derby, who had died at eight-thirty the night before. Edward Henry had suffered a severe bout of influenza in 1891 and never fully recovered. His usual robust health deteriorated and he died of "affectation of the heart." He was buried at Knowsley Hall on 27 April. The *Daily Citizen* reported that, "as the late Earl left no children, his brother, Baron Stanley of Preston, Canada's present Governor General, who was already a peer in his own right, succeeds to the title and is the new Earl of Derby."[10]

* * *

It would take several months for the new Earl of Derby to complete his responsibilities to Canada, and he and Lady Constance, now the Countess of Derby, returned to England on 15 July, 1893.

Although his term as Governor General was nearing its end anyway, in April Lord Frederick Stanley sent a telegram to Sir John Thompson, Prime Minister of Canada, announcing his need to resign in order to return to the family estate at Knowsley:

> *My dear Sir John,*
>
> *With feelings of regret such as you can imagine, I send you a telegram to inform you that I have asked the Queen and Lord Ripon11 to allow me to resign my present office at some not very distant date.*
>
> *[I hope] you will allow me the right, if necessary for any urgent business, to leave a little sooner than August.*
>
> *The loss we have experienced is a heavy one, both for the country and for our family. Men of my brother's ability and honesty are not to be found every day.*
>
> *I shall always remain deeply indebted to you for your valuable advice and friendly assistance, at all times so freely and willingly rendered during the stormy times*

which during the past five years, we have successfully weathered together.

I cannot say how deeply I shall feel the severance of my connection with Canada.[12]

Lord Ripon, Secretary of State for the Colonies, wrote:

... in dealing with the many difficult and delicate questions which have arisen in connection with Canada during your term of office, it has been the greatest satisfaction to Her Majesty's government to have the services of a statesman of your Lordship's experience and attainments.[13]

* * *

As early as October 1889, it had been announced that the Earl of Fife would succeed Stanley as the Dominion of Canada's next governor general. In June of that year, Fife had married Princess Louise — the Princess Royal, the granddaughter of Queen Victoria and daughter of the Prince of Wales, who later would reign as King Edward VII. As the *Qu'appelle Vidette* reported, "Queen Victoria has expressed a desire that, to add importance to ⌊the Earl of Fife's⌋ rank, he shall be assigned the Governor Generalship of Canada, as she did in the case of her son-in-law, the Marquis of Lorne."[14]

In the autumn of 1892, a story in *The Citizen* noted, "It is rumoured Lord Stanley will not remain in Canada his full term, but will return to England to assist his friend, the Marquis of Salisbury, in the next general election and enter the British Cabinet should the Conservative party win the election."[15]

As it turned out, the Earl of Fife did not replace Lord Stanley as governor general. In fact, on 20 April, 1893, *The Globe* announced:

The Earl of Aberdeen has been appointed Governor General of Canada. His term will not, however, begin until September. Until then, Lord Stanley will continue in office. The new viceroy is now on his way to Canada, but will not come to Ottawa until Lord Stanley has departed. He will spend the summer between the World's Fair at Chicago, in

which Lady Aberdeen has taken special interest, and his
British Columbia ranch.[16]

Nor did Stanley resign early because of the British election. Instead, the un-expected death of Stanley's elder brother was the reason for his departure.

As *The Citizen* alluded, even before Sir John Campbell Hamilton, the 1st Marquess of Aberdeen, assumed his vice regal post, he was well acquainted with Canada. While on a world tour with Lady Aberdeen in 1890, the couple spent a substantial amount of time in the Dominion, falling in love with the young country to such an extent that in 1891 they purchased Coldstream Ranch, a sizable cattle ranch on the outskirts of Vernon in British Columbia's beautiful Okanagan Valley. The ranch was renamed Guisachan by Lord and Lady Aberdeen.

* * *

Before the Stanleys returned to England after five years in Canada, there was one very important matter to handle. His Royal Highness Prince George, Duke of York,17 was marrying Princess Victoria Mary [a.k.a. May] of Teck at Buckingham Palace on 6 July, 1893. The Countess of Derby selected the gift to be sent on behalf of the citizens of Canada: a sleigh, built by the B. Ledoux Carriage Company of Montreal, complete with black-bear robes for the warmth of its passengers.[18]

* * *

While a downpour drenched the capital on 11 July, 1893, Lord Stanley stepped from his office in the Eastern Block of the Parliament Buildings and gave his farewell address to Parliament, beginning with an expression of gratitude to the City of Ottawa:

> *The five years in which we lived here seemed to be as five*
> *hours, now that it was gone. The acquaintance which we*
> *made five years ago soon ripened into friendship, and*
> *friendship into intimacy. Not one cloud arising to darken a*
> *serene sky or one obstacle occurring to mar that intimacy.*[19]

A who's who of Ottawa political society was on hand to bid adieu to Lord and Lady Stanley, including Ottawa Mayor Olivier Durocher, the aldermen, Sir Henry Strong of the Supreme Court of Canada, vice regal physician Sir James Grant and and Lady Grant, Sir Sandford Fleming, and Stanley Cup trustee Sheriff John Sweetland.

Stanley continued to lavish his praise, referring to the substantial progress made in the city during his term of office. He mentioned the houses built and streets laid, as well as the "improved mode of locomotion which set an example to other leading cities in the Dominion and showed the wisdom in selecting Ottawa as the capital of the Dominion."[20]

> *I am also thankful that as Governor General, I have dealt with public affairs as best subserved the well-being of the Dominion. It is not easy for one who has passed twenty years in public life to divest himself of the prejudices peculiar to his position. Yet, you have been good enough to state that I have held the balance fairly between all parties and creeds of the Dominion. That I hold to be the duty of every Governor General, and I hold that it is only by a strict regard for the existence of these differences that the affairs of the country can be properly administered. I trust that in the Dominion as a whole, all discord born of racial differences may become less and less, and all true Canadians unite to make of Canada a great and prosperous country.*
> *The moment was one in which nothing but pleasing terms could be expressed for the kindness that has characterized every moment of my stay in Canada. I assure you that Lady Stanley and I will always look back upon our five years stay in Canada as the happiest period of our lives.*[21]

* * *

An exceptionally large crowd, numbering over a thousand, was gathered at the train station in Ottawa on 12 July as Lord and Lady Stanley, along with daughter Isobel and attendant Miss Lister, arrived by carriage, escorted by the Princess Louise Dragoon Guards. There, the Governor General's Foot Guards presented arms and the band played "God Save the Queen," followed by "Home Sweet Home." Several in attendance dabbed at their eyes and sang along to the line, "'mid pleasures and palaces though we may roam, be it ever so humble, there's no place like home."

Among those on the platform to bid adieu one last time were Sir James Grant, Mayor Durocher, Manitoba's Lieutenant Governor Schultz and Sir Auguste-Réal Angers, who held seats in both the House of Commons and the Senate. Lady Stanley wept openly as she received a large bouquet from Lady Grant on behalf of the Ladies' Humane Society.

The vice regal party was to travel by train to Montreal one last time in the specially outfitted car *Victoria* — the same car in which they had traversed the nation from coast to coast — which was decorated in wild flowers, roses and smilax, a climbing vine. But a rather curious incident took place:

> *As if loath to deprive the Capitol of so popular a Governor General, the four-thirty CPR train pulled out from the station yesterday, leaving His Excellency as well as Lady Stanley standing on the platform. Hundreds of enthusiastic citizens cheered as the train moved away, unaware that its departure was premature. The train had only gone as far as the first switch however when Major [Percy] Sherwood [commissioner of the Dominion Police] succeeded in attracting the attention of the driver and the cars were backed into position. It appears the conductor's cry of "All aboard!" had been lost in the din of martial music and the bawl of voices on the platform, and so the customary warning was unheard.*[22]

With the new Earl and Countess of Derby standing safely on the rear platform of the train, the band played "God Save the Queen." Three cheers and a tiger were offered one last time by those gathered, and hats and handkerchiefs were reverently waved as the train slowly pulled out of the station for a second time.

> *As the curve was rounded and the vice regal pair were lost to view, the band struck up the familiar 'Auld Lang Syne' and many a farewell glimpse of the retreating figures on the*

'Victoria' was caught by tearful eyes.

Seldom, if ever, has any Governor General of Canada received so warm an ovation on his departure from Ottawa as was accorded to His Excellency, the Earl of Derby today on his leaving by the CPR for Montreal on his way to England.[23]

The Governor General and his suite arrived in Montreal later that evening and spent the night aboard *Victoria*. Before leaving for a full itinerary of official business on 13 July, Stanley tipped the train employees handsomely.

The departing governor general was greeted by a military guard along with Mayor Alphonse Desjardins and Senator George Alexander from Ontario. Stanley inspected the Prince of Wales Rifles, then was taken by carriage to Montreal's City Hall, where he received addresses from City Council and the Corporation of the University of McGill, to which His Excellency replied in both English and French. The 16th Earl of Derby had arrived early, and many who intended to witness the Governor General's farewell missed the opportunity. Stanley then entertained the mayor and welcoming committee at the Windsor Hotel.

Before leaving Montreal, His Excellency called upon Sir John Abbott, Canada's second prime minister, at Abbott's residence at Ste. Anne de Bellevue, a community on Montreal's West Island. Abbott had stepped down as prime minister due to ill health on 24 November, 1892.

Abbott, who had accepted the prime ministerial post begrudgingly, held it for only seventeen months. His government was deemed too weak and divided to successfully address either the growing Behring Sea tug-of-war or a growing economic depression. He died in Montreal on 30 October, 1893.

Later that evening of 13 July, the Earl and Countess of Derby departed by ship for Quebec City. As the vice regal couple walked down the gangway to board the ship, Lady Constance's heel got caught in one of the square holes of the gangway platform and flicked into the St. Lawrence. Her Excellency had to board the ship with a bare foot.

Stanley and his party arrived in the provincial capital at one-thirty on the afternoon of 14 July. Greeting them at the Canadian Pacific Railway station were, among others, Mayor Jules-Joseph Fremont, Mr. Justice Christopher Salmon Patterson of the Supreme Court of Canada,[24] Quebec

Lieutenant Governor Sir Joseph-Adolphe Chapleau, Richard Reid Dobell, member of Parliament, Senator Mackenzie Bowell, and two members of the Queen's Privy Council, Sir Auguste-Réal Angers and Sir Alexandre Lacoste.

One final civic address, presented in both English and French, was delivered in the Legislative Assembly, to which Stanley replied in both languages. "I have great confidence in the future of Canada and foretell for the Dominion a great and glorious history." Stanley openly encouraged Canada to maintain its connection to Great Britain.

Between the departure of the 16th Earl of Derby and the arrival of his successor the Earl of Aberdeen, affairs were administered by Major General Montgomery, commander of Her Majesty's forces in North America. After the parties proceeded to The Citadel, Montgomery was sworn in by Mr. Justice Télesphore Fournier of the Supreme Court. Montgomery continued to reside in Halifax even as he bridged the dates between Stanley's departure and the new governor general's arrival.

The country reacted with particular warmth to the 16th Earl of Derby on his imminent departure. "The regard in which their Excellencies were held by the people of Quebec was the reason so many gathered today to say farewell and Godspeed to one of the most popular governors Canada has ever had."[25]

* * *

After leaving The Citadel for the last time, the Earl and Countess of Derby, accompanied by daughter Isobel and an entourage that included Miss Lister and aide-de-camp Willie Walsh, arrived at Quebec City's Champlain Wharf at four-thirty on Saturday, 15 July, 1893. The party boarded the Sardinian, and as the ship pulled away from the wharf, they were given a twenty-one-gun salute. Such a full military honour is afforded recipients on rare occasions. The British monarch is given a twenty-one-gun salute upon arrival in Canada, upon arrival in a province and on departure from Canada. The honour is reserved for the governor general upon taking the oath of office, on leaving the Parliament Buildings after installation ceremonies, upon arrival on Parliament Hill for Canada Day ceremonies, on arrival to open a session of Parliament, and on official departure after leaving office.26 With each blast, the Earl's smile grew more melancholy.

'*Bang!*' As the last of the twenty-one blasts was fired, the Stanleys waved one final time from the deck of the *Sardinian*, then retired to their cabin.

The *Courrier du Canada* of Quebec City bid a heartfelt goodbye to the departing governor general:

> *Rarely since our defeat has the departure of a governor been the occasion of so much homage and best wishes for the future which Providence will bestow upon them. With all our hearts, we join to them the best wishes of the people of Quebec, our readers and our own* 'bon voyage et glorieuse carriere!'[27]

* * *

On Monday, 24 July, the Sardinian arrived at Liverpool, and the Earl and Duchess of Derby proceeded immediately to Knowsley Hall, the seat of the earldom.

---

[1] Library of Parliament, Parliament of Canada website, *www.parl.gc.ca.*

[2] *Ottawa Daily Citizen* (27 February, 1893).

[3] *The Dominion Illustrated Monthly* (3 January, 1891), p.22.

[4] Kilcoursie, *Recollections Hazy But Happy.*

[5] *Ottawa Daily Journal* (6 March 1893).

[6] Ibid.

[7] *Ottawa Daily Journal* (10 March, 1893).

[8] Born Frederick Rudolph Lambart, as the son of Viscount Kilcoursie, Frederick was born into his title as Lord Kilcoursie. On his father's death in 1900, he became the 10th Earl of Cavan in 1900. See, Kilcoursie, *Recollections Hazy But Happy.*

[9] *Ottawa Daily Journal* (April 1893).

[10] *Ottawa Daily Citizen* (23 April, 1893), *edition cover page.*

[11] George Robinson, Lord Ripon, was the Secretary of State for the Colonies in the Gladstone government between 1892 and 1895.

[12] F. A. Stanley, *Letter of resignation to Prime Minister Sir John Thompson* (Ottawa: 27 April, 1893).

[13] F. A. Stanley, Letter to Ripon (22 June, 1893).

[14] *Qu'appelle Vidette* (10 October, 1889), p.3.

[15] *Ottawa Daily Citizen* (11 October, 1892), p.3.

[16] *The Globe* (Toronto: 20 April, 1893).

[17] HRH the Duke of York would later be crowned King George V.

[18] 'Royal Wedding', *The Graphic*, (London: 19 July, 1893), p.10.

[19] *Ottawa Daily Citizen* (13 July, 1893), p.8.

[20] Ibid.

21 Ibid.

22 Ibid.

23 Ibid.

24 Patterson died 24 July, 1893, ten days after this event.

25 *Ottawa Daily Citizen* (17 July, 1893), *edition cover page.*

26 From Canadian Heritage website: Ceremonial and Canadian Symbols Promotion, Honours and Salutes, *www.pch.gc.ca.*

27 Translated from *Courrier du Canada* (Quebec City: 15 July, 1893), p.2.

CHAPTER SEVENTEEN

The Earl at Knowsley

When Lord Frederick Stanley arrived in England on 24 July, 1893, it marked the first time he had set foot on home soil since his departure for Canada on 31 May, 1888. Upon his return, Stanley immediately immersed himself into his new life at Knowsley, interests that included politics, community service, horticulture and horse racing, and of course, his role as the 16th Earl of Derby.

* * *

The earldom of Derby is the second-oldest title in England's peerage. It was first assumed in 1139 by the Ferrers family, but was later forfeited and in 1138, the family of Henry III began using the title. King Henry VII conferred the earldom and Knowsley upon Thomas Stanley on 27 October, 1485, in gratitude for his help in Henry's rise to the throne. By the time Lord Frederick Stanley became the 16th Earl, his family had played a prominent role in the political and social life of England for more than five centuries.

> *The Family of the Stanleys may well be described, as it has been by all who have attempted to narrate its history, as one of the most illustrious in the whole range of the British peerage, not only on account of its great antiquity, but also on account of the important and interesting character of the events with which it is historically associated.*[1]

Knowsley Hall, located on twenty-five hundred acres of private parkland,

403

can be found seven miles from Liverpool's centre. When first built, Knowsley was a mediaeval hunting lodge, but it has since become one of the more important estates in Lancashire.

The house underwent extensive renovations courtesy of the 10th Earl, Sir James Stanley, in the early 1700s. Sir James also began amassing the extraordinary art collection displayed throughout Knowsley, a collection that is ranked second in size in all of Great Britain only to that of Queen Elizabeth II. Among the works are a number of memorials to Sir Frederick Arthur Stanley, the 16th Earl. A handsome portrait created in 1897 by Professor Hubert Herkomer, the leading portraitist of his era, is displayed proudly beside a companion portrait of Countess Constance Stanley in the state dining room.[2]

Throughout the nineteenth century, Knowsley was enlarged and altered on a regular basis, but it was during the residency of the 16th Earl that the estate underwent some of its most extensive alterations. The state dining room was redecorated extensively, and further enlargements were made to the reception rooms. The walnut drawing room was created by knocking out the walls of three eighteenth-century rooms. Electric lighting had been installed in 1892, just before Lord Frederick's arrival, and heating and plumbing were also updated.[3]

In a letter to one Reverend Whitwell Elwin, Lady Emily Lytton, a cousin of Countess Constance, offered a brief and at times unflattering sketch of what Knowsley was like during the tenure of the 16th Earl.

> *This house is enormous and very rambling. There are something over eighty bedrooms, all very small. None of the house is pretty, though some very old, but it has been so patched and pulled about by different owners, especially the last Lord Derby, that it is really hideous. It is built of a dull red brick. Then rooms are all small, with the exception of one dining-room, which is enormous and a very fine room, only terribly modernised and spoilt. Inside, it is very comfortable and nice. There is a fascinating library, a suite of little rooms lined with books and ending in a large odd-shaped room....The present owners abuse right and left what was done by the last Lord Derby, in a way which I think is very unkind and disagreeable considering that he was a brother.*

> *They have jumped into his shoes and can only abuse him.*
> *The only people in the house besides the family, which con-*
> *sists of the Derbys, Isobel, one son and a secretary, are Lady*
> *Emma Talbot, Lord Derby's sister, and her husband, neither*
> *of them at all lively. Cousin [Constance] has the family*
> *failing of abusing everybody in a very nasty way. Lord Derby*
> *is rather like a boy — very jovial and full of bad jokes, but I*
> *should say without much else.*[4]

Lady Emily was far more generous in describing the Stanleys' stables, which she characterized as "magnificent":

> *An old coachman who has been here for years and is a great*
> *rogue, although a great character, showed us round with*
> *the most tremendous pride. They have over forty magnifi-*
> *cent horses. The stables are kept spotlessly clean, which they*
> *ought to be, considering that they have twenty men to look*
> *after them.*[5]

Lest the reader get the idea that Lady Emily is softening her tone, she disclaims, "The gardens are large and ugly. Thank goodness I am not obliged to live here."[6]

The village of Knowsley sprung up around the mansion to serve the needs of Knowsley Hall. During the 16th Earl's fifteen years at the estate, the community was home to about 1,325 residents, almost all of them involved, directly or indirectly, with the Stanley home.

The estate yielded a substantial rental income for the new Earl; this, combined with the property and money he inherited from both his brother and father, along with his own personal wealth, the 16th Earl of Derby was one of the wealthiest people on the planet. According to a list compiled in 1901 by *Chambers* magazine, the wealthiest was Alfred Beit, a British South African financier who grew much of his half billion dollar worth through diamond mining. Other names included New York's J. D. Rockefeller, William Waldorf Astor, who was then living in England, Pittsburgh's Andrew Carnegie, J. P. Morgan from New York, and Vienna's Baron Rothschild. In thirtieth spot was Lord Stanley, with an estimated worth of $50 million.[7]

Although the introduction of the gasoline-powered, four-wheeled auto-mobile had only occurred in 1886, the 16th Earl was an early proponent. In 1902, while living at Knowsley, Stanley owned four motor cars, each with its own driver. He had a twelve-horsepower Daimler, a ten-horsepower Georges Richard, a ten-horsepower Wolseley and a five-horsepower Locomobile.

* * *

The 16th Earl was a prominent figure in Lancashire, involving himself heavily in community affairs. On a more metropolitan level, Frederick accepted the role of Sloane Trustee of the British Museum, a position previously held by his brother. Sir Hans Sloane, who died in 1753, was a physician and naturalist who bequeathed his collection to the landmark museum.

University College Liverpool, founded by Royal Charter on 18 October, 1881, was one of the earliest civic universities. In its first constitution, the president was expected to act as the head and chief officer of the college for a term of ten years, with the possibility of being reappointed by the college's Court of Governors. The college opened in January 1882 with forty-five students, most from the immediate area, and Frederick's brother Edward, the 15th Earl, was installed as the first president. The college's governors elected Frederick to succeed his brother. Following his installation, the new Earl was enthusiastically welcomed by faculty and students alike. In an 1894 address to staff and students at the recently opened Victoria Building on Brownlow Hill, which at the time stood at the centre of the cluster of buildings that housed the university, Stanley confessed that he could boast of no university training himself, but urged the students to apply their energies and abilities in "helping forward that cause in which they were engaged, not only as individuals, but as citizens of this great country and as persons living in the age of enlightenment and refinement."[8]

In July 1903, the college received a further Royal charter, and through an Act of Parliament was granted the right to confer degrees. University College Liverpool thus became the University of Liverpool. The 16th Earl of Derby was subsequently named the first chancellor of the University of Liverpool, an office which the charter decreed he could hold "during his life or until his resignation."

The Earl demonstrated his concern for the welfare and development of the college, and later the university, in a number of ways, including an endowment of ten thousand pounds for the School of Anatomy and a further donation of five thousand pounds towards a new building for the medical school. The Liverpool Royal Infirmary Medical School, which had earlier been based at the Liverpool Royal Institution, became the nucleus of a faculty of medicine.

Lord Derby remained chancellor of the University of Liverpool until his death in 1908. "He was remembered for the gracious courtesy and the charm of his manner, which endeared him to the College and University, and for his personal kindliness to the staff and students." In 1904, the 16th Earl was presented with an honorary law degree from the university. Both his son and daughter-in-law, Edward and Alice, would also be so honoured, Edward in 1909 and Lady Alice in 1934. Stanley's son Edward, the 17th Earl of Derby, was selected to succeed his father as chancellor of the university in 1908, and he held the position until his own death in 1948.[9]

The 16th Earl also served in the prestigious, though ceremonial, role of Lord Mayor of Liverpool. The Lord Mayor is selected annually to act as a focal point within the community and to assist in promoting the city nationally and internationally. Stanley served Liverpool as Lord Mayor in 1895-96, and was succeeded by Thomas Hughes the following year. In 1911-12, Frederick's son Edward, the 17th Earl, also served as Lord Mayor of Liverpool.[10]

The Town Hall in Liverpool, which is home to that city's Lord Mayor, is one of its oldest and most historic buildings. The first town hall was built in 1515 on a spot very near the current structure. A second was built in 1673. The current town hall was constructed in 1754, then rebuilt and reopened in 1820. An extraordinary bust of Lord Frederick Stanley, the 16th Earl of Derby, sculpted by Sir William Goscombe John, proudly resides on the plinth next to one of his brother Edward, the 15th Earl, at the top of the great staircase leading to the three reception rooms and ballrooms in the town hall.[11]

> At a meeting held in the town hall on 17 June, 1901, a decision was reached that a worthy cathedral should be built in Liverpool that would be "something to speak for God."

The 16th Earl served as president of the executive committee for the construction of the Cathedral Church of
Christ in Liverpool from its inception in 1901 until his
death in 1908. The design competition attracted hundreds
of submissions from esteemed architects. In 1903, parishioners and architects alike were astounded when Stanley
and the committee selected the design of Giles Gilbert Scott,
a twenty-two-year-old student. Although he won the competition for "the best idea and the finest conception," Scott
was partnered with George F. Bodley to complete the
project. At an open-air service on 19 July, 1904, the 16th
Earl of Derby proudly looked on as King Edward VII laid
the cornerstone for what would become the largest cathedral in Britain.[12] To bring the ceremony to a close, a
thousand-voice choir sang the Hallelujah Chorus from
Handel's Messiah.[13]

In the southeast transept of the Cathedral Church of
Christ in Liverpool lies a fine bronze memorial to
Frederick Stanley. Designed by Scott, the memorial depicts
the Earl lying in Garter Robes, using a model of the cathedral as a pillow.

Those knights who have earned the Order of the
Garter are commemorated in St. George's Chapel at
Windsor Castle. The stalls that line the walls of the chapel
are reserved for the knights of the order, and the 16th Earl
of Derby, who earned his knighthood in 1897, is so installed. While the knight is still alive, a banner hangs above
the stall, while his crest and mantling are placed atop of the
helm above the stall's canopy. The crest, mantling and
banner are removed at the time of the knight's death and
replaced with a brass plate.[14]

* * *

The city of Liverpool has honoured twelve men through the dedication of
statues. Among the marble statues located within St. George's magnificent
Great Hall are William Ewart Gladstone, four-time Prime Minister of

Britain; Joseph Mayer, the founder of the Liverpool Museum; Sir Robert Peel, the founder of Britain's modern Conservative party; Edward Stanley, the 15th Earl of Derby; and, of course, Lord Frederick Stanley, the 16th Earl of Derby, whose statue was created by F. W. Pomeroy and was unveiled on 3 November, 1911, by Lord Halsbury, the Lord Chancellor of Great Britain.

* * *

Located within Lancashire and to the north-northeast of Liverpool sits Preston, an ancient town that received its Royal charter as a borough from Henry II in 1179. The charter gave Preston the right to hold a market or fair called a Guild Merchant, which meant that vendors from the borough of Preston were able to sell their wares without paying any fee. This Guild was first held in 1328 and at irregular intervals prior to 1542, after which it settled into a pattern of being held every twenty years, or roughly once a generation. For more than four hundred years, the Market Place has become the centre of Preston's commercial life, offering vendors a place to sell their wares and buyers an opportunity to shop. But the Market Place has become symbolic, too, welcoming British monarchs and offering a ceremonial place for the Preston Guild, or Preston Guild Merchant, to be held.

The historic fair is staged so infrequently that a local expression equating to "once in a blue moon" is "once every Preston Guild." Due to the rarity of the celebration, as well as the fact that large numbers of people congregated in Preston for the occasion, the Guild became a special occasion for processions and social gatherings.

In 1901–02, the 16th Earl of Derby was selected as Preston's Guild Mayor, the highest honour that the borough could bestow upon an individual. On the first of September, 1902, the 16th Earl presided over the ceremonial opening of the Guild. That day, a grand civic procession took place; embroidered banners, gleaming swords and everyone's sartorial finest were brought out for the occasion. Stanley, as the Guild Mayor, wore his robes of office and was heralded by trumpeters and mace bearers as he strode along the streets.

Following the parade, Stanley presided over a lavish banquet, which was but the first of the social events for the leading figures in Lancashire. No expense was ever spared during Guild week, and the one staged in 1902 was no different. What *was* different, though, was the evolution of the

Guild by the dawn of the twentieth century: what had been largely an agricultural fair to this date was now displaying the latest achievements in industrial development.

* * *

The 16th Earl of Derby followed more closely in his father's footsteps than did his brother. Like his father, Frederick Stanley was a great horse-racing enthusiast, a passion that had been integral to the lives of his family for generations. Frederick was a familiar figure at Liverpool race meetings, maintaining the connection with horse racing for which his father had been famous — and which he had indulged in his Canadian sojourn by appearing at the Queen's Plate. On his return to England, the new Earl joined the Jockey Club. He also founded the Stanley House Stud establishment, run in conjunction with the Knowsley Stud at the family estate. Under the 16th Earl's stewardship, the Stanley House Stud twice won the Oaks (with Canterbury Pilgrim in 1893 and Keystone II in 1906), the Ebor Handicap with Dingle Bay in 1896 and the Liverpool Cup with Bridge of Canny. In 1906 alone, Stanley House won forty-four races. On Frederick's death, his son, the 17th Earl, who had assisted his father for several years, assumed the helm of the family business and quickly established himself as arguably the most successful owner-breeder of his era.

The 16th Earl of Derby was captain of Sanningdale Golf Course, an outstanding heritage golf course less than thirty miles from central London. The King's brother, the Duke of Connaught, was president.[15]

The Stanley family also took a new love, that of hockey, back with them to England. On a frosty January in 1895, with the lake behind Buckingham Palace frozen over, the Stanley boys put together a game of ice hockey against a team from the palace. Five Stanley brothers and a friend faced a squad that included the fifty-four-year old Prince of Wales (who would succeed his mother, Queen Victoria, and rule Britain as King Edward VII), the Prince's thirty-year-old son the Duke of York (who later succeeded his father and became King George V), William Bromley-Davenport, the thirty-three-year old member of Parliament for Macclesfield, thirty-six-year old Sir Francis Astley-Corbett, Lord Mildmay and Ronald Moncrief. The Stanleys scored virtually at will, while the Palace players managed but one goal. The game was played using bandy sticks and a puck.

Prince George had toured Canada while in the Royal Navy and was gazetted for a period of time in Halifax, where it is all but certain that he would have watched hockey games being played, if not even participated. One unsubstantiated source indicated that his wife, Princess Mary [a.k.a. May] of Teck, was watching her husband play hockey in the mid-1890s when she went into labour.

Lord Kilcoursie, who had been Lord Stanley's aide-de-camp in Canada, recalls a game played on a cold winter afternoon during the winter of 1893-94. He was ordered to arrive at Buckingham Palace at three-thirty with his skates and a hockey stick. "There," remembered Kilcoursie, "I found [the future Edward VII], Queen Alexandra, three of the Stanleys, [Lady Isobel Stanley] and a few more. It was decided to play a 'quiet' game on the ornamental water [the frozen lake behind the palace]. Their Majesties kept goal, one at each end. The score was 0–0, which was as it should be."[16]

During that period of time, Hengler's Rink, which opened in 1896, was where hockey was headquartered in London, shortly to be joined by the Prince's and the short-lived Brighton and Glasgow rinks. The team assembled from the Niagara rink, which had opened in 1895, only to close in 1902, was very good, but no match for the Stanley brothers. Victor was only able to join his brothers when on leave from the Navy, but on this day, during the winter of 1896–97, he was present, although his brother Arthur was not. Nonetheless, the six Stanley brothers easily defeated the Niagara club.[17]

It would be February 1897 before the first official hockey club was formed in England. Not unlike the precedent set by Canadian rinks, the Prince's Club, an ice-skating rink which fronted onto Montpelier Square in London's Knightsbridge district, agreed to allow Major B. M. "Peter" Patton permission to form a hockey club based at the rink. Under both Royal and aristocratic patronage, ice hockey grew in popularity, and other rinks sprang up around London after the First World War. The first British ice hockey league was formed in 1903, consisting of Prince's, Cambridge University, the London Canadians, Hengler's Argylls and the Hengler's Amateur Skating Club, the latter two based in the Hengler's Rink, located where the London Palladium now stands. The first champion was the London Canadians. The league lasted but one season, as Hengler's closed during the spring of 1904.

Although these are some of the earliest hockey games played in England, several sources indicate that a game may have been played at

Windsor Castle in 1853, with Queen Victoria looking on as her husband, Prince Albert, tended goal.

* * *

During the spring of 1903, there had been suggestions that sixty-two-year-old King Edward VII was in ill health, and worry that he was suffering from depression. Yet, contrary to published reports, Edward left London on 26 March to visit the 16th Earl of Derby at his estate in Knowsley. The longtime friends attended the Grand National Steeplechase the next day. The monarch then embarked on a yachting tour.[18]

* * *

In 1893, the Royal Manchester, Liverpool and North Lancashire Agricultural Society altered its name to the less cumbersome Royal Lancashire Agricultural Society. Since that year, the Society has held an annual show, travelling to many of the towns within the county of Lancashire. The 16th Earl of Derby was the Society's president in 1894 when the show travelled to Bolton, in 1895 when the show was held in Preston; in 1899, when the show took place in Liverpool; in 1902 in Preston during the Guild; and again in 1904 and 1905. During June of the latter year, the Earl noted that the state of Canadian agriculture was much more advanced than its English counterpart. One improvement Stanley suggested, based on his Canadian experience, was a system whereby milk and other dairy products were transported from various districts to a common location, where it was tested and stored before being sold, with the profits divided among the contributing farmers.[19]

Preston's 12 Winckley Square, which had become the headquarters of the Royal Lancashire Agricultural Society, was referred to as Derby House. Although the Earl neither lived in the home nor owned it, it was so named in honour of the Society's longtime president.

* * *

The Earl and Countess of Derby also busied themselves with a great number of benevolent community events. On 26 October, 1893, for example, the 16th Earl performed the official opening of the Harris Library in Preston.

In 1890, a local resident, Mary Cross, gave a thousand pounds to help the "deaf and dumb children" of Preston, then gave five thousand pounds for the construction of a school to help these same children. Although she died before the school was opened, the Cross Deaf and Dumb School was opened by Lord Stanley in Lancashire on 28 July, 1894. The school began with sixteen pupils. In 1897, it received permission from Queen Victoria to change its name to the Royal Cross Primary School for Deaf Children. A large hall was built after the Rawstorne family donated further endowments to the school. Lady Stanley officially opened Rawstorne Hall on 29 July, 1899.[20]

Tuberculosis had claimed several thousand lives in England in the 1870s. The disease attacked the lungs of those infected and, if not treated, ultimately led to death. During the heart of the Industrial Revolution in England, the disease affected one in four citizens. It wasn't until the 1880s that tuberculosis was proven to be infectious (spitting was regarded as a prime method of spreading the tubercle bacillus). Those infected were encouraged to enter sanatoria; Baguley Sanatorium for the Treatment of Infectious Diseases was one of the first, and Frederick Stanley officially opened the hundred-bed building in Manchester on 4 October, 1902.

* * *

In 1897, Queen Victoria appointed the 16th Earl the Lord Lieutenant of Lancashire, a non-political, unpaid office he held until his death. In this role, the Earl represented the Queen at events in the county of Lancashire and was responsible for the preparation of programs for Royal visits to the county, for the presentation of awards to organizations and to individuals, and he advised Her Majesty on honours nominations.

* * *

A long-time advocate of strengthening the ties between England and the colonies, the Earl was elected president of the British Empire League in 1904. The association aimed to increase trade between England and members of the Empire, which by 1904 had grown to include Canada, Newfoundland, Australia, New Zealand, India, Singapore, Hong Kong, Burma, large portions of the Caribbean and Africa, and an assortment of other countries. The British Empire League, formed in 1895, also encouraged the establishment of cheaper and more efficient routes for travel, postal and communications, as well as a shared military and naval force between the dominions and colonies.

* * *

The Franco-British Exhibition, held between 14 May and 31 October, 1908, in a reclaimed area of west London close to Shepherd's Bush that is now called White City after the white stucco facades on most of the buildings, was a celebration of the *Entente Cordiale* signed between the two nations in 1904, and was the first international exhibition to be co-operatively organized by two countries. It attracted 8.4 million viewers over the course of its run, and was described by *The Times* as "the most remarkable exhibition ever held in the British Empire." On hand to open the fair were King Edward VII of Britain and President Armand Fallières of France, as well as the Maharaj of Nepal.

An entire modern city, complete with twenty palaces, eight halls and an artificial lake, was built on one hundred forty acres. Among the popular attractions were two colonial villages, designed to "communicate the success of colonial imposition." Visitors to the Irish village, named Ballymaclinton, were greeted by a hundred and fifty Irish colleens who demonstrated various examples of domestic advances. The Senegalese village demonstrated day-to-day life in a native village. Betraying the attitudes of the era, *The Times* commented on the "surprising cleanliness" of the Irish and noted that the Senegalese were "cleaner than they looked." The Flip-Flap Ride, an early ancestor of the London Eye, took three minutes and twenty seconds from beginning to end at a cost of sixpence. While at the top, visitors could see Windsor Castle and the Crystal Palace.[21]

Lord Stanley, the Earl of Derby, was selected president of the exhibition in 1907, although it seems unlikely that he attended: he died exactly one month after it opened.

---

[1] P. Draper, *The House of Stanley* (Ormskirk: T. Hutton Publishing, 1864), p.4.

[2] K. Shea, *Interview with Michael Pritchard*, FRPS, (Watford, England: 15 June, 2006). Pritchard is also a director at Christie's, the world-renowned auction house, in London.

[3] *Country Life* (12 July, 1913), pp.54–61.

[4] E. Lytton, *Letter to Reverend Whitwell Elwin* (14 October, 1893); Churchill, *Lord Derby*, p.41.

[5] Ibid.

[6] Ibid.

[7] *Toronto Daily Star* (9 May, 1901), p.6.

[8] Notes from Adrian Allan, University Archivist, The University of Liverpool.

[9] *For Advancement of Learning; the University of Liverpool*, 1881–1981, Thomas Kelly, Liverpool University Press, 1981

[10] Information gleaned from the City of Liverpool's official website, *www.liverpool.gov.uk*.

[11] K. Shea, *Interview with Pamela Raman*, of the Lord Mayor's Office, Liverpool Town Hall, (Liverpool: 1 May, 2006).

[12] Liverpool Cathedral encompasses 104,275 square feet, with a tower rising to a height of 331 feet. The bells have the heaviest peal of any in the world. One of the cathedral's two organs is the largest in Britain, and consists of 9,765 pipes.

[13] P. Kennerley & C. Wilkinson, *The Cathedral Church of Christ in Liverpool* (Liverpool: Bluecoat Press, 2003).

[14] F. Velde, *www.heraldica.org*.

[15] *Toronto Daily Star* (24 June, 1908), p.6.

[16] Kilcoursie, *Recollections Hazy But Happy*.

[17] B. M. Patton, *Ice Hockey* (London: George Routledge & Sons Ltd., 1936).

[18] *Toronto Daily Star* (26 March, 1902), p.10.

[19] *Toronto Daily Star* (2 June, 1905), p.14.

[20] W. Pallant, *The story of our school*, Head Masters' Log, *www.schooltrain.info*.

[21] P. Greenhalgh, 'Art, politics and society at the Franco-British Exposition of 1908', *Art History, 8, 4*, (December 1985), pp.434–452.

CHAPTER EIGHTEEN

The Death of Derby

On Monday, 15 June, 1908, *The Times* reported: "We deeply regret to announce that the Earl of Derby died suddenly last night between seven and eight o'clock from heart failure at his residence at Holwood, Keston, Kent.[1]

While returning from a walk at his estate at Holwood, sixty-seven-year-old Lord Frederick Arthur Stanley, the 16th Earl of Derby, was felled by a heart attack.

Arthur James Balfour, Stanley's longtime friend and British Prime Minister between 1902 and 1905, wrote to Lady Derby on the death of her husband, stating that Frederick had been one of his oldest and kindest friends, and "a man who had a genius for inspiring affection among those who knew him."[2]

* * *

Canadians looked back with great fondness upon Baron Stanley's term as their Governor General.

In 1840, the British army established a military post just west of Toronto to replace the aging Fort York, which had deteriorated rapidly following the War of 1812. The military post was known as New Fort, and comprised seven limestone buildings constructed around a parade square. Intended originally to be a much more important structure, New Fort remained a barracks. In 1870, Canadian forces took over the responsibility for the post; three years later, the North-West Mounted Police began to assemble and train recruits at New Fort before they were shipped off to bring law and order to the rapidly settling Canadian west.

On the occasion of the 16th Earl of Derby's departure for England in 1893, New Fort was renamed Stanley Barracks in his honour. Given Stanley's interest in sports, it is a fitting coincidence that the officers' quarters were to serve as a temporary home for Canada's Sports Hall of Fame in the mid-1950s. They later housed the Marine Museum at the Canadian National Exhibition until 1998.

In 1901, a mountain climber by the name of Edward Whymper scaled a mountain in the northeastern section of what is now known as Kootenay National Park in British Columbia. Whymper reached the summit and named the mountain after Lord Stanley. The Stanley Glacier is on the northeast face of Stanley Peak.

Likewise, the 16th Earl of Derby did not forget the young nation whose people he had served. When he learned of the massive fire that swept through Hull, Quebec, and spread across the river to Ottawa on 27 April, 1900, leaving thousands homeless, the Earl of Derby contributed £1,000 (at the time, $4,866.66 in Canadian money) to the Ottawa and Hull Relief Fund.[3]

* * *

Stanley's full title was Sir Frederick Arthur Stanley, KG[4], GCB[5], GCVO[6], PC[7], LL.D.[8], 16th Earl of Derby, 4th Baron Stanley of Bickerstaffe and 1st Baron Stanley of Preston. He was Lord Lieutenant of Lancashire, supernumerary aide-de-camp to Queen Victoria for militia from 1888 to 1901 and afterwards to the King, Honourary Colonel of the 4th Battalion King's Own Royal Lancaster Regiment from 1886, and of the 1st Volunteer Battalion Liverpool. Frederick Stanley had, among his many other positions and duties, spent twenty years in the House of Commons and had occupied many important positions in various British Cabinets, including Financial Secretary to the War Office, Secretary of State for War, Secretary of State for the Colonies and President of the Board of Trade. He was also a dearly loved governor general of Canada.

King Edward VII had been a close friend of Stanley's and sent his condolences to the 16th Earl's son Edward, who, by his father's death, immediately became the 17th Earl of Derby:

Although I have written to your poor dear afflicted Mother,
I must write you a few lines to express my deepest sympathy

with you, your brothers and sisters at the terrible loss you
have sustained! When the sad news reached me, I cannot
express how great the shock was and grief at the loss of one
of my oldest and best friends. We were born in the same
year. I had known him when he was a boy at Eton, and we
served for a few months together in the [Grenadier]
Guards. Though the suddenness of the end was fearful, still
for his sake, it is perhaps best so as he was spared a long and
painful illness. It may truly be said, 'In the midst of life we
are in death!' Your dear kind Father had, I am sure, not a
single enemy in the world and he will be deeply regretted
though never forgotten by all those who had the advantage
of knowing him and appreciating his excellent qualities.
The breaking up of your happy home must be a great blow
for you, but fortunately, you are all such a united family
that the traditions will ever remain the same.[9]

The Prince of Wales offered Edward a similar sentiment:

I have known you for so many years and we are such old
friends that I cannot express what my feelings are at such a
sad moment as this. I can only say that in your dear father,
whom I have known since I was a child, I have lost a kind
and valued friend. I think your family was the happiest and
most united one I have ever seen, therefore I can well
imagine what a terrible break up this means to you all and
how irreparable your loss is. Everyone is mourning his loss
and he will be greatly missed by his host of friends. Today
at Ascot, one heard nothing but kind and sympathetic
expressions about your dear father. We are so glad to hear
dear Lady Derby is bearing up so well. Both the Princess
and I beg to offer you and yours our deepest sympathy in
your terrible sorrow.[10]

Lady Constance, as it turned out, did not "bear up so well." She had, of
course, lost her closest companion in the world. In letters that were specifically written to be opened only after her death, the dowager countess

expressed true gratification to Edward for being the "dearest of sons" and described her deep, deep adoration for the 16th Earl:

> *I leave you [Edward] very little because you have every-thing and long may you live to enjoy the position and to be a worthy successor to Father, whose real and only object in life was to do what was right and just.*[11]

In a separate letter to all of her children, Constance thanked them for their affection and understanding:

> *... when you read this, know that I have blessed you every hour of my life. Forgive all my many faults and think of me as having tried to walk in Father's footsteps and going (I hope) to where he is — into the terrible mystery of the unknown world.*[12]

Constance Stanley survived her husband by fourteen years. She died 17 April, 1922 at the age of eighty-two.

The 16th Earl of Derby was also survived by eight of his ten children, as well as ten grandchildren. Four more grandchildren would be born in the years following his death.

On Frederick's death, his eldest son, Edward George, automatically assumed the title of 17th Earl of Derby. Like his father, he joined the Grenadier Guards and enjoyed a most successful political career. Eddy, as he was known, served as a member of Parliament and held the posts of Lord of the Treasury, Postmaster General and two stints as Secretary of State for War, and was later assigned the position of ambassador to France — in spite of not speaking the language. Like his father and grandfather before him, Edward Stanley was much loved by the people of Lancashire. On his seven-tieth birthday, for example, five thousand people gathered at Preston Public Hall, where he was showered with presents that had been bought by a remarkable eighty thousand Lancastrians, each of whom had contributed one shilling. Following the presentation of the gifts, Edward, with great emotion, addressed the crowd of well-wishers. In his speech, the 17th Earl referred to his many ancestors, including his uncle Edward Henry, who he claimed was very much "misunderstood" but was still a man loved by "a great many people." And, of course, Edward spoke of his father, whom he described as being "one of the most lovable and courteous men who ever stepped the earth."[13]

Eddy, like his father, was quite a sportsman, involving himself in several sports including horse racing, where he is acknowledged as one of the best breeders of his era. The 17th Earl served as the honorary president of the Northern Rugby Football Union beginning in 1911 — the family seat of Knowsley was a hotbed of rugby. Like his father, he too donated a trophy to sport, presenting the Lord Derby Cup to the French Rugby League in 1935 to serve as a championship trophy to be awarded to the winners of the league's knockout cup competition.[14] Edward died 4 February, 1948, at the age of eighty-two.

Captain Victor Stanley was forty-one at the time of his father's death. Sir Victor was an admiral in the Royal Navy and was appointed naval attaché to the British Embassy in St. Petersburg, and he died 9 June, 1934, at the age of sixty-seven.

Arthur Stanley, thirty-nine years old in 1908, was the member of Parliament for the Ormskirk Division. He died on 4 November, 1947, two weeks shy of his seventy-eighth birthday. Arthur's twin, Geoffrey, died on 16 March, 1871, before his second birthday. Lord and Lady Stanley lost a second child that year: infant Katherine Mary died in October 1871.

Captain Ferdinand Stanley was thirty-seven when his father died. He later served as a brigadier general in the First World War and died 17 March, 1935, at the age of sixty-four.

Lieutenant Colonel Sir George Stanley, thirty-five years of age in 1908, represented Willesden East as a Unionist before his death at the age of sixty-five on the first of July, 1938.

Colonel Algernon Stanley was eighty-eight years old when he died on 10 February, 1962. Algernon had been just thirty-four at the time of his father's passing. He rose through the military ranks, achieving the rank of colonel commandant of the 159th Welsh Brigade from 1923 to 1927.

Lady Isobel Gathorne-Hardy, Lord and Lady Stanley's sole surviving daughter, was thirty-three when her father died. She married General Sir John Francis Gathorne-Hardy on 19 December, 1898. Gathorne-Hardy served as a captain in the Second Boer War and later served a general staff officer in the First World War. After commands as a general in Egypt and India, Gathorne-Hardy was commander-in-chief at Aldershot from 1933 to

1937. Lady Isobel lived to the age of eighty-eight and died on 30 December, 1963. Today, Lady Isobel's role as one of the pioneers of women's hockey is honoured through the Isobel Gathorne-Hardy Award, which is awarded to an active player in Canada — at any level of the game — whose values, leadership and personal traits are representative of all female athletes. The award recognizes a player who has demonstrated strong community involvement and dedication to the game of hockey.[15]

The youngest child, Lieutenant Colonel Frederick William Stanley, served in the South African War, as did his brother Algernon. William — or Billy, as he was known — married Lady Alexandra Acheson, goddaughter of Queen Victoria, on 17 June, 1905. William was thirty when his father passed away, and died 9 August, 1942, at sixty-four years of age.[16]

Lord Stanley's only sister, Lady Emma Stanley, married Colonel Sir Wellington Chetwynd-Talbot, sergeant at arms to the House of Lords, but was widowed in 1898. She died on 23 August, 1928.

* * *

The body of the 16th Earl of Derby was returned to his beloved Knowsley for burial. He was interred in the family crypt in St. Mary's Knowsley, located on Knowsley Lane. Construction of the church began in 1841, and the house of worship was consecrated by John Birch, the Bishop of Chester, on 6 June, 1844. The long, storied affiliation between St. Mary's Knowsley and the Earl of Derby began with the 13th Earl, Lord Stanley's grandfather, who financed the construction of the church, which cost twenty thousand pounds. A memorial chapel to the 14th Earl, Frederick's father, was built in 1871, two years after his death. An effigy of the 14th Earl is located in the Derby Chapel.

* * *

Lord Stanley, the Earl of Derby, served both England, country of his birth, and Canada, his adopted home for five years, with dignity and class. Although he never attained the eminence of either his father or brother, he upheld the Stanley family tradition as a leading British nobleman and the head of a family whose lineage is both ancient and illustrious.

[1] *The Times* (London: 15 June, 1908), p.12.

[2] P. B.Waite, 'Frederick Arthur Stanley', *Dictionary of Canadian Biography On-Line.*

[3] *Toronto Daily Star* (7 May, 1900), p.10.

[4] Knight of the Garter.

[5] Knight Grand Cross of the Order of the Bath.

[6] Knight Grand Cross of the Royal Victorian Order.

[7] Privy Councillor

[8] Honorary law degrees from Queen's University, Kingston, Ontario and the University of Liverpool, United Kingdom.

[9] King Edward VII, *Letter to Edward George Stanley* (15 June, 1908); Churchill, *Lord Derby*, p.92–3.

[10] The Prince of Wales, *Letter to Edward George Stanley* (16 June, 1908); Churchill, *Lord Derby*, p.93.

[11] C. Stanley, *Letter to Edward George Stanley* (July, 1908); Churchill, *Lord Derby*, p.400.

[12] C. Stanley, *Letter to her Children* (July, 1908); Churchill, *Lord Derby*, p.401.

[13] E. G. Stanley, 'Speech', *The Preston Guardian* (6 April, 1935); Churchill, *Lord Derby*, pp.601–2.

[14] K. Shea, *Interview with Dr. Tony Collins*, Archivist, *Rugby Football League*, (2006).

[15] Hockey Canada website, *www.hockeycanada.ca.*

[16] See, *www.thepeerage.com*, p.1385.

Epilogue

The Stanley Cup has endured and its legacy grown steadily since 16 May, 1893, when the *Montreal Gazette* ran a story that described the "Governor General's Cup" as a handsome trophy that had been presented to the M.A.A.A. the night before.[1]

> *Hockey evolved along with the changing times. The fledgling sport had outgrown the frozen ponds and lakes of its early days and as the sport was better organized, moved into covered rinks[2], forced the introduction of rules and established early stars.*

The game was tremendously exciting, and many who witnessed it for the first time would look on in wide-eyed amazement. George Meagher, the Montreal-born world figure-skating champion in 1891 — and no stranger to Lord Stanley and the Rideau Hall Rink — wrote:

> *It would be difficult to conceive a wilder, more madly fascinating and gloriously exciting game than 'hockey'. From marbles to football, I have played them all, and it has been my experience that in hockey, the player's mental and physical powers are given a wider scope than in any other game. The clashing of sticks, the stamping of feet, the yah-yahs of the admirers when a long and well-aimed shot for goal is fired, or perhaps when one player more cunning for the time than the rest, by his superior judgement and surprising*

ability, darts with the puck, gently coaxing it from one side to the other while travelling at lightning speed through an entire line of adversaries until finally, like a pistol shot, it cracks through the goals, when a thousand, yes, five thousand throats shout and scream until the pandemonium reminds one of a dynamite factory cutting loose!

Through the late nineteenth century, hockey was strictly and proudly an amateur sport; the British tradition of sport for sport's sake was strongly adhered to. But as the game evolved, it grew more competitive, and the added lure of the Stanley Cup championship increased the stakes. A win-at-all-costs ethic began to take hold, and teams surreptitiously began paying the most skilled players. Whispers of professionalism were heard in various Canadian towns — sometimes, under the guise of providing players with jobs. It wasn't until 1904, when the International Hockey League[3] was formed, that a league openly paid its players. This development was definitely not well received by bastions of amateurism such as the Ontario Hockey Association. OHA president John Ross Robertson stated:

> *For self preservation, the stand of the Ontario Hockey Association against the professionalism of Pittsburgh, Houghton, Calumet and the Soo [Sault Ste. Marie, Michigan and Sault Ste. Marie, Ontario] must be uncompromisingly antagonistic. Any player who figures on any of these teams must be banished from Ontario hockey.*[4]

But the die had been cast, and within two years, several Canadian leagues followed suit and embraced professionalism. By 1906, the situation necessitated a change in the administration of the Stanley Cup, which had originally been earmarked for the top amateur hockey team in Canada; it was thenceforth awarded simply to the best hockey team in Canada. To provide a championship trophy for teams that were purely amateur, the Allan Cup was inaugurated in 1908. In 1910, the Stanley Cup's trustees allowed the trophy to be awarded exclusively to professional teams. The trophy ceased to be a challenge cup in 1915, when the Pacific Coast Hockey Association and National Hockey Association worked out an agreement whereby their respective champs would play off for the Cup.

In 1907, following the death of Sheriff John Sweetland, the surviving trustee of the Stanley Cup, Philip Ross, invited William Foran to succeed him. Within a few years, Ross and Foran were faced with a dilemma. In 1914, the New Westminster Royals of the Pacific Coast Hockey Association moved to Portland, Oregon. This raised the possibility that the Stanley Cup might be won by an American team, which contravened the original condition that the Cup was for the champions of Canada. The trustees responded by altering the regulations to allow the Stanley Cup to be competed for by those American teams that were affiliated with a Canadian league. "The Stanley Cup is not emblematic of the Canadian honours but of the hockey championship of the world," a 1915 article in the *Ottawa Daily Citizen* maintained. "Hence, if Portland and Seattle were to win and carry out the usual arrangement of a bond for its safekeeping, they would be allowed to retain the trophy the customary length of time."[5] In 1916, Portland competed for the Cup, and in 1917, the PCHA's Seattle Metropolitans defeated the National Hockey Association's Montreal Canadiens to become the first U.S.-based team to win the Stanley Cup.

From the National Hockey League's formation in 1917 until 1926, the Cup was awarded to the winner of a playoff between the NHL and the Pacific Coast Hockey Association (beginning in 192x, the Western Canada Hockey League also entered Stanley Cup competition). When the western pro leagues folded, the NHL assumed effective control of the Stanley Cup, and trusteeship of the Cup was transferred to the league in 1947, with the proviso that it would retain the Cup as long as it continued to be "the world's leading professional hockey league as determined by its playing calibre."

* * *

Sweetland and Ross were both appointed by Lord Stanley himself to serve as trustees of the Stanley Cup in 1893. An original provision held that, "Should either trustee resign or otherwise drop out, the remaining trustee shall nominate a substitute."[6] To succeed Sweetland, Ross therefore nominated William Foran, who served as a trustee from 6 May, 1907, until his death on 30 November, 1945. An aging Ross, feeling it was time to step aside, replaced himself with J. Cooper Smeaton, who served from 24 February, 1946, until 3 October, 1978.

Following the death of Foran, Smeaton nominated former NHL President Mervyn "Red" Dutton as a trustee, and the former New York Americans star served from 30 March, 1950, until 15 March, 1987. On Smeaton's death, Dutton nominated another former NHL President — this time, Clarence Campbell. Campbell was a trustee from 19 January, 1979, until 24 June, 1984. Following the death of former president Clarence Campbell, Red Dutton nominated Supreme Court Justice Willard "Bud" Estey as a trustee, and he served in that capacity from 16 August, 1984, until his death on 25 January, 2002.

Today's two trustees are Brian O'Neill, who was nominated by Estey following the death of Red Dutton, and Ian "Scotty" Morrison, who was O'Neill's nominee to replace Justice Estey. O'Neill, who has been a trustee since 5 May, 1988, was hired as the NHL's director of administration in 1966 and was later promoted to executive vice-president of the league. He was inducted into the Hockey Hall of Fame as a builder in 1994. Morrison, a former on-ice official, was appointed the NHL's referee-in-chief in 1965. He was promoted to Vice-President, Officiating in 1981. In 1986, NHL President John Ziegler named Morrison to the position of Vice-President, Project Development of the NHL and president of the Hockey Hall of Fame. In 1991, Morrison was appointed chairman and chief executive officer of the Hall, posts he held until his retirement in 1998. A year later, he was inducted into the Hockey Hall of Fame in 1999, and he has been a Stanley Cup trustee since 18 March, 2002.

* * *

With the era of Stanley Cup challenges long since ended, the role of the trustees has become primarily ceremonial. In a 1976 letter to Cooper Smeaton, Red Dutton wrote:

> *Lefty Reid [curator of the Hockey Hall of Fame] obtained a copy of the Trusteeship signed by yourself, Mr. Ross and Mr. Campbell and I can see why Clarence has not given much consideration to the Trusteeship, as it gives the NHL a pretty good hold on the Cup. I cannot see that you and I have very much say in what happens. God knows we have not had much to do with it in the past and it would appear*

that we are not going to have much to do with it in the future. I am not going to worry any more and I don't think you should.[7]

That sentiment would change during 2004–05, when the NHL locked out its players and ultimately cancelled the season. Trustees Brian O'Neill and Scotty Morrison were placed on the hot seat, forced to consider who, if anyone, should be allowed to play for the Stanley Cup.

* * *

One of Lord Stanley's conditions called for the name of each Stanley Cup-winning team, and the year of their championship, to be engraved on a silver ring fitted onto the trophy for that purpose. But by 1902, the silver ring had been filled; when the members of the Montreal Amateur Athletic Association won the Stanley Cup championship on 4 February, 1903, they engraved their team's name directly onto the outside of the bowl, a practice that continued until that was also full. The series between the Ottawa Silver Seven and the Montreal Wanderers in March 1906, as well as the series between the Wanderers and the New Glasgow Cubs in December of that year, are commemorated in an engraving that completely circles the outer rim of the original Stanley Cup. The January and March 1907 series between the Wanderers and Kenora Thistles are engraved inside the Cup.

The Wanderers were so proud of the title they won on March 25, 1907, that they had the names of each player and officer, twenty in all, engraved inside the bowl of the Stanley Cup. This bold move was noted by the Ottawa Senators after they wrestled the title from the Wanderers, who had won three times to that point, in 1909. The *Toronto Daily Star* reported:

> *When [Ottawa Senators] President D'Arcy McGee removed the Stanley Cup from its case, he was rather flabbergasted to find a veritable directory of the city of Montreal scratched or engraved on every available space the exterior or anterior of the cup offered. All spaces allotted for the inscription of a victorious team in a Cup game have been used up, and the engraver had to fall back on the scroll work and interior for the purpose. Occupying practically the whole of the inside of*

the bowl, engraved in very prominent letters, are the names of the Wanderer team of 1907, and every officer and member of the club, thank you. Perhaps the Wanderers considered this their license, but the liberty was never given to them by the trustees.[8]

In their defence, the Wanderers explained that the engraving, commissioned by owner James Strachan, was meant as a tribute to one of their players, Hod Stuart, who had died on 23 June, 1907, after diving headfirst into the Bay of Quinte near Belleville, Ontario, breaking his neck and drowning. The tragic accident occurred just three months after he helped lead the Wanderers to the Stanley Cup championship. And as a result, although it angered McGee and the Senators at the time, a new tradition had been born.

In 1924, the Montreal Canadiens, champions of the National Hockey League, defeated the Vancouver Maroons of the Pacific Coast Hockey Association, then trumped the Calgary Tigers of the Western Hockey League to capture the Stanley Cup championship. The Canadiens had the names of every player, as well as everyone affiliated with the team, engraved on the Cup. The practice has been repeated by every single team to win the Cup since.

The allure of winning the Stanley Cup is not simply about the bragging rights associated with being part of a championship hockey team; it's also about being part of a lasting legacy, by having one's name inscribed for perpetuity on hockey's greatest championship trophy, to be recalled by generations to come, alongside some of the greatest players ever to have played the game. Orr, Gretzky, Howe, Richard, Roy, and a host of others have been immortalized on the silver bands of the Stanley Cup.

Henri Richard, who hoisted the Cup on eleven occasions, more than any other player in NHL history, admitted:

All those years, all I ever wanted to do was skate around the ice with the Cup. I watched Butch Bouchard do it. I watched Maurice, my brother, and I watched Jean Beliveau, too. They told me it was the greatest feeling in the world. Now I know what they meant.[9]

"It's a great-looking trophy, the best in all of sports," said Mathieu Schneider, whose name was engraved on the trophy as a member of the 1993 Montreal Canadiens. [10]

"Just to see the Stanley Cup on the ice is an amazing experience," explained Mario Lemieux, who won back-to-back championships with Pittsburgh in the early 1990s. "You can't really describe the feeling once you lift the Cup in the air. That is one moment I'll remember fifty years from now. Just incredible."[11]

Slava Fetisov gave the Stanley Cup an almost mystical aura when he said, "this Cup has so much positive energy, it's incredible. People can feel this when they hold the Cup."[12]

"Hockey, more than any other sport, has placed its emphasis on trophies and cups," summarized former NHL President Clarence Campbell. "Ever since 1893, the world of hockey has revolved around the Stanley Cup. And the history of pro hockey is the history of the Stanley Cup."[13]

* * *

The names on the Cup are not limited to those of players and others officially connected with championship teams. When one examines closely the original Cup donated by Lord Stanley, it is astonishing to see the number of names that have been secretively, randomly — and clearly unofficially — carved into the Stanley Cup with nails or knives. Some are connected to intriguing stories; others are long-forgotten curiosities. For instance, the identity of B. Morris of the Ottawa Social Club, and his connection to the Stanley Cup, is a mystery unlikely ever to be unravelled. Similarly, we are unlikely to learn much about S. Van Sickle or H. L. Linall, who carved their names into the Stanley Cup in 1907, anytime soon; but they, like F. Brandt, J. M. Kirkpatrick, G. C. Donaldson and J. E. Pigeon probably went to their graves boasting that they had their names on the Stanley Cup.

Anamae Lynch and Hazel Roach may be the first women to have their names engraved on the Cup, although the official honour goes to Marguerite Norris, who, as president of the Detroit Red Wings, had her name added in 1955.

Bruce Ridpath of the Ottawa Senators made certain he got his name on the Stanley Cup by carving it in himself. At some point, Bunny Cook scratched his name onto the Cup in large letters, only to have it officially engraved — his nickname shortened to "Bun" — as a member of the New York Ranger squads of 1928 and 1933.

During the summer of 1925, youngsters Lynn and Muzz Patrick were looking through boxes in the basement of their home in Victoria, British Columbia, when they found the Stanley Cup. Their father, Lester, had been manager of the Victoria Cougars, who won the Cup on March 30 of that year. The rascals found a nail and scratched their names into the surface of the beautiful trophy. Little did they know it at that time, but fifteen years later, both Lynn and Muzz would have their names engraved legitimately as members of the 1939-40 New York Rangers.[14]

Although Fred "Cyclone" Taylor ensured that his sterling career would be recalled for all time through his exploits on the ice, he nonetheless further secured his legacy by carving "Fred W. Taylor" in large script across Ottawa's official 1904 engraving on the outside of the Cup.

And what of Bow Wow? It remains a mystery whether or not one of the Quebec Bulldogs carved the dog's name on the underside of the Cup after either of the team's championships in 1912 or 1913.

P. T. Garner added "Long Live Canadiens" to his name. The S. Broda who scratched his name inside the Stanley Cup might very well be Stan Broda, brother of Turk, a five-time Stanley Cup champion. Someone named Stubbs added their surname on the outside of the Cup, in the decorative fluting. Beneath the crest of Lord Stanley, engraved with a penknife, is the name of Weldy Young, who starred with Ottawa in the 1890s, then heard the siren song of the Klondike Gold Rush and ended up organizing the team from Dawson City that challenged the Ottawa Silver Seven for the Stanley Cup in January 1905. By travelling 6,400 kilometres to play a hockey series, Dawson City captured the nation's imagination, although they lost 9–2 on 13 January and 23–2 on the sixteenth before the remainder of the best-of-five series was cancelled.

* * *

In 1911, when the trophy was only eighteen years old, there was already talk that it should be replaced. According to the Toronto *Daily News,*

> *Hearing that there was talk of replacing the cup with a more pretentious piece of silverware, the Honourable*

Arthur Stanley and his brother, Lord Derby [Edward Stanley], came to the decision that they would offer a new cup to the hockey teams of Canada to replace the old cup. They wrote offering to give one thousand dollars to be used in the purchase of a new trophy....

The trustees are of the opinion that the old cup should be retained. It is still in good condition and would last for many years yet, and they feel that it has a claim in the hockey world for its long service. The Stanley Cup has been in existence for eighteen years, and in that time, over fifty matches have been played for its possession, exclusive of games in the NHA.[15]

* * *

On the instruction of NHL President Clarence Campbell, a duplicate of the Stanley Cup was created in 1967. The previous trophy had been made from nickel-based alloys, which had hardened and become brittle over the years. There was a fear that, in time, the Cup could be dropped and would shatter like china.

The duplicate, known as the Presentation Cup, was made by Carl Petersen using a special silver alloy. The assignment was kept under tight wraps: besides Campbell, Petersen and his immediate family, only NHL Executive Director Brian O'Neill and Lefty Reid, the curator of the Hockey Hall of Fame, were aware that a replica was being produced.

After he created the exact copy, Lord Stanley's original Cup sat on Petersen's desk for three years. On 22 August, 1970, O'Neill asked Petersen to return the original Cup, and he did, three days later — walking unnoticed into the Hall of Fame with the trophy under his arm.

* * *

"I've held women and babies and jewels and money, but nothing will ever feel as good as holding that Cup," proclaimed Wayne Gretzky.[16] To the uninitiated, it is almost incomprehensible why a 114-year-old silver trophy, dented, scratched and purchased for less than $50 by its benefactor, elicits the adoration of generations of hockey fans from around the world.

Nonetheless, the Cup's fame has grown far beyond Canada and the United States. It has taken to the road so that fans may get closer to it. On August 16, 1997, the Stanley Cup travelled to Russia for the first time, accompanied by Viacheslav Fetisov, Vyacheslav Kozlov and Igor Larionov of the Stanley Cup champion Detroit Red Wings. "I didn't know what it would be like in Moscow," admitted Fetisov. "I knew they televised the Stanley Cup final in Russia the last few years. I knew the Red Wings had a lot of fans in Russia because of the Russian Five [Fetisov, Kozlov and Larionov, as well as Sergei Fedorov and Vladimir Konstantinov]. But the reaction was incredible! From people in Russia, ordinary fans, to the Prime Minister and President Yeltsin, everyone wanted to see the Cup."[17]

It rained steadily as the plane carrying the Stanley Cup touched down in Moscow at close to two o'clock in the morning. Nonetheless, a thousand fans waited patiently and excitedly to see the Stanley Cup.[18]

And fans have come from around the world to see the Stanley Cup. In November 2005, the United Arab Emirates hockey team flew to Toronto for a contest against a team of former National Hockey League stars. The captain of the fledgling UAE team, Faisal Saeed Al Suwaidi, was on the verge of tears when he stepped into the Great Hall of the Hockey Hall of Fame and gazed at the Cup, in person, for the first time. "The game is a labour of love, and it is a dream come true for us to be here in the Hall of Fame and seeing the Stanley Cup," he said. He and his teammates took turns having their photographs taken embracing the Cup; they also posed for numerous group pictures surrounding Lord Stanley's legacy. When one considers that the United Arab Emirates occupy eighty-three thousand square miles, four-fifths of which is desert, it seems an unlikely place for anyone to develop a passion for hockey, let alone such a reverence for the sport's most cherished award.

* * *

Hockey's Stanley Cup emerged during an era when sports of all descriptions developed into serious competitions; as the twentieth century approached, an array of new trophies was created. The FA Cup, also known as the Football Association Challenge Cup, made its debut as the championship trophy for English soccer in 1872. The Calcutta Cup was instituted in 1879 for the winning side in an annual rugby match between the national teams of England and Scotland.

The Ashes is a hotly contested cricket match played every second year between England and Australia. It dates back to 1882. The award consists of an urn, which purportedly contains the ashes of burned bails[19] from an early match, and is therefore not so much a trophy. It remains at all times in a museum at Lord's Cricket Grounds in London. Tennis players have competed at Wimbledon since 1886 (for the Ladies' Singles Trophy) and 1887 (for the Gentlemen's Singles Trophy), making "The Championships" the world's oldest tennis tournament.

In terms of North America's sporting history, however, the Stanley Cup has few peers. It is one year older than baseball's Temple Cup, which was awarded between 1894 and 1897. Now preserved at the National Baseball Hall of Fame and Museum in Cooperstown, New York, the Temple Cup was awarded to the victor of a postseason series between the first- and second-place clubs in the National League. In terms of trophies that are still competed for, the Stanley Cup is seven years older than the prestigious Davis Cup, which has been contested annually since 1900 — originally to the winner of a team competition between the United States and Great Britain, but which now encompasses countries from all over the world. The Stanley Cup is also older than the Canadian Lacrosse Association's Minto Cup (1901), the Canadian Football League's Grey Cup (1909), golf's Walker Cup (1922), and what is arguably the best-known trophy in the world, soccer's World Cup (1930).

The Stanley Cup is, however, pre-dated by the America's Cup, the Holy Grail of yacht racing. This silver pitcher, first contested in 1851, is the grandaddy of all sporting trophies. The America's Cup is held every three years — like the Davis Cup, it began as a battle between American and British sailors, but has since gone global. In fact, the Stanley Cup is not even the oldest hockey trophy. The Bedouin Cup, also known as the Birks Carnival Cup, was awarded to the winners of the tournaments staged during the Montreal Winter Carnival, beginning in 1883. When the Carnival ceased to be staged, the trophy was retired, and since 1889 has resided at Montreal's McGill University.

The OHA Championship Cup, more commonly known at the time as the Cosby Cup, was donated by the Ontario Hockey Association's first president, Lieutenant Colonel A. M. Cosby, two years before the Stanley Cup was commissioned. In what was a common custom for sports trophies during the era, the Cosby Cup was given permanently to Queen's University after the school's hockey team won the championship in three consecutive years — 1895, 1896 and 1897.

The Stanley Cup is, however, the oldest hockey trophy still in contention, and it has surely become one of the highest-profile awards to be found anywhere in the sporting world.

* * *

As the Right Honourable Adrienne Clarkson, Canada's twenty-sixth governor general (from 1999 to 2005), continues, there is a long tradition of vice regal support for "excellence in Canadian culture." The Office of the Governor General sponsors awards for adult and children's literature, the performing and visual arts, architecture, journalism and the teaching of Canadian history. And Stanley's successors have donated championship trophies for lacrosse (the Minto Cup) and Canadian football (the Grey Cup). Like the Stanley Cup, these latter trophies are not administered by the governor general. Still, the eyes of many Canadians were turned towards Madame Clarkson during the 2005-06 hockey season, when representatives for the National Hockey League's owners and players proved unable to negotiate a collective-bargaining agreement. The league locked out the players, and as the stalemate continued, the NHL season was ultimately scrapped. As a result, there was no competition for the Stanley Cup.

> *Everybody in Canada was upset by what happened with the NHL. We all talked a lot about it. We asked, "What is going to happen to the Cup if the league doesn't play?" That started me thinking that the Cup should be given to the women [the National Women's Hockey League], who were playing. People said, "That's interesting," and that played out in the press.*

Such a presentation never came to pass, but the idea did prompt Clarkson to follow Lord Stanley's lead.

> *A couple of people wrote to me and said, "Don't bother*

> *with that. If you want to give a trophy for women's hockey,*
> *make it the Clarkson Cup." I consulted a couple of people*
> *and they said, "What a great idea! Let's do that." So I put*
> *that into motion. All I really want to do is reward excel-*
> *lence in women's hockey.... I'm modelling myself on Lord*
> *Stanley in that this is a personal gift of me, as ex-Governor*
> *General, to the nation and to women's hockey. It is my gift*
> *and it will be forever attached to me because I have given*
> *it; there is not a sponsor.*

As Lord Stanley had a cup created in 1893 for the amateur hockey championship of Canada, the Clarkson Cup has now been created specifically for
women's hockey. "It is very interesting and has a lot of the north in it,"
smiled Madame Clarkson. "Some Inuit artists worked in silver on it. These
Inuit artists are graduates of Arctic College and are very acknowledged
artists. They made it very special."

> *I've modelled everything on Lord Stanley because he comes*
> *from a time where to give something like that was a natural*
> *thing for a governor general to do. In our modern times,*
> *that the Governor General can do that, it recalls to us that*
> *there is a standard that you can come up to with a personal*
> *touch and a sense of belonging. I will feel always, as long as*
> *I'm alive, that when the Clarkson Cup is given out, it will*
> *be something I will be deeply personally interested in. I will*
> *have to make sure that it is safeguarded for excellence in*
> *women's hockey and therefore there will be a structure set*
> *up with trustees so that when I die, there will be a natural*
> *way in which this Cup will continue to be given. I think this*
> *will be very valuable to the nation. All these little girls*
> *playing hockey now will have something to think about*
> *that they would one day, perhaps, be on a team that won*
> *the Clarkson Cup.*[20]

Adrienne Clarkson presented the trophy for the first time at a news conference on Monday, 10 July, 2006, to the Canadian women's Olympic hockey
team, gold medallists at the Winter Games in Turin, Italy, in 2006. In future,

the trophy will be awarded to the team that wins the national championship of women's hockey.[21]

* * *

In April 2004, the Canadian Broadcasting Corporation asked Canadians to select "The Greatest Canadian." To be eligible, nominees had to have made a significant contribution to Canada. In October of that year, after counting 1,200,000 votes, the CBC listed the one hundred greatest Canadians. Lord Stanley of Preston placed ninety-fifth on the list. The ranking, not overly impressive, signifies that the former governor general is revered for little more than his donation of hockey's championship trophy, the Stanley Cup. As the CBC put it, "Today, the Stanley Cup has become the most important award in professional hockey."[22]

* * *

In the spring of 2006, the Stanley Cup was at the centre of a family reunion of sorts. On the morning of 19 April, it was officially introduced to Sir Edward Richard William John Stanley, the 19th and current Earl of Derby, the great-great-grandson of Lord Frederick Stanley. It was the first time the Earl had seen the Stanley Cup in person, although he certainly knew of its significance. Sir Edward, who also carries the title Baron Stanley of Preston, lives at Knowsley Hall, the same estate near Liverpool in which Lord Frederick lived out the final years of his life after returning from Canada. "I know from Canadian people I see that ice hockey over there [in Canada] seems to be the equivalent of [English soccer's] FA Cup," he stated.

The 19th Earl greatly enjoyed seeing and holding the trophy.

> *It was really quite exciting because, in the last year or so with all the players' disputes, the Stanley Cup has been something that has been very much in the forefront of the news, and something I've come to learn a lot more about and really learned a lot about its significance. You get wrapped up in these stories. I'm terribly proud of this long family history and proud that my great-great-grandfather should have given such a wonderful thing, so I'm really excited to see it.*

The Earl then lifted the Cup. A photographer cajoled him to pose for a picture with it hoisted over his head. "I'd love to," he responded, "but I haven't won it, and that is a privilege reserved for champions." Sir Edward recalled being given a book about the Stanley Cup when he was eight or nine years of age, and it was then that he realized his family's connection to "the great sport of ice hockey."[23]

The Stanley Cup was purchased in 1893 from G. R. Collis & Company at 130 Regent Street in London's West End. Today, that address houses a very fine jeweller called Boodles, or as the business has been known for over two hundred years, Boodles & Dunthorne. On this visit, the Stanley Cup was taken to the shop and placed in its windows. As a hundred or so staff, customers and bystanders looked on, the 19th Earl of Derby and Tim Joiner, the Lord Mayor of Westminster, each tugged on a cord to unveil a plaque that explains the location's place in history:

> *City of Westminster:*
> *Lord Stanley of Preston purchased*
> *the original Stanley Cup from a silversmith*
> *on this site in 1892 for the people of Canada*
> *to commemorate amateur and professional ice hockey.*
> *The Cup is now in the Hockey Hall of Fame in Toronto.*

Warm applause followed, and those attending the ceremony chuckled as double-decker buses slowed to a crawl to allow tourists to lean over the side and capture a photograph of the occasion.

* * *

Life in Canada during the latter half of the nineteenth century was intimately connected with that of Great Britain. "Canada, especially Ontario, was British then [in the 1890s] to an extent that today's Canadian could scarcely imagine," wrote revered sports journalist Scott Young. "Speeches from public platforms were afloat with almost religious fervour for British fair play, British common law and British educational standards."[24]

The Dominion of Canada inherited its legal, social, political and educational system from the Mother Country, and retained a formal link to Great Britain through the Queen's representative, the Governor General of

Canada. Changes were underway even during Lord Stanley's lifetime, as the young nation took its first steps towards self-determination. This was certainly true where sports were concerned, as such perennial favourites as horse racing, rugby, cricket and rowing were challenged in popularity by more recent — and more North American — pastimes such as baseball, football, lacrosse and, of course, hockey. Lord Stanley may have been every inch the Englishman in his attitudes and tastes, but by recognizing hockey, not only as a competitive sport to play but also an exciting sport to watch, he unintentionally gave it Royal approval; in the process, it was elevated from a game played enthusiastically by an enlightened few to a sport that was quickly embraced by the masses.

Lord Stanley of Preston had no comprehension of the immense impact his gift would have on the country he left behind. In 1945, Stanley was inducted as on of fourteen charter members of the Hockey Hall of Fame, as a builder of the sport. The Stanley Cup, bitterly contested and more highly prized than any other award in hockey, remains the enduring legacy of Lord Frederick Arthur Stanley, the 16th Earl of Derby.

---

[1] *Montreal Gazette* (16 May, 1893), p.8.

[2] Although the rinks were covered, they still housed surfaces of natural ice; seasons were limited to the months from December to March, and a team's full schedule of games generally lasted fewer than ten games.

[3] Perhaps because professionalism was so controversial, some contemporary newspaper accounts made a point of referring to the league as the International Professional Hockey League.

[4] See, *Copper Country Evening News* (c.1904), as quoted on 'Copper Country Hockey History', www.cchockey history.org.

[5] *Ottawa Daily Citizen* (9 December, 1915), p.9.

[6] Hockey Hall of Fame Archives.

[7] M. Dutton, *Letter to J. C. Smeaton*, Hockey Hall of Fame, (20 July, 1976).

[8] *Toronto Daily Star* (March 17, 1909).

[9] K. Shea, *Interview with Henri Richard*, Hockey Hall of Fame, www.hhof.com.

[10] K. Samuelson, 'Interview with Mathieu Schneider', NHL.com (April 20, 2006).

[11] M. Lemieux & T. McMillan, *Mario Lemieux: The Final Period* (Pittsburgh: Reich Publishing, 1997), p.73.

[12] M. Ulmer, *If the Cup Could Talk* (Chelsea: Sleeping Bear Press, 2000), p.118.

[13] Rev. Ed Hird, as quoted in *Deep Cove Crier* (July 1999).

[14] M. Dunnell, 'The Stanley Cup Mystique', D. Diamond, R. Dinger, J. Duplacey & E. Zweig (*eds*), *Total Stanley Cup* (Toronto: Total Sports Canada, 2000), p.1.

[15] *Toronto Daily News* (11 December, 1911).

[16] W. Gretzky & R. Reilly, *Gretzky* (Toronto: HarperCollinsCanada, 1990), p.80.

[17] Ulmer, *If the Cup Could Talk*, p.118.

[18] K. Shea, *Interview with Phil Pritchard*, the Hockey Hall of Fame's Cup Keeper, (2 June, 2006).

[19] In cricket, bails are the two smaller sticks placed on top of the three stumps to form a wicket.

[20] Shea, *Interview with Adrienne Clarkson*.

[21] *Toronto Star* (Toronto: 11 July, 2006), p.E3.

[22] The Greatest Canadian (Toronto: Canadian Broadcasting Corporation, 2005). *<television programme>*

[23] P. Pritchard, *Conversation with the 19th Earl of Derby* (London: 19 April, 2006).

[24] Young, *100 Years of Dropping the Puck*, p.37.

Acknowledgements

The Hockey Hall of Fame has played an integral role in the creation of this book, from the vast files in the Resource Centre, to the entire staff, who have all been so supportive. Special thanks to Phillip Pritchard, who has been through every step of this journey, suggesting ideas, guiding searches and encouraging the writing. Many thanks, as well, to Craig Campbell, who assisted with the photographs, Danielle Siciliano and Miragh Addis for their help with research materials, Peter Jagla for guidance and contractual items and Tyler Wolosewich, who was helpful, as always, in accessing items needed in producing *Lord Stanley: The Man Behind the Cup*.

This is Kevin Shea's fifth book with the family at H.B. Fenn and Company, and the on-going support and friendship of Jordan Fenn, publisher, has been wonderful. No one does sports books like Fenn Publishing, and for lovers of the game, we thank you from the bottom of our hearts for allowing us to tell Stanley's story.

The content of Lord Stanley is one thing of which we're very proud, but what you see in your hands is largely the work of Laura Brunton, designer for H.B. Fenn. Her creative vision, meticulous care and long hours resulted in a book whose presentation is as pleasing to the authors as the content itself. A heartfelt thank you to you, Laura.

Lloyd Davis is not only a terrific editor, having now polished the burrs from four of Kevin's books, but is also a hockey historian with a key eye for fact-checking, and is extended sincere thanks.

For background material on Lord Frederick Stanley, the 16th Earl of Derby, many offered substantial help and invaluable assistance.

A world of thanks to The Honourable Adrienne Clarkson for allowing the authors access to her unique insight into the role, lives and history of the Governor General. Miss Clarkson's assistant, Alyson Atkinson, was also most helpful.

The 19th Earl of Derby, Edward Stanley, was most gracious in his support of this biography and his role was greatly appreciated.

The Society for International Hockey Research (SIHR) provided a great deal of information through its membership, including incredible assistance from Bill Fitsell. Others who contributed research are James Duplacey, Pastor Glen Goodhand, Professor Stephen Hardy, Martin Harris, Morey Holzman, Paul Kitchen, Leonard Kotylo, Paul Patskou, Michel Vigneault, Earl Zukerman and Eric Zweig.

So many others are to be recognized as well:
- James Amos, head of marketing for Boodle and Dunthorne, London, England
- Tim Burgess, who assisted immeasurably in answering geography questions regarding the United Kingdom
- Robin Myers, Modern Archivist of Corpus Christi College, University of Cambridge, England, who assisted with information from the Derby-Gathorne-Hardy papers
- Arthur Zimmerman of the Canadian Antique Phonograph Society (CAPS)
- Barbara Brown, Manager of Radio Licensing for the Canadian Broadcasting Corporation, for permission to use the interview of George M. Robinson from the CBC radio program, 'Voice of the Pioneer, originally broadcast on 22 December, 1968
- Linda Cobon from the Canadian Nation Exhibition (CNE), Toronto, Ontario
- the Canadian Pacific Railway Archives, Montreal, Quebec
- Michael Pritchard, FRPS, Watford, Hertfordshire, England and a director at Christie's auction house, London, England
- Sandra Mast, Archives Assistant at the Churchill Archives Centre, Churchill College, Cambridge, England
- Jordan Dibe for contributions to library research
- Penny Hatfield, the Archivist, Eton College Library, Eton, England
- Margaret Houghton, Archivist, Hamilton Public Library, Hamilton, Ontario
- Emma Heslewood, Keeper of Social History, Harris Museum,

Preston, England
-Jenny Moran, Liverpool Cathedral, Liverpool, England
-Pamela Raman of The Lord Mayor's Office, Liverpool Town Hall
-V.W. Barley of Mappin & Webb, London, England
-Sophie Deschamps, McCord Museum, Montreal, Quebec
-Toronto's Metro Reference Library
-Sharon May, Community Development Coordinator for the City of Moose Jaw, Saskatchewan
-National Archives of Canada in Ottawa, Ontario
-Janet McGowan, National Capital Commission, Ottawa, Ontario
-Michael Oesch, who while walking across Canada, stopped at the City of Vancouver Archives to assist with research
-Allison Neill, Director of Media Relations for The Ottawa Hospital, Ottawa, Ontario
-Henk Pardoel, Communications Co-ordinator, Sports Information Office, Queen's University, Kingston, Ontario
-Jackie Carberry, Club Historian at Ottawa's Rideau Curling Club
-France Langlois, former Media Relations Officer, Rideau Hall, Ottawa
-Ian Ross regarding P.D. Ross
-the Royal Hamilton Yacht Club, Hamilton, Ontario
-Dr. Tony Collins, Archivist, Rugby Football League, Leeds, England
-Hugh Reekie, president of the St. Andrew's Society of Ottawa
-Dale Shea, who provided material regarding Stanley Park in Vancouver
-J. Edgar LeBlanc, the current proprietor of Stanley House in New Richmond, Quebec, which he and his wife Lucille have lovingly restored as The Stanley House Inn
-Erik Janssen, Sunset + Vine Productions, London, England
-Adrian Allan, University Archivist of Liverpool University Library at The University of Liverpool, Liverpool, England
-Catherine Holmes, Reference Assistant, Saskatchewan Archives Board, University of Regina, Saskatchewan
-Louis Cauz, Historian/Archivist for Woodbine Entertainment Group, Toronto, Ontario.
-York University's Microfiche Centre, Toronto, Ontario

* * *

Kevin Shea's acknowledgements:

As time marches on, a vision of what and who are truly important in one's life becomes more and more defined. This passion I have discovered for researching and writing about hockey has been nurtured and encouraged through many years by a handful of people with whom I share my love and thanks.

There are so many adjustments that need to take place during a couple's first year together and to patiently accept the intense amount of time required to write this book, I send all my love to Nancy for her encouragement and patience. Thanks, too, to Jordan, Katie and Meghan, along with Pippin and Iris, for their support. I also send my love to my mother and stepfather, Margaret and Gerry England, for unconditional love and extraordinary support through each and every one of my endeavours. As youngsters, my brother Dale sat with me on the couch sharing a bowl of potato chips, a glass of ginger ale and the excitement of *Hockey Night in Canada* every Saturday. He has shared the passion for hockey since the beginning and deserves great thanks, sent along, too, to my sister-in-law LoriLee and their kids, Ethan, Dylan and Ferron. I have frequently been told that I have the greatest friends in the world, and am proud to include Maureen and Tim Burgess, Andrea Orlick, Cam Gardiner, Steve Waxman, Kim Cooke and Bill Nairn on that list, lending an ear when necessary, jumping into the fray when required, but always supporting the dream with extraordinary friendship. Although he is no longer with us, there is no one who would be more proud of me than my Dad. Not a day goes by that I don't think of him. And finally, to my project partner, Jason Wilson — late nights, frantic schedules, commiserating and celebrating were all included on this path together. Your contributions to areas with which I was not well-versed were outstanding, and your knowledge, simply incredible. I cannot adequately thank you, Jason, and want you to know that it was a pleasure creating *Lord Stanley: The Man Behind the Cup* with you.

J. Jason Wilson's acknowledgements:

There are so many people that I would like to thank for their help in the making of this book. First off, I'd like to thank Kevin for believing in my skills as a historian and giving me an opportunity to be part of something that I feel is so important. Next, my beautiful wife Alana, who gave me all the support I needed when I needed it and, quite rightly, a wide berth when I was, er, grumpy. Cyclone and Maisy: thank you for never once eating my work relating to this book. My sister Julie: thanks for buying Goldblatt, Burt & Devaney's *The Stanley Cup* for me for Christmas 1977 — it rather started the ball rolling. A special thanks to Mom for all the love and countless "cuppa's" and sundry. And a very special thanks to Dad — working on machines that seemingly were built shortly after Gutenberg's Printing Press was invented — Johnny patiently copied and scanned some 1,200 letters and documents in a bid to make my life a little easier, something he always does! Finally, I'd like to thank Frederick Arthur Stanley, the man who gave us Canadian boys a silver cup to covet and dream about. Long dismissed as politically uninteresting and un-ambitious, both Kevin and I found Stanley to be exactly the opposite. I'll leave the book with the burden of explanation, but I'll say here that it was a pleasure to write about this gentle, dog-loving man who always put his family first — there is much to be admired about Lord Stanley.

ℬibliography

SELECT BIBLIOGRAPHY

J. J. Bagley, *The Earls of Derby, 1485–1985* (London: Didgwick & Jackson, 1985).

P. Bailey, *Leisure and Class in Victorian England: Rational Recreation and the Contest for Control, 1830–1855* (London: Routledge & Kegan Paul, 1978).

J. Barman, *Stanley Park's Secret* (Madeira Park, British Columbia: Harbour Publishing, 2005).

P. Berton, *The Impossible Railway* (New York: Knopf, 1972).

The Best of Akwesasne Notes: How Democracy Came to St. Regis & The Thunderwater Movement (Akwesasne: Akwesasne Notes Newspaper, 1974). <*booklet*>

M. Bliss, *Plague: A Story of Smallpox in Montreal* (Toronto: Harper Collins, 1991),

A. Briggs, *The Age of Improvement: 1783-1867* (London: Longman, {1959} 1979).

John Buchan, *Lord Minto: A Memoir* (London: T. Nelson, 1924).

Canadian Encyclopedia (Edmonton: Hertig Publishers, 1988).

The Canadian Journal of Lady Aberdeen: 1893-1898 (Toronto: The Champlain Society, 1960).

J. Candow (*ed*), *Industry and Society in Nova Scotia: An Illustrated History* (Black Point, NS: Fernwood Books, 2001).

L. Cauz, *The Plate: A Royal Tradition* (Toronto: Deneay, 1984).

R. S. Churchill, *Lord Derby: King of Lancashire—The Official Life of Edward, Seventeenth Earl of Derby, 1865-1948* (London: Heinemann, 1959).

J. E. Collins, *Canada under the Administration of Lord Lorne* (Toronto: Rose Publishing Company, 1884).

F. Cosentino, *The Renfrew Millionaires: The Valley Boys of Winter 1910* (Burnstown: General Store Publishing House, 1990).

J. Cowan, *Canada's Governors General: 1867–1952* (Toronto: York Publishing Toronto).

CPR, *Transcontinental Route* (Canadian Pacific Railway, Eastern Division & Western Division: 1889).

D. Creighton, *John A. Macdonald: The Old Chieftain* (Toronto: Macmillan Company of Canada Ltd., 1955).

D. Diamond, J. Duplacey, R. Dinger, E. Fitzsimmons, I. Kuperman & E. Zweig (eds) *Total Hockey: The Official Encyclopaedia of the National Hockey League, Second Edition,* (Toronto: Dan Diamond and Associates, 2000).

D. Diamond, R. Dinger, J. Duplacey, E. Zweig, (*ed*) *Total Stanley Cup* (Toronto: Total Sports Canada, 2000).

P. Draper, *The House of Stanley* (Ormskirk: T. Hutton Publishing, 1864).

The Marchioness of Dufferin & H. G. Ava (Hamilton), Marchioness of Hamilton-Temple-Blackwood, *My Canadian journal, 1872-8: Extracts from my letters home written while Lord Dufferin was Governor-General* (Toronto: Coles Publishing Company, {1891} 1969).

F. Espinasse, *Lancashire Worthies* (London: Simpkin, Marshall, & Co. Stationers Hall Court, 1874).

A. Farrell, *Hockey: Canada's Royal Winter Game* (Montreal: 1899).

N. Ferguson, *The Pity of War: Explaining World War I* (New York: Basic Books, 1999).

M. Filey, *Toronto Sketches—The Way We Were* (Toronto: Dundurn Press, 2000).

J.W. Fitsell, *Hockey's Captains, Colonels and Kings* (Erin: Boston Mills Press, 1987).

P. Fussell, *The Great War and Modern Memory* (Oxford: Oxford University Press, 1975).

J. A. Gemmill (*ed*), *The Canadian Parliamentary Companion* (Ottawa: J. Durie & Son, 1889).

S. Gibson, *More Than an Island: A History of the Toronto Island* (Toronto: Irwin, 1984).

D. Godfrey & B. Y. Card (*ed*), *The Diaries of Charles Ora Card: The Canadian Years, 1886-1903* (Salt Lake City: University of Utah Press, 1993).

Rev. H. H. Gowen, *Pioneer Church Work in British Columbia: Being a Memoir of the Episcopate of Acton Windeyer Sillitoe, First Bishop of New Westminster* (London: Mowbray, 1899).

W. Gretzky & R. Reilly, *Gretzky* (Toronto: HarperCollinsCanada, 1990).

R. Gruneau and D.Whitson, *Hockey Night in Canada: Sport, Identities and Cultural Politics* (Toronto: Garamond Press, 1993).

D. Guay, *L'Histoire du Hockey au Quebec* (Quebec: G. Morin, 1980).

D. Hodge, *The Kids Book of Canada's Railway and How the CPR Was Built* (Toronto: Kids Can Press, 2000).

C. Howell, *Blood, Sweat and Cheers: Sport and The Making of Modern Canada* (Toronto: Univesity of Toronto Press, 2001).

R. H. Hubbard, *Rideau Hall: An Illustrated History of Government House, Ottawa, from Victorian Times to the Present Day* (Montreal: McGill-Queen's, 1977).

D. Jenish, *The Stanley Cup* (Toronto: McClelland & Stewart, 1992).

C. H. Keeling, *Marvel by the Mersey: The First Book to be Devoted to the Knowsley Menagerie, the Remarkable Zoological Collection Owned by the 13th Earl of Derby* (Shalford, Knowsley Estate: Clam Publications, publication date unknown).

B. Kidd, *The Struggle for Canadian Sport* (Toronto: University of Toronto Press, 1996).

Lord Kilcoursie, *Recollections Hazy But Happy* (unpublished memoirs of Lord Kilcoursie, Earl of Cavan).

G. Kitson Clark, 'The Electorate and the Repeal of the Corn Laws', *Transactions of the Royal Historical Society* (London: 1951).

W. D. Jones, *Lord Derby and Victorian Consevatism* (Athens: The University of Georgia Press, 1956).

T. E. Kebbel, *Life of the Earl of Derby, K G.* (London: W. H. Allen & Co., 1890).

P. Kennerley & C. Wilkinson, *The Cathedral Church of Christ in Liverpool* (Liverpool: Bluecoat Press, 2003).

L. Laclaré, *Lord Stanley and the Demonstration of the Edison Perfected Phonograph in Canada, 1888* (British Institute of Recorded Sound: April-July, 1973), p.198.

E. Lear, *A Book of Nonsense*, third edition, (London: Routledge, Warne & Routledge, 1861).

M. Lemieux & T. McMillan, *Mario Lemieux: The Final Period* (Pittsburgh: Reich Publishing, 1997), p.73.

C. H. Little, *A Short History of the Rideau Curling Club: 1888-1978* (Ottawa: The Club, 1979).

The Life of Sir John A. Macdonald (Toronto: Morang & Company, 1908).

M. MacMillan, M. Harris & A. Desjardins, *Canada's House: Rideau Hall and the Invention of a Canadian Home* (Toronto: Alfred A. Knopf Canada, 2004).

J. A. MacIntosh, P. D. McIntosh, J. McLaverty, R. Fleming (*eds*), *One Hundred Years History of the St. Andrew's Society of Toronto: 1836-1936* (Toronto: Murray Printing Company, 1936).

A. Metcalfe, *Canada Learns to Play: The Emergence of Organized Sport, 1807–1914* (Toronto: McClelland & Stewart Inc., 1987).

W. S. MacNutt, *Days of Lorne: from the private papers of the Marquis of Lorne, 1878–1883* in the possession of the Duke of Argyll at Inveraray Castle, Scotland, (Fredericton, 1955).

D. McDonald, *Lord Strathcona: a biography of Donald Alexander Smith* (Toronto: Dundurn Press, 1996).

BIBLIOGRAPHY

A. B. McLeod & P. Mcgeachie, *Land of Promise: Robert Burnaby's Letters from Colonial British Columbia, 1858-1868* (Burnaby: City of Burnaby, 2002).

G. Meagher, *Lessons in Skating* (Toronto: George N. Morang & Company, Ltd., 1900).

M. Miller, *Homer Watson: The Man of Doon* (Toronto: Summerhill Press Ltd., 1988).

M. Moss, *Manliness and Militarism: Educating Young Boys in Ontario for War* (Toronto: Oxford University Press, 2001).

M. Mott, 'Inferior Exhibitions, Superior Ceremonies: The Nature and Meaning of the Hockey Games of the Winnipeg Victorias, 1890–1903', *5th Canadian Symposium on the History of Sport and Physical Education* (Toronto: 1982).

J. Noonan, *Canada's Governors General* (Ottawa: Borealis Book Publishers, 2002).

D. Owram, *Promise of Eden: The Canadian Expansionist Movement and the Idea of the West – 1856-1900* (Toronto: University of Toronto Press, 1980).

B. M. Patton, *Ice Hockey* (London: George Routledge & Sons Ltd., 1936).

W. Pollard, *The Stanleys of Knowsley: A History of That Noble Family including a Sketch of the Political and Public Lives of the Rt. Hon. The Earl of Derby, K.G. and the Rt. Hon. Lord Stanley, M.P.* (Liverpool: Edward Howell, 1868).

J. Pope, *Memoirs of the Right Honourable Sir John Alexander Macdonald, G.C.B., First Prime Minister of the Dominion of Canada, 2* (London: 1894), p.259.

C. G. Roberts & A. L. Tunnel (*eds*), *Canadian Who's Who, 1936–37* (London: Times Publishing Company, 1936).

H. Roxborough, *The Stanley Cup Story* (Toronto: McGraw Hill Ryerson Limited, 1971).

G. Saintsbury, *The Earl of Derby* (London: Sampson Low, Martson & Company, 1892).

T. H. Sanderson and E. S. Roscoe (*eds*), *Speeches and Addresses of Edward Henry 15th Earl of Derby K. G.,* (2 Vols., 1894).

E. O. S. Scholefield, *British Columbia from the earliest times to the present, I & II*, (Vancouver: S. J. Clarke Publishing Company, 1914), p.483.

Scottish Battles (Newtongrange, Midlothian: Lang Syne Publishing Ltd., 1985).

D. A. G. Seglins, *Just Part of the Game: Violence, Hockey and Masculinity in Central Canada, 1890–1910* (Kingston: Queen's University, 1995).

C. Smythe and S. Young, *If You Can't Beat 'Em in the Alley: The Memoirs of the Late Conn Smythe* (Toronto: McClelland and Stewart, 1981).

E. Stanley, *Journal of a Tour in America: 1824-1825* (London: Privately Printed, 1930).

J. H. Thompson, 'Forging the Prairie West', *The Illustrated History of Canada* (Toronto: Oxford University Press, Don Mills, 1998).

J. Thorburn & A. E. Cameron, *History of the First Century of the St. Andrew's Society of Ottawa: 1846-1946* (Ottawa, published privately, 1946).

M. Ulmer, *If the Cup Could Talk* (Chelsea: Sleeping Bear Press, 2000), p.118.

J. Vincent (*ed*), *Later Derby Diaries: Home Rule, Liberal Unionism and Aristocratic Life in Late Victorian England* (Bristol: University of Bristol, 1981).

J. Vincent, *Disraeli* (London: Oxford Paperbacks, 1990).

J. Vincent, *A Selection From: The Diaries of Edward Henry Stanley, 15th Earl of Derby (1826-93)* (London: Offices of the Royal Historical Society, 1994).

A. O. Wheeler, *The Selkirk Range* (Ottawa: Government Printing Office, 1905).

A. D. White, *A History of the Warfare of Science with Theology in Christendom* (New York: D. Appleton & Company, 1896).

S. Young, *100 Years of Dropping the Puck* (Toronto: McClelland and Stewart, 1989).

A. E. Zimmerman, Canadian Antique Phonograph Society, *Lord Stanley and Edison's Perfected Phonograph at the Toronto Industrial Exhibition* (Toronto: November, 1888).

NEWSPAPERS & PERIODICALS

Alberta History
Antique Phonograph News
Art History
Brandon Mail
British Colonist (Vancouver)
British Whig (Kingston)
Brooklyn Eagle
Buffalo Courier
Burlington Free Press
Le Canada (Ottawa)
Canadian Antique Phonograph Society
Canadian History News: Canada's Past in Perspective
Canadian Historical Review
Canadian Illustrated News
Canadian Post (Lindsay)
Canadian Rail
Le Canadien
Copper Country Evening News
Country Life
Courrier du Canada (Quebec)
Daily Mercury (Quebec)
Deep Cove Crier
Dominion Illustrated Monthly (Montreal)
Empire
l'Etendard (Montreal)
Evening Journal (Ottawa)
The Graphic (London)
Halifax Morning Herald
Hamilton Spectator
Harpers Young People
The Hindu
International Journal of the History of Sport
Journal of Contemporary History
Journal of Sports History
Kingston Daily News
Leeds Mercury
Legion Magazine
Macleans Magazine
MacLeod Gazette
Manchester Courier
Manitoba Free Press
Manitoba Liberal
Montreal Daily Star
Montreal Daily Witness
Montreal Gazette
Montreal Star

BIBLIOGRAPHY

Murray's Magazine
New York Sun
Ottawa Daily Citizen
Ottawa Evening Journal
Outing
Peterborough Examiner
Preston Guardian
Progress (Saint John)
Qu'Appelle Vidette (Fort Qu'Appelle)
Qu'Appelle Progress
Regina Leader
Renfrew Journal
The Rider and Driver (New York)
Sault Ste. Marie Star
Society for International Hockey Research (SIHR) Journal (Toronto)
Sports History Review
Stanley Estates Newsletter
The Times (London)
Toronto Daily Mail
Toronto Daily Star
Toronto Empire
Toronto Evening News
Toronto Evening Telegram
Toronto Globe
Toronto World
TWA Ambassador
Vancouver News Advertiser
Vancouver World
Victoria Daily Colonist

ORAL REPORTS

Jackie Carberry
Louis Cauz
Adrienne Clarkson
Dr. Tony Collins
Bill Fitsell
Penny Hatfield
Henk Pardoel
Michael Pritchard
Phil Pritchard
Pamela Raman
19th Earl of Derby
John Todorovic

Lord Stanley

COLLECTIONS

The Diary of P. D. Ross from the National Archives of Canada.

Lady Stanley's Journal from the National Archives of Canada.

Lord Stanley Papers from the National Archives of Canada.

Lord Stanley of Preston Papers from the Public Archives of Canada in London.

Gathorne-Hardy Papers from the National Archives of Canada.

Hansard – report of debates in the House of Commons (London: New Series, XIX).

All Collections housed at the Hockey Hall of Fame.

Lansdowne Papers from the National Archives of Canada.

Sir John A. Macdonald Papers from the National Archives of Canada.

John A. Macdonald, *House of Commons Debates.*

Board Minutes of the Montreal Amateur Athletic Association.

E. H. Stanley, *Personal Diary.*

The Earl and the Pussycat, the 13th Earl of Derby's Life and Legacy – from Liverpool's Walker Art Gallery.

City of Vancouver Archives.

Index

INDEX

INDEX

Lord Stanley

INDEX